WEBSTER'S
ENGLISH/SPANISH
ESPAÑOL/INGLÉS
DICTIONARY

Watermill Press

a *prep.* at; to
a-ba-ce-rí-a *f.* grocery
a-ba-ce-ro *m.* grocer
á-ba-co *m.* abacus
a-bad *m.* abbot
a-ba-de-sa *f.* abbess
a-ba-dí-a *f.* abbey
a-ba-jo *adv.* beneath; down; below; *prep.* down
a-ba-lan-zar *v.* to hurl
a-ban-de-ra-mien-to *m.* registration (nautical)
a-ban-de-rar *v.* to register
a-ban-do-na-do, -da *adj.* derelict; careless
a-ban-do-nar *v.* to desert; forsake; abandon; give up
a-ban-do-no *m.* abandonment; neglect
a-ba-ni-car *v.* to fan
a-ba-ni-co *m.* fan
a-ba-ra-jar *v.* to catch
a-ba-ra-tar *v.* to lower; become cheaper
a-bar-car *v.* to embrace; comprise; encompass
a-ba-ti-do, -da *adj.* downcast; dejected; despondently; glum
a-ba-ti-mien-to *m.* dejection
a-ba-tir(se) *v.* to knock down; depress; discourage
ab-di-var *v.* to abdicate
ab-do-men *m.* abdomen
ab-do-min-al *adj.* abdominal
a-be-dul *m.* birch
a-be-ja *f.* bee
a-be-jo-rro *m.* bumblebee
a-be-jón *m.* hornet
a-be-rra-cion *f.* aberration
a-ber-tu-ra *f.* aperture; gap
a-be-to *m.* fir
a-bier-ta-mem-te *adv.* outright
a-bier-to, -ta *adj.* open; clear
a-bi-ga-rra-do, -da *adj.* many-colored variegated; motley
a-bis-mal *adj.* abysmal
a-bis-mo *m.* abyss
ab-ju-rar *v.* to abjure
a-blan-dar(se) *v., n.* to soften; mollify

a-bla-tivo *m.* ablative
a-blu-ción *f.* ablution
ab-ne-ga-ción *f.* abnegation
ab-ne-gar *v.* to renounce; abnegate
a-bo-car *v.* to decant
a-bo-car-dar *v.* to ream
a-bo-chor-na-do, -da *adj.* suffocating
a-bo-chor-nar *v.* to blush; suffocate
a-bo-fe-tear *v.* to slap
a-bo-ga-cí-a *f.* bar; law; advocacy
a-bo-ga-do *m.* attorney; counsel; lawyer
a-bo-gar *v.* to plead; to advocate
a-bo-len-go *m.* ancestry
a-bo-li-ción *f.* abolition
a-bo-li-cio-nis-ta *m., f.* abolitionist
a-bo-lir *v.* to abolish
a-bo-lla-du-ra *f.* dent
a-bo-llar *v.* to emboss; dent
a-bo-mi-na-ble *adj.* abominable
a-bo-mi-na-ción *f.* abomination
a-bo-mi-nar *v.* to abominate; loathe
a-bo-nar *v.* to fertilize; give credit
a-bo-no *m.* manure; fertilizer; subscription; guarantee
a-bo-ri-gen *adj. m., pl.* aboriginal
a-bo-rre-cer *v.* to hate; abhor
a-bo-rre-ci-ble *adj.* detestable; abhorrent; loathsome; hateful
a-bo-rree-ci-mien-to *m.* hate; hatred; abhorrence; loathing
a-bor-tar *v.* to abort
a-bor-tivo, a *adj.* abortive
a-bor-to *m.* abortion
a-bo-to-nar *v.* to button up
a-bo-za-lar *v.* to muzzle
a-bra *f.* cove
a-bra-sion *f.* abrasion
a-bra-si-vo *adj.* abrasive

a-bra-za-de-ra *f.* clamp; brace

a-bra-zar(se) *v.* to hug; cuddle; embrace

a-bra-zo *m.* hug; embrace

a-bre-car-tas *m.* letter opener

a-bre-var *v.* to soak; water

a-bre-via-ción *f.* abbreviation

a-bre-viar *v.* to abridge; abbreviate; curtail; condense

a-bri-gar(se) *v.* to shelter; harbor; protect

a-bri-go *m.* shelter; coat; overcoat

a-bril *m.* April

a-bri-llan-tar *v.* to cut into parts; polish; brighten

a-brir(se) *v.* to open up; to spread out; open

a-bro-char *v.* to button up; fasten; buckle

a-bro-ga-ción *f.* abrogation

a-bro-gar *v.* abrogate; repeal

a-bru-ma-dor, a *adj.* crushing

a-bru-mar *v.* to overwhelm

a-brup-to, -ta *adj.* abrupt; steep; blunt

a-bru-ta-do, -da *adj.* bestial

abs-ce-so *m.* abscess

ab-so-lu-ción *f.* absolution

ab-so-lu-to, -ta *adj.* complete; absolute

ab-sol-ven-te *adj.* absolving

ab-sol-ver *v.* to acquit; clear; absolve

ab-sor-ben-cia *f.* absorbence

ab-sor-ben-te *m.* absorbent

ab-sor-ber *v.* to soak up; engross; absorb

ab-sor-ción *f.* absorption

ab-sor-to, -ta *adj.* abosrbed; intent

abs-ten-cion *f.* abstention

abs-te-ner-se *v.* to abstain; refrain

abs-ti-nen-cia *f.* abstinence

abs-trac-to, -ta *adj.* abstract

abs-tra-er *v.* to abstract

abs-tru-so, -sa *adj.* abstruse

ab-sur-di-dad *f.* absurdity

ab-sur-do, -da *adj.* silly; pre-

posterous; absurd

a-bue-la *f.* grandmother-

a-bue-lo *m.* grandfather; grandparent

a-bun-da-mien-to *m.* abundance

a-bun-dan-cia *f.* abundance; amplitude

a-bun-dan-te *adj.* plentiful; aboundant; ample

a-bun-dar *v.* to abound

a-bun-do-so *adj.* abundant

a-bu-rri-do *adj.* boring; bored

a-bu-rri-mien-to *m.* boredom

a-bu-rrir *v.* to bore

a-bu-sar *v.* to misuse; maltreat; abuse; impose

a-bu-si-vo, a *adj.* abusive

a-bu-so *m.* encroachment; abuse

ab-yec-ción *f.* abjectness

ab-yec-to, -ta *adj.* abject

a-cá *adv.* here

a-ca-ba-do, -da *adj.* end; conclusion

a-ca-bar *v.* to accomplish; end; fail

a-ca-de-mia *f.* academy

a-ca-dé-mi-co *adj.* academic

a-ca-li-zar *v.* to alkalize

a-cam-par *v.* to camp

a-ca-ri-ciar *v.* to pet; pat

a-ca-rrear *v.* to cart

a-ca-rreo *m.* cartage

ac-ce-der *v.* to accede

ac-ce-si-ble *adj.* accessible

ac-ce-so *m.* approach; access

ac-ce-so-rio, a *m.* accessory

ac-ci-den-ta-do, a *adj.* uneven; broken; eventful

ac-ci-den-te *m.* casualty; accident

ac-ción *f.* movement; action

a-ce-bo *m.* holly

a-ce-char *v.* to lurk; watch for

a-cei-te *m.* oil

a-cei-tu-na *f.* olive

a-ce-le-rar(se) *v.* to speed; accelerate

a-cen-to *v.* stress; emphasis; accent

a-cen-tuar(se) v. to emphasize; accent; stress

a-cep-tar v. adopt; accept; agree to something

a-cer-car(se) v. to bring near

a-ce-ro n.m. steel

a-cer-ti-jo m. riddle

a-cé-ti-co adj. acetic

a-ce-to-na f. acetone

á-ci-do m. acid

á-ci-do bo-ri-co m. boric acid

á-ci-do ci-tri-co m. citric acid

á-ci-do sul-fu-ri-co m. sulphuric acid

a-cla-ma-ción f. acclaim

a-cla-ra-ción f. clarification

a-cla-rar v. to clear; to clarify; to rinse

a-cli-ma-tar v. acclimate

ac-ne m. acne

a-co-bar-dar(se) v. to flinch; unnerve; cringe

a-co-gi-da f. welcome; shelter

a-col-char v. pad

a-có-li-to m. altar boy; acolyte

a-co-me-ter v. attempt; undertake; overcome; attack

a-co-mo-da-di-zo adj. easygoing

a-co-mo-da-dor m. usher f. usherette

a-co-mo-dar v. to suit; to accommodate; put up

a-com-pa-ñan-te m. escort mus. accompanist

a-com-pa-ñar v. to escort; attend; go with; accompany

a-con-di-cio-na-d or de ai-re m. air conditioner

a-con-se-jar(se) v. to take advice; advise; counsel

a-con-te-cer v. to chance; to happen

a-con-te-ci-mien-to m. occasion; event; occurrence; happening

a-cor-dar(se) v. to agree on; remember; agree

a-cor-de m. chord; in tune; harmony; in accord

a-cor-deón m. accordion

a-cor-near v. to gore

a-co-rra-lar v. to round up; corral; intimidate; pen

a-cor-tar(se) v. to clip; shorten; lessen; obstruct

a-co-sar v. to harass; pursue; beset

a-cos-tar(se) v. to lie down; go to bed

a-cos-tum-brar(se) v. to be accustomed to; be used to; habituate

a-cre adj. acrid; sour

a-cre-cen-tar v. to advance; increase

a-cre-dor m. creditor

a-cri-mo-nia f. bitterness

a-cró-ba-ta n.m.f. acrobat

ac-ti-tud f. pose; position; attitude

ac-ti-var v. to activate

ac-ti-vi-dad f. movement; nimbleness; activity

ac-ti-vo, -va adj. alive; brisk; active; quick

ac-to m. event; act; function

ac-tor m. actor

ac-triz f. actress

ac-tual adj. instant; actual

ac-tual-men-te adv. at present; now; actually

ac-tuar v. perform; act; set in action

a-cua-rio m. aquarium

a-cu-á-til adj. aquatic

a-cu-chi-llar v. to slash; hack; knife

a-cue-duc-to m. aqueduct

a-cueo, a adj. watery

a-cuer-do m. remembrance; resolution; agreement; accord

a-cu-mu-lar v. to amass; stock-pile; accumulate; congest

a-cu-ña-cion f. coinage

a-cu-ñar v. to coin; mint

a-cu-sar v. to impeach; charge; indict; accuse

a-cús-ti-ca f. acoustics

a-chi-car v. diminish;

humble; bail

a-chis-pa-do, -da adj. tipsy

a-da-gio m. proverb; adage

a-da-lid m. commander

a-dap-ta-ble adj. adaptable; versatile

a-dap-ta-ción f. adaptation

a-dap-tar v. to fit; adapt; adapt oneself to; adjust

a-de-cua-do, -da adj. fit; suitable; adequate

a-de-fe-sio n. something gaudy; extravagance

a-de-ha-la f. tip; bonus

a-de-lan-ta-do, -da adj. fast; advanced

a-de-lan-tar(se) v. to further; proceed; overtake

a-de-lan-te adv. forwards; forward

a-de-lan-to m. progress; advance

a-del-ga-zar(se) v. to lose weight; taper; make thin; attenuate; slim down

a-de-mán m. attitude; gesture

a-de-más adv. besides; moreover; in addition

a-den-tro adv. inside; within

a-dep-to m. adept

a-de-re-zar v. to adorn; garnish

a-de-re-zo m. finery; adornment; dressing

a-des-trar v. to train

a-deu-dar v. to debit; owe

ad-he-ren-cia f. bond; adherence

ad-he-ren-te adj. adherent; adhesive

ad-he-rir(se) v. to cling; adhere; stick

ad-he-sión f. adherence

ad-he-si-vo, -va adj. ahesive

a-di-ción f. addition

a-di-cio-nal adj. more; extra; additional

a-dic-to, -ta adj. addicted

a-dies-trar(se) v. to exercise; train; practise

a-diós m. farewell; goodbye; good day

a-di-po-so, a m. fat; adipose

a-di-ta-men-to m. attachment; addition

a-di-ti-vo m. additive

a-di-vi-nar v. to foretell; to guess

ad-je-ti-vo m. adjective

ad-ju-di-ca-ción m. award; adjudgment

ad-ju-di-car(se) v. to allot; to award

ad-jun-tar v. to annex

ad-mi-nis-tra-ción f. administration; management

ad-mi-nis-tra-dor, -ra m. administrator; steward; manager

ad-mi-nis-trar v. to manage; dispense; administer

ad-mi-nis-tra-ti-vo, -va adj. administrative

ad-mi-ra-ble adj. fine; excellent; admirable

ad-mi-ra-ción f. admiration

ad-mi-rar(se) v. to wonder; admire; amaze

ad-mi-si-ble adj. acceptable; admissible

ad-mi-sión f. input; admission

ad-mi-tir v. to acknowledge; permit; admit

a-do-be m. adobe

a-do-les-cen-cia f. adolescence

a-dop-tar v. to embrace

a-dop-ti-vo, -va adj. adoptive

a-do-ra-ble adj. adorable

a-do-ra-ción f. adoration

a-do-rar v. to worship; adore

a-dor-me-cer(se) v. to fall asleep; drowse

a-dor-mi-de-ra f. poppy

a-dor-na-mien-to m. adornment

a-dor-nar v. to adorn; deck; ecorate; grace

a-dor-no m. adornment; ornament; array

ad-qui-rir v. to obtain; secure; acquire

a-dre-na-li-na f. adrenaline

ads-cri-bir v. assign; ascribe

a-dua-na f. customs

a-dua-ne-ro *m.* customs

a-du-cir *v.* to cite; adduce

a-du-ja-da *adj.* coiled

a-du-la-ción *f.* flattery; adulation

a-du-la-dor, a *m.* flatterer

a-du-lar *v.* to flatter; adulate

a-dul-te-ra-ción *f.* adulteration

a-dul-te-ra-dor, a *m.* adulterator

a-dul-te-rar *v.* to adulterate

a-dul-te-rio *m.* adultery

a-dul-to, -ta *m.* adult

a-dul-zar *v.* to make sweet

ad-ver-bi-al *adj.* adverbial

ad-ver-bio *m.* adverb

ad-ver-sa-rio *m.* opponent; adversary

ad-ver-si-dad *f.* adversity

ad-ver-so, -sa *adj.* averse; unfavorable; adverse

ad-ver-ti-do, -da *adj.* skillful; informed; intelligent; capable; sagacious

ad-ver-tir *v.* to notify; advise; caution; take notice of something; observe

ad-ya-cen-te *adj.* adjacent

ae-ra-ción *f.* aeration

aé-reo, -rea *adj.* aerial

ae-ro-di-na-mi-co *adj.* aerodynamic

ae-ro-náu-ti-ca, -co *f.* aeronautics

ae-ro-pla-no *n.* airplane; aeroplane

ae-ro-puer-to *m.* airport

a-fa-bi-li-dad *f.* affability

a-fa-ble *adj.* affable; genial; kind

a-fán *m.* anxiety; travail

a-fa-nar *v.* to urge; toil; strive

a-fa-no-so, -sa *adj.* anxious

a-fec-ción *f.* fondness; affection

a-fec-ta-ción *f.* pretense; affectation

a-fec-ta-do, -da *adj.* affected

a-fec-tar *v.* to affect

a-fec-to *m.* affection

a-fec-tuo-sa-men-te *adv.* fondly; affectionately

a-fec-tuo-so *adj.* affectionate

a-fei-ta-do, -da *m.* shave

a-fei-tar *v.* to shave

a-fei-te *m.* shave; cosmetic

a-fe-rrar(se) *v.* to grasp; furl

a-fian-zar *v.* to bail; clinch; quaranty

a-fi-ción *f.* liking; affection; inclination

a-fi-cio-na-do, -da *m.* fan; amateur; fancier

a-fi-jo, -ja *m.* affix

a-fi-lar(se) *v.* to sharpen

a-fi-liar(se) *v.* to join; affiliate; adopt

a-fin *adj.* related; contiguous; adjacent

a-fi-na-ción *f.* refining; tuning

a-fi-nar *v.* to refine; polish; complete; tune

a-fi-ni-dad *f.* affinity; relationship

a-fir-mar(se) *v.* to secure; assert; contend; affirm; make fast

a-fir-ma-ti-vo *adj.* affirmative

a-flic-ción *f.* anxiety; bereavement; afflication

a-fli-gi-do *adj.* stricken

a-fli-gir(se) *v.* to afflict

a-flo-jar(se) *v.* to loosen; slacken; weaken

a-flo-rar *v.* to emerge; sift

a-fluen-cia *f.* affluence; crowd; jam; fluency; abundance

a-fluen-te *adj.* affluent

a-fo-rar *v.* to appraise; guage; measure

a-fo-ris-mo *m.* aphorism; maxim

a-for-tu-na-do, -da *adj.* prosperous; lucky; fortunate

a-fren-ta *f.* to insult; affront

a-fren-tar(se) *v.* insult; affront; be affronted

a-fro-di-sia-co *adj.* aphrodisiac

a-fue-ra *adv.* outside; outkirts; suburbs

a-ga-char(se) *v.* to crouch; squat; bow down

a-ga-lla f. gill
a-ga-rrar(se) v. to grasp; seize; clutch; clinch
a-ga-rre m. gripping
a-ga-rro m. grip; lutch; grab
a-ga-rro-tar v. to compress; bind tightly
a-ga-sa-ja-dor adj. attentive
a-ga-sa-jar v. to entertain; fondle; welcoming
a-gen-cia f. bureau; agency
a-gen-ciar v. to obtain
a-gen-cio-so adj. industrious
a-gen-da f. diary; notebook
a-gen-te m. officer; agent
a-gil adj. nimble; agile; lithe; active; lithesome
a-gi-li-dad f. agility
a-gi-a-ción f. flurry; flutter; stir; excitement; agitation
a-gi-tar(se) v. to stir up; churn; flutter; shake
a-glo-me-ra-ción f. agglomeration
a-glo-me-ra-do adj. agglomerate
a-glo-me-rar v. agglomerate
a-glu-ti-na-ción f. agglutination
a-glu-ti-nan-te m. cement
a-glu-ti-nar v. to agglutinate
a-go-nia f. pain; agony
a-go-ni-oso adj. persistent
a-go-rar v. to foretell
a-gos-tar v. to consume
a-gos-to m. August; harvest
a-go-ta-mien-to m. exhaurstion; depletion
a-go-tar(se) v. to drain; give out; tire; exhaust
a-gra-cia-do, a adj. attractive
a-gra-ciar v. to award; grace
a-gra-da-ble adj. gracious; nice; pleasant; agreeable; delightful
a-gra-dar v. to please
a-gra-de-cer(se) v. to appreciate; acknowledge; thank
a-gra-de-ci-do, -da adj. thankful; grateful
a-gra-do m. liking; taste
a-gran-dar v. to grow bigger
a-gra-va-ción f. aggravation

a-gra-van-te adj. aggravating
a-gra-viar v. to harm; wrong
a-gra-vio m. offence; injury; grievance; harm
a-gra-vio-so adj. injurious; offensive; insulting
a-gre-dir v. to assault
a-gre-sión f. aggression
a-gre-si-vo adj. aggressive
a-gre-sor, a m. aggressor
a-griar v. to annoy; sour
a-gri-cul-tu-ra f. farming
a-grie-tar v. to split
a-gri-men-su-ra f. surveying
a-grio, a adj. acid; sour
a-gro m. farming
a-gro-no-mi-co, -ca adj. agro-nomical
a-gru-pa-ción f. group
a-gru-par(se) v. to cluster; bunch; group
a-gua f. water
a-gua-ca-te m. avocado
a-gua-do, -da adj. diluted
a-gua-ma-ri-na f. aquamarine
a-guan-tar(se) v. to support; endure; hold
a-guan-te m. endurance
a-guar-dar v. to await
a-gu-de-za f. acumen; keenness; sharpness; brightness
a-gu-di-zar v. to sharpen
a-gu-do, -da adj. sharp
a-güe-ro m. omen
a-gue-rri-do, a adj. seasoned
a-gui-la f. eagle
a-gu-ja f. needle
a-gu-je-ro m. hole
a-guo-so, -sa adj. watery
a-gu-zar v. to sharpen
a-hi adv. there
a-hi-ja-da f. goddaughter
a-hi-ja-do m. godson
a-hi-jar v. to adopt
a-hi-la-do-do adj. faint; soft
a-hi-lar v. to faint
a-hi-to, -ta adj. stuffed
a-ho-gar v. to oppress; drown; choke
a-ho-ra adv. now
a-hor-ca-jar(se) v. to straddle

a-hor-mar v. to fit
a-ho-rrar v. to spare
a-ho-rro m. savings
a-hue-va-do adj. egg-shaped
a-hu-ma-do, -da adj. smoky; cured; smoked
a-hu-mar v. to cure; smoke
ai-rar v. to annoy; anger
ai-re m. aspect; air
ai-re-a-do adj. aired out
ai-re-ar(se) v. to air; cool
ai-re-o m. ventilation
ais-la-do, -da adj. alone
ais-lar v. to seclude; isolate
a-ja-do, -da adj. withered
a-jar v. to mar; spoil
a-je-dre-cis-ta f., m. chess player
a-je-drez m. chess
a-jen-jo m. bitterness
a-je-no, -na adj. alien; strange; foreign
a-je-tre-o m. agitation
a-jo m. garlic
a-jo-bo m. burden
a-jus-tar v. to settle; adapt; adjust; fix; tighten
a-jus-te m. fitting; accommodation
a-jus-ti-cia-mien-to m. execution
a-jus-ti-ciar v. to execute
a-la f. wing
a-la-ban-za f. praise
a-la-bar v. to commend
a-la-bas-tro m. alabaster
a-la-crán m. scorpion
a-la-cri-dad f. eagerness
a-la-do, -da adj. winged
a-lam-bre m. wire
á-la-mo m. poplar
a-lar-de-o m. bragging
a-lar-gar(se) v. to rejoice; cheer; lengthen; extend
a-lar-ma f. alarm
a-lar-ma-dor, a adj. alarming
a-lar-mar v. to alarm
al-ba f. daybreak
al-ba-ri-co-que m. apricot
al-ber-ca f. tank
al-ber-gar v. to cherish
al-bi-no, -na adj. albino
al-bo-ro-ta-do, -da adj. rowdy; excited
al-bo-ro-tar v. to excite; incite
al-bo-ro-zo m. joy
al-ca-cho-fa f. artichoke
al-cal-de m. mayor
al-ca-li-no, a adj. alkaline
al-ca-loi-de m. alkaloid
al-can-for m. camphor
al-can-zar v. to attain; reach; pass; grasp
al-cau-cil m. artichoke
al-cá-zar m. castle
al-ce m. moose
al-co-ba f. bedroom
al-co-hoi m. alcohol
al-co-hó-li-co adj. alcoholic
a-le-a-to-rio adj. uncertain
a-le-go-ri-a f. allergy
a-le-grar v. to happy; cheer; rejoice
a-le-gre adj. joyous; gay; glad
a-le-gre-men-te adv. gaily
a-le-gri-a f. gladness; gaiety
a-le-grón m. joy
a-le-ja-mien-to m. distance; withdrawal; estrangement
a-le-la-do adj. bewildered
a-len-ta-dor, ra adj. encouraging
a-len-tar v. to animate
a-ler-gia f. allergy
a-ler-gi-co, -ca adj. allergic
a-ler-tar v. to alert; warn
a-le-te-o m. flapping
al-fa-bé-ti-co adj. alphabetical
al-fa-be-to m. alphabet
al-fa-re-rí-a f. pottery
al-fi-le-rar v. to pin
al-fom-bra f. carpet
al-fom-brar v. to carpet
al-for-za f. pleat
al-ge-bra f. algebra
al-go pron. anything; something
al-go-dón m. cotton
al-guien pron. someone; anyone
al-gún adj. some
al-gu-no, a pron. anybody
al-ha-ja f. gem
al-ho-ce-ma f. lavender

aliado 9 amigo

a-lia-do, -da *m.* ally
a-lian-za *f.* alliance
a-li-bi *m.* alibi
a-lie-na-ble *adj.* alienable
a-lie-na-ción *f.* alienation
a-lie-nar *v.* to alienate
a-lien-to *m.* courage
a-li-ge-rar(se) *v.* to relieve
a-li-men-tar *v.* to feed
a-li-men-ti-cio *adj.* nutritious
a-li-men-to *m.* food
a-li-ne-a-ción *f.* alignment
a-li-ñar *v.* to tidy
a-li-ño *m.* tidiness
a-li-sar *v.* to smooth
a-lis-tar *v.* to list
a-li-viar *v.* to alleviate; allay
a-li-vio *m.* easing
al-ma *f.* spirit
al-má-ci-ga *f.* nursery
al-me-ja *f.* calm
al-men-dro, a *m.* almond tree
al-mi-dón *m.* starch
al-mi-do-nar *v.* to starch
al-miz-cle *m.* musk
al-mo-ha-da *f.* pillow
al-mor-zar *v.* to lunch
al-muer-zo *m.* lunch
a-lo-ca-do, -da *adj.* crazy
a-lo-cu-ción *f.* allocution
a-lo-jar(se) *v.* to house
a-lon-gar *v.* to stretch; to make longer
al-pi-no *adj.* alpine
al-qui-lar *v.* to hire; rent
al-qui-mia *f.* alchemy
al-qui-mis-ta *m.* alchemist
al-re-de-dor, ra *adv.* around *prep.* round
al-ta-men-te *adv.* extremely
al-tar *m.* altar
al-té-ra-ción *f.* alteration
al-ter-ca-ción *f.* altercation
al-ter-na-do *adj.* alternate
al-ter-nar *v.* rotate; alternate
al-ter-na-ti-va *f.* alternative
al-ti-me-trí-a *f.* altimetry
al-ti-tud *f.* altitude
al-to, -ta *adj.* upper; high
al-truis-ta *adj.* altruistic
al-tu-ra *f.* elevation; height
a-lu-ci-nar *v.* to hallucinate
a-lu-ci-na-to-rio *adj.* hallu-cinatory
a-lu-dir *v.* to allude
a-lum-bra-do *m.* lightening
a-lu-mi-nio *m.* aluminum
a-lum-no, -na *m.* student; alumnus
a-lu-sión *f.* allusion
al-za-do *adj.* elevated
al-zar *v.* to hoist; lift up; raise
a-llá *adv.* there
a-lla-nar *v.* overcome; flatten
a-lle-ga-do, -da *adj.* related; close; near
a-llí *adv.* there
a-ma-bi-li-dad *f.* kindness
a-ma-ble *adj.* lovable; amiable; kindly
a-ma-do *adj.* beloved
a-ma-es-trar *v.* to train
a-ma-ne-cer *v.* to nurse
a-ma-ne-ci-da *f.* daybreak
a-man-ser *v.* to soothe; tame
a-ma-na-do *adj.* skillful; fixed
a-ma-ño *m.* skill
a-ma-po-la *f.* poppy
a-mar *v.* to love
a-mar-gar *v.* to make bitter
a-mar-gor *m.* bitterness
a-ma-ri-llo, a *m.* yellow
a-ma-rrar *v.* to fasten; tie
a-ma-teur *adj.* amateur
a-ma-tis-ta *f.* amethyst
ám-bar *m.* amber
am-bi-ción *f.* ambition
am-bi-cio-so *adj.* ambitious
am-bien-ta-ción *f.* atmo-sphere
am-bi-gue-dad *f.* ambiguity
am-bi-guo *adj.* uncertain; ambiguous
am-bu-lan-cia *f.* ambulance
am-bu-lan-te *adj.* ambu-latory
am-bu-lar *v.* amble
a-me-ba *f.* amoeba
a-me-na-za *f.* threat
a-me-na-zar *v.* to menace
a-me-ni-dad *f.* amenity
a-me-ri-ca-no *adj.* American
a-mi-ga *f.* girl friend
a-mi-gar *v.* to reconcile
a-mig-da-la *f.* tonsil
a-mi-go *m.* boy friend

a-mi-la-na-do *adj.* intimidated

a-mi-la-nar *v.* to discourage; intimidate; scare; frighten

a-mis-to-so, a *adj.* friendly

a-mo *m.* master; boss

a-mo-lar *v.* to sharpen

a-mol-dar *v.* to adjust; mold

a-mon-to-nar(se) *v.* to amass; hoard; huddle

amor *m.* lover

a-mo-ra-li-dad *f.* amorality

a-mo-ro-so, -sa *adj.* amorous; loving

am-pa-rar *v.* defend; protect

am-pliar *v.* expand; increase

am-pli-fi-ca-ción *f.* amplification

am-pli-fi-car *v.* to amplify

am-po-lle-ta *f.* hourglass

am-pu-ta-ción *f.* amputation

am-pu-tar *v.* to amputate

a-na-car-do *m.* cashew

a-na-de *m.* duck

a-na-gra-ma *f.* anagram

a-nal-ge-si-co *adj.* analgesic

a-na-li-sis *m.* analysis

a-na-lis-ta *m.* analyst

a-na-li-ti-co *adj.* analytical

a-na-li-zar *v.* to analyze

a-na-lo-gi-a *f.* analogy

a-na-na *m.* pineapple

a-na-quel *m.* shelf

a-na-ran-ja-do, a *adj.* orange

a-nar-quis-ta *m.*, *f.* anarchist

a-na-to-mi-a *f.* anatomy

a-na-to-mi-co *adj.* anatomic

an-cia-no, -na *adj.* aged

an-cla *f.* anchor

an-cho *adj.* broad

an-cho-a *f.* anchovy

an-dar *v.* to go; ambulate

an-dra-jo-so, -sa *adj.* ragged

an-droi-de *m.* android

a-nec-do-ta *f.* anecdote

a-ne-gar *v.* to flood

a-ne-mi-co, -ca *adj.* anemic

a-nes-te-siar *v.* anesthetize

an-gel *m.* angel

an-ge-li-co, -ca *adj.* angelical

an-go-ra *adj.* angora

an-gui-la *f.* eel

an-gu-lo *m.* angle

an-gu-lo-so *adj.* angular

an-gu-rri *f.* greed

an-gus-tiar *v.* to anguish

an-he-lar *v.* to long for; yearn

a-ni-llo *m.* ring

a-ni-ma-ción *f.* animation

a-ni-ma-do, -da *adj.* lively; animate

a-ni-mal *m.* animal

a-ni-mar *v.* to become animated; enliven

a-ni-qui-lar *v.* to destroy; annihilate

a-ni-ver-sa-rio, -ria *adj.* anniversary

a-no-che *adv.* last night

a-no-ni-mo *adj.* anonymous

a-nor-mal *adj.* subnormal; abnormal

a-no-ta-ción *f.* note

a-no-tar *v.* to note

an-sar *m.* goose

an-sia *f.* yearning

an-siar *v.* to long for

an-sie-dad *f.* anxiety

an-te *prep.* before

an-te-bra-zo *m.* forearm

an-te-ce-der *v.* to anteceed

an-te-de-cir *v.* to predict

an-te-pa-sa-do *m.* ancestor

an-te-rior *adj.* proir; anterior

an-tes de *adv.* before

an-ti-a-ci-do *adj.* antacid

an-ti-bio-ti-co *m.* antibiotic

an-ti-ci-pa-do *adj.* advanced

an-ti-ci-par *v.* advance

an-ti-cuer-po *m.* antibody

an-ti-do-to *m.* antidote

an-ti-guo *adj.* ancient; antique

an-ti-lo-pe *m.* antelope

an-ti-na-tu-ral *adj.* unnatural

an-ti-sep-ti-co *m.* antiseptic

an-ti-so-cial *adj.* antisocial

an-ti-to-xi-co *adj.* antitoxic

an-to-ni-mia *f.* antonymy

an-tro-poi-de *adj.* anthropoid

a-nual *adj.* annual

a-nua-rio *m.* annual

a-nu-blar *v.* to cloud

a-nu-lar *v.* to cancel

a-nun-cia-ción *f.* announcement

a-nun-cian-te *m.* advertiser

a-nun-ciar *v.* to announce

an-zue-lo *m.* fishhook

a-na-di-do *m.* addition

a-na-dir *v.* to add

a-ne-jo, -ja *adj.* old; mature

a-nil *adj., m.* indigo

a-ño *m.* year

a-pa-bu-llar *v.* to squash

a-pa-ci-ble *adj.* gentle

a-pa-ci-guar(se) *v.* appease

a-pa-dri-nar *v.* to support

a-pa-le-o *m.* thrashing

a-pa-nar *v.* to mend; to seize; grasp; repair

a-pa-ra-to *m.* apparatus

a-pa-ra-to-so *adj.* ostentatious

a-par-car *v.* to park

a-pa-ra-cer(se) *v.* to haunt; to come

a-pa-re-jar *v.* to prepare

a-pa-ren-te *adj.* seeming

a-pa-ri-ción *f.* appearance

a-par-ta-do *adj.* isolated

a-par-ta-men-to *m.* apartment

a-par-tar(se) *v.* to divide; to remove

a-par-te *adv.* aside; apart

a-pa-sio-nar *v.* to excite

a-pa-ti-a *f.* apathy

a-pa-ti-co, -ca *adj.* apathetic

a-pe-ar *v.* to chock; fell

a-pe-la-ble *adj.* appealable

a-pe-lar *v.* to appeal

a-pe-lli-dar *v.* to name; called

a-pe-lli-do *m.* name

a-pe-nar *v.* pained; to grieve

a-pen-di-ci-tis *m.* appendictis

a-pe-ro *m.* gear

a-pes-tar *v.* to annoy; infect

a-pe-ten-cia *f.* appetite

ape-ti-to *m.* appetite

a-pe-ti-to-so, a *adj.* delicious

a-pio *m.* celery

a-pla-car *v.* to placate

a-pla-nar *v.* to flatten; stun

a-plas-tar(se) *v.* to flatten

a-plau-dir *v.* to clap; applaud

a-plau-so *m.* clapping

a-pli-ca-ble *adj.* applicable

a-pli-ca-ción *f.* application

a-pli-car *v.* to apply

a-po-ca-do, -da *adj.* timid

a-po-de-rar(se) *v.* empower

a-po-do *m.* nickname

a-po-li-ti-co *adj.* apolitical

a-po-rre-ar(se) *v.* to beat

a-por-tar *v.* to bring; arrive

a-po-sen-to *m.* lodging

a-po-si-ción *f.* apposition

a-pos-tol *m.* apostle

a-pos-tro-fo *m.* apostrophe

a-po-te-ca-rio *m.* apothecary

a-po-te-o-sis *f.* apothesis

a-po-yar(se) *v.* to rest on; to support

a-po-yo *m.* support

a-pre-cia-ción *f.* appreciation

a-pre-ciar *v.* to value; appreciate

a-pre-cio *m.* attention; appraisal

a-pre-hen-der *v.* to seize

a-pre-hen-sión *f.* comprehension; apprehension

a-pren-der *v.* to learn

a-pren-sión *f.* suspicion

a-pre-sar *v.* to seize

a-pre-su-rar *v.* to hurry

a-pre-tar *v.* to crowd; clutch

a-pro-ba-do, a *adj.* approved

a-pro-bar *v.* to pass

a-pro-pia-do *adj.* appropriate

a-pro-piar(se) *v.* appropriate

a-pro-vi-sio-nar *v.* provision

a-pro-xi-mar(se) *v.* to approximate

ap-ti-tud *f.* talent; aptitude

a-pues-to *f.* wager

a-pun-tar(se) *v.* to aim; point

a-pun-te *m.* notation; note

a-pu-rar(se) *v.* to worry

a-que-jar *v.* to distress

a-quel *adj.* that; those

a-quel *pron.* that one

a-qui *adv.* now; here; then

a-quie-tar *v.* to soothe; to calm down

a-ra *f.* altar

a-ra-na *f.* spider

ar-bi-trar *v.* unpire; arbitrate

ar-bi-tra-rio, a *adj.* arbitrary

ar-bi-tro, -tra *m.* arbitrator

ar-bol *m.* tree
ar-bo-re-to *m.* arboretum
ar-bus-to *m.* shrub
ar-ca-da *f.* arcade
ar-ca-is-ta *f.* archaist
ar-can-gel *m.* archangel
ar-ce *m.* maple tree
ar-co *m.* arch
ar-chi-du-que *m.* archduke
ar-chi-du-que-sa *f.* archduchess
ar-chi-var *v.* to file
ar-chi-vo *m.* archives
ar-der(se) *v.* to burn
ar-dien-te *adj.* ardent; burning
ar-di-lla *f.* squirrel
ar-dor *m.* heat
ar-duo *adj.* arduous
a-re-a *f.* area
a-re-no-so *adj.* sandy
a-ren-que *m.* herring
ar-gen-tar *v.* to silver-plate
ar-gen-ta-rio *m.* silversmith
ar-go-lla *f.* ring
ar-guir *v.* to prove; argue
ar-gu-men-tar *v.* to argue
a-ri-do *adj.* dry
a-ris-co, -ca *adj.* wild; unfriendly; surly; churlish
a-ris-to-cra-cia *f.* aristocracy
a-ris-to-cra-ta *f.,m.* aristocrat
a-rit-me-ti-co *adj.* arithmetic
ar-le-quin *m.* harlequin
ar-ma *f.* weapon
ar-ma-do *adj.* armed
ar-mar *v.* to assemble; reinforce; arm; equip
ar-ma-rio, a *m.* buffet; closet
ar-mi-no *m.* ermine
ar-mis-ti-cio *m.* armistice
ar-mo-ni-a *f.* accord
ar-mo-ni-co *m., adj.* harmonicar
ar-mo-ni-zar *v.* to harmonize
a-ro *m.* hoop; ring
a-ro-ma *m.* fragrance
a-ro-mar *v.* to scent; perfume
a-ro-ma-ti-co *adj.* aromatic
a-ro-ma-ti-zar *v.* to perfume; scent
a-ro-mo-so *adj.* aromatic
ar-pis-ta *m., f.* harpist

ar-que-o-lo-gi-a *f.* archaelogy
ar-qui-tec-to *m., f.* architect
ar-qui-tec-tu-ra *f.* architecture
a-rra-ci-ma-do *adj.* bunched
a-rran-car *v.* to seize; pull up; obtain; stem
a-rra-sar *v.* to clear; level
a-rras-trar(se) *v.* to pull; to crawl; to draw
a-rre-ar *v.* to harness; herd
a-rre-ba-ta-dor *adj.* exciting
a-rre-ba-to *m.* rage
a-rre-ci-fe *m.* reef
a-rre-gla-do *adj.* neat
a-rre-glar(se) *v.* order; settle
a-rre-glo *m.* understanding; arrangement
a-rre-me-dar *v.* to copy
a-rre-me-ter *v.* to attack
a-rren-dar *v.* to rent
a-rre-o *m.* drove; herd
a-rre-pen-tir-se *v.* to regret
a-rres-ta-do *adj.* arrested
a-rres-to *m.* arrest
a-rri-ba *adv.* above
a-rri-bar *intr.* to arrive
a-rri-bis-ta, -to *adj.* social-climbing
a-rri-bo *m.* arrival
a-rrien-do *m.* renting
a-rries-ga-do, -da *adj.* hazardous; daring
a-rries-gar(se) *v.* to venture; jeopardize; risk
a-rri-mar *v.* to draw or bring near
a-rri-mo *m.* partition
a-rrin-co-na-do *adj.* distant
a-rrin-co-nar *tr.* to corner; to place in a corner
a-rris-ca-mien-to, -ta *m.* boldness; daring
a-rris-car *v.* to fold up; to turn up
a-rrit-mia *f.* lack of rhythm
a-rro-ba-mien-to *m.* rapture; ecstasy
a-rro-bar *v.* to enrapture
a-rro-di-llar(se) *v.* to kneel
a-rro-gan-te *adj.* proud; arrogant
a-rro-jar(se) *v.* to fling; emit;

throw

a-rro-jo, -ja *m.* boldness

a-rro-lla-dor, ra *adj.* overwhelming

a-rro-liar *v.* to carry or sweep away

a-rro-par *v.* to tuck in; to wrap with clothing

a-rro-rro *m.* lullaby

a-rro-yo *m.* brook; stream

a-rroz *m.* rice pudding

a-rro-zal *m.* rice paddy or rice field

a-rru-ga *f.* crease; fold; wrinkle line

a-rru-ga-do *adj.* wrinkled

a-rru-gar(se) *v.* to rumple; wrinkle

a-mui-nar *v.* to destroy

a-rru-lla-dor *adj.* soothing

a-rru-llar *v.* to lull to sleep; to coo

a-rru-ma-co *m.* caress

a-rrum-bar *v.* to neglect; to put or cast aside

ar-se-nal *m.* storehouse; shipyard

ar-se-ni-co *m.* arsenic

ar-te *f.* craft; art

ar-te-fac-to *m.* appliance

ar-te-ria *f.* artery

ar-te-ro *adj.* sly; cunning

ar-te-sa-ni-a *f.* craftsmanship

ar-te-sa-no *m,f.* craftswoman or craftsman

ar-ti-cu-la-ción *f.* joint

ar-ti-cu-lar *v.* to articulate

ar-tis-ta *f., m.* artist

ar-ti-fi-cio, -cia *m.* item; article; thing

ar-ti-fi-cial *adj.* artificial

ar-tis-ti-co *adj.* artistic

ar-tri-tis *f.* arthritis

ar-zo-bis-po *m.* archbishop

as *m.* ace

a-sa-do *m.* roasted meat; barbecue

a-sa-dor *m.* grill

a-sa-la-ria-do, -da *adj.* salaried worker

a-sa-la-riar *v.* to set a salary for someone

a-sal-ta-dor, a *m.f.* assailant

a-sal-tar *v.* to attack

a-sal-to *m.* attack

a-sam-ble-a *f.* conference; meeting

a-sam-ble-is-ta *m.f.* assembly member

as-cen-den-cia *f.* ancestry

as-cen-den-te *adj.* ascending

as-cen-der *v.* to promote; ascend

as-cen-sión *f.* rise; ascension

as-cen-so *m.* ascent; promotion

as-cen-sor, a *m.* lift; elevator

as-cen-so-ris-ta *m., f.* one who operates an elevator

as-co *m.* disgust

a-se-ar *v.* to clean; to wash

a-se-char *v.* to trap

a-se-diar *v.* to bother; to pester

a-se-dio *m.* siege

a-se-gu-ra-do *adj.* insured

a-se-gu-rar(se) *v.* to fasten; assure; secure

a-se-me-jar(se) *v.* to resemble

a-sen-ta-de-ras *f.pl.* buttocks; behind

a-sen-ta-do *adj.* judicious

a-sen-tar *v.* to record

a-sen-ti-mien-to *m.* consent

a-sen-tir *intr.* to agree

a-se-o *m.* tidiness; neatness

a-se-qui-ble *adj.* understandable

a-ser-ción *f.* affirmation

a-se-rra-de-ro *m.* sawmill

a-se-rrar *v.* to saw

a-se-rrin *m.* sawdust

a-se-si-nar *v.* to murder

a-se-si-na-to *m.* murder; *pol* assassination

a-se-si-no *adj.* murderous *pol* assassin

a-se-sor, ra *adj.* advisory, advising

a-se-so-rar *v.* to advise

a-ses-tar *v.* to aim

a-se-ve-rar *v.* to assert

a-se-ve-ra-ti-vo *adj.* affirmative; assertive

a-se-xua-do *adj.* asexual

as-fal-tar *v.* to asphalt

as-fal-to *m.* asphalt

as-fi-xai *f.* suffocation

as-fi-xiar *v.* to asphyxiate

a-si *adv.* so

a-sien-to *m.* seat

a-sig-nar *v.* allot; assign

a-sig-nar *v.* to appoint; to assign

a-sig-na-cion *f.* course or subject in school

a-si-lar *tr.* to give shelter

a-si-lo *m.* asylum

a-si-mi-lar(se) *v.* assimilate

a-si-mis-mo *adj.* in a like manner; likewise

a-sir(se) *v.* grip; hold on to

a-sis-ten-cia *f.* attendance

a-sis-ten-cial *adj.* relier; assisting

a-sis-tir *intr.* to accompnay; to aid; to attend

as-ma *f.* asthma

as-ma-ti-co *adj.* & *m.f.* asthmatic

as-na-da *f.* stupidity

a-so-cia-cion *f.* association

a-so-cia-do *adj.* associated

a-so-ciar(se) *v.* to associate with

a-so-la-dor *adj.* ravaging

a-so-lar *v.* to scorch

a-so-le-a-mien-to *m.* sunstroke

a-so-le-ar *v.* to place in the sun

a-so-mar *v.* to show; *intr.* to appear

a-som-brar(se) *v.* to amaze; to astonish

as-pi-rar *v.* to breathe; inhale

as-pi-ri-na *f.* aspirin

as-tro-lo-gia *f.* astrology

as-tro-no-mia *f.* astronomy

as-tu-ta *adj.* artful; sly; canny; cunning

a-sun-to *m.* issue; concern

a-ta-car *v.* to assault; charge

a-ta-que *m.* attack

a-tar(se) *v.* to rope; tie; brace

a-ten-cion *f.* attention

a-ten-der *v.* to heed; attend

a-tes-ti-guar *v.* to testify

a-tie-sar(se) *v.* to tighten

at-le-ta *f.,* *m.* athlete

at-le-ti-co, a *adj.* athletic

a-to-mi-co *adj.* atomic

a-to-mo *m.* atom

a-trac-cion *f.* attraction

a-trac-ti-vo *adj.* engaging

a-traer *v.* to engage; lure

a-tras *adv.* aback; back

a-tra-sa-do *adj.* backwards

a-tri-buir *v.* to ascribe

a-tro-ci-dad *f.* atrocity

a-tur-dir(se) *v.* to daze; muddle; bewilder

au-di-cion *f.* audition

au-gus-to *adj.* August

au-men-tar(se) *v.* to augment; enhance

au-men-to *m.* raise; increase

aun *adv.* still

aun-que *conj.* although

au-sen-te *adj.* missing

au-ten-ti-ci-dad *f.* authenticity

au-to-bus *m.* bus

a-to-gra-fo *m.* autograph

au-to-mo-vil *m.* car

au-to-ri-za-cion *f.* authorization

a-van-zar(se) *v.* to advance

a-ve *f.* bird

a-ve-ni-da *f.* avenue

a-ven-tu-ra *f.* adventure

a-ver-sion *f.* aversion

a-via-cion *f.* aviation

a-vion *m.* plane; airplane

a-yu-da *f.* aid; help

a-yu-dar *v.* to assist; help

a-zo-rar *v.* to alarm

a-zo-rra-do *adj.* foxy

a-zo-ta-do *adj.* multicolored

a-so-tar *v.* to beat upon

a-zo-te *m.* spanking; whip

a-zu-car *m.* sugar

a-zu-ca-ra-do *adj.* sweet

a-zu-tre *m.* sulphur

a-zul *m.* blue

a-zu-la-do *adj.* bluish

a-zu-lar *v.* color or dye blue

a-zu-le-jo *m.* glazed tile

ba-ba f. spittle
ba-bar-se tr. to dribble
ba-ba-za f. slime
ba-bear v. to drool
ba-bel m. confusion
ba-be-ro m. bib
ba-bie-ca adj. m.f. simple person
ba-bor m. port
ba-bo-se-ar v. to slobber
ba-ca-la-o m. cod
ba-ca-nal a. bacchanalian
ba-ci-lo m. bacillus
bac-te-ria f. bacterium
bac-te-rio-lo-gi-a f. bacteriology
bac-te-rio-lo-go, a m.f. bacteriologist
ba-che m. pothole
ba-da-jo m. bell clapper
ba-du-la-que adj. & m. follish person
ba-ga-je m. luggage
ba-ga-te-la f. trinket; trifle
ba-gre m. catfish
ba-hi-a f. bay
bai-la-dor m. dancer
bai-lar v. to dance
bai-la-ri-na f. ballerina
bai-le m. ball; dance
ba-ja f. drop
ba-jar(se) v. to fall; lower
ba-je-za f. lowliness
ba-jo, -ja adv. below; adj. low; short; small
ba-jon m. decline mus bassoonist
ba-la f. bale
ba-la-da f. ballad
ba-la-di adj. trivial
ba-la-dro m. shout
ba-la-dron adj. boasting
ba-la-dro-na-da f. boast
ba-la-dro-ne-ar v. to brag; to boast
ba-lan-cear(se) v. to teeter
ba-lan-ce-o m. rocking
ba-lan-za f. scale
ba-lar v. to bleat
bal-bu-ce-ar v. to babble
bal-con m. balcony
ba-li-do m. bleat
ba-lis-ti-ca f. ballistics

ba-lis-ti-co adj. ballistic
ba-lon-ces-to m. basketball
ba-lon-ma-no m. handball
ba-lon-vo-le-a m. volleyball
ba-lo-ta f. ballot
bal-sa f. balsa
bal-sa-mo m. balsam
ba-luar-te m. bastion
ba-lle-na f. whale
ba-lle-na-to m. whale calf
ba-lle-ne-ro, -ra adj. whaling
ba-lles-ta f. crossbow
ba-lles-te-ar v. to shoot with a crossbow
ba-lles-te-ria f. archery
bam-ba-le-ar v. to sway
bam-bo-le-om m. wobble
ba-llet m. ballet
bam-bu m. bamboo
ba-na-na f. banana
ban-ca f. banking
ban-ca-rro-ta f. bankruptcy
ban-co m. bank; band; pew; bench
ban-da-da f. flock; group
ban-de-ra f. ensign; flag
ban-de-ja f. tray
ban-de-ro-la f. pennant
ban-di-do m. bandit
ban-do-le-ro m. bandit
ban-que-ta f. stool
ban-que-te m. feast
ban-que-tear v. to feast
ba-ñar(se) v. to bathe
ba-ño m. bathtub
ba-ra-jar v. to shuffle
ba-ra-to adv. cheaply; adj. inexpensive; cheap
bar-ba f. beard
bar-ba-coa f. barbecue
bar-ba-do adj. bearded
bar-ba-ri-dad f. outrage
bar-ba-ra f., -ro m. savage
bar-bear v. to shave
bar-be-ro m. barber
bar-be-lla f. chin
bar-bo-tar v. to mutter, mumble
bar-bo-te-o m. murmuring
bar-bu-do adj. heavily bearded
bar-bu-lla f. chatter; jabbering

bar-ca f. small boat
bar-ca-za f. launch
bar-co m. ship; boat
ba-ri-to-no m. baritone
bar-niz m. glaze; varnish; lacquer
bar-ni-zar v. varnish; lacquer
ba-ro-me-tro m. barometer
ba-ron m. baron
ba-ro-ne-sa f. baroness
ba-rra f. bar
ba-rra-ca f. booth
ba-rrer v. to sweep
ba-rre-ra f. barricade
ba-rri-ga f. belly
ba-rril m. barrel
ba-rrio m. neighborhood
ba-sal-to m. basalt
ba-sar v. to base
ba-se f. foundation
ba-si-co adj. basal
ba-si-li-ca f. basilica
bas-quet-bol m. basketball
bas-tan-te adj. sufficient
bas-tar v. to suffice
bas-tar-dear v. to debase
bas-to adj. rough
bas-ton m. baton; stick
ba-su-ra f. rubbish
ba-ta f. negligee
ba-ta-lla f. battle
ba-ta-llar v. to battle
ba-ta-llon m. battalion
ba-te-ria f. battery
ba-ti-do m. batter
ba-tir(se) v. to churn
ba-tu-ta f. baton
baul m. trunk
bau-tis-mo m. christening
bau-ti-zar v. to baptize
ba-ya f. berry
ba-yo adj. bay
ba-zar m. bazaar
ba-zu-ca f. bazooka
bea-ti-fi-car v. to beatify
bea-ti-fi-co adj. beatific
bea-ti-tud f. beatitude
be-be m. baby
be-ber v. to drink
be-bi-da f. beverage
be-ca f. scholarship
be-ce-rro m. calf
be-far v. to taunt

beige m. beige
beis-bol m. baseball
be-li-co-so, -sa adj. warlike
be-li-ge-ran-te adj. belligerent
be-lle-za f. beauty
be-llo adj. beautiful
be-mol m. flat
ben-de-cir v. to bless
ben-di-ción f. blessing
ben-di-to adj. holy
be-ne-fi-ciar(se) v. to benefit
be-ne-fi-cio-so adj. beneficial
be-ne-fi-co adj. charitable
be-ne-vo-lo adj. benevolent
ben-ga-la f. flare
be-nig-ni-dad f. kindness
be-nig-no adj. kind; mild
be-rrin-che m. tantrum
be-sar(se) v. to smooch
be-so, -sa m. kiss
bes-tia f. animal
bes-tial adj. bestial
Bi-blia f. Bible
bi-bli-co adj. Biblical
bi-blio-gra-fia f. bibliography
bi-blio-gra-fo, -fa m. bibliographer
bi-blio-te-ca f. library
bi-ceps m. biceps
bi-ci-cle-ta f. bicycle
bi-ci-clis-ta m., f. bicyclist
bi-cho m. bug
bien m. good
bien-ve-ni-da f. greeting
bi-fur-car-se v. to fork
bi-go-te m. mustache
bi-la-te-ral adj. bilateral
bi-lio-so adj. bilious
bi-lis f. bile
bi-llar m. billiards
bi-lle-te m. bill
bi-llon m. trillion
bi-na-rio adj. binary
bio-gra-fia f. biography
bio-gra-fi-co adj. biographic
bio-gra-fo m. biographer
bio-lo-gia f. biology
bio-lo-gi-co adj. biological
bio-lo-go m. biologist
biop-sia f. biopsy
bi-sa-bue-la f. -lo m. great-grandmother; -father

bi-se-car v. to bisect
bi-sec-cion f. bisection
bi-son-te m. bison
biz-guear v. to squint
blan-co adj. blank; white
blan-dir v. to flourish
blan-do adj. supple; soft
blan-quear v. to whiten
blas-fe-mar v. to swear
blas-fe-mia f. profanity
blin-da-do adj. armored
blo-que m. block
blo-quear v. to block
blu-sa f. blouse
bo-bo m. fool; ninny
bo-ca f. mouth
bo-ca-di-llo m. sandwich
bo-ca-do m. bite
bo-da f. marriage
bo-de-ga f. wine cellar
boi-co-teo m. boycott
bo-la f. fib; ball
bo-le-tin m. bulletin
bo-li-che m. bowling
bo-li-ta f. pellet
bol-sa f. bag; pouch
bol-si-llo m. pocket
bol-sis-ta m. stockbroker
bol-so m. handbag
bo-llo m. bump
bom-ba f. pump
bom-bar-de-ro m. bomber
bom-bear v. to pad; pump
bom-bi-lla f. bulb
bom-bon m. sweet
bon-dad f. kindness
bon-da-do-so, -sa adj. good
bo-ni-to, -ta adj. pretty
bo-quea-da f. gasp
bo-qui-lla f. nozzle
bor-de m. edge
bor-di-llo m. curb
bo-rra-cho m. drunkard
bo-rra-dor m. eraser
bos-que m. woods
bos-que-jar v. to outline
bo-ta f. wine bag
bo-ta-ni-ca f. botany
bo-te m. jackpot
bo-te-lla f. bottle
bo-ti-ca-rio m. druggist
bo-tin m. loot
bo-ton m. stud

bo-to-nes m. bellhop
bo-ve-da f. vault
bo-vi-no, -na adj. bovine
bo-xea-dor m. boxer
bo-xear v. to box
bo-ya f. buoy
bo-yan-te adj. buoyant
bo-zal m. muzzle
bra-man-te m. twine
bra-mar v. to bluster
bra-mi-do m. bellow
bra-vo, -va adj. brave
bra-za-do m. armful
bra-zo m. arm
bre-ve adj. short
bre-ve-dad f. conciseness
bri-bon adj. lazy
bri-llan-te adj. bright; shiny
bri-llar v. to glow; beam
bri-llo m. glow; shine
brin-car v. to jump; gambol
brio m. jauntiness
bri-sa f. breeze
bro-ca-do m. brocade
bro-che m. brooch
bro-mear(se) v. to joke
bro-mis-ta f. joker
bron-ce m. bronze
bron-cea-do m. suntan; bronze
bron-ce-ar v. to tan; to bronze
bron-co adj. coarse; rough
bron-quial adj. bronchial
bron-quio m. bronchial tube
bron-qui-tis f. bronchitis
bro-quel m. small sheild
bro-ta-du-ra f. budding; sprouting
bro-tar v. to bud
bru-je-ri-a f. witchcraft
bru-jo m. wizard
bru-ju-la f. compass
bru-mo-so adj. foggy; misty
bru-ni-du-ra f. polishing; burnishing
bru-nir v. to burnish; to polish
brus-co, -ca adj. sudden
bru-to m. beast; brute
bu-bon m. swelling or very large tumor
bu-ce-ar v. to swim under water

bu-cle *m.* curl; ringlet
bu-din *m.* pudding
bue-na-ven-tu-ra *f.* good luck; good fortune
bue-no, a *adj.* sound; good
buey *m.* ox
bu-fa-lo *m.* buffalo
bu-fan-da *f.* muffler; scarf
bu-fon *m.* clown; buffoon
bu-ho-ne-ro *m.* hawker; peddler
bui-tre *m.* vulture
bu-jia *f.* candle
bul-bo *m.* bulb
bu-le-var *m.* boulevard
bul-to *m.* mass; heft
bu-lla *f.* uproar; brawl; ctowd; mob
bu-lli-cio *m.* riot; racket; hubbub
bu-llir *v.* to boil
bu-me-ran-ang *m.* boomerrang
bu-nue-io *m.* fried dough
bu-que *m.* vessel; ship
bu-que *m.* bouquet
bur-bu-ja *f.* bubble
bur-de-os *adj.* deep red in color
bur-do *adj.* rough; coarse
bur-gue-si-a *f.* middle class
bu-ri-lar *v.* to engrave
bur-la *f.* taunt; joke
bur-lar(se) *v.* to gibe; joke
bur-les-co *adj.* burlesque
bu-ro-cra-ta *f.* bureaucrat
bu-rra *f.* stupid woman
bu-rro *m.* donkey; burro
bur-sa *f.* rubbish
bur-sa-til *adj.* stock market
bus-ca *f.* search
bus-ca-pie *m.* feeler
bus-car *v.* to look or search for
bus-ca-vi-das *m.f.* busybody
bus-que-da *f.* search
bus-to *m.* bust; chest
bu-ta-ca *f.* armchair
bu-ta-no *m.* butane
bu-ti-le-no *m.* butylene
bu-zo *m.* deep-sea diver
bu-zon *m.* mailbox

ca-bal *adj.* fair; precise
ca-ba-la *f. relig.* cabala
ca-bal-gar *v.* to ride on horseback
ca-bal-ga-ta *f.* cavalcade
ca-ba-lle-ria *f. milit.* cavalry
ca-ba-lle-ri-za *f.* stable
ca-ba-lle-ro *m.* gentleman
ca-ba-lle-te *m.* easel; sawhorse
ca-ba-lli-to, -ta *m.* pony, small horse
ca-ba-llo *m.* horse
ca-ba-llón *f.* ridge
ca-ba-na *f.* cabin
ca-ba-ret *m.* cabaret; night club
ca-be-ci-lla *m.* ringleader
ca-be-lle-ra *f.* head of hair
ca-be-llo *m.* hair
ca-ber *v.* to fit
ca-bes-tri-llo *m.* sling
ca-bes-tro *m.* halter
ca-be-za *f.* skull; head
ca-be-zón, o-na *adj.* bigheaded
ca-be-zo-ta *m.f. coll.* mule
ca-bil-dear *v.* to lobby
ca-bil-do *m.* town council
ca-ble *m.* cable
ca-ble-gra-fiar *v.* to cable
ca-ble-gra-ma *m.* cablegram
ca-ble-vi-sion *f.* cable television
ca-bo *m.* corporal; cape;
ca-bra *f.* goat
ca-brio *m.* rafter
ca-bri-to *m.* young goat, kid
ca-bro-na-da *f. coll.* dirty trick
ca-ca-hue-te *m.* peanut
ca-cao *m.* cocoa
ca-ca-re-ar *v.* to crow; cackle
ca-ca-tua *f.* cockatoo
ca-ce-ro-la *f.* casserole
ca-ci-que *m.* Indian chief
ca-ci-que-ar *intr. coll.* to order people around
ca-co *m.* burglar
cac-to *m.* cactus
ca-cha-lo-te *m.* sperm whale

ca-char v. to split; to chip
ca-cha-sa f. sluggish
ca-che-ar v. to frisk, to search
ca-che-mi-ra f. cashmere
ca-che-te-ar v. Amer. to slap; hit
ca-che-ti-na f. fist fight
ca-che-tu-do adj. plump or chubby-cheeks
ca-cho-rro m. puppy
ca-da adj. every; each
ca-dal-so m. platform
ca-da-ver m. body; corpse
ca-da-ve-ri-co adj. cadaverous
ca-de-na f. chain
ca-den-cia f. rhythm; cadence
ca-de-ra f. hip, hip joint
ca-de-te m. cadet
ca-du-co, a adj. lapse; to expire
caer(se) v. to fall
ca-fe m. coffee; cafe
ca-fe-i-na f. caffeine
ca-fe-tal m. coffee plantation
ca-fe-te-ri-a f. cafeteria; cafe
cai-da f. downfall; tumble
cai-man m. alligator
ca-ja f. cabinet; chest
ca-je-ro m. cashier; teller
ca-jis-ta m.f. typesetter
cal f. lime
ca-la f. cove
ca-la-ba-za f. pumpkin; gourd; squash
ca-la-bo-zo m. jail; underground prison cell
ca-la-dor m. mech. driller
ca-la-fa-te-ar v. to calk; caulk
ca-la-mar m. squid
ca-lam-bre m. cramp
ca-la-mi-dad f. calamity; misfortune
ca-la-mi-to-so adj. calamitous
ca-la-na f. character; nature
ca-lar(se) v. to swoop; to penetrate
cal-ce-te-ria f. hosiery
cal-ce-tin m. sock

cal-ci-fi-ca-ction f. calcification
cal-ci-fi-car(se) v. to calcify
cal-cio m. calcium
cal-co m. tracing
cal-co-ma-ni-a f. decal
cal-cu-la-dor, ra m.f. calculator
cal-cu-lar v. to estimate; calculate
cal-cu-lis-ta m.f. planner; calculator
cal-cu-lo m. calculation
cal-de-ra f. boiler
cal-do m. soup; broth; stock
ca-le-fac-ción f. heating; heat
ca-le-fac-tor m. heater
ca-len-da-rio m. calendar; schedule
ca-len-ta-dor adj. warming; heating
ca-len-tar(se) v. to heat or to warm
ca-lien-te adj. warm; hot
ca-li-na f. haze
ca-lip-so m. calypso
cal-ma f. calm
cal-man-te adj. sedative m. tranquilizer
cal-mar(se) v. to soothe; to calm; to settle
ca-lo-frí-o m. chill; feaver
ca-lor m. warmth; heat
ca-lo-ria f. calorie
ca-lo-ri-co adj. caloric
ca-lum-nia f. slander; calumny
ca-lum-nia-dor, ra adj. slanderous
ca-lu-ro-so adj. warm; hot
cal-va-rio m. relig. Clavary
cal-vi-cie f. baldness
cal-vo adj. bald
cal-za-da f. causeway; drive; highway; road
cal-zo-nes m. shoehorn
cal-zo-nes m., pl. trousers
ca-lla-do adj. silent; quiet
ca-llar(se) v. to keep quiet; hush
ca-lle f. street
ca-lle-jue-la f. alley

ca-llo *m.* callus; corn
ca-ma *f.* bed
ca-ma-da *f.* litter; brood
ca-ma-feo *m.* cameo
ca-ma-ra *f.* room; chamber
ca-ma-ra-da *m.,f.* comrade
ca-ma-re-ra *f.* waitress
ca-ma-re-ro *m.* waiter
ca-ma-ro-te *m.* cabin
cam-biar(se) *v.* to change; to alter
cam-bia-vi-a *m.* rail switch
cam-bio *m.* shift; change
cam-bis-ta *m.f.* broker, moneychanger
ca-me-le-ar *v. coll.* deceive
ca-me-lia *f.* camellia
ca-me-llo *m.* camel
ca-me-ro, a *adj.* double
ca-mi-lla *f.* stretcher
ca-mi-nar *v.* to walk; to travel
ca-mi-na-ta *f.* hike; walk
ca-mi-no *m.* route; road
ca-mion *m.* truck
ca-mio-ne-ro, a *m.f.* truck driver
ca-mio-ne-ta *f.* van
ca-mi-sa *f.* shirt
ca-mi-se-ta *f.* tee-shirt; undershirt
ca-mi-so-la *f.* camisole
ca-mi-son *m.* nightgown
ca-mo-rra *f. coll.* squabble
ca-mo-rre-ar *v. coll* to quarrel; squabble
cam-pa-men-to *m.* camp
cam-pa-na *f.* bell
cam-pa-na *f.* campaign
cam-pe-si-no, -na *adj.* country; peasant
cam-pes-tre *adj.* rural
cam-pis-ta *m.,f* camper
cam-po *m.* country; field
cam-po-san-to *m.* graveyard; cementery
ca-mu-fla-je *m.* camouflage
ca-mu-flar *v.* to camouflage
ca-nal *m.* canal; channel
ca-na-le-te *m.* paddle
ca-nas-ta *f.* hamper; basket
can-ce-la-ción *f.* cancellation
can-ce-lar *v.* to cancel
can-cer *m.* cancer

can-ci-ller *m.* chancellor
can-ci-lle-ri-a *f.* chancellery
can-ción *f.* song
can-cio-ne-ro *m. mus.* songbook
can-cro *m. med.* cancer
can-da-do *m.* padlock
can-del-la *f.* candle
can-de-le-ro *m.* candlestick
can-di-da-to *m.* candidate
can-di-da-tu-ra *f.* candidacy
can-di-do *adj.* unsophisticated
ca-ne-la *f.* cinnamon
ca-ne-ion *m.* roof gutter
ca-ne-lo-nes *m., pl.* canneloni
ca-ne-su *m.* bodice; yoke
can-gre-jo *m.* crab
can-gu-ro *m.* kangaroo
can-ni-bal *m.* cannibal
ca-ni-ca *f.* marble
ca-ni-no *adj.* canine
ca-ni-cu-la *f.* midsummer heat; dog days of summer
ca-ni-lla *f. anat.* shinbone
ca-ni-lli-ta *m.* newspaper boy
ca-ni-no, a *adj.& m.* canine
can-je *m.* trade; exchange
can-je-a-ble *adj.* exchangeable
can-je-ar *v.* to trade; exchange
ca-no, a *adj.* gray-haired
ca-noa *f.* canoe; rowboat
ca-non *m.* canon
can-sa-do *adj.* weary; tired; rundown
can-san-cio *m.* tiredness
can-sar(se) *v.* to weary; tire
can-ta-lu-po *m.* cantaloupe
can-tan-te *m.,f.* singer
can-tar *v.* to sing; chant *m.* song
can-te-ra *f.* pit; quarry
can-ti-dad *f.* quantity; amount
can-tim-plo-ra *f.* canteen
can-to *m.* singing; croak
can-tu-rrear *v.* to croon; hum
ca-na *f.* cane; reed
ca-no *m.* pipe; spout

ca-non *m.* cannon; barrel

ca-os *m.* chaos

ca-pa *f.* cape; coating; layer

ca-pa-ci-dad *f.* capacity; capability

ca-pa-taz *m.* foreman

ca-paz *adj.* roomy; capable

cap-cio-so *adj.* deceitful

ca-pe-llan *m.* chaplain

ca-pe-ru-za *f.* hood

ca-pi-lar *adj. & m.* capillary

ca-pi-la-ri-dad *f.* capillarity

ca-pi-lla *f.* chapel

ca-pi-llo *m.* baby bonnet; cap

ca-pi-ro-ta-zo *m.* flip as with the finger

ca-pi-tal *m.* capital

ca-pi-ta-lis-mo *m.* capitalism

ca-pi-ta-lis-mo *m.* capitalism

ca-pi-tan *m.* captain

ca-pi-to-lio *m.* capitol

ca-pi-tu-lo *m.* chapter

ca-po *m.* bonnet; hood

ca-pon *adj.* casterated

ca-pri-cho *m.* whim; fancy; quick

ca-pri-cho-so *adj.* temperamental; whimsical

cap-su-la *f.* capsule

cap-tu-ra *f.* capture; catch

ca-pu-cha *f.* hood

ca-pu-llo *m.* cocoon

ca-qui *m.* khaki

ca-ra *f.* face

ca-ra-col *m.* snail

ca-rac-ter *m.* nature; character

ca-rac-te-ris-ti-co, -ca *adj.* typical

ca-rac-te-ri-za-do, a *adj.* distinguished

ca-rac-te-ri-za-dor, ra *adj.* distinguishing

ca-rac-te-ri-zar *v.* to characterize

ca-ra-cu *m. Amer.* bone marrow

ca-ram-ba-no *m.* icicle

ca-ra-me-li-zar *v.* to cover with caramel

ca-ra-me-lo *m.* caramel

ca-ra-va-na *f.* caravan

car-bo-hi-dra-to *m.* carbohydrate

car-bon *m.* coal

car-bo-na-to *m.* carbonate

car-bo-no *m.* carbon

car-nun-co *m.* carbuncle

car-bu-ra-dor *m.* carburetor

car-bu-ran-te *m.* fuel

car-cel *f.* prison; jail

car-de-nal *m.* cardinal

car-dia-co *adj.* cardiac

ca-re-cer *v.* to lack

ca-ren-cia *f.* need; lack

ca-rey *m.* sea turtle

car-ga *f.* burden; load

car-ga-de-ro *m.* loading platform

car-ga-men-to *m.* cargo

car-gar(se) *v.* to burden; load

car-go *m.* charge; burden; load

ca-riar-se *v.* to decay

ca-ri-dad *f.* charity

ca-ri-no, a *m.* affection; love

ca-ri-ta-ti-vo *adj.* charitable

car-nal *adj.* carnal

car-na-val *m.* carnival

car-ne *f.* pulp; flesh; meat

car-ne-ar *v. Amer.* to slaughter

car-ni-ce-ria *f.* slaughter; bloodshed

car-ni-ce-ro *m.* butcher

car-pe-ta *f.* folder

car-pin-te-ria *f.* carpentry

car-pin-te-ro *m.* carpenter

ca-rre-ra *f.* career; race

ca-rre-ro *m.* carrier

ca-rre-ta-je *m.* cartage

ca-rre-te *m.* reel; spool; coil; bobbin

ca-rrc-te-ra *f.* road; highway

ca-rro-za *f.* coach; chariot

ca-rrua-je *m.* carriage

ca-rru-sel *m.* merry-go-round

car-ta *f.* card; letter

car-ta-pa-cio *m.* notebook

car-tel *m.* poster

car-te-le-ra *f.* billboard

car-te-ra *f.* billfold; wallet

car-te-ro *m.* postman

car-ti-la-go *m.* gristle; cartilage

car-to-gra-fi-a *f.* mapmaking; cartography

car-to-gra-lo, a *m., f.* mapmaker, cartographer

car-ton *m.* cardboard

car-tu-cho *m.* cartridge

ca-sa *f.* home; house

ca-sa-ca *f.* dress coat

ca-sa-do, a *adj.* married

casar(se) *v.* wed; to marry

cas-ca-bel *m.* small bell

cas-ca-be-le-ar *v.* to jingle

cas-ca-do, a *adj.* cracked; decrepit

cas-ca-da *f.* cascade

cas-ca-jo *m.* gravel

cas-ca-ra *f.* hull; shell; skin; rind

ca-se-ta *f.* cottage

ca-se-te *m.f.* tape cartridge; cassette

cas-co-te *m.* rubble

ca-si *adv.* almost

ca-si-mir *m.* cashmere

ca-si-no *m.* casino

ca-so *m.* happening; case

cas-pa *f.* dandruff

cas-ta *f.* breed; caste; cast

cas-ta-ne-te-ar *v.* to chatter

cas-ti-dad *f.* chastity

cas-ti-gar *v.* to punish

cas-ti-llo *m.* castle

cas-tor *m.* beaver

cas-tra-cion *f.* castration

ca-sual *adj.* accidental; coincidental

ca-sua-li-dad *f.* coincidence; chance

ca-ta-le-jo *m.* small telescope; spyglass

ca-ta-lo-gar *v.* to catalog; catalogue

ca-tar *v.* to taste; to sample

ca-ta-ra-ta *f.* waterfall; cataract

ca-tas-tro-fe *f.* catastrophe

ca-te-dral *f.* cathedral

ca-te-go-ria *f.* category

ca-ter-va *f.* gang

ca-te-ter *m.* catheter

ca-tin-ga *f.* body odor

ca-tor-ce *adj.* fourteen

ca-tre *m.* cot made of canvas

cau-ce *m.* channel; riverbed; ditch

cau-cion *f.* bail; caution

cau-cho *m.* rubber; rubber tree or plant

cau-di-llo *m.* leader

cau-sa *f.* cause

cau-te-la *f.* cautiously

cau-te-la *f.* caution

cau-te-lo-so, a *adj.* cautions

cau-te-ri-zar *v.* captivating

cau-ti-ve-rio *m.* captivity

cau-ti-vo, a *adj. & m.f* captive

cau-to, a *adj.* cautions

ca-var *v.* to dig

ca-ver-na *f.* cave, cavern

ca-vial/viar *m.* caviar

ca-vi-dad *f.* cavity

ca-vi-la-cion *f.* rumination, pondering

ca-vi-lar *intr.* to ruminate; ponder

ca-za *f.* hunt game

ca-za-dor, ra *adj.* hunting

ca-zar *v.* to hunt

ca-zo *m.* ladle

ca-zue-la *m.* small shark

ce-bar *v.* to fatten

ce-bo-lla *f.* onion

ce-bra *f.* zebra

ce-ce-o *m.* lisp

ce-dro *m.* cedar

ce-du-la *f.* document

ce-fi-ro *m.* zephyr

ce-gar *v.* to blind

ce-gue-dad-ra *f.* blindness

ce-ja *f.* eyebrow

ce-jar *intr.* to back up

ce-la-da *f.* ambush

ce-la-dor, ra *adj.* vigilant; watchful

ce-lar *v.* to comply with something

cel-da *f.* cell

ce-le-bra-cion *f.* celebration

ce-le-bran-te *adj.* celebrating

ce-le-brar *v.* to celebrate

ce-le-bre *adj.* famous; celebrated

ce-le-bri-dad f. celebrity
ce-le-ri-dad f. speed
ce-les-te adj. sky-blue
ce-les-tial adj. heavenly
ce-les-ti-na f. madam; procuress
ce-li-ba-to m. celibacy
ce-li-be adj. & m.f. celibate
ce-lo-tan m. cellophane
ce-lo-si-a f. latticework
ce-lo-so, a adj. zealous
ce-lu-la f. cell
ce-lu-loi-de m. celluloid
ce-lu-lo-so adj. cellulous
ce-llis-ca f. sleet
ce-men-te-rio m. cemetery
ce-men-to m. cement
ce-na f. supper; dinner
ce-na-gal m. swamp
ce-nar intr. to have dinner
cen-ca-rro m. cowbell
ce-ni-ce-ro m. ashtray
ce-nit m. zenith
cen-sor m. censor
cen-su-rar v. to censor
cen-te-lla f. flash
cen-te-lle-an-te adj. sparkling
cen-te-na f. one hundred
cen-te-nar m. one hundred
cen-te-no m. rye
cen-te-si-mo adj. hundredth
cen-ti-gra-do adj. centigrade
cen-ti-me-tro m. centimeter
cen-ti-me-tro, a adj. hundredth
cen-ti-ne-la m.f. sentry
cen-to-lla f. spider crab
cen-tra-do, a adj. centered
cen-tral adj. central
cen-tra-li-zar v. to centralize
cen-trar v. to center
cen-tri-co adj. central
cen-tro m. core; middle; center
ce-nir v. to encircle; to bind; to be tight on
ce-no m. frown
ce-pa f. stump
ce-pi-llo m. brush
ce-ra f. wax
ce-ra-mi-ca f. ceramics

cer-ca adv. near; close
cer-ca f. fence
cer-ca-ni-a f. nearness pl. outskirts
cer-ca-no adj. near; close
cer-car v. to surround; to fence something in
cer-ce-nar v. to cut
cer-cio-rar v. to assure
cer-co m. circle
cer-da f. pig; sow
cer-do m. pig
cer-do-so adj. bristly
ce-real m. cereal
ce-re-bral adj. cerebral
ce-re-bro m. brain
ce-re-mo-nia f. ceremony
ce-re-mo-nial m. cermonial
ce-re-za f. cherry
ce-ri-lla f. match
ce-ro m. zero
ce-rra-do adj. shut
ce-rra-du-ra f. lock
ce-rrar(se) v. to close; seal
ce-rro-jo m. bolt
cer-ti-fi-ca-do m. certificate
cer-ti-fi-car v. to certify
cer-va-to m. fawn
cer-ve-za f. ale; beer
ce-sar v. to cease
ce-sion f. grant; cession
ces-ped m. grass; sod; lawn
ces-ta f. basket
ce-tri-no adj. sallow
ci-cli-co adj. cyclic
ci-clis-ta m., f. cyclist
ci-clo m. circle
ci-clon m. cyclone
ci-cu-ta f. hemlock
cie-go adj. sightless; blind
cie-lo m. heaven; sky
cien adj. hundred
cie-na-ga f. swamp
cien-cia f. science
cien-ti-fi-co m. scientist
cien-to a., m. hundred
cie-rre m. snap
cier-ta-men-te adv. certainly
cier-to, -ta adj. certain; sure
cier-vo m. hart; stag
ci-fra f. figure; cipher
ci-frar v. to cipher
ci-ga-rri-llo m. cigarette

ci-lin-dro *m.* cylinder

ci-ma *f.* crest; summit; top

cin-co *adj.* five

cin-cuen-ta *adj.* fifty

ci⁻ne *m.* movies

cin-ta *f.* reel; tape; ribbon

cin-to *m.* girdle

cin-tu-ron *m.* belt

ci-pres *m.* cypress

cir-co *m.* circus

cir-cu-la-ción *f.* circulation

cir-cu-lar *adj.* circular

cir-cu-lo *m.* circle

cir-cun-ci-dar *v.* to circumcise

cir-cun-ci-sion *f.* circumcision

ci-rio *m.* candle; taper

ci-rro *m.* cirrus

ci-rue-la *f.* plum

ci-ru-gia *f.* surgery

ci-ru-ja-no *m.* surgeon

cis-ne *m.* swan

ci-ta *f.* meeting; date; appointment

ci-ta-cion *f.* citation; subpena

ci-tar(se) *v.* to quote; summon

clu-dad *f.* town; city

ciu-da-da-no *m.* citizen

ci-vi-co *adj.* civic

ci-vil *adj.* civilian; civil

ci-vi-li-za-cion *f.* civilazation

cal-mor *m.* outcry; noise

cla-mo-ro-so *adj.* clamorous

clan *m.* clan

cla-ra-men-te *adv.* clearly

cla-ri-dad *f.* clearness; clarity

cla-ri-fi-ca-ción *f.* clarification

cla-ri-fi-car *v.* to clarify

cla-rin *m.* bugle

cla-ri-ne-te *m.* clarinet

cla-ro *adj.* clear; light; lucid

cla-se *f.* grade; class; sort

cla-si-co *adj.* classic; classical

cla-si-fi-ca-ción *f.* classification

cla-si-fi-car(se) *v.* to classify; class

cla-var(se) *v.* to nail; to

thrust; stick

cla-ve *adj.* key

cla-vel *m.* carnation

cla-vi-za *f.* peg

cla-vo *m.* spike; nail

cle-men-cia *f.* mercy; clemency

cle-men-te *adj.* clement

cle-ri-cal *adj.* clerical

cle-ri-go *m.* priest; parson

cle-ro *m.* ministry; clergy

clien-te *m., f.* client; customer; patron

cli-ma *m.* climate

cli-max *m.* climax

cli-ni-ca *f.* clinic

clo-quear *v.* to cluck

clo-ro *m.* chlorine

coac-ción *f.* compulsion; constraint

coa-gu-la-ción *f.* coagulation

coa-gu-lar(se) *v.* to coagulate; clot

coa-li-ción *f.* coalition

co-bal-to *m.* cobalt

co-bar-de *adj.* cowardly

co-bra *f.* cobra

co-bra-dor, a *m.* conductor

co-brar(se) *v.* cash; receive

co-bre *m.* copper

co-bro *m.* recovery

co-cai-na *f.* cocaine

co-cer *v.* to bake; cook

co-cien-te *m.* quotient

co-ci-na *f.* kitchen; stove

co-ci-nar *v.* to cook

co-co *m.* coconut

co-co-dri-lo *m.* crocodile

coc-tel *m.* cocktail

co-che *m.* automobile

co-di-cia *f.* greed

codi-ciar *v.* to covet

co-di-cio-so *adj.* greedy

co-di-fi-car *v.* to codify

co-di-go *m.* code

co-do *m.* elbow

co-e-du-ca-ción *f.* coeducation

coe-ta-neo *m.* contemporary

co-fra-dia *f.* gang

co-fre *m.* chest

co-ger *v.* get; choose; take

co-gi-da *f.* toss; catch

co-he-char v. to bribe
co-he-cho m. bribery
co-he-ren-te adj. coherent
co-he-te m. rocket
coin-ci-den-te adj. coincidental
coin-ci-dir v. to coincide
coi-to m. intercourse
co-jear v. to hobble
co-je-ra f. limp
co-jin m. cushion
co-jo adj. lame
col f. cabbage
co-la f. tail
co-la-bo-ra-ción f. collaboration
co-la-no-rar v. to collaborte
co-la-dor m. strainer
co-lap-so m. collapse
col-cha f. quilt; spread
col-chon m. mattress
co-lec-ción f. collection
co-lec-cio-nar v. to collect
co-le-ga m. colleague
co-le-gio m. academy; college; high school
col-ga-du-ra f. drape
co-li-bri m. hummingbird
co-li-co f. colic
co-li-flor f. cauliflower
co-li-na f. hill
col-me-nar f. hive; beehive
col-mi-llo m. fang; tusk
col-mo m. height; climax
co-lo-ca-ción f. location; situation
co-lo-car(se) v. to place; locate; put
co-lon m. colon
co-lo-nia f. colony
co-lo-nial adj. colonial
co-lo-no m. settler
co-lor m. color
co-lo-re-te m. rouge
co-lum-na f. pillar
co-lum-mis-ta m., f. columnist
co-lim-piar(se) v. to swing
co-lu-sion f. colusion
co-ma f. comma
co-ma-dre f. gossip
co-man-dan-te f. commander

co-man-dar v. to command
co-ma-to-so adj. comatose
com-ba f. bend
com-bar(se) v. to bend; sag
com-ba-te m. fight
com-ba-tir(se) v. to combat
com-bi-na-ción f. combination
com-bi-nar(se) v. to blend; combine
com-bus-ti-ble adj. combustible
com-pe-ler v. to compel
com-pen-sa-ción f. compensation
com-pe-ten-cia f. competence
com-pe-tir f. compilation
com-pi-lar v. to compile
com-pin-che m. chum
com-pla-cer(se) v. to please; humor
com-ple-men-to n. complement
com-ple-tar v. to complete
com-ple-to adj. full; absolute; thorough; complete
com-pli-ca-ción f. complication
com-pli-car(se) v. to involve
com-pli-ce m. accessory
com-po-ner(se) v. to make; compose
com-por-ta-mien-to m. behavior
com-por-tar(se) v. to behave
com-po-si-ciona f. composition
com-prar v. purchase; trade
com-pre-hen-sión f. comprehesnion
com-pren-der v. understand
com-pren-si-vo adj. comprehensive
com-pre-sion f. compression
com-pri-mir v. to compress
com-pro-ba-ción f. proof
com-pro-bar v. to verify
com-pues-to m. compound
com-pul-sion f. compulsion
com-pu-ta-dor m. computer
com-pu-tar v. to compute

co-mun *adj.* common
con *prep* towards; with; by
con-ca-vi-dad *f.* hollow
con-ce-bir *v.* to conceive
con-ce-der *v.* allow; accord
con-ce-jo *m.* council
con-cen-tra-ción *f.* concentration
con-cen-trar(se) *v.* to concentrate
con-cep-ción *f.* conception
con-cep-to *m.* concept; notion
con-ce-sion *f.* allowance; concession
con-cien-cia *f.* conscience
con-cier-to *m.* concert
con-cluir(se) *v.* to end; conclude
con-cor-dar *v.* to tally; agree
con-cor-dia *f.* concord
con-cre-to *adj.* concrete
con-cu-bi-na *f.* concurence; turnout
con-cu-rrir *v.* to meet; concur
con-cur-san-te *m., f.* participant
con-cur-so *m.* contest
con-da-do *m.* county
con-de *m.* county
con-de *m.* earl; count
con-de-co-rar *v.* to decorate
con-de-na *f.* sentence
con-de-na-ción *f.* condemnation
con-de-sa *f.* countess
con-di-ción *f.* state; condition
con-di-ció-nal *adj.* conditional
con-di-ció-nar *v.* to condition
con-di-men-to *m.* condiment; seasoning
con-do-len-cia *f.* condolence
con-do-nar *v.* to condone
con-du-cir(se) *v.* to steer; lead; conduct; drive
con-duc-ta *f.* behavior
con-duc-to *m.* duct; conduit
co-nec-tar *v.* to connect
co-ne-ji-to *m.* bunny
co-ne-jo *m.* rabbit
co-ne-xion *f.* connection

con-fec-ción *f.* confection
con-fec-cio-nar *v.* to make up; concoct
con-fe-de-ra-ción *f.* confederation; confederacy
con-fe-ren-cia *f.* lecture; conference
con-fe-rir *v.* to grant; bestow
con-fe-sar(se) *v.* to confess; admit
con-fe-sion *f.* confession; avowal
con-fe-sio-na-rio *m.* confessional
con-fe-so *m.* confessor
con-fe-ti *m.* confetti
con-fia-ble *adj.* reliable
con-fian-za *f.* dependence; confidence
con-fiar *v.* trust; rely; confide
con-fi-den-cial *adj.* confidential
con-fi-gu-ra-ción *f.* configuration
con-fin *m.* confines; bound
con-fir-ma-ción *f.* corroboration
con-fir-mar *v.*, ratify; confirm
con-fis-ca-ción *f.* confiscation
con-fis-car *v.* to confiscate
con-fia-gra-ción *f.* conflagration
con-flic-to *m.* clash; conflict
con-for-mar(se) *v.* to adjust; conform
con-for-me *adj.* similar; agreeable
con-for-mi-dad *f.* conformity
con-for-tar *v.* to comfort
con-fron-ta-ción *f.* confrontation
con-fron-tar *v.* to confront
con-fun-dir(se) *v.* to confound; perplex; puzzle; baffle
con-fu-sion *f.* mess; jumble; confusion
con-fu-tar *v.* to disprove; confute
con-ge-la-ción *f.* frostbite
con-ge-lar(se) *v.* to freeze; congeal

con-ge-ni-to *adj.* congenital

con-ges-tion *f.* congestion

con-glo-me-ra-do *m.* conglomerate

con-gre-gar(se) *v.* to flock; assemble

con-gre-so *m.* convention; congress

con-je-tu-ra *f.* surmise; guess; conjecture

con-je-tu-rar *v.* conjecture

con-ju-gar(se) *v.* conjugate

con-jun-ción *f.* conjunction

con-jun-to *m.* whole; ensemble

con-ju-rar *v.* to conjure

con-me-mo-ra-ción *f.* commemoration

con-me-mo-rar *v.* to commemorate

con-me-mo-ra-ti-vo *adj.* memorial

con-mo-cion *f.* stir; concussion; commotion

con-mo-ve-dor *adj.* stirring

con-mo-ver-(se) *v.* to shake; move; thril

co-no *m.* cone

cons-truc-ti-vo *adj.* constructive

cons-truir *v.* to build; structure; construct

con-sue-lo *m.* consolation

con-sul-tar *v.* to consult

con-su-mar *v.* to carry out

con-su-mi-dor *m.* consumer

con-su-mir(se) *v.* to waste away; consume

con-su-mo *m.* consumption

con-sun-cion *f.* consumption

con-tac-to *m.* contact

con-ta-giar(se) *v.* to catch; infect

con-ta-gio *m.* contagion

con-ta-gio-so *adj.* catching

con-ta-mi-na-ción *f.* pollution; contamination

con-ta-mi-nar(se) *v.* to contaminate

con-tar(se) *v.* to number; count; relate; tell

con-tem-pla-ción *f.* contemplation

con-tem-plar *v.* to view; meditate

con-tem-po-ra-neo *adj.* contemporary

con-ten-der *v.* to strive; conten; contest

con-ten-dien-te *v.* contestant

con-te-ner(se) *v.* to hold; include; contain

con-te-ni-do *m.* content

con-ten-to *adj.* happy; contented

con-tes-ta-ción *f.* answer

con-tes-tar *v.* reply; answer

con-tien-da *f.* contest; strife; struggle

con-ti-guo *adj.* adjacent

con-ti-nen-tal *adj.* continental

con-ti-nen-te *m.* mainland; continet; container

con-tin-gen-cia *f.* contingency

con-ti-nua-ción *f.* continuation

con-ti-nuar *v.* to continue

con-ti-nuo *adj.* constant; perpetual; continuous

con-to-near(se) *v.* to strut

con-tor-no *m.* contour; outline

con-tra *prep.* versus; against *adv.* against

con-tra-ba-jo *m.* bass

con-tra-ban-dis-ta *m., f.* smuggler

con-tra-ban-do *m.* smuggling; contraband

con-trac-ción *f.* contraction

con-tra-de-cir *v.* to contradict

con-tra-dic-cion *f.* contradiction

con-traer(se) *v.* to contract

con-tral-to *m., f.* alto; contralto

con-tra-rie-dad *f.* snag; vexation

con-tra-rio *adj.* adverse; contrary

con-tras-tar *v.* contrast

con-tras-te *m.* contrast

con-tra-tiem-po *m.* upset; mishap

con-tra-to *m.* contract; agreement

con-tra-ven-ta-na *f.* shutter

con-tri-bu-ción *f.* task; contribution

con-tri-buir *v.* to contribute

con-trol *m.* control

con-tro-lar *v.* to control

con-tro-ver-sia *f.* controversy

con-tu-sion *f.* bruise; contusion

con-va-le-cen-cía *f.* convalescence

con-va-le-cer *v.* convalesce

con-va-le-cien-te *m., f.* convalescent

con-ven-cer *v.* to satisfy

con-ven-ción *f.* convention

con-ven-ció-nal *adj.* conventional

con-ve-nien-cia *f.* expediency

con-ve-nien-te *adj.* handy; fitting; convenient

con-ve-nir(se) *v.* agree; befit

con-ven-to *m.* abbey

con-ver-gir *v.* to converge

con-ver-sa-ción *f.* conversation

con-ver-sar *v.* to converse

con-ver-tir(se) *v.* to turn into

con-ve-xo *adj.* convex

con-vic-cion *f.* conviction

con-vi-da-do *m.* guest

con-vi-dar(se) *v.* to invite

con-vi-te *m.* invitation

con-vo-ca-ción *f.* convocation

con-vo-car *v.* to summon

con-voy *m.* convoy

con-vul-sion *f.* convulsion

co-nac *m.* brandy

co-o-pe-ra-cion *f.* teamwork

co-o-pe-rar *v.* to cooperate

co-or-di-na-ción *f.* coordination

co-or-di-nar *v.* to coordinate

co-pa *f.* goblet

co-pe-te *m.* tuft

co-pia *f.* imitation; copy

co-piar *v.* to copy

co-pio-so *adj.* copious

co-que-ta *f.* coquette

co-que-tear *v.* to flirt

co-ral *adj.* choral

co-ra-zon *m.* heart

co-ra-zo-na-da *f.* hunch

cor-ba-ta *f.* tie

cor-cel *m.* steed

cor-che-te *m.* clasp

cor-cho *m.* cork

cor-de-ro *m.* lamb

cor-don *m.* cord

co-reo-gra-fo *m.* choreographer

cor-ne-ta *f.* bugler

cor-ni-sa *f.* cornice

co-ro *m.* chorus

co-ro-la *f.* corolla

co-ro-na *f.* crown

co-ro-nar *v.* to crown

co-ro-na-ria *f.* coronary

cor-pi-no *m.* bodice

cor-po-ral *adj.* corporal

cor-po-reo *adj.* bodily

corps *m., pl.* corps

co-rral *m.* corral

co-rrea *f.* strap

co-rrec-ción *f.* propriety

co-rrec-to, -ta *adj.* right

co-rre-dor *m.* broker

co-rre-gir(se) *v.* stream; run

co-rre-ria *f.* foray

co-rres-pon-der(se) *v.* to concern

co-rrien-te *adj.* current

co-rroer(se) *v.* to erode

co-rrom-per(se) *v.* to rot

co-rro-sion *f.* corrosion

co-rro-si-vo *adj.* corrosive

co-rrup-ción *f.* corruption

cor-se *m.* corset

cor-ta-do *adj.* abrupt

cor-ta-du-ra *f.* slit

cor-tan-te *adj.* edged

cor-tar(se) *v.* chop; cut; clip

cor-te *m.* court

cor-tes *adj.* civil; polite

cor-te-sia *f.* civility

cor-ti-jo *m.* grange

cor-to *adj.* brief

co-sa *f.* affair

co-se-cha *f.* crop

co-ser *v.* to sew

cos-me-ti-co *adj.* cosmetic

cos-mos *m.* cosmos
cos-qui-llear *v.* to tickle
cos-ta *f.* cost
cos-tar *v.* to cost
cos-te *m.* price
cos-ti-lla *f.* rib
cos-to-so, -sa *adj.* expensive
cos-tum-bre *f.* custom
cos-tu-ra *f.* joint
co-ti-dia-no *adj.* daily
co-yo-te *m.* coyote
cra-neo *m.* skull
cra-so *adj.* thick
cra-ter *m.* crater
crea-cion *f.* creation
crea-dor *m.* creator
crear *v.* to make; create
cre-cer(se) *v.* to increase
cre-cien-te *m.* crescent
cre-ci-mien-to *m.* growth
cre-di-to *m.* credit
cre-do *m.* credo
cre-du-lo *adj.* credulous
creen-cia *f.* faith
creer(se) *v.* to think
crei-ble *adj.* plausible
cre-ma *f.* cream
cre-sa *f.* maggot
cres-po *adj.* crisp
cre-ta *f.* chalk
cria-da *f.* maid
criar(se) *v.* to raise; nurse
cri-men *m.* felony
crip-ta *f.* crypt
cri-sis *f.* breakdown
cri-sol *m.* crucibile
cris-tal *m.* crystal; glass
cris-tian-nis-mo *m.* Christianity
Christo *m.* Christ
cri-te-rio *m.* criterion
cri-ti-ca *f.* censure; criticism
cri-ti-car *v.* to criticize
cri-ti-co, -ca *adj.* critical
cro-ma-ti-co *adj.* chromatic
cro-mo *m.* chrome
cro-ni-ca *f.* chronicle
cro-ni-co *adj.* chronic
cro-no-me-trar *v.* to tell time
cro-quet *m.* croquet
cro-que-ta *f.* croquette
cru-ce *m.* intersection
cru-ci-fi-car *v.* to crucify

cru-ci-fi-xion *f.* crucifixion
cru-do *adj.* crude; raw
cruel *adj.* heartless; cruel
cru-ji-do *m.* crack
cru-jir *v.* to crunch
cruz *f.* cross
cru-za-da *f.* crusade
cru-za-do, -da *m.* crusader
cru-zar(se) *v.* to cross
cua-dra-do *m.* square
cua-dran-te *m.* quadrant
cua-drar(se) *v.* to tally
cua-dri-lon-go *m.* oblong
cua-dro *m.* square; picture
cua-ja-da *f.* curd
cual *adv.* as; *pron.* which
cua-li-dad *f.* quality
cual-quier *adj.* any; either
cuan *adv.* how
cuan-do *prep.* when; *adv.* when; since
cuan-ti-a *f.* amount
cuan-to *adj.* as much as
cuan-to *adj.* how much?
cua-ren-ta *adj.* forty
cua-ren-ta-vo *adj.* fortieth
cua-res-ma *f.* Lent
cuar-te-ar *v.* to cut up; to quarter
cuar-tel *m. Mil.* barracks
cuar-to *m.* quarter; fourth
cuar-zo *m.* quartz
cua-si *adv.* almost
cua-te *adj.* twin; alike
cua-tre-re-ar *v.* to rustle or steal
cua-tre-ro *adj.* to steal horses
cua-tro *m.* four
cua-tro-cien-tos *adj.* four hundred
cu-be-ta *f.* bucket
cu-bier-to *f.* casing; cover
cu-bil *m.* den
cu-bi-le-te *m.* tumbler
cu-bo *m.* pailful
cu-brir(se) *v.* to conceal; to cover
cu-ca-ra-cha *f.* cockroach
cu-co *adj.* cute
cu-cha-ra *f.* spoon
cu-cha-ra-da *f.* spoonful
cu-che-ta *f.* cabin

cu-chi-che-ar *intr.* to whisper

cu-chi-che-o *m.* whispering

cu-cha-ri-lla *f.* teaspoon

cu-chi-lla *m.* knife

cue-le *m.* collar

cuen-ta *f.* count; bill

cuen-ta-go-tas *m.* eyedropper

cuen-te-ro *adj.* gossipy

cuen-tis-ta *m.* storyteller

cuen-to *m.* tale

cuer-da *f.* cord

cuer-do *adj. & m.f.* sensible; sane person

cuer-no *m.* horn

cue-ro *m.* hide

cuer-pe-ar *intr.* to dodge something

cuer-po *m.* body

cuer-vo *m.* crow

cues-ta *f.* hill; slope

cues-tión *f.* question

cues-tio-na-bel *adj.* debatable; questionable

cues-tio-nar *v.* to debate; discuss

cues-tio-na-rio *m.* questionaire

cue-va *f.* cave

cui-da-do *m.* heed

cui-da-dor *m., f.* caretaker

cui-da-do-so *adj.* careful

cui-dar(se) *v.* to look after

cui-ta *f.* grief

cu-lan-tro *m.* coriander

cu-le-bra *f.* snake

cu-le-bri-lla *f. MED.* ringworm

cu-li-na-rio, a *adj.* culinary

cul-mi-na-ción *f.* culmination

cul-mi-nan-te *adj.* culminating

cul-mi-nar *v.* to culminate

cul-pa *f.* fault

cul-pa-bi-li-dad *f.* guilt

cul-pa-ble *adj.* guilty

cul-par *v.* to criticize; to accuse

cul-ti-va-cion *f.* cultivation

cul-ti-var *v.* farm; to cultivate

cul-ti-vo *m.* cultivation

cul-to *adj.* cultured

cul-tu-ra *f.* culture

cum-bre *f.* peak; top

cum-plea-nos *m.* birthday

cum-pli-do, -da *adj.* perfect; complete

cum-pli-dor *adj.* reliable; trustworthy

cum-pli-men-tar *v.* to compliment

cum-pli-mien-to *m.* fulfillment

cum-plir *v.* to accomplish

cun-dir *intr.* to expand; to spread

cu-ña-da *f.* sister-in-law

cu-ña-do *m.* brother-in-law

cup-le *m.* popular song

cu-po *m.* quota

cu-pon *m.* coupon

cu-ra *f.* cure

cu-ra-ble *adj.* curable

cu-ra-ción *f.* treatment, cure

cu-ran-de-ro, a *m., f.* quack

cu-rar(se) *v.* to heal; recover

cu-ria *f.* court

cu-rio-se-ar *intr.* to pry, snoop

cu-rio-si-dad *adj.* curiosity

cu-rio-so *adj.* curious

cu-rri-cu-lum vi-tae *m.* resume

cur-sar *v.* to study

cur-si *adj.* vulgar

cur-si-vo *adj.* cursive

cur-so *m.* course

cur-ti-do *m.* tanning as in leather

cur-ti-dor *m.* tanner

cur-tiem-bre *m.* tannery

cur-tir(se) *v.* to coarsen

cur-va *f.* bend; curve

cur-va-do, a *adj.* bent; curved

cur-var *v.* to curve

cur-va-tu-ra *f.* curvature

cus-to-dia *f.* keeping

cus-to-diar *v.* to protect; to watch over

cus-to-dio *adj. & m.* guardian

cu-ti-cu-la *f.* curicle

cu-tis *m.* complexion; skin

da-ble *adj.* feasible; possible

dac-ti-lo-gra-ti-a *f.* typewriting; typing

dac-ti-lo-gra-fo *m.f.* typist

da-di-va *f.* gift; present

da-di-vo-si-dad *f.* liberality; generosity

da-di-vo-so, a *adj.* lavish; generous

da-do *m.* die

dal-to-nis-mo *m.* color-blindness

da-ma *f.* lady

da-mi-se-la *f.* damsel

dam-ni-fi-car *v.* to harm; to damage

dam-ni-fi-ca-do, a *adj.* harmed; damaged

dan-za *f.* dance

da-ñar(se) *v.* to hurt; to damage

da-ni-no, -na *adj.* harmful; damaging

da-no *m.* damage

dar(se) *v.* to give; allow

dar-do *m.* arrow; dart

dar-se-na *f.* dock; inner harbor; port

da-ta *f.* items; date

de-tar *v.* to date

da-to *m.* fact

de *prep.* of; frow; with

de-am-bu-lar *intr.* to roam or wander around

de-ba-jo *adv.* underneath; below

de-ba-te *m.* discussion; debate

de-ba-tir *v.* to discuss; to debate

de-be *m.* debit

de-ber *v.* to owe *m.* obligation or duty

de-bi-da-men-te *adv.* duly; properly

de-bi-do *adj.* fitting; due

de-bil *adj.* feeble; weak; faint

de-bi-li-dad *f.* weakness

de-bi-li-tar *tr. & reflex* to weaken

de-but *m.* opening; debut

de-bu-tan-te *f.* debutant *adj.*

beginning

de-ca-den-cia *f.* decline; decadence

de-ca-den-te *adj. & m.f.* decadent

de-ca-er *v.* to decay

de-cal-mien-to *m.* feebleness, weakness; dejection

de-ca-no *m.* dean

de-can-ta-ción *f.* pouring off

de-can-tar *v.* to pour off; to decant

de-ca-pi-tar *v.* to behead

de-cen-cia *f.* decency

de-ce-nio *m.* decade

de-cen-te *adj.* decent

de-cep-ción *f.* deception; disappointment

de-cep-cio-nar *v.* to disappoint

de-ce-so *m.* death; decease

de-ci-di-do, a *adj.* resolute; determined

de-ci-dir *v.* to resolve

de-ci-mal *adj.* decimal

de-cir *v.* to state; say

de-ci-sion *f.* decision; verdict; ruling

de-ci-si-vo *adj.* crucial; conclusive; decisive

de-cla-mar *tr. & intri.* to recite

de-cla-ra-ción *f.* declaration; statement; evidence

de-cla-ra-da-men-te *adv.* openly; manifestly

de-cla-rar(se) *v.* to propose; declare

de-cli-na-cion *f.* decline

de-cli-nar *v.* to decline; to refuse

de-cli-ve *m.* incline; slope

de-co-lo-ra-ción *f.* discoloration

de-co-lo-ran-te *m.* decolorant

de-co-lo-rar *v.* to fade; to discolor

de-co-mi-sar *v.* to seize; confiscation

de-co-ra-do *m.* scenery or set in a theater

de-co-ra-dor, ra *adj.*

ornamental; decorative

de-co-rar v. to decorate

de-co-ra-ti-vo, a adj. ornamental; decorative

de-co-ro m. honor; respect

de-co-ro-so, a adj. decent; honorable

de-cre-cer v. to diminish

de-cre-ci-mien-to m. decrease

de-cre-pi-to, -ta adj. aged; decrepit

de-cre-tar v. to decree; order

de-dal m. thimble

de-di-car(se) v. to devote

de-do m. finger

de-du-cir v. to conclude; deduce; subtract

de-fa-mar v. to defame

de-fec-ción f. defection

de-fec-to m. flaw; defect

de-fec-tuo-so, a adj. faulty; defective

de-fen-der v. to defend

de-fen-sa f. defense

de-fen-sor m. supporter

de-fe-ren-cia f. difference

de-fi-cien-cia f. lacking; deficient

de-fi-ni-ción f. definition; determination

de-fi-nir v. to define

de-for-mar(se) v. to loose shape

de-frau-da-ción f. cheating; fraud

de-frau-dar v. to cheat

de-fun-ción f. death; demise

de-ge-ne-rar v. to decline; to degenerate

de-go-lla-de-ro m. windpipe; throat

de-go-llar v. to cut the throat

de-gra-dar(se) v. to demean

de-gus-ta-ción f. sampling; tasting

dei-dad f. deify

de-ja-do, a adj. negligent; careless

de-jar(se) v. to quit; let

de-jo m. abandonmnet

del contr. of de and el

de-lan-ta adv. ahead; before; in front

de-lan-te-ro adj. forward; front

de-la-tar v. to inform; to denounce, expose

de-le-ga-ción f. delegation

de-le-gar v. to delegate

de-lei-ta-ble adj. enjoyable; delightful

de-lei-tar(se) v. to delight

del-ga-do adj. thin; slim

de-li-be-ra-do, a adj. intentional; deliberate

de-li-ca-do, -da adj. sensitive

de-li-cia f. pleasure; delight

de-lin-cuen-te adj. delinquent

de-li-ne-ar v. to outline; delineate

de-li-ran-te adj. delirious

de-li-rar v. to rave; to be delirious

de-man-da f. challenge; demand

de-man-dar v. to demand; to ask for

de-ma-si-a f. surplus; more than what is needed

de-ma-sia-do adv. too much

de-me-ri-to m. demerit

de-mo-cra-cia f. democracy

de-mo-le-dor, ra adj. demolishing

de-mo-ler v. to demolish; to destroy

de-mo-li-ción f. destruction

de-mo-nio m. devil; demon

de-mo-ra f. wait; delay

de-mo-rar(se) v. to delay

de-mos-trar v. to display; to demonstrate

de-mos-tra-ti-vo, a adj. & m. demonstrative

de-mu-dar v. to change

de-ne-gar v. to reject; to refuse

de-no-da-do, a adj. bold

de-no-mi-na-ción f. denomination

de-no-mi-na-dor, ra adj. denominating

de-nos-tar v. to insult; to

abuse

de-no-tar v. to denote

den-si-dad f. density

den-so adj. thick; dense

den-ta-du-ra f. denture

den-tal adj. dental

den-te-lle-ar v. to bite; to nibble

den-te-ra f. jealousy; envy

den-ti-fri-co m. toothpaste

den-tis-ta m., f. dentist

den-tro adv. within; inside

de-nue-do m. courage; bravery

de-nues-to m. insult

de-nun-ciar v. to denounce

de-pa-rar v. to supply

de-par-ta-men-to m. office; department; section

de-par-tir v. to converse; to talk

de-pen-den-cia f. dependence; kinship; reliance

de-pen-der v. to depend

de-plo-rar v. deplore

de-po-ner v. depose; to put aside

de-por-ta-ción f. deportation

de-por-tar v. to exile; deport

de-por-te m. sport

de-po-si-tar v. to bank

de-po-si-to m. deposit

de-pra-va-ción f. corruption

de-pra-va-do, a adj. corrupted

de-pra-var v. to deprave

de-pre-car v. to implore

de-pre-ca-to-rio adj. imploring

de-pre-ciar v. to depreciate

de-pre-dar v. to pillage

de-pre-sion f. slump; depression

de-pri-mi-do adj. depressed

de-pri-mir v. to depress

de-re-cho adj. right; upright

de-ri-var(se) v. drift

der-ma-to-lo-gi-a f. dermatology

der-ma-to-lo-go m., f. dermatologist

de-rra-mar(se) v. to overflow; to spill

de-rri-bar v. to overthrow; to knock down

de-rro-char v. to waste

de-rro-che m. squandering

de-rro-tar(se) v. to ruin

des-a-co-plar v. disconnect

des-a-fiar v. to defy

des-a-fio m. challenge

des-a-gra-dar v. to displease

des-a-hu-ciar v. to evict

des-ai-re m. slight

des-a-len-tar v. to dishearten

des-a-ni-mar(se) v. dismay

des-a-ni-mo m. depression

des-a-pro-bar v. disapprove

des-a-rre-glar(se) v. derange

des-a-rre-glo m. disorder

des-a-rro-llar(se) v. to unfold

des-a-rro-llo m. development

des-a-so-sie-go m. unrest

des-as-tre m. disaster

des-a-tar(se) v. to undo

des-a-ten-to adj. unthinking

des-a-ti-no m. blunder

des-a-yu-nar(se) v. breakfast

des-a-yu-no m. breakfast

des-ca-li-fi-car v. disqualify

des-can-sar v. to rest

des-can-so m. rest

des-ca-ra-do adj. brazen

des-car-gar(se) v. to unload

des-cen-den-te adj. downward

des-cen-der v. descent

des-ci-frar v. to decipher

des-co-lo-rar(se) v. fade

des-com-po-ner(se) v. to decompose

des-con-cer-tar(se) v. to embarrass

des-con-fiar v. to distrust

des-co-no-cer v. to disavow

des-con-ten-to m. discontent

des-con-ti-nuar v. to discontinue

des-cot-tes adj. impolite

des-co-ser(se) v. to come apart

des-cri-bir v. to describe

des-crip-ción f. description

des-cu-brir v. to find

des-cui-da-do adj. remiss

des-cui-dar *v.* to neglect
des-de *prep.* since; from
des-de-nar *v.* to disdain
des-di-cha *f.* unhappiness
de-sea-ble *adj.* elegible
de-sear *v.* hope; wish; desire
des-e-char *v.* to reject
des-em-bo-car *v.* to land
des-em-bol-sar *v.* disburse
des-en-cov-var *v.* to unbend
des-en-la-ce *m.* ending
de-seo *m.* craving
de-ser-tar *v.* to defect
de-ser-tor *m.* deserter
des-es-pe-rar *v.* to despair
des-fal-car *v.* to embezzle
des-fi-gu-rar *v.* to blemish; to disfigure
des-fi-le *m.* parade
des-ga-rrar(se) *v.* to tear
des-gas-te *m.* waste
des-gra-cia *f.* misfortune
des-gra-cia-do *m.* unfortunate
des-ha-cer(se) *v.* to unwrap
des-he-lar(se) *v.* to thaw
des-hi-dra-ta-cion *f.* dehydration
des-hon-ra *f.* disgrace
des-hon-rar *v.* to disgrace
des-i-gual *adj.* irregular
des-in-flar *v.* to deflate
des-in-te-res *m.* disinterest
de-sis-tir *v.* to desist
des-leal *adj.* disloyal
des-li-zar(se) *v.* to glide
des-lo-car(se) *v.* dislocate
des-lum-brar *v.* to blind
des-lus-trar(se) *v.* to dull
des-lus-tre *m.* tarnish
des-ma-yo *m.* swoon
des-mi-ga-jar(se) *v.* crumble
des-mon-tar(se) *v.* to dismantle
des-na-tar *v.* to skim
des-nu-dar(se) *v.* to undress
des-nu-do, a *adj.* nude; bare
des-nu-tri-ción *f.* malnutrition
des-o-be-de-cer *v.* to disobey
des-o-cu-pa-do *adj.* free
des-o-do-ri-zar *v.* deodorize
de-so-la-ción *f.* desolation

des-or-den *m.* mess
des-or-ga-ni-zar *v.* to disrupt
des-pa-cio *adv.* slowly
des-pa-char *v.* to speed
des-pe-dir(se) *v.* to dismiss; to see off
des-pei-na-do *adj.* unkempt
des-per-di-ciar *v.* to waste
des-per-tar(se) *v.* to awaken; to wake up
des-pier-to *adj.* awake
des-ple-gar(se) *v.* to unfold
des-po-jar(se) *v.* to strip
des-po-sar(se) *v.* to marry
des-pre-cia-ble *adj.* vile; worthless
des-pre-ciar(se) *v.* to scorn
des-pues *adv.* after; later
des-te-rrar *v.* to banish
des-te-tar(se) *v.* to wean
des-ti-lar *v.* to distill
des-tre-za *f.* dexterity; skill
des-truc-cion *f.* destruction
des-truir *v.* to destroy
des-u-nir *v.* to disunite
des-va-ne-cer(se) *v.* vanish
des-ver-gon-za-do *adj.* unabashed
des-viar(se) *v.* to divert; wander
de-ta-lla-do *adj.* elaborate
de-ta-llar *v.* to itemize
de-ta-lle *m.* detail
de-tec-ti-ve *m.* sleuth
de-ten-ción *f.* arrest
de-te-ner(se) *v.* to arrest
de-te-rio-rar(se) *v.* to decay
de-ter-mi-nar *v.* to decide
de-tes-tar *v.* to hate
de-tras *adv.* aback; behind
deu-da *f.* debt
de-va-nar *v.* to wind
de-vas-tar *v.* to devastate
de-vo-cion *f.* devotion
de-vol-ver *v.* to refund; return
de-vo-rar *v.* to devour
dia *m.* day
dia-blo *m.* devil
dia-co-no *m.* deacon
dia-frag-ma *m.* diaphragm
diag-nos-ti-car *v.* to diagnose
dia-gra-ma *m.* diagram
dia-lec-to *m.* dialect

dia-man-te *m.* diamond
dia-rio *m.* daily
di-bu-jan-te *m.* cartoonist
di-bu-jar *v.* to sketch
dic-cio-na-rio *m.* dictionary
di-ciem-bre *m.* December
dic-ta-dor *m.* dictator
dic-tar *v.* to dictate
di-cho *m.* remark; saying
die-ci-nue-ve *adj.* nineteen
die-cio-cho *adj.* eighteen
die-ci-séis *adj.* sixteen
die-ci-sie-te *adj.* seventeen
dien-te *m.* tooth
diez *adj.* ten
di-fe-ren-cia *f.* difference
dife-ren-te *adj.* different
di-fe-rir *v.* to defer
di-fí-cil *adj.* hard; difficult
di-fun-to *adj.* deceased
di-fu-so *adj.* widespread
di-ge-rir *v.* to digest
di-ges-tion *f.* digestion
di-gi-to *m.* digit
dig-ni-dad *f.* dignity
di-la-tar(se) *v.* to dilate
di-li-gen-te *adj.* diligent
di-luir *v.* to dilute
di-lu-viar *v.* to pour
di-men-sion *f.* dimension
di-nas-tia *f.* dynasty
di-ne-ro *m.* money
dios *m.* god
dio-sa *f.* goddess
di-plo-ma-cia *f.* diplomacy
di-rec-ción *f.* direction
di-rec-ta-men-te *adv.* straight
di-rec-to *adj.* straight
di-ri-gir(se) *v.* to lead; control
dis-cer-nir *v.* to discern
dis-ci-pli-na *f.* discipline
dis-ci-pli-nar *v.* discipline
dis-co *m.* record
dis-cre-par *v.* to disagree
dis-cre-to *adj.* discreet
dis-cul-pa *f.* excuse
dis-cul-par *v.* to excuse
dis-cu-sion *f.* discussion
dis-cu-tir *v.* to argue
di-se-mi-nar *v.* to spread
di-se-nar *v.* to design
dis-fraz *m.* costume

dis-fra-zar *v.* to disguise
dis-gus-tar(se) *v.* to annoy
dis-gus-to *m.* displeasure
dis-lo-ca-ción *f.* dislocation
di-sol-var(se) *v.* to dissolve
dis-per-sar(se0 *v.* to dispel
dis-po-ner(se) *v.* ready
dis-pues-to *adj.* willing
dis-pu-ta *f.* dispute
dis-pu-tar *v.* fight; quarrel
dis-tan-te *adj.* distant
dis-tin-guir *v.* distinguish
dis-traer(se) *v.* to divert; dis-tract
dis-tri-buir *v.* to distribute
dis-tur-bio *m.* trouble
di-sua-dir *v.* to deter
di-van *m.* couch
di-ver-gir *v.* to diverge
di-ver-sion *f.* amusement
di-ver-so *adj.* varied; different
di-vi-dir(se) *v.* to split; divide
di-vi-no *adj.* divine
di-vor-ciar(se) *v.* to divorce
do-blar(se) *v.* fold; double
do-ce *adj.* twelve
do-ce-na *f.* dozen
do-cil *adj.* meek
do-lar *m.* dollar
do-ler(se) *v.* to pain; hurt
do-lor *m.* ache; pain
do-mes-ti-car(se) *v.* to domesticate
do-min-go *m.* Sunday
do-nan-te *m.* donor
do-ñar *v.* to donate
don-de *adv.* where
dor-mir(se) *v.* to sleep
dos *adj.* two
dra-gon *m.* dragon
dra-ma-ti-co *adj.* dramatic
dro-ga *f.* drug
du-cha *f.* shower
du-char-se *v.* to shower
du-dar *v.* to hesitate; doubt
due-na *f.* owner; master
dul-ce *m.* candy
duo-de-ci-mo *adj.* twelfth
du-pli-car(se) *v.* to duplicate
du-que-sa *f.* duchess
du-ra-de-ro *adj.* durable
du-ran-te *prep.* during
du-ro *adj.* stiff; hard

e-ba-no *m.* ebony
e-brie-dad *f.* inebriation
e-brio *m.* drunk
e-clec-ti-co *adj.* eclectic
e-cle-sias-ti-co *adj.* ecclesiastic
e-clip-sar *v.* eclipse
e-clip-se *m.* eclipse
e-co *m.* echo
e-co-lo-gia *f.* ecology
e-co-no-mia *f.* economy
e-co-no-mis-ta *m.* economist
e-co-no-mi-zar *v.* economize
e-cua-ción *f.* equation
e-cua-dor *m.* equator
e-cua-ni-me *adj.* impartial
e-cua-to-rial *adj.* equatorial
ec-ze-ma *m.* eczema
e-cha-da *f.* toss
e-char(se) *v.* throw; cast away
e-dad *f.* age
e-di-cion *f.* edition
e-dic-to *m.* edict
e-di-fi-car *v.* edify
e-di-tar *v.* edict
e-di-tor *m.* editor
e-di-to-rial *m.* editorial
e-du-ca-ción *f.* education
e-du-car *v.* instruct; teach; train; educate
e-fe-bo *m.* adolescent
e-fec-ti-vi-dad *f.* effectiveness
e-fec-to *m.* result; impact; effect
e-fec-tuar *v.* contrive; effect
e-fi-ca-cia *f.* efficacy
e-fi-cien-cia *f.* efficiency
e-fi-cien-te *adj.* efficient
e-fu-sion *f.* effusion
e-fu-si-vo *adj.* effusive
e-go *m.* ego
e-gre-sar *v.* graduate
e-je-cu-ción *f.* execution
e-je-cu-tar *v.* execute
e-je-cu-ti-vo *adj.* executive
e-jem-plar *m.* example
e-jem-pli-fi-car *v.* exemplify
e-jem-plo *m.* example
e-jer-cer *v.* exercise
e-jer-ci-cio *m.* drill; exercise; practice
e-jer-ci-to *m.* army

e-lec-to *adj.* elect
e-lec-to-ra-do *m.* electorate
e-lec-tri-ci-dad *f.* electricity
e-lec-tri-fi-car *v.* to electrify
e-lec-tro-cu-tar *v.* to electrocute
e-lec-trom *m.* electron
e-le-fan-te *m.* elephant
e-le-gan-cia *f.* grace
e-le-gan-te *adj.* elegant
e-le-gi-do *adj.* chosen
e-le-gir *v.* to choose; elect
e-le-men-tal *adj.* elementary; essential; elemental
e-le-va-ción *f.* elevation
e-le-va-do *adj.* high
e-le-var(se) *v.* to elevate; lift
e-li-mi-nar *v.* to eliminate
e-lip-se *f.* ellipse
e-lip-ti-co *adj.* elliptical
e-li-xir *m.* elixir
e-lo-cuen-cia *f.* eloquence
e-lo-cuen-te *adj.* eloquent
e-lo-giar *v.* to eulogize
e-lu-ci-dar *v.* to elucidate
e-lu-dir *v.* to elude
e-lla *pron., f.* she
e-llas *pl. pron., f.* them; they
e-llo *pron.* it
e-llos *pl. pron., m.* them; they
e-ma-nar *v.* to emanate
e-man-ci-par *v.* to emancipate
em-ba-ja-da *f.* embassy
em-ba-ja-dor *m.* ambassador
em-bal-sa-mar *v.* to embalm
em-ba-ra-za-da *adj.* pregnant
em-ba-ra-zo, -za *m.* embarrassment; pregnancy
em-bar-car(se) *v.* to embark
em-bar-que *m.* shipment
em-bas-tar *v.* to tack; quilt
em-be-ber *v.* to wet; absorb
em-be-lle-cer *v.* to embellish
em-bes-tir *v.* to attack
em-blan-que-cer *v.* to bleach
em-ble-ma *m.* emblem
em-bo-lia *f.* embolism
em-bo-rra-char(se) *v.* to get drunk
em-bos-car *v.* to ambush
em-bo-ta-do, -da *adj.* dull
em-bo-tar *v.* to dull

em-bo-te-llar v. to bottle
em-bra-vs-cer v. to infuriate
em-bria-gar(se) v. to intoxi-
cate
em-brion m. embryo
em-bro-llar v. to embroil
e-mer-gen-cia f. emergency
e-mi-gra-do m. emigrant
e-mi-grar v. to emigrate
e-mi-sa-rio m. emissary
e-mi-sion f. issue
e-mi-tir v. to give off; emit
e-mo-ción f. feeling; emotion
e-mo-cio-nar v. to affect
e-mo-ti-vo, -a adj. emotional
em-pal-mar v. to splice; join
em-pa-par(se) v. to drench;
wet
em-pa-pe-la-do m. lining
em-pa-pe-lar v. to line with
paper
em-pa-re-da-do m. recluse;
captive; prisoner
em-pa-tar v. to tie
em-pa-te m. impediment;
draw; connection
em-pe-ci-na-do adj. obstinate
em-pe-ci-nar v. to be
obstinate
em-pe-llar v. to push
em-pe-no m. patron; pledge;
insistence
em-peo-rar(se) v. to become
worse
em-pe-ra-dor m. emperor
em-pe-ra-triz f. empress
em-pe-ro conj. however
em-pe-zar v. to start; begin
em-pi-ri-co adj. empirical
em-plas-tar v. to hamper;
plaster
em-plas-to m. plaster
em-ple-a-do m. employee
em-ple-a-dor m. employer
em-ple-ar(se) v. to employ
em-pleo m. job; work
em-plu-mar v. to feater
em-po-bre-ci-do adj. im-
poverished
em-pren-der v. to begin
em-pre-sa f. company; busi-
ness
em-pre-sa-rio m. director

em-pu-jar v. to thrust; push
em-pu-je m. push
e-mu-la-ción f. emulation
e-mul-sión f. emulsion
en prep. in
e-na-je-na-ble adj. alienable
e-na-je-na-ción f. alienation
e-na-je-nar v. to alienate
e-na-no m. dwarf
e-nar-de-cer v. to ignite
en-ca-be-za-mien-to m.
heading; caption
en-ca-be-zar v. to enroll; to
head
en-ca-jar v. to force; insert
en-ca-je m. insertion; lace
en-ca-lle-cer v. to develop a
callous
en-can-di-lar v. to excite; stir
en-can-ta-do adj. happy;
delighted
en-can-ta-dor adj. charming;
enchanting
en-can-ta-mién-to m. en-
chantment
en-can-tar v. to charm; to
enchant
en-can-to m. enchantment
en-ca-po-ta-do adj. cloudy
en-ca-po-tar v. to become
overcasted
en-ca-ra-mar v. to elevate; to
raise; to promote
en-ca-rar v. to confront
en-car-gar v. to advise; place
in charge; request
en-car-go m. assignment;
task; job
en-car-na-ción f. incarnation
en-car-nar v. to heal; to mix;
to embody
en-car-ni-za-do adj. bloody
en-ca-rri-llar v. to guide
en-ce-fa-li-tis f. encephalitis
en-cen-de-dor m. lighter
en-cen-der(se) v. to ignite
en-ce-rar v. to polish
en-ce-rrar(se) v. to confine
en-ci-clo-pe-dia f. en-
cyclopedia
en-cie-rro m. closing;
seclusion; enclosure
en-ci-ma adv. above

en-ci-ma de *adv.* upon
en-cin-ta *adj.* pregnant
en-co-co-rar *v.* to annoy
en-co-ger *v.* to shrink; contract; become smaller
en-co-gi-mien-to *m.* shrinkage; contraction
en-co-lar *v.* to glue
en-co-men-dar(se) *v.* to commend
en-co-miar *v.* to extol
en-co-nar *v.* to irritate; anger
en-con-trar(se) *v.* to find; encounter
en-cor-var *v.* to curve
en-cru-ci-ja-da *f.* intersection
en-cua-der-nar *v.* to bind
en-cua-drar *v.* to frame
en-cu-brir *v.* to hide
en-cuen-tro *m.* meeting; collision; encounter
en-cues-ta *f.* inquiry
en-cum-brar *v.* to honor; to lift; to raise
en-cur-tir *v.* to preserve
en-chi-la-da *f.* enchilada
en-chu-far *v.* to couple; to connect; to merge
en-chu-fe *m.* plug; connection; socket
en-de-ble *adj.* weak
en-de-mi-co *adj.* endemic
en-de-re-zar *v.* to direct; to straighten
en-dia-bla-do *adj.* diabolical
en-di-bia *f.* endive
en-do-sa-ble *adj.* endorsable
en-do-san-te *m.* endorser
en-do-sar *v.* to endorse
en-do-so *m.* endorsement
en-dul-zar *v.* to make sweet
en-du-re-cer(se) *v.* toughen
e-ne-mi-go *m.* enemy
e-ne-mis-tad *f.* animosity
en-ner-gia *f.* energy
e-ner-gi-co *adj.* energetic
e-ne-ro *m.* January
e-ner-va-ción *f.* enervation
e-ner-var *v.* to weaken
en-fa-dar *v.* to annoy; to make angry
en-fa-sis *m.* stress; emphasis

en-fer-mar *v.* to become ill
en-fer-me-dad *f.* sickness
en-fer-me-ra *f.* nurse
en-fer-mo *adj.* ill
en-fer-vo-ri-zar *v.* to encourage; to enliven
en-fi-lar *v.* to string; to point; direct
en-fo-car(se) *v.* to focus
en-fren-te *adv.* in front of
en-friar(se) *v.* to cool
en-fu-re-cer *v.* to make furious; to infuriate
en-gan-char *v.* to persuade
en-gan-che *m.* hook
en-ga-na-di-zo *adj.* credulous
en-ga-nar(se) *v.* to fool; to deceive
en-ga-no *m.* mistake; trick; error; fraud
en-ga-no-so *adj.* tricking; deceitful; deceiving
en-gar-zar *v.* to curl; to mount; to thread
en-gas-te *m.* mounting
en-gen-drar *v.* to breed
en-gen-dro *m.* fetus
en-go-la-do *adj.* arrogant
en-go-lle-ta-do *adj.* proud
en-go-mar *v.* to glue
en-gor-de *m.* fattening
en-go-rro-so *adj.* troublesome
en-gra-nar *v.* to link; connect
en-gran-de-cer *v.* to praise; increase; heighten; augment; be promoted; exaggerate
en-gra-pa-do-ra *f.* stapler
en-gra-sa-do *m.* lubricant
en-gra-se *m.* lubricant
en-gre-í-do *adj.* arrogant
en-gro-sar *v.* to swell; to enlarge
en-ha-ci-nar *v.* to heap
en-he-brar *v.* to connect; to string; to link
en-hi-lar *v.* to arrange; guide; thread; order
e-nig-ma-ti-co *adj.* enigmatic
en-jam-brar *v.* to swarm
en-jam-bre *m.* swarm
en-ju-gar *v.* to settle; dry

en-jui-ciar v. to examine; to indict; to judge

en-jun-dia f. fat; grease; vitality

en-la-ce m. liaison; link; junction; connection

en-lar-dar v. to baste

en-la-zar v. to connect; to rope; to lace; to lasso

en-lo-que-cer v. to make insane; to drive crazy

en-lo-sa-dor m. tiler

en-lu-cir v. to plaster

en-lu-tar v. to sadden; darken

en-men-da-ble adj. amendable

en-men-da-ción f. amendment

en-ne-gre-cer v. to darken

en-no-ble-cer v. to ennoble

e-no-jar(se) v. to anger one

e-no-jo m. annoyance

e-no-jo-so, -sa adj. annoying

e-no-lo-go m. oenologist

e-nor-me adj. very large; enormous

e-nor-me-men-te adv. enormously

en-ra-ma-da f. arbor

en-ra-sar v. to smooth; level

en-re-da-dor m. gossip

en-re-dar(se) v. to mesh; mix

en-re-do m. muddle; snarl; mess

en-re-ve-sa-do adj. complicated

en-ri-que-cer(se) v. to enrich

en-ris-car v. to lift

en-ro-je-cer v. to turn red; to make red; to redden

en-ro-lar v. to recruit

en-ro-llar v. to involve; entangle

en-ros-car v. to twist

en-sa-la-da f. salad

en-sa-la-de-ra f. bowel for salad

en-sal-zar v. to exalt

en-sam-blar v. to connect

en-san-char v. to extend; to broaden; to expand

en-san-che m. expansion

en-sa-yar v. to practice; train

en-sa-yo m. test

en-sa-na-da f. inlet

en-se-nan-za f. tuition

en-se-nar v. to instruct; to tell; to teach

en-si-mis-ma-do adj. pensive

en-si-mis-ma-mien-to m. vanity; pensiveness

en-som-bre-cer v. to eclipse; to darken

en-sor-de-cer v. to make deaf

en-su-ciar(se) v. to make soiled

en-sue-no m. daydream

en-ta-bla-do m. floor

en-ta-llar v. to engrave; to carve; to groove

en-ten-de-dor, -a adj. sharp; expert

en-ten-der(se) v. to understand

en-ten-di-mien-to m. understanding

en-te-ra-men-te adv. totally; entirely

en-te-rar(se) v. to learn

en-te-re-za f. fortitude; integrity

en-te-ri-zo adj. entire

en-te-ro adj. whole; entire

en-ti-dad f. concern; entity

en-tie-rro m. funeral; burial; grave; internment

en-tin-ta-do m. inking

en-tin-tar v. to ink

en-to-mo-lo-gi-a f. entomolgy

en-to-nar v. to modulate; to intone

en-ton-ces adv. then

en-tor-no m. enviroment

en-tor-pe-cer v. to deaden; to obstruct; to dull

en-tra-da f. entrance

en-tram-par v. to snare; to trick; to entangle

en-tran-te adj. coming; next

en-tra-na-ble adj. beloved; close; dear

en-trar v. to go into; to enter

en-tre prep. among; between

en-tre-ca-no adj. graying

en-tre-cor-tar v. to interrupt

en-tre-ga *f.* delivery

en-tre-gar-(se) *v.* to deliver to

en-tre-na-dor *m.* coach

en-tre-na-mien-to *m.* coaching

en-tre-nar *v.* to train

en-tre-ta-llar *v.* to impede; to carve; to engrave

en-tre-te-ner-(se) *v.* to entertain

en-tre-te-ní-do *adj.* entertaining

en-tre-ver *v.* to surmise

en-tre-ve-ro *m.* jumble

en-tre-vis-tar *v.* to interview

en-tu-bar *v.* to put a tube into

en-tuer-to *m.* injustice

en-tur-biar *v.* to cloud

en-tu-sias-mar *v.* to enthuse

en-tu-sias-mo *m.* enthusiasm

e-nu-me-ra-ción *f.* enumeration

en-nu-me-rar *v.* to enumerate

e-nun-cia-ción *f.* enunciation

e-nun-ciar *v.* to enunciate

en-va-sar *v.* to package; to bottle

en-va-se *m.* packaging

en-ver-gar *v.* to fasten

en-via-do *m.* envoy

en-viar *v.* to send

en-vi-dia *f.* envy

en-vi-diar *v.* to envy

en-vi-dio-so *adj.* envious

en-ví-o *m.* dispatch; package; sending

en-vol-tu-ra *m.* wrapper

en-vol-ven-te *adj.* enveloping

en-vol-ver-(se) *v.* to wrap up

en-ye-sar *v.* to plaster

en-zi-ma *f.* enzyme

e-on *m.* eon

e-pi-cen-tro *m.* epicenter

e-pi-co *f.* epic

e-pi-de-mia *f.* epidemic

e-pi-de-mi-co *adj.* epidemic

e-pi-der-mi-co *adj.* epidermic

e-pi-glo-tis *f.* epiglottis

e-pi-lep-sia *f.* epilepsy

e-pi-lo-go *m.* epilogue

e-pi-so-dio *m.* episode

e-pi-te-lio *m.* epithelium

e-po-ca *f.* age; time period

e-po-pe-ya *f.* epic

e-qui-dad *f.* equity

e-qui-la-te-ro *adj.* equilateral

e-qui-li-bra-do *adj.* well-balanced; reasonable

e-qui-li-brar *v.* to balance

e-qui-li-brio *m.* equilibrium

e-qui-li-bris-ta *f.* acrobat

e-qui-no *adj.* equine

e-qui-pa-je *m.* baggage

e-qui-par *v.* to equip

e-qui-pa-rar *v.* to compare

e-qui-po *m.* team

e-qui-ta-ti-vo *adj.* fair

e-qui-va-len-te *adj.* equivalent

e-qui-vo-ca-do *adj.* being wrong

e-qui-vo-car-(se) *v.* to error

e-qui-vo-co *adj.* equivocal

er-bio *m.* erbium

e-rec-to *adj.* erect

er-guir *v.* to lift up

e-ri-gir *v.* to erect

e-ro-sión *f.* erosion

e-ro-ti-co *adj.* erotic

e-rra-di-car *v.* to uproot; to eradicate

e-rra-do *adj.* mistaken

e-rran-te *adj.* errant

e-rrar-(se) *v.* to wander; to miss; to roam; to fail

e-rro-ne-o *adj.* erroneous

e-ruc-to *m.* burp

e-ru-di-ción *f.* erudition

e-rup-ción *f.* eruption

e-sa *adj.* that

es-bel-to *adj.* slender

es-bo-zo *m.* outline

es-ca-bel *m.* footstool; stool

es-ca-bro-so *adj.* rough; rugged

es-ca-la *f.* range; ladder

es-ca-lar *v.* to climb; to scale

es-ca-le-ra *f.* stairs; staircase

es-cal-far *v.* to poach

es-ca-lo-nar *v.* to stagger

es-ca-par-(se) *v.* to escape; to get away

es-car-pa-do, -a *adj.* short;

abrupt
es-ca-so *adj.* scarce
es-ce-na *f.* scene
es-cla-vi-zar *v.* to put into slavery
es-cla-vo, -a *m.* slave
es-co-ba *f.* broom
es-co-ger *v.* decide; choose
es-con-der(se) *v.* to hide
es-cor-pión *m.* scorpion
es-cri-bir *v.* to write
es-cu-char *v.* to listen
es-cue-la *f.* school
es-cul-pir *v.* to carve
es-cul-tu-ra *f.* sculpture
e-se *adj.* that; e-sos *pl.* those
e-sen-cial *adj.* essential
es-for-zar(se) *v.* to strive for
es-fuer-zo *m.* exertion; attempt
es-mal-te *m.* enamel
es-me-ral-da *f.* emerald
e-so *pron.* that
e-so-fa-go *m.* esophagus
es-pa-ciar(se) *v.* spread out
es-pa-cio *m.* space
es-pa-da *f.* sword
es-pa-gue-ti *m.* spaghetti
es-pal-da *f.* back
es-pas-mo *m.* spasm
es-pas-ti-co *adj.* spastic
es-pe-cial *adj.* special
es-pe-cia-li-dad *f.* speciality
es-pe-cia-li-zar(se) *v.* to specialize
es-pe-ci-fi-car *v.* to specify
es-pe-ci-men *m.* specimen
es-pec-ta-dor *m.* witness
es-pe-jo *m.* mirror
es-pe-ra *f.* wait
es-pe-rar *v.* to hope; wait
es-piar *v.* to spy
es-pi-na *f.* spine
es-pi-na-zo *m.* backbone
es-pi-ni-lla *f.* shin
es-pi-ral *adj.* spiral
es-pi-rar *v.* to exhale
es-plen-di-do *adj.* splendid
es-plen-dor *m.* splendor
es-pon-ta-neo *adj.* spontaneous
es-po-sa *f.* wife
es-po-so *m.* husband

es-que-le-to *m.* skeleton
es-qui *m.* ski
es-quiar *v.* to ski
es-qui-na *f.* corner
es-ta *adj., f.* this
es-ta *pron., f.* this
es-ta-ble-cer(se) *v.* to settle, to establish
es-ta-ción *f.* station; season
es-ta-dio *m.* stadium
es-ta-do *m.* state
es-ta-llar *v.* to explode
es-tam-par *v.* to stamp
es-tam-pi-da *f.* stampede
es-tan-car(se) *v.* to stagnate
es-tan-dar-te *m.* standard
es-tar *v.* to lie; to be
es-ta-tua *f.* statue
es-ta-tu-ra *f.* stature
es-te *adj.* east
es-te *pron.* this; *pl.* these
es-te-ri-li-dad *f.* sterility
es-ti-bar *v.* to stow
es-ti-lo *m.* style
es-ti-mar(se) *v.* to estimate
es-ti-mu-lar *v.* to stimulate
es-ti-rar *v.* to stretch
es-to-ma-go *m.* stomach
es-tor-bar *v.* block; impede
es-tor-nu-dar *v.* to sneeze
es-tor-nu-do *m.* sneeze
es-tran-gu-lar *v.* to choke
es-tra-te-gia *f.* strategy
es-tra-ti-fi-car(se) *v.* to stratify
es-tre-char(se) *v.* to narrow
es-tre-lla *f.* star
es-tre-llar)se *v.* smash into
es-tre-me-cer(se) *v.* to shake
es-tric-to *adj.* strict
es-tro-pa-jo *m.* mop
es-tro-pear(se) *v.* to ruin
es-truc-tu-ra *f.* form
es-truen-do *m.* thunder
es-tu-dian-te *m., f.* student
es-tu-diar *v.* to study
es-tu-dio *m.* studio
es-tu-fa *f.* stove
es-tu-pen-do *adj.* stupendous
es-tu-pi-do *adj.* stupid
es-ter-ño *adj.* eternity
e-ti-que-ta *f.* label
eu-fo-ria *f.* euphoria
e-va-cua-ción *f.* evacuation

e-va-cuar v. to evacuate
e-va-dir v. to avoid; dodge
e-va-lua-ción f. evaluation
e-va-po-ra-ción f. evaporation
e-va-po-rar(se) v. evaporate
e-va-sion f. evasion
e-vi-den-cia f. evidence
e-vi-den-te adj. obvious
e-vi-tar v. to shun
e-vo-car v. to evoke
e-o-lu-ción f. evolution
ex-ac-ta-men-te adv. exactly
ex-a-ge-ra-ción f. exaggeration
ex-a-ge-rar v. to exaggerate
ex-a-men m. test; quiz
ex-a-mi-nar(se) v. examine
ex-ca-va-ción f. excavation
ex-ce-der(se) v. to surpass
ex-ce-len-cia f. excellence
ex-ce-len-te adj. excellent
ex-cep-to prep. unless
ex-ci-tar(se) v. to arouse
ex-cla-ma-ción f. exclamation
ex-cla-mar v. to exclaim
ex-cluir v. to exclude
ex-clu-sion f. exclusion
ex-cu-sa f. excuse
ex-cu-sar v. to excuse
ex-ha-lar v. to exhale
ex-i-gir v. to require
ex-is-tir v. to exist
ex-pan-sion f. expansion
ex-pen-der v. to expend
ex-pe-rien-cia f. experience
ex-pe-ri-men-tar v. to experiment
ex-per-to m. expert
ex-pli-ca-cion f. explanation
ex-pli-car(se) v. to explain
ex-plo-ra-ción f. exploration
ex-plo-rar v. to explore
ex-por-ta-ción f. export
ex-por-tar v. to export
ex-pre-sar(se) v. tell; express
ex-pre-sion f. expression
ex-pul-sar v. to put out; expel
ex-ten-der(se) v. expand out
ex-te-rior adj. exterior
ex-tran-je-ro m. alien
ex-tra-ño adj. odd; strange
ex-tre-mo adj. extreme

fa-bri-ca f. mill
fa-bri-ca-ción f. manufacture
fa-bri-car v. to manufacture
fa-bu-la f. fiction; fable
fa-bu-lo-sa-men-te adv. fabulously
fa-bu-lo-so adj. fabulous
fac-ción f. feature; faction
fa-ce-ta f. facet
fa-cil adj. simple
fa-fi-li-dad f. chance; facility
fa-ci-li-tar v. to expedite; to facilitate
fac-ti-ble adj. feasible
fac-tor m. factor
fac-to-ri-a f. foundry; factory
fac-tu-ra-cion f. invoicing
fac-tu-rar v. to invoice
fa-cul-tad f. power
fa-cul-tar v. to empower
fa-cha f. appearance
fai-san m. pheasant
fa-ja f. sash; band
fa-ja-du-ra f. belting
fa-jar v. to belt; wrap
fa-lan-ge f. phalanx
fa-laz adj. deceptive
fal-da f. skirt
fal-don m. tail
fa-li-co adj. phallic
fal-se-dad f. untruth; lie
fal-si-fi-car v. to misrepresent
fal-so adj. dishonest
fal-ta f. fault; shortage; flaw; want; lack
fal-tar v. to fail; to need
fal-to adj. wanting; wretched; short
fa-llar v. to fail
fa-llo adj. judgment; void; decision; ruling
fa-ma f. fame
fa-me-li-co adj. famished
fa-mi-lia f. family
fa-mi-liar adj. familiar; casual; familial
fa-mo-so adj. well-known
fa-na-ti-zar v. to fanaticize
fan-fa-rron adj. showy; bragging
fan-go m. mud
fan-go-si-dad f. muddiness
fan-ta-se-ar v. to dream

fan-ta-sia *f.* fantasy

fan-tas-ti-co *adj.* bizarre; fanciful

fa-ran-du-la *f.* business; theater

fa-ra-on *m.* pharaoh

far-do *m.* bale; pack

fa-rin-ge *f.* pharynx

far-ma-ceu-ti-co *m.* pharmacist

far-ma-cia *f.* pharmacy

fa-ro *m.* beacon; light; lighthouse

fa-rol *m.* light; lantern

far-sa *f.* farçe

fas-ci-na-ción *f.* fascination

fas-ci-nan-te *adj.* fascinating

fas-ci-nar *v.* to intrigue; to fascinate

fas-cis-ta *m.* fascist

fas-ti-diar(se) *v.* to hassel; to annoy; to bother

fas-ti-dio *m.* annoyance; repugnance

fas-ti-dio-so *adj.* annoying; tedious; bothersome

fas-to *m.* splendor

fas-tuo-si-dad *f.* splendor

fa-tal *adj.* fatal

fa-ta-li-dad *f.* fatality

fa-tal-men-te *adv.* unhappily; wretchedly

fa-ti-ga *f.* fatigue

fa-ti-gar(se) *v.* to fatigue; tire

fa-ti-go-so *adj.* tiring; fatigued; tired

fa-tuo *m.* fool

fau-na *f.* fauna

fa-vor *m.* favor

fa-vo-ra-ble *adj.* favorable

fa-vo-re-cer *v.* to favor; to help another; to support

fa-vo-ri-to *adj.* favorite

fe *f.* trust; faith

fe-bre-ro *m.* February

fe-bril *adj.* hectic

fe-cu-la *f.* starch

fe-cun-di-dad *f.* fertility

fe-cha *f.* date

fe-char *v.* to date

fe-de-ra-ción *f.* federation

fe-de-ral *adj.* federal

fe-de-ra-lis-ta *adj.* federalist

fe-de-rar *v.* to federate

fe-li-ci-dad *f.* bliss; happiness; felicity

fe-li-ci-ta-ción *f.* congratulation

fe-li-ci-tar *v.* to congratulate

fe-li-no *adj.* feline

fe-liz *adj.* happy

fel-po *m.* rug

fel-po-so *adj.* plush

fel-pu-do *m.* rug

fe-me-ni-no *adj.* feminine

fe-mi-nis-ta *adj.* feminist

fe-mur *m.* femur

fe-ne-cer *v.* to pass away; to settle; to finish

fe-no-bar-bi-tal *m.* phenobarbital

fe-nol *m.* phenol

feo *adj.* ugly

fe-ria *f.* fair; market

fe-ria-do *adj.* holiday

fe-ri-no, -a *adj.* ferocious; fierce

fer-men-ta-cion *f.* fermentation

fer-men-tar *v.* to ferment

fe-ro-ci-dad *f.* ferocity

fe-roz *adj.* fierce

fe-rre-o *adj.* iron

fe-rro-ca-rril *m.* railway

fer-til *adj.* rich

fer-ti-li-zan-te *adj.* fertilizing

fer-ti-li-zar *v.* to fertilize

fer-vi-do *adj.* fervid

fer-vor *m.* fervor

fes-te-jar *v.* to celebrate; to entertain; to court

fes-tin *m.* feast

fes-ti-val *m.* festival

fes-ti-vo, -va *adj.* merry; festive; witty

fe-tal *adj.* fetal

fe-ti-che *m.* fetish

fe-ti-dez *f.* fetidness

fe-to *m.* fetus

feu-dal *adj.* feudal

feu-da-lis-mo *adj.* feudalism

fia-ble *adj.* dependable

fia-dor *m.* bail

fian-za *f.* guarantor; security

fiar *v.* to entrust; to guaranty

fias-co *m.* fiasco

fi-bro-ma *m.* fibroma
fi-bro-so *adj.* stringy; fibrous
fic-ción *f.* fiction
fic-ti-cio *adj.* fictitious
fi-cha *f.* chip; token
fi-de-dig-no *adj.* trustworthy
fi-dei-co-mi-so *m.* trust
fi-de-li-dad *f.* accuracy; fidelity
fie-bre *f.* fever
fiel *adj.* true; loyal; honest; faithful; trustworthy
fiel-tro *m.* felt
fie-re-za *f.* ferocity; deformity; fierceness
fies-ta *f.* feast; party
fi-gu-ra *f.* shape; figure; character
fi-gu-ra-ción *f.* figuration
fi-gu-ra-do *adj.* figurative
fi-gu-rar(se) *v.* to figure
fi-gu-ra-ti-vo *adj.* figurative
fi-ja-dor *adj.* fixative
fi-ja-men-te *adv.* firmly
fi-jar(se) *v.* to determine; set
fi-jo *adj.* permanent; set; steady; fixed
fi-la *f.* row; file; tier
fi-la-men-to *m.* filament
fi-lan-tro-po *m.* philanthropist
fi-la-te-lis-ta *m.* philatelist
fi-li-gra-na *f.* filigree
fil-mar *v.* to film
fil-mi-co *adj.* movie; film
fi-lo *m.* edge
fi-lo-lo-gi-a *f.* philology
fi-lo-so-fi-a *f.* philosophy
fi-lo-so-fo *m.* philosopher
fil-tra-ción *f.* filtration
fil-trar(se) *v.* to strain; filter
fil-tro *m.* filter
fin *m.* finish
fi-nal *adj.* ending; last; end; final
fi-na-li-dad *f.* finality
fi-na-lis-ta *m.* finalist
fi-na-li-zar *v.* to conclude
fi-nal-men-te *adv.* finally
fin-ca *f.* land; farm
fi-ne-za *f.* politeness; fineness; affection
fin-gir(se) *v.* pretend; sham

fi-ni-to *adj.* finite
fi-no *adj.* acute; fine; elegant; delicate
fir-ma *f.* firm
fir-ma-men-to *m.* firmament
fir-mar *v.* to sign something
fir-me *adj.* hard; strong; firm
fis-ca-li-zar *v.* to investigate; to oversee; to snoop
fi-si-co *adj.* physical
fi-sio-lo-gi-a *f.* physiology
fi-sio-lo-go *m.* physiologist
fi-sion *f.* fission
fis-tu-la *f.* fistula
fi-su-ra *f.* fissure
fla-co *adj.* skinny; gaunt
fla-ge-la-do *adj.* flagellate
fla-gran-te *adj.* flagrant
fla-me-ar *v.* to flame
flan-co *m.* side
fla-que-ar *v.* to weaken
fla-que-za *f.* weakness; leanness
flau-ta *f.* flute
flau-tin *m.* piccolo
flau-tis-ta *f.* flutist
fle-bi-tis *f.* phlebitis
fle-cha *f.* arrow
fle-ma *f.* phlegm
fle-te *m.* cargo; freight
fle-xi-bi-li-dad *f.* flexibility
fle-xi-ble *adj.* flexible
fle-xor *adj.* flexor
flo-je-dad *f.* laziness; debility
flo-je-ra *f.* carelessness
flo-jo *adj.* limp; weak
flor *f.* blossom; flower; bloom
flo-re-cer *v.* bloom; prosper
flo-reo *m.* flourish
flo-ris-ta *m., f.* florist
flo-tar *v.* to float
fluc-tua-ción *f.* vacilation
fluc-tuar *v.* to fluctuate
flui-do *adj.* fluid
fluir *v.* to flow
fo-co *m.* focus
fo-li-cu-lo *m.* follicle
fo-lla-je *m.* foliage
fo-lle-to *m.* brochure
fo-men-tar *v.* to encourage
fon-ta-ne-ro *m.* plumber
for-jar *v.* to forge

for-ma *f.* shape; form
for-ma-ción *f.* formation
for-ma-li-dad *f.* formality
for-mar(se) *v.* make; shape
for-ta-le-cer(se) *v.* to fortify
for-ta-le-za *f.* fortress
for-tui-to *adj.* casual
for-tu-na *f.* fortune
for-zar *v.* to strain; force
fo-sil *m.* fossil
fo-to *f.* picture; photograph
fo-to-gra-fía *f.* photography
fra-ca-sar *v.* to fail
frac-ción *f.* fraction
frac-tu-ra *f.* break; fracture
frac-tu-rar(se) *v.* to fracture
frá-gil *adj.* frail
fran-ca-men-te *adv.* frankly
fran-ces *adj.* French
fran-co *adj.* open; candid
fran-que-za *f.* frankness
fra-se *f.* sentence
fra-ter-ni-dad *f.* fraternity
frau-de *m.* deception
frecuen-cia *f.* frequency
fre-cuen-te *adj.* frequent
fre-gar *v.* to wash; scrub
freirse *v.* to fry
fre-nar *n.* brake
fren-te *f.* front; forehead
fres-co *adj.* fresh
fric-ción *f.* friction
frio *adj.* cold; frigid
fron-tal *adj.* frontal
fron-te-ra *f.* border; limit
fro-tar(se) *v.* to chafe
frun-cir *v.* to gather
frus-tra-cion *f.* frustration
frus-trar(se) *v.* to frustrate
fue-go *m.* fire
fuen-te *f.* spring; fountain
fue-ra *adv.* outside; off
fuer-te *m.* sturdy; strong
fuer-za *f.* power; force
fu-gar-se *v.* to abscond
ful-gu-rar *v.* to gleam
fu-mar *v.* to smoke
fun-da-cion *f.* foundation
fun-dar(se) *v.* to establish
fun-dir(se) *v.* to fuse
fu-ria *f.* fury
fu-rio-so *adj.* furious
fu-tu-ro *m.* future

ga-ban *m.* topcoat
ga-bar-di-na *f.* gabardine
ga-bi-ne-te *m.* boudoir
ga-ce-la *f.* gazelle
ga-ce-ta *f.* gazette
ga-chi *f.* girl
ga-cho *adj.* floppy; bent
ga-fas *f.* glasses
ga-ga *adj.* foolish
gal-te-ro *adj.* gaudy
ga-jo *m.* section; bunch
ga-lac-ti-co *adj.* galactic
ga-la-na-men-te *adv.* elegantly
ga-la-ni-a *f.* elegance
ga-lan-te *adj.* gallant
ga-lan-te-o *m.* flirting; courting another
ga-len-te-ri-a *f.* generosity; grace
ga-lar-do-nar *v.* to reward
ga-la-xia *f.* galaxy
ga-le-on *m.* gallon
ga-le-ra *f.* galley
ga-le-ría *f.* gallery
ga-li-ma-ti-as *m.* nonsense
ga-lon *m.* gallon
ga-lo-pan-te *adj.* galloping
ga-lo-par *v.* to gallop
ga-lo-pe *m.* gallop
gal-va-ni-zar *v.* to galvanize
ga-llar-dí-a *f.* gallantry; grace; elegance
ga-llar-do *adj.* graceful; brave
ga-lle-ta *f.* cracker
ga-lli-na *f.* chicken; hen
ga-lli-ne-ro *m.* henhouse; coop
ga-llo *m.* cock; rooster
ga-ma *f.* gamut
gam-ba-do *adj.* bowlegged
gam-be-te-ar *v.* to prance
ga-na *f.* longing; appetite
ga-na-de-ro *m.* cattle
ga-na-do *m.* livestock
ga-nan-cia *f.* profit
ga-nar *v.* to earn; to win
gan-cho *m.* hook
gan-du-le-rí-a *f.* laziness
gan-glio *m.* ganglion
gan-go-so *adj.* nasal
gan-gre-na *f.* gangrene

ga-no-so *adj.* anxious

gan-so *m.* goose

ga-ra-ba-to *m.* grapple

ga-ra-je *m.* garage

ga-ran-tia *f.* warrant; guaranty

ga-ran-tir *v.* to defend; to guarantee

ga-ra-tu-sa *f.* compliment

gar-ban-zo *m.* chickpea

gar-be-ar *v.* to steal; to rob

gar-bi-llo *m.* sieve

gar-bo-so *adj.* graceful; generous

gar-fa *f.* claw

gar-ga-je-ar *v.* to spit

gar-gan-ta *f.* neck

gar-ga-ra *f.* gargling

gar-ga-ri-zar *v.* to gargle

gar-go-la *f.* gargoyle

gar-gue-ro *m.* trachea

ga-rra *f.* talon

ga-rra-fal *adj.* enormous

ga-rra-pa-ta *f.* mite

ga-rra-pi-nar *v.* to grab

ga-rron *m.* claw

ga-ruar *v.* to drizzle

gas *m.* gas

ga-sa *f.* guaze

ga-si-fi-car *v.* to gasify

ga-so-li-na *f.* gas

gas-ta-do, -a *adj.* threadbare; exhausted

gas-tar *v.* to exhaust; to spend; to squander; wear

gas-tri-co *adj.* gastric

gas-tri-tis *f.* gastritis

gas-tro-no-mia *f.* gastronomy

gas-tro-no-mi-co *adj.* gastronomic

ga-te-ar *v.* to climb; to swipe

ga-ti-llo *m.* hammer

ga-to *m.* cat

ga-tu-no *adj.* catlike

gau-cho *adj.* gaucho

ga-ve-ta *f.* drawer

ga-vio-ta *f.* gull

ga-za-pi-na *f.* brawl

gaz-na-te *m.* windpipe; throat

gei-ser *m.* geyser

ge-la-ti-na *f.* gelatin

ge-ma *f.* gem

ge-mi-do *m.* groan

ge-ne-a-lo-gi-a *f.* genealogy

ge-ne-ra-cion *f.* generation

ge-ne-ral *m.* general

ge-ne-ra-li-dad *f.* generality

ge-ne-ra-li-za-cion *f.* generalization

ge-ne-ra-li-zar *v.* generalize

ge-ne-ra-ti-vo *adj.* generative

ge-ne-ri-ca-men-te *adv.* generically

ge-ne-ri-co *adj.* generic

ge-ne-ro-si-dad *f.* generosity

ge-ne-ro-so, -a *adj.* fine; generous

ge-nial *adj.* genial; inspired; pleasant

ge-nio *m.* genius; disposition

ge-no-ci-dio *m.* genocide

ge-no-ti-po *m.* genotype

gen-te *f.* nation; people

gen-til *adj.* genteel; excellent; polite

gen-ti-o *m.* mob

ge-nui-no *adj.* real; true; genuine

ge-o-fi-si-co *adj.* geophysical

ge-o-gra-fia *f.* geography

ge-o-gra-fo *m., f.* geographer

ge-o-lo-gia *f.* geology

ge-o-lo-go *m., f.* geologist

ge-o-me-tria *f.* geometry

ge-ra-nio *m.* geranium

ge-ren-te *m., f.* director

ge-ria-tri-co *adj.* geriatric

ger-ma-nio *m.* germanium

ger-men *m.* germ

ger-mi-na-cion *f.* germination

ger-mi-nar *v.* to germinate

ge-ron-to-lo-gia *f.* gerontology

ges-ta-cion *f.* gestation

ges-ti-cu-la-cion *f.* gesture; grimace

ges-ti-cu-lar *v.* to gesture

gey-ser *m.* geyser

gi-bar *v.* to curve

gi-bon *m.* gibbon

gi-gan-ta *f.* sunflower

gi-gan-te *m.* giant

gi-go-lo *m.* gigolo
gim-na-sía *f.* gymnastics
gim-nas-ta *f., m.* gymnast
gi-mo-te-ar *v.* to whine
gi-ne-co-lo-gia *f.* gynecology
gin-gi-vi-tis *f.* gingivitis
gi-rar *v.* rotate; spin; gyrate
gi-ra-to-rio *adj.* rotating
gi-ro *m.* rotation; turn
gi-ros-co-pio *m.* gyroscope
gi-ta-nes-co *adj.* gypsy-like
gla-cia-cion *f.* glaciation
gla-cial *adj.* glacial; icy
gla-ciar *adj.* glacial
gla-dia-dor *m.* gladiator
glan-du-la *f.* gland
gla-se-ar *v.* to glaze
glau-co-ma *m.* glaucoma
glo-bal *adj.* global
glo-bo *m.* globe
glo-glo *m.* gurgle
glo-ria *f.* glory
glo-ri-fi-ca-cion *f.* glorification
glo-ri-fi-car(se) *v.* to glorify
glo-rio-so *adj.* glorious
glo-sa *f.* gloss
glo-sar *v.* to gloss
glo-sa-rio *m.* glossary
glo-tis *f.* glottis
glu-co-sa *f.* glucose
glu-ti-no-so *adj.* glutinous
go-ber-na-cion *f.* government
go-ber-na-dor *m.* governor
go-ber-nar *v.* to govern
go-bier-no *n.* government
go-la *f.* throat
golf *m.* golf
gol-fo *m.* golf
go-lo-si-na *f.* craving; delicacy; longing
gol-pe *m.* blow; hit
gol-pear *v.* to slug; hit; beat
gol-pe-te-ar *v.* to pummel; hit; to pound; to beat
gó-ma *f.* rubber; gum; rubber band
go-mo-so *adj.* gummy
gon-do-la *f.* gondola
gon-do-le-ro *m.* gondolier
go-no-co-co *m.* gonococcus
gor-do *adj.* fat

gor-go-te-o *m.* gurgle
go-ri-la *m.* gorilla
go-te-o *m.* dripping
go-zar *v.* to enjoy; to rejoice
gra-bar *v.* to engrave
gra-cía *f.* kindness; charm; pardon
gra-cío-so *adj.* funny; charming; amusing
gra-do *m.* step; grade; stair
gra-dual *adj.* gradual
gra-fi-to *m.* graphite
gra-ma-ti-co *adj.* grammatical
gra-na-te *m., adj.* garnet
gra-ni-ti-co *adj.* granite
gran-je-ro *m., f.* farmer
gra-pa *f.* staple
gra-ti-fi-car *v.* to gratify
gra-ve *adj.* serious; important; grave
gre-ga-rio *adj.* gregarious
gris *adj.* grey
gri-tar *v.* to yell; to cry
gri-to *m.* yell; scream
gro-se-ria *f.* roughness; stupidity; vulgarity
gro-se-ro *adj.* vulgar; coarse
gro-tes-co *adj.* grotesque
grue-so *adj.* fat; coarse
gru-nir *v.* to grumble; grunt
gru-po *m.* bunch
guan-te *m.* glove
guan-te-ro *m.* glove maker
gua-pe-ton *adj.* bold; flashy
gua-pe-za *f.* daring
gua-po *adj.* flashy; good-looking
guar-da *f.* custody; guard
guar-dar(se) *v.* keep; guard
guar-día *f.* guard
guar-dian *m., f.* guardian
guar-ne-cer *v.* border; supply
gu-ber-na-men-tal *adj.* governmental
gue-rra *f.* war
gue-rre-ar *v.* to fight
gui-a *m., f.* leader; guide
guiar *v.* to steer; to guide
gui-ta-rra *f.* guitar
gu-sa-no *m.* worm
gus-tar *v.* to like
gus-to *m.* zest; taste

ha-ber *v.* to have
ha-bil *adj.* skillful
ha-bi-li-dad *f.* ability; skill
ha-bi-ta-cion *f.* habitation; lodging
ha-bi-tar *v.* to dwell
ha-bi-tual *adj.* habitual
ha-bi-tuar *v.* to habituate
ha-bla *f.* speech
ha-bla-do *adj.* spoken
ha-bla-du-ri-a *f.* gossip; chatter
ha-blar *v.* to talk; to speak
ha-ce *adv.* ago
ha-cer(se) *v.* to act; to become; to force; compose
ha-cia *prep.* about; to
ha-cien-da *f.* ranch
ha-ci-na *f.* pile
ha-ci-nar *v.* to pile up
ha-da *f.* fairy
ha-do *m.* fate
ha-la-gue-no *adj.* promising; attractive; pleasing
ha-lar *v.* to tow something
hal-con *m.* falcon
hal-co-ne-ri-a *f.* falconry
hal-co-ne-ro *m.* falconer
ha-llar(se) *v.* to locate
ham-bre *f.* hunger
ham-brien-to *adj.* hungry; starved
ham-bur-gue-sa *f.* hamburger
ha-ra-po-so *adj.* tattered
ha-ren *m.* harem
har-tar *v.* to annoy; to stuff
has-ta *prep.* till
has-tiar *v.* to annoy; to sicken
he-bra *f.* filament; thread
he-chi-ce-ro *m., f.* charmer; sorceress; sorcerer
he-chi-zo *m.* charm; spell
he-der *v.* to stink; smell bad
he-dor *m.* stink
he-la-do *m.* ice cream
he-lar *v.* to freeze
he-li-cop-te-ro *m.* helicopter
he-lio *m.* helium
he-li-puer-to *m.* heliport
hem-bra *f.* female; woman
he-mo-fi-lia *f.* hemophilia
he-mo-glo-bi-na *f.* hemoglobin

he-mo-rra-gia *f.* hemorrhage
hen-der(se) *v.* to crack
he-nil *m.* hayloft
he-no *m.* hay
he-pa-ti-tis *f.* hepatitis
her-ba-rio *adj.* herbal
he-re-di-ta-rio *adj.* hereditary
he-ren-cia *f.* heritage
he-ri-da *f.* wound
he-rir *v.* hurt; injure; wound
her-ma-na *f.* sister
her-man-dad *f.* sisterhood; brotherhood; league
her-ma-no *m.* brother
her-mo-se-ar *v.* to beautify
her-mo-so, -a *adj.* beautiful
her-nia *f.* hernia
he-roi-co *adj.* heroic
he-ro-i-na *f.* heroine
her-pes *m.* herpes
he-rre-ro *m.* blacksmith
he-rrin *m.* rust
he-rrum-brar *v.* to rust
her-vor *m.* boiling
he-si-ta-cion *f.* hesitation
he-si-tar *v.* to hesitate
he-xa-go-no *adj.* hexagonal
hi-ber-na-cion *f.* hibernation
hi-ber-nar *v.* to hibernate
hi-bri-do *m.* hybrid
hi-dra-ta-cion *f.* hydration
hi-dra-tar *v.* to hydrate
hi-dro-car-bu-ro *m.* hydrocarbon
hi-dro-fo-bia *f.* hydrophobia
hi-dro-ge-no *m.* hydrogen
hi-dro-te-ra-pia *f.* hydrotherapy
hi-dro-xi-do *m.* hydroxide
hie-dra *f.* ivy
hie-lo *m.* ice
hier-ba *f.* grass
hi-gie-ne *f.* hygiene
hi-gie-ni-co *adj.* hygienic
hi-ja *f.* daughter
hi-jas-tra *f.* stepdaughter
hi-jas-tro *m.* stepson
hi-jo *m.* son
hi-la-dor *m., f.* spinner
hi-lar *v.* to spin
hi-le-ro *m.* current
hi-lo *m.* filament; thread

hi-men *m.* hymen
him-no *m.* hymn
hin-char *v.* to exaggerate; to swell; to blow up
hi-no-jo *m.* knee
hi-per-bo-la *f.* hyperbola
hi-per-sen-si-ble *adj.* hypersensitive
hi-per-ter-mía *f.* hyperthermia
hip-no-sis *f.* hypnosis
hip-no-tis-mo *m.* hypnotism
hip-no-ti-zar *v.* to hypnotize
hi-po-con-drí-a *f.* hypochondria
hi-po-cre-sí-a *f.* hypocrisy
hi-po-cri-ta *f., m.* hypocrite
hi-po-te-ca *f.* mortgage
hi-po-te-car *v.* to mortgage
hi-po-ter-mia *f.* hypothermia
his-te-ria *f.* hysteria
his-to-ria *f.* story; history
his-to-rial *adj.* historical
ho-ci-car *v.* smooch; nuzzle
hoc-key *m.* hockey
ho-gue-ra *f.* bonfire
ho-ja *f.* petal; leaf; sheet
ho-jo-so *adj.* leafy
hol-gan-za *f.* leisure
ho-lo-caus-to *m.* holocuast
hom-bre *m.* man
hom-bre-ra *f.* shoulder pad
hom-bri-llo *m.* yoke
hom-bro *m.* shoulder
ho-mi-ci-da *adj.* homicidal
ho-mi-ci-dio *m.* homocide
ho-mo-ge-nei-zar *v.* to homogenize
ho-mo-ni-mia *f.* homonymy
hon-do *adj.* intense; deep
hon-do-na-da *f.* gorge
ho-nes-ti-dad *f.* honesty
hon-go *m.* mushroom
ho-nor *m.* honor
ho-no-ra-ble *adj.* honorable
hon-ra-dez *f.* honesty
hon-ra-do *adj.* honest
hon-ro-so *adj.* honorable
ho-ra *f.* time; hour
hor-con *m.* pitchfork
ho-ri-zon-tal *adj.* horizontal
ho-ri-zon-te *m.* horizon
hor-mi-go-ne-ra *f.* cement

hor-mo-na *f.* hormone
hor-ne-ar *v.* to bake
hor-ne-ro *f., m.* baker
hor-ni-llo *m.* stove
hor-no *m.* oven
ho-ros-co-po *m.* horoscope
ho-rren-do *adj.* horrendous
ho-rri-ble *adj.* awful; horrible
ho-rri-do *adj.* horrid
ho-rri-fi-car *v.* to horrify
ho-rror *m.* terror; horror
hor-ti-co-la *adj.* horticultural
hor-ti-cul-tu-ra *f.* horticulture
hos-pi-tal *m.* hospital
hos-pi-ta-li-zar *v.* hospitalize
hos-te-rí-a *f.* hostel; inn
hos-ti-gar *v.* to harass; whip
hos-til *adj.* hostile
hos-ti-li-dad *f.* hostility
ho-tel *m.* hotel
hoy *m.* today
ho-ya *f.* hole
hue-co *adj.* deep; hollow
hue-lla *f.* print; footprint
huer-ta *f.* garden
hue-sa *f.* grave
hue-su-do *adj.* bony
hue-vo *m.* egg
huir(se) *v.* to flee; to escape; to avoid; to run from
hu-ma-nar *v.* to humanize
hu-ma-ni-dad *f.* humanity
hu-ma-ni-zar *v.* to humanize
hu-ma-no *m.* human
hu-me-ar *v.* to steam; smoke
hu-me-dad *f.* humidity
hu-me-do *adj.* humid
hu-me-ro *m.* humerus
hu-mil-dad *f.* humility
hu-mi-lla-cion *f.* humiliation
hu-mi-llan-te *adj.* humiliating
hu-mí-llo *m.* pride
hu-mo *m.* smoke
hu-mo-ris-mo *m.* wit
hu-mo-so *adj.* smoky
hun-dir *v.* ruin; sink; plunge
hu-ra-can *m.* hurricane
hur-gon *m.* poker
hu-ron *m.* ferret
hur-tar(se) *v.* to steal; take
hur-to *m.* robbery
hus-me-ar *v.* to pry
hus-me-o *m.* prying

i-bis *f.* ibis
i-ce-berg *m.* iceberg
i-co-no *m.* icon
i-co-no-gra-fía *f.* iconography
ic-te-ri-cia *f.* jaundice
ic-tio-lo-go *m.* ichthyologist
i-dea *f.* notion; thought; image; idea; picture
i-de-al *m.* ideal
i-de-a-lis-ta *adj.* idealist
i-de-a-li-zar *v.* to idealize
i-de-ar *v.* to invent; to plan; to design
i-den-ti-co *adj.* identical
i-den-ti-dad *f.* identity
i-den-ti-fi-ca-ble *adj.* identifiable
i-den-ti-fi-ca-cion *f.* identification
i-den-ti-fi-car *v.* to identify
i-de-o-lo-gí-co *adj.* ideological
i-di-lio *m.* idyll
i-dio-ma-ti-co *adj.* idiomatic
i-dio-sin-cra-sia *f.* idiosyncrasy
i-dio-ta *f., m.* idiot, *adj.* idiotic; foolish
i-do-la-trar *v.* to idolize
i-do-la-tri-a *f.* idolatry
i-do-lo *m.* idol
i-gle-sia *f.* church
ig-ni-cion *f.* ignition
ig-no-mi-nio-so *adj.* ignominious
ig-no-ran-cia *f.* ignorance
ig-no-ran-te *adj.* ignorant; unaware; uneducated
ig-no-to *adj.* undiscovered
i-gual *adj.* level; even; alike; like
i-gua-la-mien-to *m.* equalization
i-gua-lar *v.* to make equal; to equate; to smooth
i-gual-dad *f.* equality
i-gual-men-te *adv.* too; equally
i-gua-na *m.* iguana
i-la-cion *f.* cohesiveness
i-le-gal *adj.* unlawful; illegal; against the law
i-le-ga-li-dad *f.* illegality
i-le-gi-ble *adj.* illegible
i-le-tra-do *adj.* illiterate
i-lo-gi-co *adj.* illogical
i-lu-mi-na-cion *f.* illumination
i-lu-mi-na-dor *adj.* illuminative
i-lu-mi-nar *v.* light; illuminate
i-lu-sion *f.* illusion
i-lu-so-rio *adj.* illusory
i-lus-tra-cion *f.* illustration
i-lus-tra-dor *adj.* illustrative
i-lus-trar *v.* to illustrate
i-lus-tre *adj.* illustrious
i-ma-gi-na-ble *adj.* imaginable
i-ma-gi-na-cion *f.* imagination
i-ma-gi-nar(se) *v.* to think up; to conceive
i-ma-gi-na-tí-vo *adj.* imaginative
i-ma-nar *v.* to magnetize
im-be-ci-li-dad *f.* imbecility
i-mi-ta-ble *adj.* imitable
i-mi-ta-cion *f.* imitation
i-mi-tar *v.* to imitate
im-pa-cién-cia *f.* impatience
im-pa-cien-te *adj.* impatient
im-par-cial *adj.* impartial
im-par-tir *v.* to concede
im-pa-si-ble *adj.* impassive
im-pe-ca-ble *adj.* impeccable
im-pe-di-men-to *m.* impediment
im-pe-dir *v.* to deter; hinder
im-pen-sa-ble *adj.* inimaginable; unthinkable
im-pe-rar *v.* to reign
im-per-do-na-ble *adj.* inexcusable
im-per-fec-cion *f.* imperfection
im-pe-rial *adj.* imperial
im-per-me-a-bi-li-dad *f.* impermeability
im-per-me-a-ble *m.* raincoat
im-per-so-nal *adj.* impersonal
im-pe-ti-go *m.* impetigo
im-pe-tu *m.* energy; impetus
im-pe-tuo-so *adj.* impetuous; violent

im-pla-ca-ble *adj.* implacable
im-plan-tar *v.* to implant
im-pli-ca-cion *f.* implication; consequence
im-pli-car *v.* mean; implicate
im-plo-rar *v.* to invoke
im-po-ner *v.* to charge; to inspire; to inform
im-po-pu-lar *adj.* unpopular
im-por-ta-cion *f.* importation
im-por-tan-cia *f.* authority; importance
im-por-tan-te *adj.* important
im-por-tu-nar *v.* to importune
im-por-tu-no *adj.* inopportune
im-po-si-bi-li-dad *f.* impossibility
im-po-si-ble *adj.* impossible; difficult
im-pos-tor *m.* impostor
im-po-ten-cia *f.* impotence
im-prac-ti-ca-ble *adj.* unfeasible; impracticable
im-pre-ci-so *adj.* imprecise
im-preg-nar *v.* to impregnate
im-pre-sion *f.* impression
im-pre-sio-nan-te *adj.* impressive
im-pre-vis-to *adj.* unexpected; sudden
im-pri-mir *v.* to stamp; print; to imprint
im-pro-ba-ble *adj.* improbable
im-pro-duc-ti-vo *adj.* unproductive
im-pro-vi-sa-cion *f.* improvisation
im-pu-den-cia *f.* impudence
im-pug-nar *v.* to impugn
im-pul-sar *v.* to drive; impel
im-pul-sion *f.* impulse
im-pul-so *m.* impulse
im-pu-ni-dad *f.* impunity
im-pu-re-za *f.* impurity
im-pu-ro *adj.* impure
i-nac-cion *f.* inaction
i-na-cep-ta-ble *adj.* unacceptable
i-nac-ti-vo *adj.* inactive
in-a-de-cua-do *adj.* inadequate

i-nad-ver-ten-cia *f.* carelessness; inadvertence
i-nal-te-ra-ble *adj.* unalterable
i-na-ne *adj.* insane
i-na-ni-dad *f.* inanity
i-na-pli-ca-ble *adj.* inapplicable
i-na-ten-cion *f.* inattention
i-na-ten-to *adj.* unattentive
in-ca-pa-ci-dad *f.* incapacity
in-ca-pa-ci-tar *v.* to incapacitate
in-ca-paz *adj.* unable; incapable
in-cen-dio *m.* fire
in-cen-ti-vo *m.* incentive
in-ces-to *m.* incest
in-cien-so *m.* incense
in-cier-to *adj.* vague; uncertain; doubtful
in-ci-ne-rar *v.* to incinerate
in-ci-sion *f.* incision
in-ci-tar *v.* to urge; to incite
in-cle-men-te *adj.* inclement
in-cli-na-cion *f.* slant; inclination; slope
in-cli-nar(se) *v.* to slant; to sway; to incline; persuade
in-cluir *v.* to contain; include
in-clu-sion *f.* inclusion
in-clu-si-vo *adj.* inclusive
in-co-he-ren-te *adj.* incoherent
in-co-mi-ble *adj.* inedible
in-com-pa-ti-ble *adj.* incompatible
in-com-ple-to *adj.* incomplete
in-con-clu-so *adj.* inconclusive
in-cons-tan-te *adj.* fickle
in-cor-po-ral *adj.* incorporeal
in-cor-po-rar *v.* incorporate
in-co-rrec-to *adj.* incorrect
in-co-rrup-to *adj.* incorrupt
in-cre-du-lo *adj.* incredulous
in-cre-i-ble *adj.* incredible
in-cre-men-tar *v.* to increase
in-cre-men-to *m.* increase
in-cre-par *v.* to reprimand
in-cri-mi-nar *v.* to incriminate
in-crus-tar *v.* to encrust

in-cu-ba-cion f. incubation
in-cu-bar v. to incubate
in-cul-car v. to inculcate
in-cu-ra-ble adj. incurable
in-cu-rrir v. to incur
in-de-cen-te adj. indecent
in-de-ci-sion f. indecision
in-de-ci-so adj. indecisive
in-de-fen-so adj. defenseless
in-de-le-ble adj. indelible
in-dem-ne adj. unhurt
in-de-pen-di-zar v. to liberate
in-de-se-a-ble adj. undersirable
in-di-ca-cion f. sign; indication; direction
in-di-car v. to show; indicate
in-di-fe-ren-te adj. indifferent
in-di-gen-cia f. indigence
in-di-gen-te adj. indigent
in-di-ges-tion f. indigestion
in-dig-nar v. to infuriate
in-dig-no adj. despicable
in-di-go m. indigo
in-di-rec-to adj. hint; indirect
in-dis-cre-cion f. indiscretion
in-dis-cu-ti-ble adj. indisputable
in-dis-tin-to adj. indistinct
in-di-vi-dual adj. individual
in-di-vi-duo m. individual
in-di-vi-si-ble adj. indivisible
in-do-cil adj. indocile
in-do-ci-li-dad f. unruliness
in-do-len-cia f. indolence
in-do-len-te adj. indolent
in-do-ma-ble adj. uncontrollable; untamable
in-do-mi-to adj. untamable; indomitable
in-duc-cion f. induction
in-du-cir v. to induce
in-du-da-ble adj. certain
in-dul-gen-te adj. indulgent
in-dus-tria f. industry
in-dus-trial adj. industrial
in-dus-tria-li-zar v. to become industrialize
in-dus-trio-so adj. industrious
i-ne-fa-ble adj. ineffable
i-ne-fi-caz adj. ineffective
i-nep-ti-tud f. ineptitude
i-nep-to adj. inept

i-ner-cia f. inertia
i-ner-te adj. inert
i-nes-pe-ra-do adj. unexpected
i-nes-ta-ble adj. unstable
i-ne-vi-ta-ble adj. inevitable
i-ne-xis-ten-te adj. nonexistent; not existing
i-nex-plo-ra-do adj. unexplored
in-fa-li-ble adj. infallible
in-fa-mar v. to slander
in-fa-mia f. infamy
in-fan-cia f. infancy
in-fan-te m. baby; infant
in-fan-til adj. childish; baby
in-far-to m. infarction
in-fa-tuar v. to become conceited
in-fec-cion f. infection
in-fec-cio-so adj. infectious
in-fec-tar(se) v. to infect
in-fe-liz adj. wretched
in-fe-ren-cia f. inference
in-fe-rior adj. under; inferior
in-fe-rio-ri-dad f. inferiority
in-fe-rir v. to inflict; to infer
in-fes-tar v. to infest
in-fiel adj. disloyal
in-fier-no m. hell
in-fil-trar v. to infiltrate
in-fi-mo adj. worst; lowest
in-fi-ni-to m., adj. infinite
in-fla-cion f. inflation
in-fla-ma-ble adj. inflammable
in-fla-mar v. to inflame
in-flar v. to inflate
in-fle-xi-ble adj. rigid; unyielding
in-fluen-cia f. influence
in-flue-ciar v. to influence
in-flu-jo m. influence
in-for-ma-cion f. information
in-for-mal adj. informal
in-for-mar(se) v. to report; to inform; to find out
in-for-me adj. formless
in-for-tu-nio m. misfortune
in-fra-rro-jo adj. infared
in-fre-cuen-te adj. infrequent
in-fruc-tuo-so adj. fruitless
in-fun-dir v. to arouse

in-fu-sion f. infusion
in-ge-nie-ria f. engineering
in-ge-nie-ro m. engineer
in-ge-nio-so adj. witty; clever
in-ge-rir v. to ingest
in-ges-tion f. ingestion
in-gles m. English
in-gra-to adj. thankless
in-gre-dien-te m. ingredient
in-gre-so m. entrance
in-ha-bi-li-dad f. incompetence
in-ha-lar v. to inhale
in-he-ren-te adj. inherent
in-hi-bir v. to inhibit
in-hu-ma-no adj. inhuman
i-ni-cia-cion f. initiation
i-ni-cial adj. initial
i-ni-ciar v. to initiate
i-ni-cio m. beginning
i-ni-gua-la-do adj. unequaled
i-ni-mi-ta-ble adj. inimitable
in-je-rir v. to insert
in-jer-to m. transplant
in-ju-ria f. injury
in-jus-ti-cia f. injustice
in-jus-to adj. unjust
in-ma-du-ro adj. immature
in-me-mo-rial adj. immemorial
in-men-so adj. immense
in-mer-sion f. immersion
in-mi-grar v. to immigrate
in-mi-nen-te adj. imminent
in-mo-des-to adj. immodest
in-mo-lar v. to immolate
in-mo-ral adj. immoral
in-mor-tal adj. immortal
in-mo-vi-ble adj. immovable
in-mo-vil adj. immobile
in-mum-do adj. filthy
in-mu-ni-dad f. immunity
in-mu-ni-zar v. to immunize
in-mu-ta-ble adj. immutable
in-no-ble adj. ignoble
in-no-va-cion f. innovation
in-no-var v. to innovate
i-no-cen-cia f. innocence
i-no-cen-te adj. innocent
i-no-cu-lar v. to inoculate
i-no-cuo adj. innocuous
i-no-pe-ra-ble adj. inoperable
i-nor-ga-ni-co adj. inorganic

in-quie-tar v. to alarm
in-quie-tud f. uneasiness
in-qui-li-no m., f. tenant
in-qui-rir v. to probe
in-sa-no adj. insane
ins-cri-bir(se) v. to record; to engrave
ins-crip-cion f. record; inscription
in-sec-to m. insect
in-se-gu-ro adj. insecure
in-sen-si-ble adj. unfeeling; unconscious; insensible
in-ser-cion f. insertion
in-ser-tar v. to insert
in-sig-nia f. emblem
in-sin-ce-ro adj. insincere
in-sis-ten-te adj. insistent
in-sis-tir v. to insist
in-so-len-cia f. insolence
ins-pec-cion f. inspection
ins-pi-rar v. to inspire
ins-truc-cion f. instruction
ins-truir(se) v. to teach; to learn; to instruct
in-su-li-na f. insulin
in-sul-tar v. to insult
in-tac-to adj. together; intact
in-te-li-gen-cia f. intellect; intelligence
in-te-li-gen-te adj. smart; intelligent
in-ten-si-fi-car v. to intensify
in-te-re-sar(se) v. to concern
in-te-rior m. inside
in-ter-no adj. inside
in-te-rrup-cion f. interruption
in-ter-ve-nir v. to mediate; to intervene
in-ti-mo adj. intimate
in-tor-duc-cion f. introduction
in-va-dir v. to invade
in-va-sion f. invasion
in-ven-cion f. invention
in-ven-tar v. to contrive; to think up; to invent
in-ves-tir v. to invest
in-vier-no m. winter
ir(se) v. to depart; to leave
i-rre-gu-lar adj. irregular
is-la f. island
iz-quier-do, -a adj. left

ja-ba-li *m.* boar
ja-ba-li-na *f.* javelin
ja-bon *m.* soap
ja-bo-na-do *m.* wash
ja-bo-nar *v.* to lather up
ja-bo-ne-ro *m., f.* soapmaker
ja-ca *f.* nag; pony
ja-ca-re-ro *adj.* lively
ja-co *m.* nag
jac-tan-cia *f.* arrogance; bragging; boast
jac-tan-cio-so *adj.* arrogant
jac-tar-se *v.* to brag
ja-de *m.* jade
ja-de-ar *v.* to gasp for air
ja-diar *v.* to hoe
ja-guar *m.* jaguar
ja-lar *v.* to pull on
ja-le-a *f.* jelly
ja-le-ar *v.* to urge one
ja-leo *m.* racket; uproar
ja-lo-nar *v.* to mark
ja-más *adv.* never; ever; never again
jam-ba *f.* jamb
ja-mel-go *m.* nag
ja-mon *m.* ham
ja-que *m.* check
ja-que-ar *v.* to check
ja-ra-be *m.* syrup
ja-ra-near *v.* to carouse
jar-ca *f.* acacia
jar-din *m.* garden
jar-di-ne-ra *f.* gardener
jar-di-ne-ro *m.* gardener
ja-rra *f.* mug; pitcher
ja-rro *m.* flagon
ja-rron *m.* vase
jas-pe *m.* jasper
au-la *f.* cell; cage
az-min *m.* jasmine
je-fa *f.* master; boss
je-fe *m.* head; boss; master
je-mi-que-ar *v.* to whine
jen-gi-bre *m.* ginger
je-rar-qui-a *f.* hierarchy
je-re-mias *m., f.* complainer
jer-ga *f.* jargon; slang
je-ri-gon-za *f.* gibberish
je-rin-gar *v.* to pester
je-rin-ga-zo *m.* injection
je-ro-gli-fi-co *m.* hieroglyph
jer-sey *m.* sweater

ji-fia *f.* swordfish
jin-da *f.* fright
ji-ne-te *m.* equestrian; horseman
ji-ne-te-ar *v.* to ride a horse
ji-par *v.* to pant
ji-ra *f.* excursion
ji-ra-fa *f.* giraffe
jo-co-si-dad *f.* joke; wit
jo-co-so *adj.* jocular
jo-cun-di-dad *f.* jocundity
jo-fai-na *f.* washbowel
jor-na-da *f.* trip
jor-nal *m.* wage
jo-ro-ba *f.* hump
jo-ro-bar *v.* to annoy; bother
jo-rrar *v.* to haul
jo-ven *m.* youth
jo-vial *adj.* jovial
jo-ya *f.* gem; jewel
jo-ye-ra *f.* box for jewelry
jo-ye-ria *f.* jewelry store
jo-ye-ro *m.* jeweler
ju-bi-la-do *m., f* retired one
ju-bi-lar(se) *v.* to retire
ju-bi-leo *m.* jubilee
ju-bi-lo *m.* joy
ju-bi-lo-so *adj.* joyful
ju-día *f.* bean
jue-go *m.* play; game
jue-ves *m.* Tuesday
juez *m.* judge
ju-gar *v.* to game; to play
ju-gue-tear *v.* to play
ju-gue-ton *adj.* playful
jui-cio *m.* verdict; judgment
ju-lio *m.* July
jun-co *m.* junk
ju-nio *m.* June
jun-ta *f.* union
jun-ta-men-te *adv.* together
jun-tar(se) *v.* to connect; join
jun-to *adv.* together
ju-ra-do *m.* jury
ju-rar *v.* to vow; swear; curse
ju-ris-ta *f.* jurist
jus-ta-men-te *adv.* fairly
jus-ti-cia *f.* justice
jus-ti-fi-car *v.* to warrant
jus-to *adj.* fair
ju-ve-nil *adj.* youth
ju-ven-tud *f.* youth
juz-gar *v.* to try; to judge

ki-lo *m.* kilogram
ki-lo-ci-clo *m.* kilocycle
ki-lo-gra-mo *m.* kilogram
ki-lo-me-tri-co *adj.* kilometric
ki-ló-me-tro *m.* kilometer
ki-lo-va-tio *m.* kilowatt
kirsch *m.* cherry-brandy
kum-mel *m.* cumin brandy

la *def. article* the
la-be-rin-to *m.* labyrinth
la-bia *f.* elloquence
la-bio *m.* lip
la-bor *f.* work
la-bo-ra-ble *adj.* working
la-bo-ral *adj.* labor
la-bo-rar *v.* to work
la-bo-ra-to-rio *m.* laboratory
la-bo-re-ar *v.* to work
la-bo-rio-so *adj.* arduous
la-bra-do, -da *adj.* plowed; cultivated; wrought
la-bra-dor, ra *adj.* farming *m.* farmer; peasant
la-bran-za *f.* farmland; farm
la-brar *v.* to carve; work; plow; cultivate; tool
la-ca *f.* shellac; lacquer; hair spray
la-ca-yo *m.* valet; attendant
la-ce-ra-cion *f.* laceration
la-ce-rar *v.* to injure; lacerate
la-ce-ria *f.* want; toil
la-cio *adj.* limp; straight
la-co-ni-co, -ca *adj.* laconic
la-cra *f.* scar
la-cre *m.* a sealing wax
la-cri-mó-ge-no, -na *adj.* tear producing
la-cri-mo-so, -sa *adj.* tearful; sad; sorrowful
lac-ta-cion *f.* nursing
lac-tan-cia *f.* lactation
lac-tar *v.* to suckle
lac-ti-co, -ca *adj.* lactic
lac-to-sa *f.* lactose
la-de-ar *v.* to tilt
la-de-o *m.* inclination
la-de-ra *f.* slope

la-di-no, -na *adj.* astute
la-do *m.* room; side; protection de next to; beside; along side
la-drar *v.* to snarl at something; to growl
la-dri-llo *m.* brick
la-dron *m.* robber
la-dro-ne-ri-a *f.* theft
la-gar-ti-ja *f.* a small lizard
la-gar-to *m.* lizard
la-go *m.* lake
lá-gri-ma *f.* tear
la-gri-me-ar *v.* to tear; to weep; to cry
la-gri-mo-so, -sa *adj.* tearful; watery
la-gu-na *f.* lagoon
lai-cal *adj.* laical
la-ja *f.* slab of stone
la-me-du-ra *f.* licking
la-men-ta-ble *adj.* lamentable
la-men-ta-ción *f.* lamentation
la-men-tar *v.* to be sorry for; to regret something
la-men-to *m.* lament
la-men-to-so, -sa *adj.* mournful
la-mer *v.* to lap up
la-me-ta-da *f.* lick
la-mi-do, -da *adj.* polished
la-mi-na-cion *f.* lamination
lá-mi-nar *v.* to laminate
lám-pa-ra *f.* lamp
lam-pa-ri-lla *f.* little or small lamp
lam-pa-ron *m.* stain
lam-pi-ño, -ña *adj.* hairless
la-na *f.* wool
la-na-do, -na *adj.* fleecy
lan-ce *m.* argument; move; occurrence
lan-ce-ar *v.* to lance
lan-ce-ta *f.* lancet
lan-cha *f.* boat
lan-che-ro *m.* boatman
lan-chon *m.* barge
la-ne-ro, -ra *adj.* woolen
lan-gui-de-cer *v.* to languish
lan-gui-dez *f.* feebleness; lethargy

lán-gui-do, -da *adj.* languid
lan-guor *m.* languor
la-no-li-na *f.* lanolin
la-no-so, -sa *adj.* woolly
lan-za *f.* spear
lan-za-da *f.* wound due to a lance
lan-za-mien-to *m.* throwing
lan-zar *v.* to hurl; to fire; to release; to vomit; to throw; to shoot
lá-pi-da *f.* tombstone
la-pi-da-rio, -ria *adj.* concise; lapidary
lá-piz *m.* pencil
lap-so, -sa *m.* interval; lapse
la-que-ar *v.* to varnish
lar-do *m.* fat; lard
lar-gar *v.* to let go; to dismiss; to release; to hurl; to throw
lar-go *adj.* lengthy; long; abundant
lar-gor *m.* length
lar-gue-za *f.* length
lar-gui-ru-cho, -cha *adj.* lanky
la-rin-ge *f.* larynx
la-rin-gi-tis *f.* laryngitis
lar-va *f.* larva
lar-val *adj.* larval
las *pron.* them; *art.* the
la-ser *m.* laser
la-si-tud *f.* lassitude
la-so *adj.* weak; limp
lás-ti-ma *f.* compassion; shame; pity
las-ti-ma-du-ra *f.* wound
las-ti-mar *v.* to hurt; to offend; to injure
las-ti-me-ro, -ra *adj.* pitiful
la-ta *f.* can; tin can; pest
la-te-ar *v.* to bend
la-ten-te *adj.* latent
la-te-ral *adj.* lateral
la-ti-do *m.* beating; throbbing; beat
la-tien-te *adj.* throbbing
la-ti-gue-ar *v.* to whip; to crack the whip
la-tir *v.* to throb
la-ti-tud *f.* breadth; extent; width; scope

la-ti-tu-di-nal *adj.* latitudinal
la-to, -ta *adj.* wide
la-tón *m.* brass
la-to-ne-ro *m.* brassworker
la-to-so, -sa *adj.* bothersome
la-tro-ci-nio *m.* theft
lau-da-ble *adj.* laudable
lau-de *f.* tonbstone
lau-do *m.* verdict
lau-rel *m.* bay; laurel
lau-re-o *adj.* laurel
la-va *f.* lava
la-va-ble *adj.* washable
la-va-da *f.* washing
la-va-de-ro *m.* laundry
la-va-do *m.* wash
la-va-dor *m.* washer
la-van-da *f.* lavender
la-van-de-ra *f.* laundrywoman
la-van-de-ro *m.* laundryman
la-va-pla-tos *m.* dishwasher
la-var *v.* to wash; to clean
la-va-ti-va *f.* enema
la-xar *v.* to slacken
la-xa-ti-vo *adj.* laxative
la-zar *v.* to rope
la-za-ri-no, -na *adj.* leprous
la-zo *m.* lasso; knot; trap; snare
le *pron.* him
le-al *adj.* faithful
le-al-tad *f.* loyalty
lec-ción *f.* lession
lac-tor, a *adj.* reading
lec-tu-ra *f.* reading
le-cha-da *f.* grout; whitewash
le-char *v.* to milk
le-che *f.* milk
le-che-río, -ría *adj.* dairy; milky
le-cho *m.* layer; bed
le-cho-so *adj.* milky
le-chu-ga *f.* lettuce
le-er *v.* to read
le-ga-ción *f.* legation
le-ga-do *m.* legacy
le-ga-jo *m.* file
le-gal *adj.* legal
le-ga-li-dad *f.* legality
le-ga-lis-ta *f.* legalist
le-ga-li-za-cion *f.* legalization
le-ga-li-zar *v.* to legalize

le-gar v. to delegate; to bequeathe
le-gi-ble adj. legible
le-gion f. legion
le-gis-la-cion f. legislation
le-gis-la-dor m. legislator
le-gis-la-tu-ra f. legislative
le-jos adv. far away
len-gua f. language
le-on m. lion
le-o-na f. lioness
le-o-par-do m. leopard
les pron. for them; for you
le-tal adj. lethal
le-tra f. letter
le-van-tar v. to lift up; erect
ley f. rule; law
li-be-ra-ción f. liberation
li-be-ral adj. liberal
li-ber-tad f. freedom
li-bre adj. single; open; free
li-bro m. book
li-gar v. to commit; bind
li-mi-ta-ción f. limitation
li-mi-ta-do adj. limited
li-mi-tar v. to restrict; limit
li-món m. lemon
lim-piar v. to clear; clean
lim-pie-za f. neatness; cleaning
lim-pio adj. pure; clean
lí-ne-a f. outline; line; boundary
lis-ta f. list
lis-to adj. ready
li-tro m. liter
li-via-no, -naadj. faithless; light
li-vi-dez f. lividness
li-vi-do adj. livid
lo def. article the
lo-a f. praise
lo-a-ble adj. praiseworthy
lo-ar v. to praise
lo-ba f. the female wolf
lo-bo m. the male wolf
lo-bre-go adj. somber; dark
ló-bu-lo m. lobe
lo-ca-cion f. leasing
lo-cal adj. local
lo-ca-li-dad f. locality
lo-ca-li-zar v. to find; to locate

lo-cion f. lotion
lo-co adj. crazy; extraordinary
lo-grar v. to take; obtain
lo-ro m. parrot
los pron. them; art. the
lu-ci-do adj. shining
lu-cir v. to illuminate; to light
lue-go adv. later; then
lu-na f. moon
lu-nar adj. lunar
lus-trar v. to shine
luz f. day; light

ma-ca-bro adj. funeral
ma-ca-dam m. macadam
ma-ca-rrón m. macaroon
ma-ce-ra-cion f. maceration
ma-ce-rar v. to macerate
ma-ce-ta f. flowerpot or holder
ma-ci-len-to, -ta adj. lean; thin; emaciated
ma-ci-zo, -za adj. solid
ma-cro-bio-ti-co f. macrobiotics
ma-cu-la f. spot
ma-cha-ca f. pounder
ma-cha-ca-dor, -ra adj. pounding
ma-cha-car v. to beat; to pound; to bother
ma-cha-con, -ona adj. tiresome f., m pest
ma-cha-da f. stupidity
ma-cha-do m. hatchet
ma-che-te m. machete
ma-che-te-ar v. to injure or cut with a machete
ma-cho adj. manly; male; tough; virile
ma-chu-ca-du-ra f. beating; bruising
ma-chu-car v. to beat
ma-de-ra f. timber; wood; lumber
ma-de-ra-da f. raft
ma-de-re-ri-a f. lumberyard
ma-de-re-ro, -ra adj. timber

ma-de-ro *m.* log
ma-dras-tra *f.* stepmother
ma-dre *f.* mom; mother
ma-dre-sel-va *f.* honeysuckle
ma-dri-gue-ra *f.* hole; burrow; lair
ma-dri-na *f.* bridesmaid; godmother; patroness
ma-dru-ga-dor, -ra *m., f.* early riser
ma-dru-gar *v.* to anticipate; to get up early
ma-du-ra-cion *f.* ripening
ma-du-ra-dor, a *adj.* ripening
ma-du-rar *v.* to mature; to ripen; to maturate
ma-du-rez *f.* maturity, ripeness
ma-es-tre *m.* master
ma-es-tro, -tra *adj.* expert; teacher; master
ma-gan-ce-ri-a *f.* trickery
ma-gia *f.* magic
má-gi-co, -ca *adj.* magic
ma-gis-tra-do *m.* magistrate
ma-gis-tral *adj.* imposing; masterful; magisterial
mag-na-te *m.* magnate
mag-ne-sia *f.* magnesia
mag-ne-sio *m.* magnesium
mag-né-ti-co, -ca *adj.* magnetic
mag-ne-tis-mo *m.* magnetism
mag-ne-to-fo-ni-co, -ca *adj.* magnetic
mag-ni-fi-ca-dor, -ra *adj.* magnifying
mag-ni-fi-car *v.* to exalt; to magnify; to glorify
mag-ni-fi-cen-cia *f.* magnificence
mag-ni-fi-cen-te *adj.* magnificent
mag-ni-fi-co, -ca *adj.* excellent; magnificent
mag-ni-tud *f.* size; importance; magnitude
mag-no-lia *f.* magnolia
ma-go, -ga *adj.* magic
ma-gu-llar *v.* to batter
ma-íz *m.* corn
ma-ja-de-ro, -ra *adj.* foolish

ma-ja-du-ra *f.* pounding
ma-jar *v.* to pound; to bother; to mash
ma-jes-tad *f.* grandeur; majesty
ma-jo, -ja *adj.* showy; attractive; flashy; nice
mal *adj.* bad; evil; disease
mal *adv.* wrongly; badly
ma-la-bar *v.* to juggle
ma-la-ba-ris-ta *m.* juggler
ma-la-cos-tum-bra-do, a *adj.* ill-mannered; have poor or bad habits; spoiled
ma-lan-drin, a *adj.* evil
ma-la-ria *f.* malaria
ma-la-ven-tu-ra *f.* misfortune
ma-la-ven-tu-ran-za *f.* misfortune
mal-ba-ra-tar *v.* to squander
mal-co-mer *v.* to eat badly or poorly
mal-co-mi-do *adj.* underfed
mal-con-ten-to, -ta *adj.* unhappy; rebellious
mal-cria-do, -da *adj.* ill-bred
mal-criar *v.* to spoil
mal-dad *f.* evil
mal-de-cir *v.* to slander; to curse
mal-di-ci-en-te *adj.* defaming; slandering *m., f.* curser; slanderer
mal-di-ción *f.* curse
mal-di-to, -ta *adj.* wicked; bad
ma-le-a-bi-li-dad *f.* malleability
ma-le-a-ble *adj.* malleable
ma-le-an-te *adj.* corrputing; wicked
ma-le-ar *v.* to ruin; to corrupt; to pervert
ma-le-di-cen-cia *f.* slander
ma-le-fi-cen-cia *f.* evil
ma-le-fi-cen-te *adj.* maleficent
ma-les-tar *m.* uneasiness; malaise
ma-le-ta *f.* suitcase; baggage; luggage
ma-le-vo-len-cia *f.* malevolence

mal-for-ma-cion *f.* malformation

mal-gas-tar *v.* to waste

mal-ha-da-do, -da *adj.* unfortunate

mal-he-rir *v.* to injure

mal-hu-mo-ra-do, -da *adj.* bad-tempered

mal-hu-mo-rar *v.* to irritate; to bother; to annoy

ma-li-cia *f.* cunning; wickedness; slyness

ma-li-cio-so, -sa *adj.* malicious; cunning

ma-lig-ni-dad *f.* malignancy

ma-lig-no, -na *adj.* malignant

mal-mi-ra-do, -da *adj.* disfavored

ma-lo *adj.* harmful; nasty; bad

ma-lo-grar *v.* to fail; to lose; to waste

ma-lo-gro *m.* failure

mal-pa-rar *v.* to harm; to damage

mal-quis-tar *v.* to estrange

mal-quis-to, -ta *adj.* unpopular

mal-so-nan-te *adj.* harsh

mal-tra-ta-mien-to *m.* mistreatment

mal-tra-tar *v.* to mistreat

mal-va-do, -da *adj.* wicked

mal-ver-sa-dor, -a *m., f.* embezzler

mal-ver-sar *v.* to embezzle

ma-má *f.* mommy

ma-mar *v.* to nurse; to suck

ma-ma-rio, -ia *adj.* mammary

ma-me-lon *m.* nipple

ma-na-da *f.* herd; bunch

ma-na-de-ro, -a *m., f.* spring

ma-nan-te *adj.* running

ma-nar *v.* to flow

man-car *v.* to disable

man-ci-lla *f.* blemish

man-ci-llar *v.* to blemish

man-ci-par *v.* to enslave

man-co *adj.* one-armed; disabled

man-co-mu-nar *v.* to join together; to combine

man-co-mu-ni-dad *f.* union; association

man-cha *f.* blot; stain

man-char *v.* to stain; to spot; to soil

man-da *f.* bequest

man-da-do *m.* errand; task; order

man-da-mien-to *m.* command; order

man-dar *v.* to leave; order

man-da-ri-na *f.* mandarin orange

man-da-to *m.* trust; command; order

man-dí-bu-la *f.* mandible

man-do *m.* leadership; power

man-do-lin *f.* mandolin

man-dria *adj.* timid; worthless; useless

man-dril *m.* mandrill

ma-ne-ar *v.* to hobble around

ma-ne-ja-ble *adj.* manageable

ma-ne-jar *v.* to handle; to manage

ma-ne-jo *m.* operation; handling; management

ma-ne-ra *f.* style; way; manner; type

man-ga *f.* strainer; hose

man-ga-ne-so *m.* manganese

man-gar *v.* to swipe; to mooch

man-gos-ta *f.* mongoose

man-gue-ar *v.* to startle

man-gue-ra *f.* garden hose

man-gui-ta *f.* cover

ma-ní *m.* peanut

ma-ni-a *f.* habit; craze

ma-ni-a-co, -ca *adj.* maniac

ma-ni-fes-ta-ción *f.* manifestation

ma-ni-fes-tar *v.* to reveal; to manifest

ma-ni-fies-to, -ta *adj.* manifest

ma-ni-lla *f.* bracelet

ma-ni-pu-la-ción *f.* manipulation

ma-ni-pu-la-dor, a *m.* manipulator

ma-ni-pu-lar v. to manipulate; to manage

ma-ni-quí m. mannequin

ma-no f. hand

ma-no-jo m. handful; bunch

ma-no-se-ar v. to touch

man-so, -sa adj. mild; tame

man-ta f. shawl; blanket

man-te-ca f. fat; lard

man-tel m. tablecloth

man-te-nen-cia f. support; maintenance

man-te-ner v. to support; to keep; to feed; to maintain

man-te-ni-mien-to m. support; sustenance

man-te-que-ri-a f. dairy

man-te-que-ro m. dairyman

man-te-qui-lla f. butter

man-to m. mantle; robe; cloak; cover

ma-nual adj. manual

ma-nu-fac-tu-rar v. to manufacture

ma-nu-ten-ción f. maintenance

man-za-na f. apple

man-za-nar m. apple orchard

man-za-no m. apple tree

ma-ña f. dexterity; skill

ma-ña-na f. morning

ma-ne-ar v. to manage

ma-ñe-ro adj. shrewd

ma-pa f. map

ma-pa-che m. raccoon

ma-que-ar v. to varnish

ma-qui-na f. machine

ma-qui-na-ción f. machination

ma-qui-na-dor m., f. schemer

ma-qui-nar v. to scheme

ma-qui-nis-ta m. machinist

mar m. sea; tide

ma-ra-ton m. marathon

ma-ra-vi-lla f. marvel; astonishment; wonder

ma-ra-vi-llar v. to astonish; to be amazed

ma-ra-vi-llo-so, -sa adj. marvelous

mar-ca f. brand; mark; stamp; trademark

mar-ca-do adj. notable

mar-ca-dor, -ra adj. marking

mar-car v. to stamp; to mark; to note

mar-cia¹ adj. military; martial

mar-co m. mark; standard

mar-cha f. march; velosity; speed; progress

mar-char v. to run; walk

mar-chi-tar v. to weaken; to wilt; to languish

mar-chi-to, -ta adj. wilted

ma-re-ar v. to sail; to bother

ma-re-ja-da f. turbulence

ma-re-o m. nausea

mar-ga-ri-na f. margarine

mar-ga-ri-ta f. daisy

mar-gen m. fringe; margin

mar-gi-nal adj. marginal

mar-gi-nar v. to marginate

ma-ri-dar v. to wed

ma-ri-do m. spouse

ma-ri-nar v. to marinate

ma-ri-ne-ria f. saloring

ma-ri-ne-ro, -ra adj. marine; seaworthy

ma-ri-no adj. marine

ma-ri-po-sa f. butterfly

ma-ri-qui-ta f. ladybug

ma-ris-cal m. marshal

ma-ris-co m. crustacean

ma-ri-tal adj. marital

ma-rí-ti-mo, -ma adj. maritine

már-mol m. marble

mar-qués m. marquis

ma-rra-no adj. filthy

ma-rrar v. to fail; to miss something

ma-rrón adj. brown

ma-rru-lle-ro, -ra m., f. conniver

mar-so-pa f. porpoise

mar-su-pial adj. marsupial

mar-tes m. Tuesday

mar-ti-llar v. to hammer

mar-ti-llo m. hammer

már-tir m., f. martyr

mar-ti-rio m. martyrdom

mar-zo m. March

mas adv. rather; more

ma-sa-crar v. to massacre

ma-sa-cre m. massacre
ma-sa-je m. massage
ma-sa-jis-ta m. masseur
mas-car v. to chew
más-ca-ra f. disguise
mas-ca-ra-da f. masquerade
mas-co-ta f. mascot
mas-cu-li-ni-dad f. masculinity
mas-cu-li-no adj. manly; male
ma-si-vo, -va adj. massive
mas-ti-car v. to masticate; to ruminate
más-til m. mast
mas-toi-des adj. mastoid
ma-ta f. shrub
ma-ta-dor, -ra m., f. killer
ma-ta-fue-go m. fire extinguisher
ma-tan-za f. massacre; killing; slaughtering
ma-tar v. to extinguish; to kill; to slaughter
ma-ta-ri-fe m. slaughterer
ma-ta-se-llar v. to cancel
ma-te-ma-ti-co, -ca adj. mathematical
ma-te-ria f. matter
ma-te-rial adj. material
ma-te-ria-li-dad f. materiality
ma-te-ria-lis-ta adj. materialistic
ma-ter-nal adj. maternal
ma-ter-ni-dad f. maternity
ma-ter-no adj. motherly
ma-ti-nal adj. morning
ma-tiz m. tint
ma-ti-zar v. to tint
ma-tre-ro, -ra adj. shrewd
ma-triar-ca-do m. matriarchy
ma-triar-cal adj. matriarchal
ma-tri-ci-dio m. matricide
ma-tri-cu-la f. list
ma-tri-cu-la-cion f. registration
ma-tri-cu-lar v. to natriculate
ma-tri-mo-nial adj. matrimonial
ma-tri-mo-nio m. matrimony
ma-triz f. uterus
ma-tro-na f. matron
ma-tro-nal adj. matronly

ma-xi-ma-men-te adv. chiefly
ma-xi-me adv. principally
ma-xi-mo adj. maximum
ma-yo m. May
ma-yo-ne-sa f. mayonnaise
ma-yor adj. greatest; larger; older
ma-yo-ría f. majority
ma-yo-ri-dad f. majority
ma-yus-cu-lo, -la adj. important; capital
maz-mo-rra f. dungeon
ma-zo m. bunch
me pron. me
me-ca-ni-co, -ca adj. mechanical
me-ca-ni-zar v. to mechanize
me-ce-do-ra f. rocking chair
me-cer v. to sway; to rock
me-cha f. match; wick
me-che-ra f. shoplifter
me-chón m. tuft
me-da-lla f. medal
me-da-llon m. medallion
me-dia f. stocking
me-dia-dor, -ra m., f. mediator
me-dia-ne-ro, -ra adj. mediating
me-dia-no-che f. midnight
me-diar v. to intercede
me-di-ca-cion f. medication
me-di-car v. to medicate
me-di-ci-na f. medicine
me-di-ci-nal adj. medicinal
me-di-ci-nar v. to cure or treat with medicine
mé-di-co, -ca m., f. doctor
me-di-da f. measurement
me-die-val adj. medieval
me-dio adj. middle; half
me-dio-cre adj. mediocre
me-dio-cri-dad f. mediocrity
me-dio-dí-a m. noon
me-dir v. to weigh; measure
me-di-ta-ción f. meditation
me-di-tar v. meditate
me-di-ta-ti-vo, -va adj. meditative
me-dium m. medium
me-drar v. to thrive; prosper

me-dro-so, -sa adj. timorous
me-du-la f. medulla
me-du-sa f. jellyfish
me-ga-fo-no m. megaphone
me-ga-tón m. megaton
me-ji-lla f. cheek
me-jor adj. superior; better
me-jo-ra f. betterment
me-jo-rar v. to make better
me-jo-ría f. improvement
me-lan-có-li-a f. melancholy
me-la-za f. molasses
me-lin-dre-ria f. affectation
me-lo-co-tón m. peach
me-lo-co-to-ne-ro m. peach tree
me-lo-dia f. tune
me-lo-di-co adj. tuneful
me-lo-dio-so, -sa adj. melodious
me-lo-dra-ma m. melodrama
me-lo-dra-ma-ti-co, -ca adj. melodramatic
me-lón m. melon
me-lo-te m. molasses
me-llar v. to nick; to chip
mem-bra-na f. membrane
me-mo-ra-ble v. memorable
me-mo-rar v. to recall
me-mo-ria f. remembrance; memory
me-mo-rial m. memorial
me-mo-ri-za-cion f. memorization
me-mo-ri-zar v. to memorize
men-ción f. mention
men-cio-nar v. to mention
me-ne-ar v. to sway
men-gua f. poverty
men-gua-do adj. decreased; timid
men-guar v. to wane; to diminish
me-nin-gi-tis f. meningitis
me-no-pau-sia f. menopause
me-nor adj. lesser; least; less; younger
me-nos adv. least; less
me-nos-ca-bar v. to impair
me-nos-ca-bo m. damage; diminishing
me-nos-pre-cia-ble adj.
despicable
me-nos-pre-cio m. underestimation; contempt
men-sa-je m. message
men-sa-je-ro, -ra adj. messenger
men-sual adj. monthly
men-su-ra f. measurement
men-su-ra-ble adj. mensurable
men-su-rar v. measure
men-ta f. mint
men-ta-do, -da adj. reowned
men-tal adj. mental
men-ta-li-dad f. mentality
men-tar v. mention
men-te f. intellect; intelligence
men-tir v. to lie
men-ti-ra f. falsehood
men-ti-ro-so, -sa adj. lying
men-tor m. mentor
me-nu-do adj. little; insignificant
mer-ca-de-o m. marketing
mer-ca-do m. marketplace
mer-can-te adj. merchant
mer-can-til adj. mercantile
mer-car v. to buy
mer-ced f. gift
mer-ce-na-rio, -ria adj. mercenary
mer-cu-rial adj. mercurial
mer-cu-rio m. mercury
me-re-ci-mien-to m. worth
me-ri-dia-no, -na adj. meridian
me-rien-da f. snack
mé-ri-to m. value; worth
me-ri-to-rio, -ria adj. meritorious
mer-mar v. to diminish
me-ro, -ra adj. pure
me-ro-de-ar v. plunder
mes m. month
me-sa f. table
me-son m. tavern
me-so-ne-ro, -ra m., f. innkeeper
me-su-ra f. moderation
me-su-ra-do, -da adj. moderate
me-ta-bo-li-co, -ca adj.

metabolic

me-ta-bo-lis-mo *m.* metabolism

me-tá-fo-ra *f.* metaphor

me-ta-fó-ri-co, -ca *adj.* metaphoric

me-tal *m.* metal

me-tá-li-co *adj.* metallic

me-ta-li-zar *v.* to metalize

me-ta-mor-fi-co, -ca *adj.* metamorphic

me-ta-no *m.* methane

me-te-o-ri-co, -ca *adj.* meteoric

me-te-o-ri-to *m.* meteorite

me-te-o-ro *m.* meteor

me-te-o-ro-lo-gi-a *f.* meteorology

me-te-o-ro-lo-gis-ta *m., f.* meteorologist

me-ter *v.* to insert into; to cause

me-ti-cu-lo-so, -sa *adj.* meticulous

me-ti-lo *m.* methyl

me-tó-di-co, -ca *adj.* methodical

mé-to-do *m.* method

me-to-do-lo-gi-a *f.* methodology

me-tri-co *adj.* metric

me-tro-po-li-ta-no, -na *adj.* metropolitan

mez-cla-dor *adj.* blending

mez-clar *v.* to mingle; blend

mez-quin-dad *f.* miserliness

mez-qui-no, -na *adj.* petty; wretched; miserly

mez-qui-ta *f.* mosque

mi *pron.* me

mi-cro-bio *m.* microbe

mi-cro-bio-lo-gia *f.* microbiology

mi-cro-fil-me *m.* microfilm

mi-cró-fo-no *m.* microphone

mi-cros-co-pi-co, -ca *adj.* microscopic

mi-cros-co-pio *m.* microscope

mie-do *m.* dread

mie-do-so, -sa *adj.* cowardly

miel *f.* honey

miel-ga *f.* alfalfa

miem-bro *m.* member

mien-tras *adv.* meanwhile *conj.* while

miér-co-les *m.* Wednesday

mies *f.* grain

mi-ga *f.* substance; scrap

mi-gra-ción *f.* migration

mi-gra-na *f.* migraine

mil *adj.* thousand

mi-la-gro *m.* miracle

mi-la-gro-so *adj.* miraculous

mi-li-cia *f.* militia

mi-li-cia-no, -na *adj.* military

mi-li-gra-mo *m.* milligram

mi-li-li-tro *m.* milliliter

mi-li-me-tro *m.* millimeter

mi-li-tar *m.* soldier

mi-lla *f.* mile

mi-llón *m.* million

mi-mar *v.* to fondle; pamper

mi-mi-co, -ca *adj.* mimic

mi-mo-so *adj.* spoiled

mi-na *f.* mine

mi-na-dor *adj.* mining

mi-nar *v.* to mine

mi-ne-ral *adj.* mineral

mi-ne-ra-lo-gis-ta *m.* mineralogist

mi-ne-rí-a *f.* mining

mi-nia-tu-ra *f.* miniature

mi-nia-tu-ris-ta *m., f.* miniaturist

mi-ni-fal-da *f.* miniskirt

mi-ni-mi-zar *v.* to minimize

mi-ni-mo, -ma *adj.* least; minimal; minute

mi-nis-te-rial *adj.* ministerial

mi-nis-te-rio *m.* ministry

mi-nis-tro *m.* minister

mi-no-rar *v.* to reduce

mi-no-ria *f.* minority

mi-no-ri-ta-rio *adj.* minority

mi-nu-cio-so, -sa *adj.* minute

mi-nús-cu-lo, -la *adj.* tiny; small

mi-nu-ta *f.* record; note

mi-nu-to *m.* minute

mi-o, -a *adj.* mine

mio-pe *adj.* myopic

mio-pí-a *f.* myopia

mi-ra *f.* sight; intention

mi-ra-do, -da *adj.* regarded; cautious

mi-ra-dor *adj.* watching
mi-rar *v.* to watch; to look at; to observe
mi-ra-sol *m.* sunflower
mi-rí-a-da *f.* myriad
mir-lo *m.* blackbird
mis-ce-lá-ne-o, -a *adj.* miscellaneous
mi-se-ra-ble *adj.* miserable; poor; miserly
mi-se-ria *f.* suffering; miserliness; misery
mi-sil *m.* missile
mi-sión *f.* mission
mi-sio-nal *adj.* missionary
mis-mo *adj.* likewise; same thing
mis-te-rio *m.* mystery
mis-te-rio-so *adj.* mysterious
mís-ti-co, -ca *adj.* mystic
mis-ti-fi-car *v.* to mystify
mis-tu-ra *f.* mixture
mi-tad *f.* half
mi-ti-ga-cion *f.* mitigation
mi-ti-gar *v.* to mitigate
mi-to *m.* myth
mi-ton *m.* mitt
mi-tra *f.* miter
mix-to, -ta *adj.* mixed
mix-tu-ra *f.* mixture
mix-tu-rar *v.* to mix up
mo-bi-lia-rio, -ria *adj.* movable
mo-bla-je *m.* furnishing
mo-blar *v.* to furnish
mo-ce-dad *f.* youth
mo-ción *f.* motion
mo-cho, -cha *adj.* hornless
mo-da *f.* fashion
mo-de-lo *m.* model
mo-de-ra-ción *f.* moderation
mo-de-ra-do *adj.* moderate
mo-de-rar *v.* to regulate; to restrain
mo-der-ni-za-ción *f.* modernization
mo-der-ni-zar *v.* to modernize
mo-der-no *adj.* modern
mo-des-tia *f.* modesty
mó-di-co, -ca *adj.* moderate
mo-di-fi-ca-ción *f.* modification

mo-di-fi-ca-dor *adj.* modifying
mo-di-fi-car *v.* to modify
mo-dis-te-ri-a *f.* shop for dresses
mo-do *m.* way
mo-do-so, -sa *adj.* well-mannered
mo-du-la-cion *f.* modulation
mo-du-la-dor, -ra *m., f.* modulator
mo-jar *v.* to drench; to dip; to wet
mol-de *m.* pattern; mold
mol-de-ar *v.* to shape
mo-lé-cu-lar *adj.* molecular
mo-ler *v.* to grind
mo-les-tar *v.* to annoy; to disrupt
mo-les-tia *f.* annoyance; trouble
mo-les-to *adj.* bothered; annoying
mo-men-to *m.* moment
mo-na *f.* a female monkey
mo-nas-te-rio *m.* monastery
mo-ni-tor *m.* monitor
mo-no *m.* male monkey
mo-no-gra-ma *m.* monogram
mons-truo *m.* monster
mons-truo-so *adj.* monstrous
mon-ta-ña *f.* mountain
mon-tar *v.* to mount
mo-nu-men-to *m.* monument
mo-ral *f.* morale
mo-ra-li-dad *f.* morality
mo-ra-li-zar *v.* to moralize
mo-rar *v.* to dwell; to live
mór-bi-do *adj.* morbid
mo-re-no *adj.* brown
mor-fi-na *f.* morphine
mo-rir *v.* to kill
mor-tal *adj.* fatal; mortal
mor-ta-li-dad *f.* mortality
mor-tuo-rio *m.* mortuary
mos-ca *f.* fly
mos-qui-to *m.* mosquito
mos-ta-za *f.* mustard
mos-trar *v.* to exhibit; to appear; to show
mo-tor *m.* engine

mo-ver *v.* to move
mo-vi-men-to *m.* movement
mu-cha-cha *f.* girl
mu-cha-cho *m.* boy
mu-cho *adj.* many; a lot
muer-te *f.* death
muer-to *adj.* dead
mu-jer *f.* female; woman
múl-ti-ple *adj.* multiple
mul-ti-pli-car *v.* to multiply
mun-do *m.* world
mu-ni-ci-pal *adj.* municipal
mu-ne-ca *f.* wrist; doll
mus-cu-lo *m.* muscle
mu-si-ca *f.* music
mu-si-cal *adj.* musical
mus-lo *m.* thigh
muy *adv.* much; greatly

na-bo *m.* turnip; mast
na-ca-ri-no *adj.* narcreous
na-cer *v.* to rise; to be born; to be concieved
na-ci-do, -da *adj.* born
na-cien-te *adj.* recent; growing; initial; nascent
na-ci-mien-to *m.* hatching; origin; birth; spring
na-ción *f.* nation
na-cio-nal *adj.* domestic; national
na-cio-na-li-dad *f.* nationality
na-cio-na-lis-ta *m., f.* nationalist
na-cio-na-li-za-cion *f.* nationalization
na-cio-na-li-zar *v.* to nationalize
na-da *pron.* no; not anything; none; nothing
na-da-dor *m., f.* swimmer
na-dar *v.* to swim
na-die *pron.* no one; nobody
nai-pe *m.* playing card
nal-ga *f.* behind; buttocks
na-ran-ja *f.* orange
na-ran-jal *m.* orange grove
na-ran-je-ro *adj.* orange
na-ran-jo *m.* orange tree

nar-có-ti-co, -ca *adj.* narcotic
nar-co-ti-zar *v.* to narcotize
na-riz *f.* nostril; nose
na-rra-cion *f.* narration; narrative
na-rra-dor, -ra *adj.* narrative
na-rrar *v.* to narrate
na-rra-ti-vo, -va *adj.* narrative
na-ta-ción *f.* swimming
na-tal *adj.* natal
na-ta-li-dad *f.* natality
Na-ti-vi-dad *f.* Christmas
na-ti-vo *adj.* inborn; native
na-to, -ta *adj.* natural
na-tu-ra *f.* nature
na-tu-ral *adj.* native; innate; natural
na-tu-ra-le-za *f.* nature
na-tu-ra-li-dad *f.* naturalness
na-tu-ra-li-za-ción *f.* naturalization
nau-fra-gar *v.* to shipwreck
náu-fra-go, -ga *adj.* shipwrecked
náu-se-a *f.* nausea
nau-se-ar *v.* to feel nauseous
náu-ti-co, -ca *adj.* nautical
na-val *adj.* naval
na-ve-ga-ble *adj.* navigable
na-ve-ga-cion *f.* navigation
na-ve-gar *v.* to sail
Na-vi-dad *f.* Christmas
na-ví-o *m.* vessel; boat
ne-bli-na *f.* fog
ne-bli-no-so, -sa *adj.* foggy
ne-bu-lo-si-dad *f.* haziness
ne-ce-dad *f.* nonsense
ne-ce-sa-rio *adj.* necessary
ne-ce-si-dad *f.* need; poverty; necessity
ne-ce-si-ta-do, -da *adj.* poor; needy
ne-ce-si-tar *v.* to want; to require; to need
ne-cio, -cia *adj.* foolish; stubborn
ne-cro-lo-gi-a *f.* necrology
nec-tar *m.* nectar
nec-ta-ri-na *f.* nectarine
ne-fri-tis *f.* nephritis
ne-ga-ble *adj.* refutable

ne-ga-ción f. denial; refusal; negation

ne-gar v. to refuse; to deny; to forbid

ne-ga-ti-vi-dad f. negativity

ne-gli-gen-cia f. disregard; negligence

ne-go-cia-ble adj. negotiable

ne-go-cia-ción f. negotiation; transaction

ne-go-ciar v. to deal; to negotiate

ne-go-cio m. job; work; business; transaction

ne-gro, -a adj. black

ne-gru-ra f. darkness

ne-gruz-co, -ca adj. dark

ne-ne, -na m., f. baby

ne-nu-far m. water lily

ne-ó-fi-to, -ta m., f. neophyte

ne-on m. neon

ne-o-na-to m. neonate

ner-vo m. nerve

ner-vio-si-dad f. nervousness

ner-vio-so, -sa adj. nervous

ner-vo-si-dad f. nervousness

ne-to, -ta adj. simple; pure

neu-má-ti-co, -ca adj. pneumatic

neu-ro-ci-ru-gi-a f. neurosurgery

neu-ro-lo-go m. neurologist

neu-ro-ti-co, -ca adj. neurotic

neu-to-nio m. newton

neu-tral adj. neutral

neu-tra-li-dad f. neutrality

neu-tra-li-zar v. to neutralize

neu-tro, -a adj. neutral

neu-trón m. neutron

ne-va-do, -da adj. snow-covered

ne-var v. to snow

ne-ve-ra f. refrigerator

ne-xo m. link

ni conj. neither; nor

ni-co-ti-na f. nicotine

ni-cho m. vault; recess

ni-dal m. nest

ni-do m. nest; liar; den

nei-bla f. mist

nie-ta f. granddaughter

nie-to m. grandson

nie-ve f. snow

ni-hi-lis-ta adj. nihilistic

ni-lon m. nylon

nim-bom. halo

ni-mio, -a adj. insignificant

nin-fa f. nymph

nin-fe-a f. water lily

nin-fo m. dandy

nin-fo-ma-ni-a f. nymphomania

nin-gu-no, -na adj. no; none

ni-ne-ri-a f. childish

ni-nez f. infancy; childhood

ni-no, -na m. f. child

ní-quel m. nickel

ni-que-lar v. to nickel

ni-ti-do, -da adj. clear

ni-tra-to m. nitrite

ni-tri-to m. nitrite

ni-tro-ge-no m. nitrogen

ni-tro-gli-ce-ri-na f. nitroglycerin

ni-vel m. height; standard

ni-ve-lar v. to make level

no adv. no

no-ble adj. honorable; noble

no-ble-za f. nobleness; nobility

no-ción f. notion

no-ci-vi-dad f. noxiousness

no-ci-vo, -va adj. noxious

noc-tur-nal adj. nocturnal

noc-tur-no, -na adj. sad; nocturnal

no-che f. night

no-du-lo m. nodule

no-gal m. walnut

no-ma-da adj. nomadic

nom-bra-mein-to m. nomination; naming

nom-brar v. to name; to nominate

nom-bre m. name

no-men-cla-tu-ra f. nomenclature

no-mi-na f. roll

no-mi-na-ción f. nomination

no-mi-nal adj. nominal

no-mi-nar v. to nominate

non adj. uneven

no-na-da f. trifle

no-no, -na adj. ninth

nor-ma f. rule

nor-mal adj. normal

nor-ma-li-dad *f.* normality

nor-ma-li-za-cion *f.* normalization

nor-ma-li-zar *v.* to normalize

no-ro-es-te *m.* northwest

nor-te *m.* north

nos *pron.* us

no-ta-ble *adj.* outstanding; notable

no-tar *v.* to observe; note

no-ti-fi-car *v.* to notify

no-ve-no *adj.* ninth

no-ven-ta *adj.* ninety

no-via *f.* girlfriend

no-vio *m.* boyfriend

nu-bo-si-dad *f.* cloudiness

nu-ca *f.* nape

nues-tro *adj.* our

nue-ve *adj.* nine

nue-vo *adj.* new

nú-me-ro *m.* number

nun-ca *adv.* not ever

nu-trir *v.* to feed

ña-me *m.* yam

ña-pa *f.* tip; bonus

ña-que *m.* junk

ñe-que *m.* vigor; *adj.* strength

ño-ñe-ria *f.* timidity

ño-ñez *f.* bashfulness

ño-ño -a *adj., m., f.* timid; bashful

ñu-do *m.* knot

o *conj.* or

o-a-sis *m.* oasis

ob-ce-ca-da-men-to *adv.* blindly

ob-ce-car *v.* to blind

o-be-de-cer *v.* to obey

o-be-dien-cia *f.* obedience

o-be-dien-te *adj.* obedient

o-ber-tu-ra *f.* overture

o-be-si-dad *f.* obesity

o-bi-ce *m.* obstacle

o-bis-po *m.* bishop

ob-je-ción *f.* objection

ob-je-ta-ble *adj.* objectionable

ob-je-tar *v.* to object

ob-je-ti-var *v.* to objectify

ob-je-ti-vi-dad *f.* objectivity

ob-je-ti-vo *adj.* objective

ob-je-to *m.* theme; object

o-bli-cuo, -cua *adj.* oblique

o-bli-ga-ción *f.* responsibility; obligation

o-bli-gar *v.* to force; to oblige; to favor

o-bli-ga-to-rio, -ria *adj.* obligatory

o-blon-go, -ga *adj.* oblong

o-bo-e *m.* oboe

o-bra *f.* work; labor

o-brar *v.* to act; to work

o-bre-ro, -ra *adj.* working

obs-ce-ni-dad *f.* obscenity

obs-ce-no, -na *adj.* obscene

ob-se-quio *m.* present; kindness; gift

ob-se-quio-so, -sa *adj.* obsequious; attentive

ob-ser-va-ción *f.* observation

ob-ser-va-dor, -ra *adj.* observing *m.*, *f.* observer

ob-ser-van-cia *f.* observance

ob-ser-var *v.* to watch; to observe

ob-se-sión *f.* obsession

ob-se-sio-nan-te *adj.* obsessive

ob-se-sio-nar *v.* to obsess about someting

ob-se-so, -sa *adj.* obsessive

obs-ta-cu-li-zar *v.* to hinder

obs-ta-cu-lo *m.* obstacle

obs-tan-te *adj.* obstructing

obs-tar *v.* to hinder; to obstruct something

obs-ti-na-ción *f.* obstinacy

obs-ti-na-do, -da *adj.* obstinate

obs-truc-ción *f.* obstruction

obs-truir *v.* to obstruct

ob-ten-cion *f.* obtaining

ob-te-ner *v.* to get; to have; to obtain

ob-tu-so, -sa *adj.* obtuse
ob-viar *v.* to prevent
ob-vio, -via *adj.* obvious
o-ca-sión *f.* cause; occasion; circumstance
o-ca-sio-nar *v.* to cause; to provoke; to occasion
oc-ci-den-tal *adj.* occidental
oc-ci-pi-tal *adj.* occipital
o-cé-a-no *m.* ocean
o-ce-a-no-gra-fí-a *f.* oceanography
o-ce-a-no-gra-fi-co, -ca *adj.* oceanographic
o-cio *m.* leisure; idleness
oc-ta-vo *adj.* eighth
oc-te-to *m.* octet
oc-to-ge-si-mo *adj.* eightieth
oc-to-go-nal *adj.* octagonal
oc-to-go-no, -na *adj.* octagonal
oc-tu-bre *m.* October
o-cul-tar *v.* to conceal; to silence; to hide
o-cu-lis-ta *m., f.* oculist
o-cul-ta-men-te *adv.* secretly
o-cul-tar *v.* to conceal; to silence; to hide
o-cul-tis-mo *m.* occultism
o-cul-to, -ta *adj.* concealed; occult
o-cu-pa-ción *f.* trade; occupation; job
o-cu-pa-do *adj.* occupied
o-cu-pan-te *adj.* occupying
o-cu-par *v.* to fill; to occupy; to employ; to pay attention to something
o-cu-rren-cia *f.* occurrence
o-cu-rrir *v.* to happen; to take place
o-chen-ta *adj.* eighty
o-chen-ta-vo, -va *adj.* eightieth
o-cho *adj.* eight
o-cho-cien-tos *adj.* eight hundred
o-da *f.* ode
o-da-lis-ca *f.* odalisque
o-diar *v.* to loathe
o-dio *m.* loathing
o-dio-so, -sa *adj.* odious
o-di-se-a *f.* odyssey

o-don-to-lo-go, -ga *m., f.* odontologist
o-es-te *m.* west
o-fen-der *v.* to hurt; offend
o-fen-sa *f.* offense
o-fen-si-vo, -va *adj.* offensive
o-fen-sor *adj.* offending
o-fer-tar *v.* to tender
o-fi-cial *m.* officer
o-fi-cia-li-dad *f.* officers
o-fi-cian-te *m.* officiant
o-fi-ci-na *f.* office
o-fi-ci-nis-ta *m., f.* office clerk
o-fi-cio *m.* work; office
o-fre-ci-mien-to *m.* offering
o-fren-da *f.* gift
o-fren-dar *v.* to give an offering for
of-tal-mo-lo-gi-a *f.* ophthalmology
of-tal-mo-lo-go *m.* ophthalmologist
o-fus-ca-cion *f.* confusion; dazzling
o-fus-car *v.* to bewilder; to blind
o-í-do *m.* ear
o-ír *v.* to listen; to hear; to attend
o-jal *m.* bottonhole
o-je-a-da *f.* glimpse
o-je-ri-za *f.* grudge
o-jo *m.* eye
o-jo-ta *f.* sandal
o-le-a-da *f.* wave
o-le-a-je *m.* waves
o-ler *v.* to smell
ol-fa-to *m.* instinct
ol-fa-to-rio, -ria *adj.* olfactory
o-li-va *f.* olive
o-li-var *m.* olive grove
o-li-vo *m.* olive tree
ol-mo *m.* elm tree
o-lor *m.* smell
o-lo-ro-so, -sa *adj.* fragrant
ol-vi-da-do, -da *adj.* forgetful; ungrateful
ol-vi-dar *v.* to omit; to forget; to leave out

ol-vi-do *m.* forgetfulness
o-lla *f.* kettle
om-bli-go *m.* navel
o-mi-sión *f.* omission
o-mi-tir *v.* to omit
óm-ni-bus *m.* omnibus
om-ni-po-ten-cia *f.* omnipotence
om-ni-po-ten-te *adj.* omnipotent
o-na-nis-mo *m.* onanism
on-ce *adj.* eleven
on-ce-no *adj.* eleventh
on-co-lo-gi-a *f.* oncology
on-de-ar *v.* to flutter; to ripple
on-du-la-ción *f.* undulation
on-du-lar *v.* to undulate
o-ne-ro-so, -sa *adj.* onerous
o-nix *f.* onyx
o-no-ma-to-pe-ya *f.* onomatopoeia
on-za *f.* ounce
on-za-vo *adj.* eleventh
o-pa *adj.* foolish
o-pa-ci-dad *f.* opacity
o-pa-co, -ca *adj.* opaque
ó-pa-lo *m.* opal
op-ción *f.* option
op-cio-nal *adj.* optional
ó-pe-ra *f.* opera
o-pe-ra-ción *f.* operation
o-pe-ran-te *adj.* operating
o-pe-rar *v.* to operate
o-pe-ra-ti-vo, -va *adj.* operative
o-pi-nion *f.* opinion
o-pio *m.* opium
o-po-ner *v.* to oppose
o-por-tu-na-men-te *adv.* opportunely
o-por-tu-ni-dad *f.* chance
o-por-tu-nis-ta *adj.* opportunist
o-por-tu-no, -na *adj.* opportune; fitting
o-po-si-cion *f.* opposition
o-po-si-tor, -ra *m., f.* opponent
o-pre-sion *f.* opression
o-pre-si-vo, -va *adj.* oppressive
o-pre-so, -sa *adj.* oppressed

o-pri-mi-do, -da *adj.* oppressed
o-pri-mir *v.* to press; to oppress
o-pro-bio *m.* disgrace
o-pro-bio-so, -sa *adj.* disgraceful
op-tar *v.* to select
óp-ti-co, -ca *adj.* optical
op-ti-mis-ta *adj.* optimistic
op-ti-mo, -ma *adj.* optimal
op-to-me-tra *m., f.* optometrist
op-to-me-tri-a *f.* optometry
o-pues-to *adj.* contrary; opposite
o-pu-len-cia *f.* opulence
o-ra *conj.* now
o-ra-ción *f.* oration; speech; sentence
o-rá-cu-lo *m.* oracle
o-ral *adj.* oral
o-ran-gu-tan *m.* orangutan
o-rar *v.* to speak
o-ra-to-rio, -ria *adj.* oratorical
or-be *m.* orb
or-den *m.* order
or-de-na-cion *f.* ordination; ordering
or-de-na-da *f.* ordinate
or-de-nar *v.* to command; to arrange; to put into order
or-de-nar *v.* to milk
or-di-nal *adj.* ordinal
or-di-na-riez *f.* commonness
or-di-na-rio *adj.* ordinary; uncouth; coarse
o-re-ar *v.* to ventilate
or-fa-na-to *m.* orphanage
or-fe-li-na-to *m.* orphanage
or-ga-ni-co *adj.* organic
or-ga-nis-mo *m.* organism
or-ga-nis-ta *m., f.* organist
or-ga-ni-za-dor, -ra *m., f.* organizer
or-ga-ni-zar *v.* to organize
ór-ga-no *m.* organ
or-gu-llo *m.* conceit
o-rien-ta-cion *f.* orientation
o-rien-tal *adj.* oriental
o-rien-tar *v.* to orient
o-ri-fi-cio *m.* opening

o-ri-gen *m.* source
o-ri-gi-nal *adj.* authentic; original; new
o-ri-gi-na-li-dad *f.* originality
o-ri-gi-nar *v.* to originate
o-ri-gi-na-ria-men-te *adv.* originally
o-ri-lla *f.* edge
o-ri-llar *v.* to edge
o-rin *m.* rust
o-ri-nal *m.* urinal
o-ri-nar *v.* to urinate
or-lar *v.* to edge
or-na-men-tal *adj.* ornamental
or-na-men-tar *v.* to ornament; to decorate
or-na-men-to *m.* ornament
or-nar *v.* to embellish
or-ni-to-lo-gi-a *f.* ornithology
or-ni-to-lo-go *m., f.* ornithologist
o-ro *m.* gold
or-ques-ta *f.* orchestra
or-ques-ta-cion *f.* orchestration
or-ques-tal *adj.* orchestral
or-ques-tar *v.* to orchestrate
or-qui-de-a *f.* orchid
or-ti-ga *f.* nettle
or-to-do-xo, -xa *adj.* orthodox
or-to-gra-fi-a *f.* orthographic
or-to-pe-di-co, -ca *adj.* orthopedic
or-to-pe-dis-ta *m., f.* orthopedist
o-ru-ga *f.* caterpillar
o-ru-jo *m.* residue
os *pron.* you
o-sa-di-a *f.* audacity
o-sa-do, -da *adj.* daring
o-sa-men-ta *f.* bones
o-sar *v.* to dare
os-ci-la-cion *f.* wavering; swinging
os-ci-lar *v.* to oscillate; to swing
os-cu-lo *m.* kiss
os-cu-re-cer *v.* to dim; to obscure; to shade
os-cu-re-ci-mien-to *m.* darkening

os-cu-ri-dad *f.* haziness; obscurity
os-cu-ro, -ra *adj.* unclear; dark; obscure
o-si-fi-car-se *v.* to ossify
os-mo-sia *f.* osmosis
o-so *m.* bear
os-ten-si-ble *adj.* ostensible
os-ten-ta-cion *f.* ostentation
os-ten-tar *v.* to flaunt; to show
os-te-o-lo-go, -ga *m., f.* osteologist
os-tra *f.* oyster
os-tra-cis-mo *m.* ostracism
o-te-ar *v.* to survey
o-to-ñal *adj.* autumnal
o-to-ño *m.* autumn
o-tor-gar *v.* to give
o-tro *adj.* other
o-va-cion *f.* ovation
o-va-cio-nar *v.* to give another an ovation
o-val *adj.* oval
o-va-lo *m.* oval
o-va-rio *m.* ovary
o-ve-ja *f.* the female sheep
o-ver-tu-ra *f.* overture
o-vi-llo *m.* snarl; ball
o-vi-no *m.* ovine
o-vu-la-cion *f.* ovulation
o-vu-lar *adj.* ovular
o-xi-da-cion *f.* oxidation
o-xi-dar *v.* to oxidize
ó-xi-do *m.* oxide
o-xi-ge-na-do, -da *adj.* oxygenated
o-xi-ge-nar *v.* to give oxygen to; to oxygenate
o-xi-ge-no *m.* oxygen
o-yen-te *adj.* listening *m., f.* listener
o-zo-no *m.* ozone

pa-be-llón *m.* banner; pavilion
pa-bi-lo *m.* candle wick
pa-bu-lo *m.* pabulum; support

pa-cer v. to graze
pa-cien-cia f. patience
pa-cien-te adj. patient
pa-ci-fi-ca-cion f. pacification
pa-ci-fi-ca-dor, -ra m., f. pacifier
pa-ci-fi-car v. to pacify
pa-ci-fi-co adj. pacific
pa-ci-fis-ta adj. pacifist
pa-cho-rra f. sluggishness
pa-de-cer v. to bear; to suffer; to endure
pa-dras-tro m. stepfather
pa-dre m. dad; father
pa-dri-llo m. stallion
pa-dri-no m. godfather
pa-ga f. payment
pa-ga-de-ro, -ra adj. payable
pa-ga-no, -na adj. pagan
pa-gar v. to repay; pay for
pá-gi-na f. page
pa-gi-nar v. to paginate
pa-go adj. paid
país m. land
pai-sa-je m. landscape
pai-sa-jis-ta adj. landscape
pa-ja f. straw
pa-jar m. barn
pa-ja-re-ra f. cage for birds
pa-ja-re-ri-a f. bird store
pá-ja-ro m. bird
pa-la- f. blade; spade; shovelful
pa-la-bra f. word
pa-la-bre-o m. chatter
pa-la-cie-go, -ga adj. magnificent
pa-la-cio m. palace
pa-la-da f. shovelful
pa-la-de-ar v. to relish
pa-la-dio m. palladium
pa-la-fre-ne-ro m. groom
pa-lan-ca f. shaft; lever
pa-lan-ga-na f. washbasin
pa-le-ar v. to shovel
pa-le-on-to-lo-gi-a f. paleontology
pa-le-ta f. trowel; palette
pa-lia-ti-vo, -va adj. palliative
pá-li-dez f. pallor
pá-li-do, -da adj. pallid
pa-li-to m. small stick

pa-li-za f. thrashing
pal-ma f. palm
pal-ma-do, -da adj. palm-shaped
pal-mar m. palm grove
pal-me-a-do, -da adj. palm-shaped
pal-me-ar v. to applaud
pal-me-ra f. palm tree
pal-mo m. palm
pal-mo-te-ar v. to applaud
pa-lo m. pole; handle
pa-lo-ma f. pigeon
pa-lo-mi-ta f. popcorn
pa-lo-te m. drumstick
pal-pa-ble adj. palpable
pal-par v. to feel
pal-pi-ta-ción f. palpitation
pal-pi-tan-te adj. palpating
pal-pi-tar v. to palpitate; to beat
pal-ta f. avocado
pa-lu-dis-mo m. malaria
pa-lur-do, -da m., f. boor
pam-pa f. pampa
pan m. bread
pa-na f. corduroy
pa-na-de-ri-a f. bakery
pa-na-de-ro, -ra m., f. baker
pa-nal m. honeycomb
pan-cre-as m. pancreas
pan-cre-a-ti-co, -ca adj. pancreatic
pa-cho, -cha adj. unruffled
pan-da f. panda
pan-de-mo-nio m. pandemonium
pan-de-ro m. tambourine
pan-di-lla f. gang
pan-fle-to m. pamphlet
pá-ni-co, -ca m., adj. panic
pa-no-ra-ma f. panorama
pa-no-ra-mi-co, -ca adj. panoramic
pan-ta-ló-nes m. slacks; pants
pan-ta-lla f. movie screen; lamp shade
pan-ta-no m. difficulty
pan-te-on m. pantheon
pan-te-ra f. panther
pan-to-mi-ma f. pantomine
pan-to-rri-lla f. calf

pa-no m. cloth
pa-no-le-ta f. scarf
pa-no-lon m. shawl
pa-nue-lo m. kerchief
pa-pa f. potato
pa-pa-ga-yo m. parrot
pa-pal adj. papal
pa-par v. to gape
pa-pa-ya f. papaya
pa-pel m. paper
pa-pe-le-ro, -ra adj. paper
pa-pe-le-ta f. card
pa-pe-ra f. goiter
pa-pi-la f. papilla
pa-pi-ro m. papyrus
pa-que-te m. packet; pack; package
pa-que-te-ri-a f. elegance
pa-qui-der-mo m. pachyderm
par adj. paired; equal
pa-ra prep. for; to; towards
pa-ra-bo-la f. parable
pa-ra-bri-sas m. windshield
pa-ra-ca-i-das f. parachute
pa-ra-di-sia-co, -ca adj. heavenly
pa-ra-do, -da adj. stopped; stationary; idle
pa-ra-do-ja f. paradox
pa-ra-do-ji-co, -ca adj. paradoxical
pa-ra-fi-na f. paraffin
pa-ra-guas m. umbrella
pa-ra-i-so m. paradise
pa-ra-je m. area
pa-ra-le-lo m. parallel
pa-ra-le-lo-gra-mo m. parallelogram
pa-ra-li-sis f. paralysis
pa-ra-li-ti-co, -ca adj. paralytic
pa-ra-li-za-cion f. paralyzation
pa-ra-li-zar v. to paralyze
pa-ra-me-di-co, -ca adj. paramedical
pa-ra-me-tro m. parameter
pa-ra-no-ia f. paranoia
pa-ra-noi-co, -ca adj. paranoid
pa-ra-ple-ji-co, -ca adj. paraplegic

pa-rar v. to halt; to check; to stop
pa-ra-si-ti-co, -ca adj. parasitic
pa-ra-si-to, -ta adj. parasitic
pa-ra-sol m. parasol
par-ce-la f. parcel
par-cial adj. partial
par-cia-li-dad f. partiality
pa-re-ar v. to pair
pa-re-cer m. view; appearance
pa-re-ci-do adj. similar
pa-red f. wall
pa-re-jo, -ja adj. equal; smooth; alike
pa-ren-te-la f. relatives
pa-ren-tes-co m. kinship
pa-ren-te-sis m. parenthesis
pa-ri-dad f. parity
pa-ri-ta-rio, -ria adj. joint
par-la-men-ta-rio adj. parliamentary
par-la-men-to m. parliament
par-lar v. to chatter
par-lo-te-o-m. chatter
pa-ro m. unemployment
pa-ro-dia f. parody
pa-ro-diar v. to parody
pa-ro-dis-ta m., f. parodist
pa-ro-xis-mo m. paroxysm
par-pa-de-ar v. to twinkle
par-pa-do m. eyelid
par-que m. park
par-que-o m. parking
par-que-dad f. moderation
pa-rra f. grapevine
pa-rra-fo m. paragraph
pa-rri-ci-dio m. parricide
pa-rro-quial adj. parochial
par-si-mo-nia f. moderation
par-si-mo-nio-so, -sa adj. parsimonious
par-te f. share; part
par-te-ra f. midwife
par-ti-ción f. partition
par-ti-ci-pa-ción f. participation
par-ti-ci-par v. to inform
par-ti-ci-pe adj. participating
par-ti-cu-la f. particle
par-ti-cu-lar adj. particular

par-ti-cu-la-ri-dad *f.* peculiarity

par-ti-cu-lar-men-te *adv.* particularly

par-ti-dis-ta *adj.* party

par-ti-da *f.* group; leaving; departure

par-ti-do *m.* party

par-tir *v.* to depart; to leave

par-ti-ti-vo, -va *adj.* partitive

par-ti-tu-ra *f.* score

pa-sa-di-zo *m.* passage

pa-sa-do *m.* past

pa-sa-dor *adj.* passing

pa-sa-je *m.* passage

pa-sa-por-te *m.* passport

pa-sar *v.* to elapse; to occur; to happen

pa-sa-tiem-po *m.* pastime

pa-se *m.* pass

pa-se-o *m.* stroll; outing

pa-sion *f.* passion

pa-so *m.* footstep; pace

pas-ta *f.* paste

pas-tel *m.* cake

pas-teu-ri-zar *v.* to pasteurize

pas-teu-ri-za-cion *f.* pasteurization

pas-to *m.* pasture; grass

pa-ta *f.* foot; leg; paw; female duck

pa-ta-da *f.* kick

pa-ta-ta *f.* potato

pa-te-ar *v.* to kick

pa-ten-tar *v.* to register

pa-ten-te *adj.* patent; evident; obvious

pa-ter-nal *adj.* paternal

pa-ter-ni-dad *f.* paternity

pa-ti-llas *f.* sideburns

pa-tin *m.* skate

pa-ti-nar *v.* to skate

pa-tion *m.* patio

pa-to *m.* duck

pa-to-lo-gia *f.* pathology

pa-to-lo-go, -ga *m., f.* pathologist

pa-triar-ca *m.* patriarch

pa-trio-ta *m., f.* patriot

pa-trió-ti-co, ca *adj.* patriotic

pa-tro-ci-nar *v.* to patronize

pa-trón *m.* host

pa-tro-nal *adj.* management

pa-tro-na-to *m.* patronage

pa-tru-llar *v.* to patrol

pau-la-ti-no, -na *adj.* gradual

pau-sa *f.* interruption

pau-ta *f.* rule

pa-va-da *f.* foolishness

pa-vi-men-ta-cion *f.* paving

pa-vi-men-to *m.* pavement

pa-vo *m.* turkey

pa-vor *m.* terror

pa-vu-ra *f.* terror

pa-ya-so *m.* clown

paz *f.* peace

paz-gua-to, -ta *adj.* foolish

pe-car *v.* to sin

pe-ce-ra *f.* aquarium

pec-ti-na *f.* pectin

pec-to-ral *adj.* pectoral

pe-cu-liar *adj.* peculiar

pe-cu-lia-ri-dad *f.* peculiarity

pe-cu-lio *m.* peculium

pe-cu-nia *f.* money

pe-char *v.* to pay

pe-cho *m.* breast; chest

pe-dal *m.* pedal

pe-da-le-o *m.* pedaling

pe-dan-te-ri-a *f.* pedantry

pe-da-zo *m.* bit; piece

pe-der-nal *m.* flint

pe-des-tal *m.* pedestal

pe-des-tre *adj.* pedestrian

pe-dia-tri-a *f.* pediatrics

pe-di-cu-lo *m.* peduncle

pe-di-gre-e *m.* pedigree

pe-dir *v.* to order; to beg; to charge

pe-dre-go-so, -sa *adj.* rocky

pe-dris-ca *f.* hail

pe-dun-cu-lo *m.* peduncle

pe-ga-di-zo, -za *adj.* catching

pe-ga-jo-so, -sa *adj.* catching; adhesive

pe-gar *v.* to glue; to attach; to cleave

pei-na-do *m.* hairdresser

pei-ne *m.* comb

pe-la-do, -da *adj.* bare; bald

pe-la-du-ra *f.* peeling

pe-la-gra *f.* pellagra

pe-lar *v.* to peel; to cut

pe-le-a-dor *adj.* fighting

pe-li-ca-no m. pelican
pe-li-cu-la f. film; movie
pe-li-gro m. danger
pe-li-gro-so adj. dangerous
pe-lo m. fur; hair
pe-lo-ta f. ball
pel-tre m. pewter
pe-lu-ca f. wig
pe-lu-do, -da adj. shaggy
pel-vis f. pelvis
pe-lliz-car v. to nibble
pe-llon m. sheepskin
pe-ña f. anxiety; penalty; distress
pe-na-cho m. crest
pe-na-do, -da adj. grieved
pe-na-li-zar v. to penalize
pe-nar v. to punish
pen-den-ciar v. to quarrel; to argue
pen-der v. to hover
pen-dien-te adj. hanging
pe-ne-tra-ble adj. penetrable
pe-ne-tra-ción f. penetration
pe-ne-tran-te adj. piercing; penetrating
pe-ne-trar v. to pierce; to penetrate
pe-ni-ci-li-na f. penicillin
pe-nin-su-la f. peninsula
pe-ni-que m. penny
pe-ni-ten-cia f. penitence
pe-ni-ten-te adj. penitent
pe-no-so adj. grievous; wearing
pen-sa-mien-to m. thought
pen-san-te adj. thinking
pen-sar v. to think about
pen-sa-ti-vo adj. thoughtful; pensie
pen-sio-nar v. to pension
pen-to-tal m. pentothal
pe-na f. circle
pe-nas-co-so, -sa adj. rocky
pe-or adj. worse
pe-pi-no m. cucumber
pep-ti-co, -ca adj. peptic
pe-que-ño adj. tiny; small
pe-ra f. pear
pe-ral m. pear tree
per-cep-ción f. perception
per-cep-ti-vo, -va adj. perceptive

per-ci-bir v. to sense; to recieve
per-cu-dir v. to dull
per-cu-sión f. percussion
per-cu-tir v. to percuss
per-cha f. hanger; prop
per-der v. to waste; to lose
pér-di-da f. waste
per-di-do adj. missing
per-diz f. partridge
per-dón m. pardon
per-do-nar v. to remit; to excuse; to pardon
per-du-rar v. to last
pe-re-cer v. to perish
pe-re-gri-na-ción f. pilgrimage
pe-re-jil m. parsley
pe-ren-ne adj. perennial
pe-re-za f. laziness
pe-re-zo-so, -sa adj. lazy
per-fec-ción f. perfection
per-fec-cio-nar v. to make something perfect
per-fec-cio-nis-ta adj. perfectionist
per-fec-to adj. perfect
pér-fi-do, -da adj. unfaithful
per-fi-lar v. to profile
per-fo-ra-ción f. perforation
per-fo-ra-dor adj. perforating
per-fo-rar v. to perforate
per-fu-mar v. to perfume
per-fu-me m. perfume
per-fu-me-ri-a f. perfumery
pe-ri-car-dio m. pericardium
pe-ri-coa f. skill
pe-ri-co m. parakeet
pe-ri-me-tro m. perimeter
pe-rio-di-ca-men-te adv. periodically
pe-rio-di-co m. periodical
pe-rio-dis-mo m. journalism
pe-rio-dis-ta m., f. journalist
pe-rio-do m. period
pe-ris-to-le f. peristalsis
pe-ri-qui-to m. parakeet
pe-ris-co-pio m. periscope
pe-ri-to-ne-o m. peritoneum
per-ju-di-car v. to harm
per-ju-di-cial adj. harmful
per-ju-rio m. perjury
per-la f. pearl

per-ma-ne-cer v. to remain

per-ma-nen-te adj. permanent

per-mi-si-ble adj. permissible

per-mi-si-vo adj. permissive

per-mi-so m. consent

per-mi-tir v. to allow; to give; to permit

per-mu-tar v. to exchange

per-ni-cio-so, -sa adj. pernicious

per-no m. pin

pe-ro conj. but

pe-ro-ne m. fibula

pe-ró-xi-do m. peroxide

per-pe-tra-cion f. perpetuation

per-pe-tuar v. to perpetuate

per-ple-ji-dad f. perplexity

per-ple-jo, -ja adj. perplexed

pe-rro m. dog

per-se-cu-cion f. persecution

per-se-guir v. to follow; to hound; to pursue

per-se-ve-ran-cia f. perseverance

per-se-ve-ran-te adj. persevering

per-sia-na f. blind

per-sig-nar v. to cross

per-sis-ten-cia f. persistence

per-sis-tir v. to persist

per-so-na f. person

per-so-na-li-dad f. personality

per-so-na-li-zar v. to personalize

per-so-ni-fi-ca-cion f. personification

pers-pec-ti-va f. perspective

per-sua-dir v. to persuade

per-sua-sion f. persuasion

per-sua-si-vo, -va adj. persuasive

per-te-ne-cer v. to belong

per-te-ne-cien-te adj. pertaining

per-ti-nen-cia f. relevancy

per-ti-nen-cia f. relevance

per-ti-nen-te adj. relevant

per-tre-char v. to equip

per-tur-ba-cion f. disturbance

per-tur-bar v. to upset

per-ver-si-dad f. perversity

per-ver-sion f. perversion

per-ver-ti-do, -da adj. perverted

pe-sa-di-lla f. nightmare

pe-sa-do adj. dull; heavy; boring

pe-sar v. to grieve

pes-ca f. fishing

pes-ca-de-ri-a f. fish market

pes-ca-di-lla f. whiting

pes-ca-do m. fish

pes-ca-dor m. fisherman

pes-car v. to fish

pe-se-bre f. manger

pe-si-mis-ta adj. pessimistic

pe-so m. weight

pes-que-ro, -ra adj. fishing

pes-ta-ña f. eyelash

pes-ta-ñe-ar v. to wink

pes-ta-ne-o m. winking

pes-te f. plague

pé-ta-lo m. petal

pe-ti-ción f. petition

pé-tre-o, -a adj. rocky

pe-tri-fi-car v. to petrify

pe-tró-le-o m. petroleum

pe-tu-lan-cia f. arrogance

pe-tu-lan-te adj. arrogant

pe-tu-nia f. petunia

pez m. fish

pia-nis-ta m., f. pianist

pia-no m. piano

piar v. to chirp

pi-can-te adj. spicy

pi-car v. to sting; to chip; to bite

pi-ca-res-co, -ca adj. mischievous

pi-ca-ro, -ra adj. wicked; sly

pi-ca-zon f. itching

pi-co m. spout; beak

pi-cor m. itching

pi-co-te-ar v. to pick; to peck

pic-to-ri-co, -ca adj. pictorial

pie m. foot

pie-dra f. stone

piel f. fur; skin

pier-na f. leg

pie-za f. piece

pi-fiar v. to miscue

pig-men-tar v. to pigment

pig-me-o adj. pygmy
pi-ja-ma m. pajamas
pi-lar m. pillar
pi-le-ta f. sink
pi-lo-tar v. to pilot
pi-lo-to m. pilot
pi-llar v. to plunder
pi-llue-lo, -la adj. mischievous
pi-men-ton m. paprika
pi-mien-ta f. pepper
pim-pan-te adj. spruce; graceful
pi-na-cu-lo m. pinnacle
pi-nar m. pine grove
pin-cel m. brush
pin-cha-du-ra f. puncture
pin-char v. to puncture
pin-cha-zo m. puncture
pin-gui-no m. penguin
pi-ño m. pine
pin-tar v. to paint
pin-to, -ta adj. speckled
pin-tor, -ra m., f. painter
pin-to-res-co, -ca adj. picturesque
pin-tu-ra f. painting
pi-ña f. pine cone
pio-jo m. louse
pio-la f. cord
pi-pa f. barrel
pi-per-min m. peppermint
pi-pe-ta f. pipette
pi-que-ta f. pick
pi-que-te m. picket
pi-ra-mi-dal adj. pyramidal
pi-rá-mi-de f. pyramid
pi-ra-ta m. pirate
pi-ri-ta f. pyrites
pi-rue-ta f. pirouette
pi-sa-da f. footprint
pi-sar v. to walk upon
pis-ci-na f. swimming pool
pi-so m. story; flat
pi-són m. tamper
pi-so-te-ar v. to trample
pis-ta f. runway; trail
pis-ta-cho m. pistachio
pis-to-la f. pistol
pis-tón m. piston
pi-ti-do m. whistling
pi-ti-llo m. cigarette
pi-to m. whistle

pi-tón m. python
pi-to-ni-sa f. pythoness
pi-tui-ta-rio, -ria adj. pituitary
pi-vo-te m. pivot
pla-ca f. plaque
pla-ce-bo m. placebo
pla-cen-ta f. placenta
pla-cen-te-ro, -ra adj. placenta
pla-cer m. gratification; pleasure
plá-ci-do adj. placid
pla-gar v. to plague
plan m. scheme; plan
plan-cha f. sheet
plan-cha-do, -da adj. ironing
plan-char v. to iron
pla-ne-ar v. to plan
pla-ne-ta f. planet
pla-ne-ta-rio, -ria adj. planetary
pla-ni-cie f. plain
pla-ni-fi-ca-cion f. planning
pla-ni-fi-car v. to plan
pla-no adj. level
plan-ta f. plant
plan-ta-cion f. plantation
plan-tar v. to plant
plan-te-ar v. to start; to expound
pla-na-do m. lament
plas-ma f. plasma
plas-mar v. to mold
plás-ti-co, -ca adj. plastic
plas-ti-fi-car v. to shellac something
pla-ta f. silver
pla-ta-for-ma f. platform
pla-ta-no m. banana
pla-te-ar v. to silver-plate
pla-te-ro m. silversmith
pla-ti-car v. to talk
pla-ti-no m. platinum
pla-to m. dish; plate
pla-to-ni-co, -ca adj. platonic
plau-si-ble adj. plausible
pla-ya f. beach
pla-ye-ro, -ra adj. beach
ple-ga-ble adj. collapsible
ple-ga-do m. folding
ple-gar v. to fold; to bend; to pleat

pleu-re-si-a f. pleursiy
pli-sa-do m. pleat
plo-me-ro m. plumber
plo-mo, -ma adj. leaden
plu-ma f. pen; feather
plu-ral adj. plural
plu-ra-li-dad f. plurality
plu-ra-li-zar v. to pluralize
plu-to-nio m. plutonium
po-bla-ción f. population
po-bla-do m. population
po-blar v. to populate
po-bre adj. poor
po-bre-za f. poverty
po-cion f. potion
po-co adv. little
po-dar v. to prune
po-der v. to be able; can
po-de-rí-o m. power
po-di-a-tra m. podiatrist
poe-ma m. poem
po-e-sí-a f. poetry
po-e-ta m. poet
poé-ti-co adj. poetical
po-e-ti-sa f. poetess
po-ker m. poker
po-lar adj. polar
po-la-ri-za-cion f. polariza-
   tion
po-la-ri-zar v. to polarize
po-len m. pollen
po-li-cia f. constable; police
po-li-cial adj. police
po-li-fo-ni-a f. polyphony
po-li-go-no m. polygon
po-li-lla f. moth
po-li-ni-za-cion f. pollination
po-li-no-mio m. polynomial
po-li-po m. polyp
po-lí-ti-ca f. policy
po-lí-ti-co adj. political
po-li-ti-zar v. to politicize
po-lo m. pole
pol-tron, -na adj. lazy
po-lu-ción f. pollution
pol-vo m. powder; dust
pól-vo-ra f. powder
po-llo m. chicken
po-ma-da f. pomade
pom-pa f. pomp
pom-po-si-dad f. pomposity
pom-po-so, -sa adj. pom-
   pous

pon-che m. punch
pon-cho m. poncho
pon-de-ra-ble adj. pon-
   derable
pon-de-rar v. to consider
po-ner v. to place; to don
pon-ti-fi-cal adj. pontifical
pon-ti-fi-car v. to pontificate
pon-zo-no-so, -sa adj.
   poisonous
po-pu-la-cho m. populace
po-pu-lar adj. popular
po-pu-la-ri-dad f. popularity
po-pu-la-ri-zar v. to
   popularize
po-pu-rri m. potpourri
po-quer m. poker
por prep. from; via; for
por-cen-ta-je m. percentage
por-cen-tual adj. percentage
por-cion f. part; portion
por-che m. porch
por-fia-do, -da adj. stubborn
po-ro-si-dad f. porosity
po-ro-so, -sa adj. porous
por-qué conj. because
por-qué m. reason
por-tal m. porch
por-tá-til adj. portable
por-ten-to-so, -sa adj. marvelous
por-ve-nir m. future
po-sar v. to rest; to lodge
pos-da-ta f. postscript
po-se-er v. to have
po-se-í-do, -da adj.
   possessed
po-se-sión f. dependency;
   possession
po-se-si-vo, -va adj. posses-
   sive
po-se-so, -sa adj. possessed
pos-fe-cha f. postdate
po-si-bi-li-dad f. possibility
po-si-bi-li-tar v. to make
   something possible
po-si-ble adj. possible
po-si-ción f. place; status
po-si-ti-vo, -va adj. positive
pos-po-ner v. to postpone
pos-ta f. slice
pos-tal adj. postal
pos-te m. post

pos-ter-ga-cion *f.* postponement

pos-te-gar *v.* to postpone

pos-te-rior *adj.* posterior

pos-te-rio-ri-dad *f.* posteriority

pos-ti-zo, -za *adj.* artificial

pos-to-pe-ra-to-rio, -ria *adj.* postoperative

pos-tor *m.* bidder

pos-trar *v.* to debilitate; to humiliate

pos-tre *m.* dessert

pos-tre-mo, -ma *adj.* final

pos-tre-ro, -ra *adj.* final

pos-tu-ra *f.* posture

po-ta-ble *adj.* potable

po-ta-sio *m.* potassium

po-te *m.* pot

po-ten-cia *f.* potency

po-ten-cial *adj.* potential

po-ten-ta-do *m.* potentate

po-ten-te *adj.* potent; powerful

po-tre-ar *v.* to frolic

po-tre-ro *m.* pasture

po-tri-llo *m.* colt

po-tro *m.* colt

prác-ti-ca *f.* custom; practice

prac-ti-car *v.* to practice

prác-ti-co *adj.* practical

pra-de-ra *f.* meadow

pra-do *m.* meadow

pre-ám-bu-lo *m.* preamble

pre-ca-rio, -ria *adj.* precarious

pre-cau-ción *f.* precaution

pre-ca-vi-do, -da *adj.* cautious

pre-ce-den-te *adj.* preceeding

pre-ce-der *v.* to forego

pre-cep-to *m.* precept

pre-cep-tor, -ra *m., f.* tutor

pre-cia-do, -da *adj.* precious

pre-cin-ta-do, -da *adj.* sealed

pre-cin-tar *v.* to stamp

pre-cio *m.* fare; cost; price

pre-cio-si-dad *f.* beauty

pre-cio-so *adj.* precious

pre-ci-pi-ta-ción *f.* precipitation

pre-ci-pi-tar *v.* to hasten

pre-ci-sa-men-te *adj.* precisely

pre-ci-sar *v.* to set; to explain

pre-ci-sión *f.* precision

pre-co-ci-dad *f.* precocity

pre-cog-ni-cion *f.* precodnition

pre-con-ce-bir *v.* to preconceive

pre-co-ni-zar *v.* to recommend something

pre-coz *adj.* precocious

pre-de-ce-sor, -ra *m., f.* predecessor

pre-de-cir *v.* to foretell

pre-des-ti-na-cion *f.* predestination

pre-de-ter-mi-nar *v.* to predetermine

pre-di-ca *f.* sermon

pre-di-ca-do *m.* predicate

pre-di-car *v.* to preach

pre-dic-ción *f.* prediction

pre-di-lec-to, -ta *adj.* favorite

pre-dio *m.* property

pre-dis-po-ner *v.* to predispose

pre-dis-po-si-cion *f.* predisposition

pre-do-mi-nan-te *adj.* predominant

pre-do-mi-nar *v.* to prevail

pre-do-mi-nio *m.* predominant

pre-es-co-lar *adj.* preschool

pre-fa-bri-ca-do, -da *adj.* prefabricated

pre-fa-bri-car *v.* to prefabricate

pre-fa-cio *m.* preface

pre-fec-tu-ra *f.* prefecture

pre-fe-ren-te *adj.* preferable

pre-fe-ren-te-men-te *adv.* preferably

pre-fe-ri-do *adj.* preferred

pre-fe-rir *v.* to prefer

pre-go-nar *v.* to divulge; to proclaim

pre-gun-ta *f.* question

pre-gun-tar *v.* to ask; to question

pre-his-to-ria *f.* prehistory

pre-his-to-ri-co, -ca *adj.* prehistoric

pre-juz-gar *v.* to prejudge

pre-lu-dio *m.* prelude

pre-ma-tu-ro-, -ra *adj.* premature

pre-me-di-ta-cion *f.* premeditation

pre-me-di-ta-da-men-te *adv.* deliberately

pre-me-di-tar *v.* to premeditate

pre-miar *v.* to reward

pre-mio *m.* prize

pre-mi-sa *f.* premise

pre-mo-ni-cion *f.* premonition

pre-mu-ra *f.* urgency

pre-na-tal *adj.* prenatal

pren-da *f.* token; guaranty

pren-der *v.* to catch

pren-sa *f.* press

pren-sar *v.* to press

pre-nup-cial *adj.* prenuptial

pre-ñez *f.* pregnancy

pre-o-cu-pa-cion *f.* concern

pre-o-cu-par *v.* to mind; to preoccupy

pre-pa-rar *v.* to ready; fix

pre-pon-de-ran-te *adj.* preponderant

pre-po-si-cion *f.* preposition

pre-po-ten-cia *f.* prepotency

pre-po-ten-te *adj.* prepotent

pre-pu-cio *m.* prepuce

pre-sa *f.* victim; capture

pres-cin-den-cia *f.* omission

pres-cin-di-ble *adj.* nonessential

pres-cin-dir *v.* to ignore

pres-cri-bir *v.* to prescribe

pre-sen-cia *f.* presence

pre-sen-ciar *v.* to witness

pre-sen-ta-cion *f.* presentation

pre-sen-tar *v.* to introduce; to feature

pre-sen-te *adj.* current

pre-ser-va-cion *f.* preservation

pre-ser-var *v.* to preserve

pre-ser-va-ti-vo, -va *adj.* preservative

pre-si-den-cia *f.* presidency

pre-si-den-cial *adj.* presidential

pre-si-den-ta *f.* president

pre-si-den-te *m.* president

pre-si-dia-rio *m.* convict

pre-si-dio *m.* prison

pre-si-dir *v.* to preside

pre-sion *f.* pressure

pre-sio-nar *v.* to press

pres-ta-cion *f.* services

pres-ta-dor, -ra *adj.* lending

pres-ta-men-te *adj.* quickly

pres-ta-mo *m.* lending

pres-tar *v.* to loan

pres-te-za *f.* promptness

pres-ti-gio *m.* prestige

pres-ti-gio-so, -sa *adj.* prestigious

pres-to, -ta *adj.* prompt

pre-su-mi-ble *adj.* presumable

pre-su-mir *y.* to presume

pre-sun-cion *f.* presumption

pre-sun-tuo-so, -sa *adj.* presumptuous

pre-su-po-ner *v.* to presuppose

pre-su-po-si-cion *f.* presupposition

pre-su-pues-ta-rio, -ria *adj.* budgetary

pre-su-ri-zar *v.* to pressurize

pre-ten-cio-so, -sa *adj.* pretentious

pre-ten-der *v.* to attempt; to pretend

pre-ten-dien-te *adj.* pretending to

pre-ten-sion *f.* desire

pre-ten-sio-so, -sa *adj.* pretentious

pre-va-le-cer *v.* to prevail

pre-va-le-cien-te *adj.* prevailing

pre-va-ler *v.* to prevail

pre-ven-cion *f.* prevention

pre-ve-nir *v.* to prepare; to prevent

pre-ven-ti-vo, -va *adj.* preventive

prez *m.* glory

pri-ma, -mo f., m. cousin
pri-ma-rio, -ria adj. primary
pri-ma-te m. primate
pri-ma-ve-ra f. spring
pri-me-ro adj. prime; first
pri-mi-ti-vo adj. primitive
pri-mo-ro-so adj. delicate;
  exquisite
prin-ce-sa f. princess
prin-ci-pa-do m. principality
prin-ci-pal adj. leading;
  master; principal
prin-ci-pal-men-te adv. principally
prin-ci-pe m. prince
prin-ci-pes-co, -ca adj.
  princely
prin-ci-pian-te, -ta adj.
  beginning
prin-ci-piar v. to begin
prin-ci-pio m. beginning
prin-go-so, -sa adj. greasy
prio-ri-dad f. priority
pri-sa f. haste
pri-sion f. prison
pri-sio-ne-ro, -ra m., f.
  prisoner
pris-ma m. prism
pris-ti-no, -na adj. pristine
pri-va-do adj. private
pri-va-ti-zar v. to privatize
pri-vi-le-gio m. privilege
pro-ba-bi-li-dad f. probability
pro-ba-ble adj. probable
pro-bar v. to prove; to try
pro-bi-dad f. probity
pro-ble-ma m. problem
pro-ble-má-ti-co, -ca adj.
  problematic
pro-bo, -ba adj. upright
pro-ce-di-mien-to m. proce-
  dure
pro-ce-sar v. to prosecute
pro-ce-sión f. procession
pro-ce-so m. action
pro-cla-ma-cion f. proclama-
  tion
pro-cla-mar v. to announce;
  to proclaim
pro-cre-a-cion f. procreation
pro-cre-ar v. to produce; to
  procreate
pro-di-gar v. to waste

pró-di-go adj. lavish;
  spendthrift
pro-di-gio-so, -sa adj. marvelous
pro-duc-cion f. turnout;
  production
pro-du-cir v. to yield; to
  produce
pro-duc-ti-vi-dad f. produc-
  tivity
pro-duc-ti-vo, -va adj. pro-
  ductive
pro-duc-to, -ta m. product
pro-fa-nar v. to disgrace
pro-fe-sar v. to teach; to
  practice
pro-fe-sion f. vocation; job;
  profession
pro-fe-sio-nal adj. profes-
  sional
pro-fe-sor, -ra m., f.
  professor; teacher
pro-fi-la-xis f. prophylaxis
pro-fun-di-dad f. profundity
pro-fun-do, -da adj.
  profound; deep
pro-fu-sion f. profusion
pro-du-so, -sa adj. profuse
pro-gra-ma m. program
pro-gra-ma-cion f.
  programming
pro-gra-mar v. to program
pro-gre-sar v. to progress
pro-gre-sion f. progress
pro-gre-sis-ta adj. progres-
  sive
pro-gre-so m. progress
pro-hi-bi-ción f. prohibition
pro-hi-bi-do, -da adj. forbid-
  den
pro-hi-bir v. to prohibit
  something
pro-hi-bi-ti-vo, -va adj.
  prohibitive
pro-li-fe-ra-cion f. prolifera-
  tion
pro-li-fe-rar v. to proliferate
pro-li-fi-co, -ca adj. prolific
pró-lo-go m. prologue
pro-lon-ga-do, -da adj. pro-
  longed
pro-lon-gar v. to lengthen
pro-me-dio m. average

pro-me-sa *f.* vow; promise
pro-me-te-dor, -ra *adj.* promising
pro-me-ter *v.* to promise
pro-mi-nen-te *adj.* prominent
pro-mi-so-rio, -ria *adj.* promising
pro-mo-ción *f.* promotion
pro-mo-cio-nar *v.* to promote
pro-mo-ve-dor, -ra *adj.* promoter; promoting
pro-mo-ver *v.* to promote
pro-no, -na *adj.* prone
pro-nom-bre *m.* pronoun
pro-no-mi-nal *adj.* pronominal
pro-nos-ti-car *v.* to predict
pron-ti-tud *f.* promptness
pron-to *adj.* prompt
pro-nun-cia-ción *f.* pronunciation
pro-nun-ciar *v.* to pronounce
pro-pa-ga-ción *f.* propagation
pro-pa-lar *v.* to divulge
pro-pen-so, -sa *adj.* prone
pro-pie-dad *f.* estate
pro-pi-na *f.* gratuity
pro-pio *adj.* proper
pro-po-ne-dor, -ra *adj.* proposing
pro-po-ner *v.* to intend
pro-por-ción *f.* proportion
pro-por-cio-nal *adj.* proportional
pro-po-si-ción *f.* motion; proposition
pro-pó-si-to *m.* purpose; intention
pro-pues-ta *f.* proposal
pro-pug-nar *v.* to advocate
pro-pul-sar *v.* to push
pro-pul-sión *f.* propulsion
pro-rra-te-ar *v.* to prorate
pró-rro-gar *v.* to extend
pro-sa *f.* prose
pro-sia-co, -ca *adj.* prosaic
pros-cri-bir *v.* to proscribe
pros-crip-ción *f.* proscription
pros-pec-to *m.* prospectus
pros-pe-rar *v.* to thrive; to prosper

pros-pe-ri-dad *f.* prosperity
pros-pe-ro, -ra *adj.* prosperous
prós-ta-ta *f.* prostate
pros-ti-tu-ción *f.* prostitution
pro-tec-ción *f.* protection
pro-tec-tor, -ra *adj.* supporting; protective
pro-te-ger *v.* to defend; to protect
pro-te-i-na *f.* protein
pro-tes-ta *f.* protest
pro-tes-tar *v.* to profess
pro-tes-to *m.* protest
protón *m.* proton
pro-to-ti-po *m.* prototype
pro-to-zo-a-rio *m.* protozoan
pro-ve-cho *m.* profit; benefit
pro-ve-cho-so *adj.* profitable
pro-veer *v.* to cater; to fill; to provide
pro-vi-den-cial *adj.* providencial
pro-vi-sión *f.* provision
pro-vo-ca-cion *f.* provocation
pro-vo-car *v.* to antagonize
próx-i-mo *adj.* near
pru-den-cia *f.* prudence
psi-co-lo-gia *f.* psychology
pu-bli-ca-ción *f.* publication
pu-bli-car *v.* to publish
pú-bli-co *m.* public
pue-blo *m.* nation; town
puer-ta *f.* entrance
pues *conj.* then; for
pul-gar *m.* thumb
pu-lir *v.* to shine; to polish
pul-món *m.* lung
pun-ta *f.* point
pun-to *m.* dot; point
pu-ro *adj.* pure
púr-pu-ra *f.* purple

quan-tum *m.* quantum
que *pron.* that; whom
qué *adj.* what; which
que-bra-cho *m.* quebracho
que-bra-da *f.* gap; ravine

que-bra-di-zo, -za *adj.* fragile

que-bra-do *adj.* rough; broken; bankrupt

que-bra-du-ra *f.* rupture; fracture; crack

que-bra-jar *v.* to crack

que-bran-ta-dor, -ra *adj.* crushing; breaking

que-bran-ta-mien-to *m.* cracking; deterioration; breaking

que-bran-tar *v.* to crush; to break; to weaken

que-bran-to *m.* sorrow; loss

que-brar *v.* to break

que-da-men-te *adv.* calmly

que-dar *v.* to stay; to be; to remain

que-do, -da *adj.* calm

que-jar-se *v.* to complain; to whine

que-ji-do *m.* groan

que-jo-so *adj.* complaining

que-ma *f.* burning

que-ma-de-ro *m.* incinerator

que-ma-do, -da *adj.* burnt; burned out

que-ma-dor, -ra *adj.* burning

que-mar *v.* to heat up; to burn

que-ma-zón *f.* burning

que-re-lla *f.* lament; quarrel

que-re-llan-te *adj.* complaining

que-rer *v.* to desire; to want *m.* love; affection

que-ri-do, -da *adj.* beloved

que-so *m.* cheese

quie-bra *f.* crack

quien *pron.* who

quie-to, -ta *adj.* quiet

quí-mi-ca *f.* chemistry

quí-mi-co *adj.* chemical

quin-ce *adj.* fifteen

quin-to *adj.* fifth

qui-tar *v.* to forbid; to remove; to take away

rá-ba-no *m.* radish

ra-bi *m.* rabbi

ra-bia *f.* rabies

ra-biar *v.* to have rabies

ra-bi-no *m.* rabbi

ra-bio-so *adj.* furious

ra-bo *m.* stem; tail

ra-cial *adj.* racial

ra-ci-mo *m.* bunch; cluster

ra-ción *f.* allowance; ration

ra-cio-nal *adj.* rational

ra-cio-na-li-dad *f.* rationality

ra-cio-na-lis-mo *m.* rationalism

ra-cio-na-lis-ta *adj.* rationalist

ra-cio-na-li-zar *v.* to rationalize about

ra-cio-nar *v.* to ration

ra-cha *f.* gust

ra-da *f.* bay

ra-dar *m.* radar

ra-dia-ción *f.* radiation

ra-diac-ti-vi-dad *f.* radioactivity

ra-diac-ti-vo, -va *adj.* radioactive

ra-dia-dor *m.* radiator

ra-dial *adj.* radial

ra-dian-te *adj.* radiant

ra-diar *v.* to radiate

ra-di-cal *adj.* radical

ra-dio *m.* radio; radius

ra-dio-di-fun-dir *v.* to broadcast

ra-dio-gra-fí-a *f.* radiography

ra-dio-gra-ma *f.* radiogram

ra-dio-lo-gí-a *f.* radiology

ra-dio-lo-go, -ga *m., f.* radiologist

ra-dios-co-pia *f.* radioscopy

ra-er *v.* to scrape

raid *m.* raid

ra-i-do, -da *adj.* worn

ra-ja *f.* splinter; crack

ra-ja-do, -da *adj.* cracked

ra-ja-du-ra *f.* crack

ra-jar *v.* to sliver; crack

ra-lo, -la *adj.* thin

ra-llar *v.* to grate

ra-ma *f.* branch

ra-ma-da *f.* grove

ra-mal *m.* flight; strand

ram-bla *f.* boulevard
ra-mi-fi-ca-cion *f.* ramification
ra-mi-fi-car-se *v.* to branch
ra-mi-lle-te *m.* cluster
ra-mo *m.* bouquet
ra-mo-ne-ar *v.* to graze
ram-pa *f.* ramp
ra-na *f.* frog
ran-ci-dez *f.* rancidity
ran-cio *adj.* rancid
ran-cho *m.* farm
ra-pa-ci-dad *f.* rapacity
ra-par *v.* to crop; to shave
ra-pi-da-men-te *adv.* rapidly
ra-pi-do *adj.* fast; express; rapid
rap-so-dia *f.* rhapsody
rap-to *m.* rapture
ra-que-ta *f.* racket
ra-qui-tis-mo *m.* rickets
ra-ra-men-te *adv.* rarely
ra-re-za *f.* rarity
ra-ro *adj.* rare; bizarre; odd
ra-sar *v.* to brush
ras-ca-cie-los *m.* skyscraper
ras-ca-du-ra *f.* scratch
ras-car *v.* to scrape
ras-ca-zon *f.* itch
ras-ga-du-ra *f.* tear
ras-gar *v.* to tear
ras-go *m.* feature; trait
ras-gon *m.* tear
ras-gu-ñar *v.* to scratch
ras-gu-no *m.* scratch
ra-so, -sa *adj.* level; flat
ras-pa-dor *m.* scraper
ras-pa-du-ra *f.* rasping
ras-pan-te *adj.* abrasive
ras-par *v.* to erase; to scrape
ras-tra *f.* trail
ras-tre-ar *v.* to trail
ras-tri-llo *m.* rake
ra-su-ra *f.* shaving
ra-su-rar *v.* to shave
ra-ta *f.* rat
ra-te-ro, -ra *m., f.* thief
ra-ti-fi-ca-cion *f.* ratification
ra-ti-fi-car *v.* ratificar
ra-ti-fi-ca-to-rio, -ria *adj.* ratifying
ra-to *m.* while
ra-ton *m.* mouse

ra-ya *f.* stripe; line
ra-yar *v.* to rule; to streak
ra-yo *m.* beam; ray
ra-yon *m.* rayon
ra-za *f.* race
ra-zon *f.* cause
ra-zo-na-ble *adj.* rational; reasonable
ra-zo-na-do, -da *adj.* reasoned
ra-zo-nar *v.* to reason
re-ac-cion *f.* reaction
re-ac-cio-nar *v.* to react
re-ac-ti-va-cion *f.* reactivation
re-ac-ti-var *v.* to reactivate
re-a-dap-ta-cion *f.* readaptation
re-a-dap-tar *v.* to readapt
re-a-fir-mar *v.* to reaffirm
re-a-jus-tar *v.* to readjust
re-a-jus-te *m.* readjustment
real *adj.* true; real; royal
re-a-le-za *f.* royalty
rea-li-dad *f.* reality
rea-lis-ta *adj.* realistic
re-a-li-za-dor, -ra *adj.* fulfilling
rea-li-zar *v.* to accomplish; to fulfil; realize
re-al-zar *v.* to enhance
re-a-ni-mar *v.* to reanimate
re-a-nu-da-cion *f.* resumption
re-a-nu-dar *v.* to resume
re-a-pa-re-cer *v.* to reappear
rea-ta *f.* rope
re-a-vi-var *v.* to revive
re-ba-ja *f.* reduction
re-ba-jar *v.* to reduce
re-ba-na-da *f.* slice
re-ba-nar *v.* to slice
re-ba-ño *m.* flock
re-be-lar-se *v.* to rebel; to revolt
re-bel-de *adj.* rebel
re-be-lion *f.* revolt
re-bor-de *m.* border
re-bo-tar *v.* to bounce
re-buz-no *m.* braying
re-ca-bar *v.* to request
re-ca-do *m.* message
re-ca-er *v.* to relapse

re-cal-car v. to squeeze

re-ca-len-ta-mien-to m. reheating

re-ca-len-tar v. to reheat

re-ca-pa-ci-tar v. to reconsider

re-ca-pi-tu-la-cion m. recapitulation

re-ca-pi-tu-lar v. to recapitulate

re-car-gar v. to overload; to reload

re-cau-dar v. to collect

re-cau-do m. collection

re-ce-lar v. to suspect

re-ce-lo m. jealousy; mistrust; suspicion

re-ce-lo-so, sa adj. suspicious

re-cep-cion f. reception

re-cep-cio-nis-ta m., f. receptionist

re-cep-ta-cu-lo m. receptacle

re-cep-ti-vi-dad f. receptivity

re-cep-ti-vo adj. receptive

re-ce-sion f. recession

re-ce-tar v. to prescribe

re-ci-bi-dor, -ra adj. receiving

re-ci-bi-mien-to m. reception

re-ci-bir v. to accept; receive

re-ci-bo m. receipt

re-ci-clar v. to recycle

re-cien adv. recently

re-cien-te adj. recent

re-cien-te-men-te adv. recently

re-cio, -cia adj. severe; strong

re-ci-pro-car v. to reciprocate

re-ci-pro-ci-dad f. reciprocity

re-ci-ta-cion f. recitation

re-ci-tar v. to recite

re-cla-ma-cion f. complaint

re-cla-ma-dor adj. claiming

re-cla-mar v. to reclaim

re-cli-nar v. to rest on

re-cluir v. to imprison

re-clu-sion f. imprisonment

re-clu-so m. recluse

re-clu-ta f. recruitment

re-clu-ta-mien-to m. recruitment

re-clu-tar v. to recruit

re-co-brar v. to regain; to recover

re-co-bro m. recovery

re-co-do m. bend

re-co-ge-dor, -ra adj. collecting

re-co-gar v. to collect; to gather; to shorten

re-co-gi-mien-to m. retirement

re-co-lec-ción f. collection

re-co-lec-tar v. to gather

re-co-men-da-ble adj. recommendable

re-co-men-da-cion f. recommendation

re-co-men-dar v. to recommend

re-com-pen-sa f. to reward

re-com-pen-sar v. to compensate

re-con-ci-lia-ble adj. reconcilalbe

re-con-ci-lia-ción f. reconciliation

re-con-ci-liar v. to reconcile

re-con-for-tar v. to comfort

re-co-no-cer v. to acknowledge

re-co-no-ci-do, -da adj. gratitude; recognition

re-con-quis-tar v. to recover

re-con-si-de-rar v. reconsider

re-cons-ti-tuir v. to reconstitute

re-cons-truc-cion f. reconstruction

re-cons-truir v. to reconstruct

re-con-tar v. to recount

re-co-pi-la-cion f. compilation

re-co-pi-la-dor m. compiler

re-co-pi-lar v. to compile

re-cor-da-cion f. memory

re-cor-dar v. to remember

re-co-rrer v. to travel

re-cor-tar v. to reduce

re-cre-a-ción f. recreation

re-cre-ar v. to re-create

re-crea-ti-vo adj. recreational

re-creo *m.* recreation

re-cri-mi-na-sion *f.* recrimination

re-cru-de-ci-mien-ti *m.* worsening

rec-tal *adj.* rectal

rec-ta-men-te *adv.* justly

rec-tan-gu-lar *adj.* rectangle

rec-tán-gu-lo *adj.* rectangular

rec-ti-fi-ca-cion *f.* rectification

rec-ti-fi-car *v.* to recify

rec-ti-tud *f.* honesty

rec-to *adj.* right; upright

re-cu-brir *v.* tocover

re-cuen-to *m.* recount

re-cuer-do *m.* menory; remembrance

re-cu-la-da *f.* backing up

re-cu-pe-ra-ble *adj.* recoverable

re-cu-pe-ra-ción *f.* recovery

re-cu-pe-rar *v.* to recover

re-cu-rren-te *adj.* recurrent

re-cu-rrir *v.* to return

re-cur-so *m.* remedy; resource

re-cu-sa-cion *f.* rejection

re-cu-sar *v.* to refuse

re-cha-za-mien-to *m.* rejection

re-cha-zar *v.* to reject; rebuff

re-cha-zo *m.* rejection

re-chi-fla *f.* hissing

re-chi-flar *v.* to hiss

re-dac-cion *f.* writing

re-dac-tar *v.* to edit

ra-da-da *f.* roundup

re-de-ci-lla *f.* mesh

re-den-ción *f.* redemption

re-dil *m.* fold

re-di-mir *v.* to redeem

re-di-to *m.* rent

re-di-tuar *v.* to yield

re-do-blar *v.* to fold

re-don-dez *f.* roundness

re-don-do, -da *adj.* round

re-duc-cion *f.* reduction

re-du-ci-do *adj.* reduced

re-du-cir *v.* to shorten; reduce

re-duc-tor, -ra *adj.* reducing

re-dun-dan-cia *f.* redundancy

re-dun-dan-te *adj.* redundant

re-dun-dar *v.* to overflow

re-e-le-gir *v.* to reelect

re-em-bol-sa-ble *adj.* reimbursable

re-em-bol-sar *v.* to reimburse

re-em-bol-so *m.* reimbursement

re-em-pla-zar *v.* to replace

re-em-pla-zo *m.* substitution

re-en-car-na-cion *f.* reincarnation

re-es-truc-tu-ra-cion *f.* restructuring

re-es-truc-tu-rar *v.* to restructure

re-fec-to-rio *m.* refectory

re-fe-ren-cia *f.* refernce

re-fe-ren-te *adj.* referring

re-fe-rir *v.* to refer; to tell

re-fi-na-do, -da *adj.* refined

re-fi-na-mien-to *m.* refinement

re-fi-nar *v.* to refine

re-fi-ne-ri-a *f.* refinery

re-fle-jar *v.* to speculate; to reflect

re-fle-xión *f.* reflection

re-fle-xi-vo, -va *adj.* reflective

re-for-ma *f.* reform

re-for-ma-cion *f.* reformation

re-for-mar *v.* to reform

re-for-ma-to-rio, -ria *adj.* reformatory

re-for-mis-ta *adj.* reformist

re-for-za-do, -da *adj.* reinforced

re-for-zar *v.* to reinforce

re-frac-ción *f.* refraction

re-frac-tar *v.* to refract

re-fre-nar *v.* to restrain

re-fres-can-te *adj.* refreshing

re-fres-car *v.* to refresh

re-fres-co *m.* refreshment

re-fri-ge-ra-ción *f.* refrigeration

re-fir-ge-ra-dor *m.* refrigerator

re-fri-ge-rar v. to refrigerate

re-fri-to, -ta adj. refried

re-fuer-zo m. reinforcement

re-fu-gia-do, -da adj. refugee

re-fu-gio m. shelter; refuge

re-ful-gen-te adj. refulgent

re-fun-fu-nar v. to grumble

re-fun-fu-no m. grumble

re-fu-ta-cion f. rebuttal

re-fu-tar v. to rebut

re-ga-la-do, -da adj. easy; dainty

re-ga-lar v. to give away

re-ga-liz m. licorice

re-ga-lo m. present

re-ga-ñar v. to argue

re-gar v. to bathe

re-ga-zo m. lap

re-ge-ne-ra-cion f. regeneration

re-ge-ne-ra-dor, -ra m., f. regenerator

re-ge-ne-rar v. to regenerate

re-gen-tar v. to direct

ré-gi-men m. regimen

re-gi-men-tar v. to regiment

re-gio, -gia adj. regal

re-gión f. area; region

re-gio-nal adj. regional

re-gio-na-lis-mo m. regionalism

re-gir v. to govern

re-gis-tra-dor, -ra m., f. register, adj. registering

re-gis-trar v. to record; to register

re-gis-tro m. search; registration; registry; register

re-gla f. rule

re-gla-men-ta-cion f. regulation

re-gla-men-tar v. to regulate

re-glar v. to regulate

re-go-ci-jo m. joy

re-go-de-o m. pleasure

re-gre-sar v. to return

re-gre-sion f. regression

re-gre-si-vo adj. regressive

re-gre-so m. return

re-gue-ro m. trail; stream

re-gu-la-cion f. regulation

re-gu-la-dor m. regulator

re-gu-lar adj. regular

re-gu-la-ri-dad f. regularity

re-gu-la-ri-zar v. to regularize

re-gu-lar-men-te adv. regularly

re-gur-gi-ta-ción f. regurgitation

re-gur-gi-tar v. to regurgitate

re-ha-bi-li-ta-ción f. rehabilitation

re-ha-bi-li-tar v. to rehabilitate

re-ha-cer v. to remake

re-ho-gar v. to brown

re-huir v. to avoid

re-hu-sar v. to refuse

re-im-pri-mir v. to reprint

rei-na f. queen

rei-na-do m. reign

rei-nan-te adj. ruling

rei-nar v. to reign

re-in-ci-den-te adj. relapsing

re-in-ci-dir v. to relapse

re-in-cor-po-ra-ción f. reincorporation

re-in-cor-po-rar v. to reincorporate

re-in-gre-sar v. to re-enter something

rei-no m. kingdom

re-ins-ta-la-ción f. reinstallation

re-ins-ta-lar v. to reinstall

re-in-te-gra-ción f. reintegration

re-in-te-grar v. to reintegrate

re-in-te-gro m. reintegration

re-ir(se) v. to laugh

rei-te-ra-ción f. reiteration

rei-te-rar v. to reiterate

rei-te-ra-ti-vo, -va adj. reiterative

rei-vin-di-car v. to recover

re-jun-tar v. to gather

re-ju-ve-ne-cer v. to rejuvenate

re-la-ción f. account; relation

re-la-cio-na-do, -da adj. related

re-la-cio-nar v. to relate

re-la-ja-ción f. relaxation

re-la-ja-do, -da *adj.* relaxed
re-la-jar *v.* to relax
re-la-mar *v.* to lick
re-lám-pa-go *m.* lightning
re-lám-pa-gue-o *m.* lightning
re-lap-so, -sa *adj.* relapsed
re-la-tar *v.* to narrate
re-la-ti-vi-dad *f.* relativity
re-la-ti-vo, -va *adj.* relative
re-la-to *m.* story; narration
re-le-gar *v.* to relegate
re-le-var *v.* to relieve; to praise
re-li-ca-rio *m.* reliquary
re-li-ve *m.* relief
re-li-gión *f.* religion
re-li-gio-si-dad *f.* religiosity
re-li-gio-so *adj.* religious
re-loj *m.* watch; clock
re-lo-je-ri-a *f.* clockmaking
re-lo-je-ro, -ra *m., f.* watchmaker
re-lu-cir *v.* to shine
re-lum-bran-te *adj.* dazzling
re-lum-brar *v.* to dazzle
re-lle-nar *v.* to refill
re-ma-llar *v.* to mend
re-mar *v.* to row
re-ma-tar *v.* to use up
re-ma-te *m.* conclusion
re-me-dar *v.* to mimic
re-me-dia-ble *adj.* remediable
re-me-diar *v.* to cure; to remedy
re-mem-bran-za *f.* remembrance
re-me-mo-ra-cion *f.* remembrance
re-me-mo-rar *v.* to remember something
re-men-dar *v.* to mend; to repair
re-mem-don, -na *m., f.*
re-mi-sión *f.* remission
re-mi-so, -sa *adj.* remiss
re-mi-tne-te *adj.* remitting
re-mi-tir *v.* to forgive; to remit; to diminish
re-mo *m.* oar
re-mo-la-cha *f.* beet
re-mol-car *v.* to tow
re-mo-lo-ne-ar *v.* to loaf

re-mol-que *m.* tow truck
re-mon-tar *v.* to remount; to surmount
re-mor-di-mien-to *m.* remorse
re-mo-to *adj.* faraway
re-mo-ver *v.* to remove; to move; to dismiss
re-mo-zar *v.* to rejuvenate
re-mu-ne-ra-ción *f.* remuneration
re-mu-ne-rar *v.* to remunerate
re-mu-ne-ra-ti-vo, -va *adj.* remunerative
re-na-ci-mien-to *m.* revival
re-nal *adj.* renal
ren-ci-lla *f.* quarrel
ren-cor *m.* spite; bitterness; rancor
ren-co-ro-so *adj.* bitter; resentful
ren-di-do *adj.* submissive; obsequious
ren-di-mien-to *m.* submissiveness; yield
ren-dir *v.* to yield; to surrender; to defeat
ren-gue-ar *v.* to limp
re-no *m.* reindeer
re-nom-bra-do, -da *adj.* renowned
re-nom-bre *m.* renown
re-no-va-ción *f.* renovation
re-no-va-do *adj.* renewed
re-no-var *v.* to renovate; to reform
ren-ta *f.* interest; rent; income
ren-ta-ble *adj.* profitable
ren-tar *v.* to rent
re-nuen-cia *f.* reluctance
re-nuen-te *adj.* reluctant
re-nun-cia *f.* renunciation
re-nun-cia-ción *f.* renunciation
re-nun-ciar *v.* to reject; to surrender; to waive; to renounce
re-ñi-dor, -ra *adj.* quarrelsome
re-ñir *v.* to fight; to quarrel with another

re-or-ga-ni-za-cion f. reorganization

re-or-ga-ni-zar v. to reorganize

re-pa-ra-ción f. repair

re-pa-ra-dor, -ra m., f. repairer

re-pa-rar v. to mend; repair

re-pa-ro m. protection; objection

re-par-ti-cion f. sharing

re-par-ti-dor, -ra m., f. distributor

re-par-tir v. to share; to apportion; to divide

re-par-to m. delivery

re-pa-sar v. to review; to revise

re-pa-so m. review

re-pa-tria-ción f. repatriation

re-pa-triar v. to repatriate

re-pe-len-te adj. repellent

re-pe-ler v. to repel

re-pen-te m. start

re-pen-ti-no, -na adj. repercussion

re-per-cu-sion f. repercussion

re-per-cu-tir v. to reverberate

re-per-to-rio m. repertoire

re-pe-ti-cion f. repetition

re-pe-tir v. to repeat

re-pe-ti-ti-vo, -va adj. repetitive

re-pi-que-te-ar v. to beat; to ring

re-pi-sa f. shelf

re-plan-tar v. to replant

re-plan-te-ar v. to restate

re-ple-to, -ta adj. full

ré-pli-ca f. answer

re-pli-car v. to reply; to respond

re-po-bla-cion f. repopulation

re-po-blar v. to repopulate

re-po-llo m. cabbage

re-po-ner v. to replace; to revive

re-por-tar v. to bring

re-por-te-ro, -ra adj. reporting

re-po-sa-do adj. quiet

re-po-sar v. to lie

re-po-si-ción f. reposition

re-po-so m. repose

re-pren-der v. to reprimand

re-pren-sión f. reprimand

re-pre-sa-lia f. reprisal

re-pre-sen-ta-ción f. representation

re-pre-sen-tan-te adj. representing

re-pre-sen-tar v. to represent; to appear to be

re-pre-sen-ta-ti-vo, -va adj. representative

re-pre-sión f. repression

re-pre-si-vo, -va adj. repressive

re-pri-men-da f. reprimand

re-pri-mir v. to repress

re-pro-char v. to reproach

re-pro-che m. rebuke; reproach

re-pro-duc-ción f. reproduction

re-pro-du-cir v. to reproduce

rep-tar v. to crawl

rep-til m. reptile

re-pú-bli-ca f. republic

re-pu-bli-ca-no, na adj. republican

re-pu-dia-cion f. repudiation

re-pu-diar v. to repudiate

re-pug-nan-cia f. repugnance

re-pug-nan-te adj. repugnant

re-pul-gar v. to hem

re-pul-sar v. to reject

re-pul-sion f. repulsion

re-pul-si-vo, -va adj. repulsive

re-pun-tar v. to turn

re-pun-te adj. turning

re-que-brar v. to break something again

re-que-ri-mien-to m. requirement

re-que-rir v. to want; to require

re-quiem m. requiem

re-qui-sar v. to requisition

re-qui-si-cion f. requisition

re-qui-si-to m. requirement

re-sa-la-do, -da adj. charming

re-sar-cir v. to indemnify

res-ba-lar v. to glide

res-ca-tar v. to rescue; to recover

res-ca-te m. rescue

res-cin-dir v. to rescind

res-ci-sion f. rescission

re-sen-ti-do, -da adj. resentful

re-sen-ti-mien-to m. resentment

re-sen-tir-se v. to feel hurt

re-se-ña f. account; inspection

re-se-ñar v. to review; to inspect

re-ser-va f. reserve

re-ser-va-ción f. reservation

re-ser-va-do, -da adj. reserved; confidential

re-ser-var v. to reserve

res-fria-do m. cold

res-friar v. to cool

res-guar-dar v. to protect

res-guar-do m. guard; protection

re-si-den-cia f. residence

re-si-den-cial adj. residential

re-si-den-te m., f. resident

re-si-dir v. to live; reside

re-si-duo m. residue

re-sig-na-ción f. resignation

re-sis-ten-cia f. endurance; resistance

re-sis-ten-te adj. resistant

re-sis-tir v. to oppose; to resist

re-so-lu-ción f. resolution

re-so-lu-to, -ta adj. resolute

re-sol-ver v. to settle; to solve; to resolve

re-so-nan-cia f. resonance

re-so-nan-te adj. resounding

re-so-nar v. to resound

re-so-pli-do m. puffing

res-pal-dar v. to back something or someone

res-pal-do m. back

res-pec-ti-vo adj. respective

res-pec-to m. respect

res-pe-ta-ble adj. respectable

res-pe-tar v. to respect

res-pe-to m. respect

res-pe-tuo-so, -sa adj. respectful

res-pi-ra-ción f. respiration

res-pi-ra-dor m. respirator

res-pi-rar v. to inhale and exhale; to breath

res-pi-ro m. respite

res-plan-dor m. glow; brightness

res-pon-der v. to reply; to respond

res-pon-sa-ble adj. responsible

res-pues-ta f. answer; response

res-que-brar v. to crack

res-que-mor m. remorse

res-ta-ble-cer v. to reestablish

res-ta-ble-ci-mien-to m. reestablishment

res-ta-llar v. to crack

res-tau-ra-ción f. restoration

res-tau-ra-dor, -ra m., f. restorer

res-tau-ran-te m. restaurant

res-tau-rar v. to restore

res-ti-tu-ción f. restitution

res-to m. remainder

res-tric-ción f. restriction

res-tric-ti-vo, -va adj. restrictive

res-trin-gir v. to restrict

re-su-ci-tar v. to resuscitate

re-sul-ta f. result

re-sul-ta-do m. issue; result

re-sul-tar v. to result

re-su-mir v. to summarize

re-sur-gir v. to reappear

re-su-rrec-ción f. resurrection

re-tar-dar v. to delay

re-ten-ción f. retention

re-te-ner v. to keep; to retain

re-ti-na f. retina

re-ti-ni-tis f. retinitis

re-ti-ra-da f. retreat

re-ti-ra-do, -da adj. retired

re-ti-rar v. to retire; to

withdraw; to retract
re-ti-ro *m.* retreat; withdrawal
re-to *m.* challenge
re-to-ñar *v.* to sprout
re-tor-cer *v.* to twist
re-tor-ci-do, -da *adj.* twisted
re-tor-ci-mien-to *m.* twisting
re-tó-ri-co, -ca *adj.* rhetorical
re-tor-nar *v.* to return
re-to-zar *v.* to frolic
re-to-zo *m.* frolic
re-to-zon, -ona *adj.* frolic-some
re-trac-ción *f.* retraction
re-trac-tar *v.* to recant; to retract
re-trac-til *adj.* retractable
re-tra-er *v.* to dissuade
re-tra-i-do, -da *adj.* withdrawn
re-trai-mien-to *m.* seclusion
re-trans-mi-tir *v.* to retransmit
re-tra-sar *v.* to delay
re-tra-to *m.* portrait
re-tre-ta *f.* retreat
re-tri-bu-ción *f.* retribution
re-tri-buir *v.* to reward
re-tro-ac-ti-vo, -va *adj.* retroactive
re-tro-gra-do, -da *adj.* retrograde
re-tros-pec-cion *f.* retrospection
re-tum-bar *v.* to resound
reu-ma-ti-co *adj.* rheumatic
reu-ma-tis-mo *m.* rheumatism
reu-nión *f.* meeting; reunion
reu-nir *v.* to gather; to mass; to meet
re-va-li-da-ción *f.* revalidation
re-va-li-dar *v.* to revalidate
re-va-lo-ri-zar *v.* to revalue
re-van-cha *f.* revenge
re-ve-la-cion *f.* revelation
re-ve-la-dor, -ra *adj.* revealing
re-ve-lar *v.* to betray; to reveal
re-ven-der *v.* to resell
re-ven-tar *v.* to blow; to burst
re-ven-tion *m.* burst
re-ver *v.* to review
re-ver-be-rar *v.* to reverberate
re-ve-ren-cia *f.* reverence
re-ve-ren-ciar *v.* to revere
re-ve-ren-do, -da *adj.* reverend
re-ve-ren-te *adj.* respectful
re-ver-so *m.* reverse
re-ver-tir *v.* to revert
re-ves-tir *v.* to cover
re-vi-sar *v.* to review
re-vi-sión *f.* revision
re-vi-sor, -ra *m., f.* inspector
re-vis-ta *f.* magazine
re-vis-te-ro, -ra *m., f.* reviewer
re-vi-ta-li-zar *v.* to revitalize
re-vi-vi-fi-car *v.* to revive
re-vi-vir *v.* to revive
re-vo-ca-ción *f.* revocation
re-vo-car *v.* to repeal; to revoke
re-vol-con *m.* fall
re-vo-lo-te-ar *v.* to flutter
re-vo-lu-ción *f.* revolution
re-vo-lu-cio-nar *v.* to revolutionize
re-vo-lu-cio-na-rio *adj.* revolutionary
re-vól-ver *v.* to revolve; to mix; to shake
re-vol-ver *m.* revolver
re-vo-que *m.* plaster
re-vue-lo *m.* commotion
rey *m.* king
re-zar *v.* to pray; to say something
re-zon-gar *v.* to grumble
ri-be-ra *f.* shore
ri-be-te-a-do *adj.* trimmed
ri-be-te-ar *v.* to hem
ri-ca-men-te *adv.* richly
ri-co *adj.* wealthy; rich
ri-di-cu-la-men-te *adv.* ridiculously
ri-di-cu-li-zar *v.* to ridicule
ri-di-cu-lo *adj.* ridiculous
riel *m.* rail
rien-da *f.* rein
ries-go *m.* danger; risk

ri-fa *f.* raffle
ri-far *v.* to raffle off
ri-fle *m.* rifle
ri-gi-do *adj.* stiff; rigid
ri-gor *m.* rigor
ri-gu-ro-so *adj.* severe; rigorous
rigorous
ri-ma *f.* rhyme
ri-mar *v.* to rhyme
rim-bom-ban-te *adj.* echoing
rin-cón *m.* corner
ri-no-ce-ron-te *m.* rhinoceros
ri-ña *f.* quarrel
ri-ñon *m.* kidney
ríó *m.* river
ri-que-za *f.* riches
ri-sa *f.* laughter
ri-si-ble *adj.* laughable
ris-tra *f.* string
ri-sue-ño, -na *adj.* smiling
rít-mi-co *adj.* rhythmical
ri-to *m.* ceremony
ri-tual *m.* ritual
ri-val *m.* rival
ri-va-li-dad *f.* rivalry
ri-va-li-zar *v.* to rival
ri-zar *v.* to curl up
ro-bar *v.* to steal
ro-ble *m.* oak
ro-bo *m.* robbery
ro-bus-te-cer *v.* to make strong; to strengthen
strong; to strengthen
ro-bus-to *adj.* hardy; strong
ro-ciar *v.* to sprinkle
ro-cin *m.* donkey
ro-cí-o *m.* sprinkle
ro-dar *v.* to tumble; to roll
ro-de-ar *v.* to circle; to ring
ro-de-o *v.* to go around
ro-de-te *m.* bun
ro-di-lla *f.* knee
ro-e-dor, -ra *adj.* gnawing
ro-er *v.* to gnaw
ro-gar *v.* to request; to pray
ro-jo *adj.* red
ro-llo *m.* roll
ro-ma-no, -na *adj.* Roman
ro-mán-ti-co *adj.* romantic
rom-bo *m.* rhombus
ro-me-ro *m.* rosemary
rom-per *v.* to smash; to break
break
ron *m.* rum

ron-car *v.* to snore
ron-co, -ca *adj.* hoarse
ron-que-ra *f.* hoarseness
ro-no-so, -sa *adj.* filthy
ro-pa *f.* clothing
ro-pe-ro *m.* closet
ro-sa *f.* rose
ro-sa-do, -da *adj.* pink
ro-sal *m.* rosebush
ro-sa-le-da *f.* rose garden
ros-bif *m.* roast beef
ros-ca *f.* circle
ros-tro *m.* face
ro-ta-ción *f.* rotation
ro-ta-to-rio, -ria *adj.* rotating
ro-ton-da *f.* rotunda
ro-tor *m.* rotor
ro-tu-la-do *m.* label
ro-tu-la-dor, -ra *adj.* labeling
ro-tu-lar *v.* to label
ro-za-mien-to *m.* rubbing
ro-zar *v.* to scrape; to skim
ru-be-o-la *f.* rubella
ru-bí *m.* ruby
ru-bi-cun-do, -da *adj.* ruddy
ru-bio *adj.* blonde
ru-bor *m.* blush
ru-bo-ri-zae-se *v.* to blush
ru-da *f.* rue
ru-de-za *f.* rudeness
ru-di-men-tal *adj.* rudimentary
tary
ru-di-men-ta-rio, -ria *adj.* rudimentary
rudimentary
ru-di-men-to *m.* rudiment
ru-do, -da *adj.* rude
rue-da *f.* wheel
rue-do *m.* hem; edge
rue-go *m.* request
ru-gi-do *m.* roar
ru-gi-dor, -ra *adj.* roaring
ru-go-so, -sa *adj.* winkled
rui-do *m.* sound; rattle; noise
rui-do-so, -sa *adj.* noisy
ruin *adj.* poor; despicable
rui-na *f.* ruin
rui-nar *v.* to ruin
rum-bo *m.* direction
ru-mor *m.* rumor
rup-tu-ra *f.* rupture
ru-ral *adj.* rural
ru-ti-lar *v.* to shine
ru-ti-na *f.* route

sá-ba-do m. Saturday
sá-ba-na f. sheet for a bed
sa-ber v. to inform; to know
sa-bi-do, -da adj. known
sa-bi-du-rí-a f. knowledge
sa-bio, -bia adj. learned
sa-ble m. saber
sa-bor m. flavor; taste
sa-bo-re-ar v. to taste
sa-bo-ta-je m. sabotage
sa-bo-te-a-dor, -ra adj. sabotaging
sa-bo-te-ar v. to sabotage
sa-bro-so adj. delightful
sa-ca-cor-chos m. corkscrew
sa-ca-pun-tas m. pencil sharpener
sa-car v. to pull out; to get out
sa-ca-ri-na f. saccharin
sa-cer-do-cio m. priesthood
sa-cer-do-te m. priest
sa-cer-do-ti-sa f. priestess
sa-co m. bag
sa-cra-men-to m. sacrament
sa-cri-fi-car v. to sacrifice
sa-cri-fi-cio m. sacrifice
sa-cri-le-gio m. sacrilege
sa-cro adj. sacred
sa-cu-di-da f. tremor; shake
sa-cu-dir v. to beat; to tug
sá-di-co, -ca adj. sadistic
sa-ga f. saga
sa-ga-ci-dad f. sagacity
sa-gaz adj. sagacious
sa-gra-do, -da adj. sacred
sa-ke m. sake
sal f. salt
sa-la f. living room of a house
sa-la-do, -da adj. salted; salty
sa-la-man-dra f. salamander
sa-laz f. salacious
sal-chi-chon m. sausage
sal-dar v. to pay off something
sal-do m. payment
sa-le-ro m. saltshaker
sa-li-da f. exit; solution
sa-lien-te adj. salient
sa-li-no, -na adj. saline

sa-lir v. to get out; to leave
sa-li-va n. saliva
sa-li-val adj. salivary
sa-li-var v. to salivate
sal-mo m. psalm
sal-món m. salmon
sa-lo-bre adj. briny
sal-pi-car v. to splash
sal-pi-men-tar v. to season
sal-sa f. sauce
sal-ta-dor m. jumper
sal-ta-mon-tes m. grasshopper
sal-tar v. to jump; to leap; to bounce
sal-te-ar v. to skip
sal-to m. jump
sa-lu-bre adj. healthful
sa-lud f. health
sa-lu-da-ble adj. healthy
sa-lu-dar v. to salute
sa-lu-ta-cion f. greeting
sal-va-ción f. salvation
sal-va-guar-dar v. to safeguard
sal-va-guar-dia f. safeguard
sal-va-ja-da f. savagery
sal-va-je adj. untamed; wild; uncivilized
sal-var v. to avoid; to save; to cover
sal-via f. sage
sal-vo adj. safe
sa-an-men-te adv. sincerely
sa-nar v. to heal
san-ción f. sanction
san-cio-nar v. to sanction
san-da-lia f. sandal
san-da-lo m. sandalwood
san-dez f. nonsense
san-dí-a f. watermelon
sa-ne-a-mien-to m. sanitation
sa-ne-ar v. to right
san-grar v. to bleed
san-gre f. blood
san-gri-a f. sangria
san-grien-to adj. bloody
san-gui-jue-la f. leech
san-gui-na-rio, -ria adj. cruel
sa-ni-dad f. healthiness
sa-ni-ta-rio, -ria adj. sanitary
sa-no adj. unharmed;

wholesome
san-ti-dad f. sanctity
san-ti-fi-car v. to sanctify
san-to adj. blessed
san-tua-rio m. sanctuary
sa-pien-cia f. wisdom
sa-pien-te adj. wise
sa-po m. toad
sa-que-ar v. to plunder
sa-que-o m. plundering
sa-ram-pión m. measles
sar-cas-mo m. sarcasm
sar-cás-ti-co adj. sarcastic
sar-di-na f. sardine
sar-do-ni-co, -ca adj. sardonic
sar-gen-to m. sergeant
sar-no-so, -sa adj. scabby
sa-rro m. crust
sar-ta f. string
sa-sa-fras m. sassafras
sa-té-li-te m. satellite
sa-ten m. satin
sa-ti-na-do, -da adj. satiny
sá-ti-ra f. satire
sa-ti-ri-co, -ca adj. satirical
sa-ti-ri-zar v. to satirize
sa-ti-ro m. satyr
sa-tis-fac-ción f. satisfaction
sa-tis-fa-cer v. to satisfy
sa-tis-fac-to-rio, -ria adj. satisfactory
sa-tu-ra-cion f. saturation
sa-tu-ra-do, -da adj. saturated
sa-tu-rar v. to saturate
sa-xó-fo-no m. saxophone
sa-yo m. tunic
sa-zon f. season
sa-zo-na-do adj. flavorful
sa-zo-nar v. to season
se pron. herself; oneself; yourself; himself
se-ba-ce-o, -a adj. sebaceous
se-bo m. fat
se-bo-rre-a f. seborrhea
se-ca-do m. drying
se-ca-do-ra f. clothes dryer
se-can-te adj. drying
se-car v. to dry
sec-ción f. section
sec-cio-nar v. to section

se-ce-sion f. secession
se-ce-sio-nis-ta adj. secessionist
se-co adj. dried
se-cre-ción f. secretion
se-cre-ta-men-te adv. secretly
se-cre-ta-ria f. secretary
se-cre-ta-rio m. secretary
se-cre-te-ar v. to whisper
se-cre-te-o m. whispering
se-cre-to m. secret
sec-ta-rio, -ria adj. sectarian
sec-tor m. sector
sec-to-rial adj. sectorial
se-cue-la f. consequence
se-cuen-cia f. sequence
se-cues-trar v. to kidnap
se-cues-tro m. kidnapping
se-cu-lar adj. secular
se-cu-la-ri-zar v. to secularize
se-cun-dar v. to second
se-cun-da-rio, -ria adj. secondary
sed f. thirst
se-da f. silk
se-dan-te adj. sedative
se-dar v. to soothe
se-dar v. to sedate
se-da-ti-vo adj. sedative
se-den-ta-rio, -ria adj. sedentary
se-di-ción f. sedition
se-dien-to, -ta adj. thirsty
se-di-men-to m. sediment
se-do-so adj. silky
se-duc-ción f. seduction
se-du-cir v. to seduce
se-duc-ti-vo, -ra adj. seductive
se-ga-dor, -ra adj. seductive
se-gar v. to mow; to harvest
se-glar adj. secular
seg-men-ta-cion f. segmentation
seg-men-to m. segment
se-gre-ga-cion f. segregation
se-gre-ga-cio-nis-ta adj. segregationist
se-gre-gar v. to segregate
se-gui-da-men-te adv. con-

tinuously
se-gui-do adj. consecutive
se-gui-dor, -ra m., f. follower
se-guir v. to chase; to follow; to watch
se-gún prep. according to
se-gun-do adj. second
se-gur m. sickle
se-gu-ra-men-te adv. probably
se-gu-ri-dad f. safety
se-gu-ro adj. sure; certain
sels adj. six
seis-cien-tos, -tas adj. six hundred
se-lec-ción f. selection
se-lec-cio-nar v. to select
se-lec-ti-vo, -va adj. selective
se-lec-to, -ta adj. select
sel-va f. woods
se-llar v. to stamp
se-llo m. stamp
se-ma-na f. week
se-ma-nal adj. weekly
se-ma-nal-men-te adv. weekly
se-ma-na-rio, -ria adj. weekly
se-man-ti-co, -ca adj. semantic
sem-bra-dor, -ra adj. sowing
sem-brar v. to sow
se-me-jan-te adj. similar
se-me-jan-za f. similarity
se-men-tar v. to seed
se-mes-tral adj. semiannual
se-mes-tre m. semester
se-miau-to-ma-ti-co, -ca adj. semiautomatic
se-mi-cir-cu-lar adj. semicircular
se-mi-cir-cu-lo m. semicircle
se-mi-fi-na-lis-ta adj. semifinalist
se-mi-lla f. seed
se-mi-lle-ro m. nursery for plants
se-mi-nal adj. seminal
se-mi-na-rio m. seminary
se-mi-na-ris-ta m. seminarian
se-mo-la f. semolina

sem-pi-ter-no, -na adj. everlasting
se-na-do m. senate
se-na-dor m. senator
sen-ci-lla-men-te adv. simply
sen-ci-llez f. simplicity
sen-ci-llo, -lla adj. simple; easy
sen-da f. path; trail
se-nil adj. senile
se-no m. cavity; hollow
sen-sa-ción f. sensation
sen-sa-cio-nal adj. sensational
sen-sa-cio-na-lis-ta adj. sensational
sen-sa-to adj. sensible
sen-si-bi-li-dad f. sensibility; sensitiveness
sen-si-bi-li-zar v. to sensitize
sen-si-ble adj. sentimental; sensitive
sen-si-ble-ri-a f. sentimentality
sen-si-ti-vo, -va adj. sensitive
sen-so-rio, -ria adj. sensorial
sen-sual adj. sensual
sen-sua-li-dad f. sensuality
sen-ta-do, -da adj. settled; seated
sen-tar v. to sit
sen-ten-cia f. sentence
sen-ten-ciar v. to sentence
sen-ten-cio-so, -sa adj. sententious
sen-ti-do, -da adj. heartfelt
sen-ti-men-tal adj. sentimental
sen-ti-mien-to m. sentiment
sen-tir v. to feel; to sense; to experience
se-ña f. signal; sign
se-ñal f. sign
se-ña-lar v. to point; to determine
se-ña-li-zar v. to put up signs
se-ñe-ro adj. solitary
se-ñor adj. Mr.; Mister
se-ño-ri-o m. domain; solemnity

se-ño-ri-ta *f.* lady; girl

se-ño-ri-to *m.* boy; young man

se-ñue-lo *m.* trap; bait

se-pa-ra-ción *f.* separation

se-pa-ra-da-men-te *adv.* separately

se-pa-ra-do *adj.* separated

se-pa-rar *v.* to divide

se-pa-ra-tis-ta *adj.* separatist

se-pe-lio *m.* burial

sep-ti-co, -ca *adj.* septic

sep-tiem-bre *m.* September

sep-ti-mo *adj.* seventh

sep-tua-ge-na-rio, -ria *adj.* septuagenarian

sep-tua-ge-si-mo, -ma *adj.* seventieth

se-pul-tar *v.* to bury

se-pul-to, -ta *adj.* buried

se-pul-tu-ra *f.* burial

se-que-dad *f.* dryness

se-quí-a *f.* drought

ser *v.* to be; to come from

se-ra-fin *m.* angel

se-re-nar *v.* to calm

se-re-na-ta *f.* serenade

se-re-ni-dad *f.* serenity

se-re-no, -na *adj.* calm

se-rial *adj.* serial

se-ria-men-te *adv.* seriously

se-rie *f.* series

se-rie-dad *f.* seriousness

se-rio *adj.* serious

ser-món *m.* sermon

ser-mo-ne-ar *v.* to lecture

ser-pien-te *f.* snake

se-rra-do, -da *adj.* sawed

se-rra-ní-a *f.* mountains

se-rrar *v.* to saw

se-rre-rí-a *f.* sawmill

se-rru-cho *m.* saw

ser-vi-cio *m.* help; service

ser-vi-dor, -ra *m., f.* servant

ser-vil *adj.* servile

ser-vi-lle-ta *f.* napkin

ser-vir *v.* to serve

se-sa-mo *m.* sesame

se-sen-ta *adj.* sexty

se-sen-ta-vo, va *adj.* sixtieth

ses-go *m.* slant

se-sión *f.* session

se-so *m.* brain

se-su-do, -da *adj.* wise

se-te-cien-tos, -tas *adj.* seven hundred

se-ten-ta *adj.* seventy

se-ten-ta-vo, -va *adj.* seventieth

se-tiem-bre *m.* September

seu-dó-ni-mo, -ma *m.* pseudonym

se-ve-ra-men-te *adv.* relentlessly; severly

se-ve-ri-dad *f.* graveness; severity

se-ve-ro, -ra *adj.* unyielding; severe

se-xa-ge-si-mo, -ma *adj.* sixtieth

sex-te-to *m.* sextet

sex-to *adj.* sixth

se-xual *adj.* sexual

se-xua-li-dad *f.* sexuality

si *conj.* if; *adv.* yes

si-bi-lan-te *adj.* sibilant

si-co-mo-ro *m.* sycamore

sie-ga *f.* harvesting

siem-bra *f.* sowing

siem-pre *adv.* forever; always

sien *f.* temple

sie-rra *f.* saw

sier-vo *m.* servant; serf

sies-ta *f.* nap in the afternoon

sie-te *adj.* seven

si-fi-lis *f.* syphilis

si-fi-li-ti-co, -ca *adj.* syphilitic

si-gi-lo *m.* secrecy

si-gla *f.* acronym

si-glo *m.* century

sig-ni-fi-ca-ción *f.* significance

sig-ni-fi-ca-do, -da *adj.* significant

sig-ni-fi-can-te *adj.* significant

sig-ni-fi-car *v.* to signify; to indicate

sig-ni-fi-ca-ti-vo, -va *adj.* significant

sig-no *m.* sign

si-guien-te *adj.* next

sí-la-ba *f.* syllable

si-la-be-ar *v.* to syllable

si-la-be-o *m.* syllabication

sil-ba-to *m.* whistle
sil-bi-do *m.* whistle
si-len-cia-dor *m.* silencer
si-len-ciar *v.* to silence
si-len-cio *m.* silence
si-len-cio-so *adj.* silent
si-li-co-na *f.* silicone
si-lo *m.* silo
si-lo-gis-ti-co, -ca *adj.* syllogistic
si-lue-ta *f.* outline
sil-ves-tre *adj.* wild
sil-vi-cul-tor *m.* forester
si-lla *f.* chair
si-llin *m.* seat
si-llón *m.* armchair
sim-bio-sis *f.* symbiosis
sim-bio-ti-co, -ca *adj.* symbiotic
sim-bo-li-zar *v.* to symbolize
sím-bo-lo *m.* symbol
si-me-tri-a *f.* symmetry
si-mé-tri-co, -ca *adj.* symmetric
si-mien-te *f.* seed
sí-mil *adj.* similar
si-mi-lar *adj.* similar
si-mi-li-tud *f.* similarity
sim-pa-tí-a *f.* congeniality; affection
sim-pá-ti-co, -ca *adj.* pleasant
sim-pa-ti-zan-te *adj.* sympathizing
sim-ple *adj.* simple
sim-ple-za *f.* simplicity
sim-pli-ci-dad *f.* simplicity
sim-pli-fi-ca-cion *f.* simplification
sim-pli-fi-car *v.* to simplify
sim-po-sio *m.* symposium
si-mu-la-cion *f.* pretense
si-mu-la-dor, -ra *m., f.* simulator
si-mul-tá-ne-o, -a *adj.* simultaneous
sin *prep.* without
si-na-go-ga *f.* synagogue
sin-ce-ri-dad *f.* sincerity
sin-ce-ro, -ra *adj.* sincere
sín-co-pa *f.* syncope
sin-co-pa-do, -da *adj.* syncopated

sin-co-pe *m.* syncope
sin-cro-ni-a *f.* synchrony
sin-cro-ni-za-cion *f.* synchronization
sin-cro-ni-zar *v.* to synchronize
sin-di-ca-li-za-ción *f.* unionization
sin-di-ca-li-zar *v.* to unionize
sin-dro-me *m.* syndrome
si-ner-gi-a *f.* synergy
sin-fo-ní-a *f.* symphony
sin-fo-ni-co, -ca *adj.* symphonic
sin-gu-lar *adj.* single
sin-gu-la-ri-zar *v.* to distinguish
sin-nú-me-ro *m.* countless
si-no *conj.* but; fate
si-no-ni-mia *f.* synonymy
si-no-ni-mo, -ma *adj.* synonymous
si-nop-sis *f.* synopsis
si-nop-ti-co, -ca *adj.* synoptic
sin-ta-xis *m.* syntax
sin-te-sis *f.* synthesis
sin-té-ti-co, -ca *adj.* synthetic
sin-te-ti-za-dor *m.* synthesizer
sin-te-ti-zar *v.* to synthesize
sin-to-ma *m.* symptom
sin-to-ma-ti-co, -ca *adj.* symptomatic
sin-to-ni-zar *v.* to tune
si-nuo-si-dad *f.* sinuosity
si-nuo-so, -sa *adj.* sinuous
si-qui-a-tra *m., f.* psychiatrist
si-quia-tri-a *f.* psychiatry
si-qui-co *adj.* psychic
si-quie-ra *adv.* at least
sir-vien-ta *f.* maid
sir-vien-te *m.* servant
sis-mi-co, -ca *adj.* seismic
sis-mo *m.* earthquake
sis-mo-gra-fo *m.* seismograph
sis-te-ma *m.* system
sis-te-ma-ti-za-ción *f.* systematization
sis-te-ma-ti-zar *v.* to systematize

sis-to-le *f.* systole
si-tio *m.* place
si-to, -ta *adj.* situated
si-tua-ción *f.* situation
si-tuar *v.* to place
so-ba-co *m.* armpit
so-bar *v.* to thrash; to knead
so-be-o *m.* strap
so-be-ra-ni-a *f.* sovereignty
so-be-ra-no, -na *adj.* sovereign
so-ber-bio, -bia *adj.* superb
so-bor-nar *v.* to bribe another
so-bor-no *m.* bribery
so-bra *f.* excess
so-bra-do, -da *adj.* plenty
so-bran-te *adj.* surplus
so-brar *v.* to surpass
so-bre *prep.* over; on; above
so-bre-a-bun-dan-cia *f.* superabundance
so-bre-a-bun-dan-te *adj.* superabundant
so-bre-car-ga *f.* overload
so-bre-car-gar *v.* to overload
so-bre-ce-jo *m.* frown
so-bre-co-ger *v.* to scare
so-bre-cu-bier-ta *f.* cover
so-bre-en-ten-di-do, -da *adj.* understood
so-bre-ex-ci-tar *v.* to overexcite
so-bre-lle-nar *v.* to overfill
so-bre-lle-var *v.* to bear
so-bre-na-tu-ral *adj.* supernatural
so-bre-nom-bre *m.* nickname
so-bren-ten-der *v.* to understand
so-bre-pa-sar *v.* to surpass
so-bre-pe-so *m.* overlaod
so-bre-pre-cio *m.* surcharge
so-bre-sa-lien-te *adj.* outstanding
so-bre-sa-lir *v.* to project
so-bre-sal-tar *v.* to startle
so-bre-fal-to *m.* fright
so-bres-cri-to *m.* address
so-bres-ti-mar *v.* to overestimate
so-bre-to-do *m.* coat; overcoat
so-bre-vi-vien-te *adj.* surviving
so-bre-vi-vir *v.* to survive
so-bri-na *f.* niece
so-bri-no *m.* nephew
so-ca-rrón, -na *m., f.* one who is sarcastic
so-ca-rro-ne-rí-a *f.* sarcasm
so-ca-var *v.* to excavate
so-cia-bi-li-dad *f.* friendliness
so-cia-ble *adj.* sociable
so-cial *adj.* social
so-cie-dad *f.* society
so-cio, -cia *m., f.* member
so-cio-e-co-no-mi-co, -ca *adj.* socioeconomic
so-cio-lo-grí-a *f.* sociology
so-cio-ló-gi-co, -ca *adj.* sociological
so-cio-lo-go, -ga *m., f.* sociologist
so-co-rrer *v.* to aid
so-co-rro *m.* aid
so-dio *m.* sodium
so-fá *f.* sofa
so-fis-ma *m.* sophism
so-fis-ta *adj.* sophistic
so-fis-ti-ca-cion *f.* sophistication
so-fis-ti-ca-do, -da *adj.* sophisticated
so-fo-ca-cion *f.* suffocation
so-fo-ca-dor, -ra *adj.* suffocating
so-fo-car *v.* to suffocate; to suppress
so-ga *f.* rope
so-ja *f.* soybean
so-juz-gar *v.* to subjugate
sol *m.* sun
so-la-men-te *adv.* only
so-la-no *m.* the east wind
so-lar *adj.* solar
so-la-rium *m.* solarium
so-laz *m.* relaxation
sol-da-do *m.* soldier
sol-da-dor *m.* solderer
sol-da-du-ra *f.* soldering
sol-dar *v.* to join
so-le-a-do *adj.* sunny
so-le-cis-mo *m.* solecism

so-le-dad f. loneliness
so-lem-ne adj. solemn
so-lem-ni-dad f. solemnity
so-le-van-tar v. to lift
so-li-ci-ta-cion f. request
so-li-ci-tan-te m., f. petitioner
so-li-ci-tar v. to ask for; to request
so-li-ci-to, -ta adj. solicitous
so-li-ci-tud f. request; solicitude
so-li-da-ri-dad f. solidarity
so-li-dez f. solidity
so-li-di-fi-ca-cion f. solidification
so-li-di-fi-car v. to solidify
só-li-do adj. solid
so-li-lo-quio m. soliloquy
so-lis-ta f. soloist
so-li-vian-tar v. to irritate
so-li-viar v. to lift something
so-lo adj. alone
sols-ti-cio m. solstice
sol-tar v. to let go; to loosen
sol-te-ro adj. single
sol-tu-ra f. confidence; looseness
so-lu-ble adj. soluable
so-lu-ción f. solution
so-lu-cio-nar v. to solve
sol-ven-cia f. solvency
sol-ven-tar v. to resolve
sol-ven-te adj. solvent
so-ma-ti-co, -ca adj. somatic
so-ma-ti-za-cion f. somatization
so-ma-ti-zar v. to somatize
som-bra f. shade
som-brar v. to shade
som-bre-ar v. to shade
som-bre-ro m. hat
som-brí-o, -a adj. sullen
so-me-ter v. to subordinate
so-me-ti-mien-to m. submission
som-no-len-cia f. somnolence
so-ña-do, -da adj. crazy
so-ñar v. to sound
soñ-da f. sounding
son-de-ar v. to sound
son-de-o m. sounding

so-ne-to m. sonnet
so-ni-do m. sound
so-no-ri-dad f. sonority
so-no-ro, -ra adj. sonority
so-no-ro, -ra adj. sound
son-re-ír v. to smile
son-rien-te adj. smiling
son-ri-sa f. smile
son-ro-jo m. blush
son-ro-sar v. to turn pink
son-sa-car v. to wheedle
so-ña-do, -da adj. dream
so-ña-dor, -ra m., f. dreamer
so-ñar v. to dream
so-ño-len-cia f. somnolence
so-ño-lien-to, -ta adj. sleepy
so-pa f. soup
so-pa-pe-ar v. to slap
so-pa-po m. slap
so-pe-sar v. to wiegh
so-pla-dor, -ra adj. blowing
so-plar v. to blow
so-por m. sleepiness
so-por-ta-ble adj. bearable
so-por-tar v. to support
so-por-te m. support
so-pra-no m. soprano
sor-ber v. to absorb
sor-be-te m. sherbet
sor-bo m. sip
sor-de-ra f. deafness
sor-di-dez f. squalor
sór-di-do, -da adj. squalid
sor-do, -da adj. deaf
sor-na f. sarcasm
sor-pren-den-te adj. surprising
sor-pren-der v. to surprise
sor-pre-sa f. surprise
sor-pre-si-vo, -va adj. unexpected
sor-ti-ja f. ring
so-se-ga-do, -da adj. peaceful
so-se-gar v. to calm one down
so-sie-go m. quiet
sos-la-yo, -ya adj. slanted
so-so, -sa adj. dull
sos-pe-cha f. suspicion
sos-pe-char v. to suspect
sos-pe-cho-so, -sa adj. suspicious

sos-tén m. support; sustenance

sos-te-ne-dor m. supporter

sos-te-ner v. to uphold; to support

sos-te-ni-do, -da adj. sustained

sos-te-ni-mien-to m. sustenance; support

so-ta-na f. soutane

so-ta-no m. basement

Sr. abbr. Señor, m. Mr.

Sra. abbr. Señora, f. Mrs.

stan-dard adj. standard

su, sus adj. her; his; its; your

sua-ve adj. sweet; soft

sua-vi-dad f. smoothness; sweetness

sua-vi-za-dor, -ra adj. softening

sua-vi-zar v. to smooth; to soften

su-bal-ter-no, -na adj. subordinate

su-ba-rren-dar v. to sublet

su-ba-rrien-do m. sublease

su-bas-ta f. auction

su-bas-tar v. to auction

sub-co-mi-sion f. subcommittee

sub-cons-cien-te adj. subconscious

sub-cu-ta-ne-o, -a adj. subcutaneous

sub-di-vi-sion f. subdivision

su-bes-ti-mar v. to underestimate

su-bi-ba-ja m. seesaw

su-bi-do, -da adj. deep

su-bir v. to raise; to go up; to come

su-bi-ta-men-te adv. suddenly

su-bi-to adj. hasty

sub-je-ti-vi-dad f. subjectivity

sub-je-ti-vo, -va adj. subjective

su-ble-var v. to annoy

su-bli-ma-ción f. sublimation

su-bli-mar v. to sublimate

su-bli-me adj. sublime

sub-ma-ri-no, -na adj. submarine

su-bor-di-na-ción f. subordination

su-bor-di-na-do, -da adj. subordinate

su-bor-di-nar v. to subordinate

sub-sa-nar v. to correct

subs-cri-bir v. to subscribe to; to sign

subs-crip-ción f. subscription

subs-crip-tor, -ra m., f. subscriber

sub-se-cuen-te adj. subsequent

sub-si-diar v. to subsidize

sub-si-dio m. subsidy

sub-sis-ten-cia f. subsistence

sub-sis-tir v. to subsist

subs-tan-cia f. substance

subs-tan-cial adj. substantial

subs-tan-ciar v. to substantiate

subs-tan-cio-so, -sa adj. substantial

subs-ti-tu-ción f. substitution

subs-ti-tuir v. to substitute

subs-ti-tu-ti-vo, -va adj. substitue

subs-trac-ción f. subtraction

subs-tra-er v. to subtract; to deduce

sub-sue-lo m. basement

sub-ter-fu-gio m. subterfuge

sub-te-rrá-ne-o, -a adj. underground

sub-ti-tu-lo m. subtitle

su-bur-ba-no, -na adj. suburban

su-bur-bio m. suburb

sub-ven-ción f. subsidy

sub-ven-cio-nar v. to subsidize

sub-yu-gar v. to subjugate

suc-ción f. suction

su-ce-da-ne-o, -a adj. substitute

su-ce-der v. to succeed

su-ce-sión f. succession

su-ce-si-va-men-te adv. successively

su-ce-si-vo, -va adj. consecutive

su-ce-so *m.* event

su-ce-sor, -ra *adj.* succeeding

su-cie-dad *f.* filth

su-cio, -cia *adj.* vile; dirty

su-cu-len-cia *f.* succulence

su-cu-len-to, -ta *adj.* succelent

su-cum-bir *v.* to succumb

sud *m.* south

su-dar *v.* to sweat

su-des-te *m.* southeast

su-do-es-te *m.* southwest

su-dor *m.* sweat

su-do-ri-fe-ro, -ra *adj.* sudoriferous

su-do-ro-so, -sa *adj.* sweaty

sue-gra *f.* mother-in-law

sue-gro *m.* father-in-law

sue-lo *m.* floor; soil; ground

suel-to, -ta *adj.* nimble; loose

sue-ño *m.* dream; sleep

sue-ro *m.* serum

suer-te *f.* luck

su-fi-cien-cia *f.* competence

su-fi-cien-te *adj.* sufficient

su-fi-jo *m.* suffix

su-fra-gio *m.* suffrage

su-fra-gis-ta *f., m.* suffragist

su-fri-do, -da *adj.* patient

su-frir *v.* to suffer; to endure something

su-ge-ren-cia *f.* suggestion

su-ge-rir *v.* to suggest

su-ges-tion *f.* suggestion

su-ges-ti-vo, -va *adj.* suggestive

sui-ci-da *adj.* suicidal

sui-ci-dio *m.* suicide

su-je-ción *f.* subjection

su-je-tar *v.* to subject; to fasten

su-je-to, -ta *adj.* subject

sul-fu-ro *m.* sulfide

su-ma-men-te *adv.* extremely

su-mar *v.* to add up

su-ma-ria-men-te *adv.* summarily

su-ma-rio, -ria *adj.* brief

su-mer-gir *v.* to submerge

su-mi-de-ro *m.* drain

su-mi-nis-trar *v.* to supply

su-mi-nis-tro *m.* supply

su-mir *v.* to submerge into something

su-mi-sion *f.* submission

su-mi-so, -sa *adj.* submissive

sun-tou-si-dad *f.* sumptuousness

sun-tuo-so, -sa *adj.* sumptuous

su-pe-di-tar *v.* to subordinate

su-pe-ra-bun-dar *v.* to superabound

su-pe-rar *v.* to surpass; to beat

su-pe-res-truc-tu-ra *f.* superstructure

su-per-fi-cial *adj.* superficial

su-per-fi-cie *f.* surface

su-per-fi-no, -na *adj.* very fine

su-per-fluo, -a *adj.* superfluous

su-pe-rin-ten-den-te *m., f.* superintendent

su-pe-rior *adj.* superior; better

su-pe-rio-ri-dad *f.* superiority

su-per-mer-ca-do *m.* supermarket

su-per-po-bla-cion *f.* overpopulation

su-per-po-ten-cia *f.* superpower

su-per-pro-duc-cion *f.* overproduction

su-per-só-ni-co, -ca *adj.* supersonic

su-pers-ti-ción *f.* superstition

su-pers-ti-cio-so, -sa *adj.* superstitious

su-per-vi-sar *v.* to supervise

su-per-vi-sion *f.* supervision

su-per-vi-ven-cia *f.* survival

su-pi-no, -na *adj.* supine

su-plan-tar *v.* to supplant

su-ple-men-tal *adj.* supplemental

su-plen-te *adj.* substitute

su-pli-car *v.* to implore

su-po-ner *v.* to imagine

something; to suppose

su-po-si-ción *f.* supposition

su-po-si-to-rio *m.* suppository

su-pre-mo, -ma *adj.* supreme

su-pri-mir *v.* to eliminate

su-pues-to, -ta *adj.* supposed; assumed

su-pu-rar *v.* to suppurate

sur *m.* south

sur-car *v.* to plow

sur-gir *v.* to arise

su-rre-a-lis-to *adj.* surrealistic

sur-ti-do, -da *m.* selection *adj.* assorted

sur-ti-dor, -ra *m.* supplier

sur-tir *v.* to supply something

sus-cep-ti-bi-li-dad *f.* susceptibility

sus-cep-ti-ble *adj.* susceptible

sus-pen-der *v.* to interrupt

sus-pen-sión *f.* suspension

sus-pen-si-vo, -va *adj.* suspensive

sus-pen-so-rio, -ria *adj.* suspensory

sus-pi-ca-cia *f.* distrust

sus-pi-caz *adj.* being distrustful

sus-pi-rar *v.* to sigh

sus-pi-ro *m.* sigh

sus-ten-ta-mien-to *m.* sustenance

sus-ten-tar *v.* to uphold; to sustain

sus-tne-to *m.* support; sustenance

sus-to *m.* scare

su-su-rran-te *adj.* rustling

su-su-rrar *v.* to murmur; to whisper

su-su-rro *m.* whisper

su-til *adj.* subtle

su-ti-le-za *f.* sublety

su-tu-ra *f.* suture

su-tu-rar *v.* to suture a wound

su-yo, -ya *adj.* their; her; his; your

ta-ba *f.* bone of the ankle

ta-ba-cal *m.* field for tobacco

ta-ba-ca-le-ro, -ra *m., f.* tabacco dealer

ta-ba-co *m.* tobacco

tá-ba-no *m.* gadfly

ta-ba-que-ri-a *f.* tobacco shop

ta-ber-na *f.* tavern

ta-ber-ná-cu-lo *m.* tabernacle

ta-ber-ne-ro, -ra *m., f.* bartender

ta-bi-que *m.* partition

ta-bla *f.* table

ta-ble-a-do, -da *m.* pleats

ta-ble-ro *m.* board

ta-ble-ta *f.* tablet

ta-bu-la-dor *m., f.* tabulator

ta-bu-re-te *m.* stool

ta-co-no, -na *adj.* stingy

tá-ci-to, -ta *adj.* tacit

ta-ci-tur-no, -na *adj.* taciturn

ta-co *m.* pad; wedge

ta-cón *m.* heel

tác-ti-co, -ca *adj.* tactical

tac-til *adj.* tactile

tac-to *m.* touch; tact

ta-cha *f.* flaw

ta-char *v.* to cross something out

ta-cho *m.* can

ta-chue-la *f.* tack

ta-fe-tán *m.* taffeta

ta-hur *m.* cardsharp

tai-ma-do, -da *adj.* crafty

ta-ja-da *f.* profit

ta-jan-te *adj.* sharp

ta-jar *v.* to slice

ta-jo *m.* cut

tal *adj.* such

ta-la *f.* ruin

ta-la-dor, -ra *adj.* cutting

ta-la-drar *v.* to drill

ta-la-dro *m.* drill

ta-lar *v.* to cut something down

tal-co *m.* talc

ta-le-ga *f.* wealth

ta-len-to *m.* talent

ta-len-to-so, -sa *adj.* talented

ta-lis-man *m.* talisman

ta-lon *m.* talon; heel
ta-lo-na-rio *m.* checkbook
ta-lla *f.* size; height
ta-lla-do, -da *adj.* engraved; carved
ta-lla-dor *m.* engraver
ta-llar *v.* to carve
ta-lle *m.* figure; shape
ta-ller *m.* shop
ta-llo *m.* stem
ta-ma-no, -na *adj.* very big
tam-ba-le-an-te *adj.* staggering
tam-ba-le-ar *v.* to stagger
tam-bien *adv.* too; also
tam-bor *m.* drum
tam-bo-ra *f.* drum
tam-bo-ril *m.* little drum
tam-bo-ri-le-ar *v.* to beat
tam-bo-ri-le-o *m.* beating
ta-miz *m.* sieve
ta-mi-zar *v.* to filter
tam-po-co *adv.* nor; niether
tan *adv.* as; so
tan-da *f.* shift; turn
tan-gen-te *adj.* tangent
tan-gi-ble *adj.* tangible
tan-go *m.* tango
tan-gue-ar *v.* to tango
tan-que *m.* tanker
tan-te-ar *v.* to consider; to test
tan-to, -ta *adj.* so many
ta-ner *v.* to play
ta-pa *f.* cover; lid
ta-pa-do *m.* coat
ta-par *v.* to block something
ta-pe-te *m.* carpet
ta-piar *v.* to wall something in
ta-pi-ce-ro, -ra *m., f.* upholsterer
ta-pio-ca *f.* tapioca
ta-piz *m.* tapestry
ta-pi-zar *v.* to upholster; to hang tapestries
ta-pon *m.* cork
ta-qui-gra-fi-a *f.* stenography
ta-qui-gra-fiar *v.* to write using shorthand
ta-qui-gra-fo, -fa *m., f.* stenographer
ta-ra *f.* defect

ta-ran-tu-la *f.* tarantula
ta-ras-car *v.* to bite
tar-dan-za *f.* delay
tar-dar *v.* to delay
tar-de *f.* afternoon
tar-di-o, -a *adj.* late
ta-ra-a *f.* homework
ta-ri-fa *f.* tariff
ta-ri-far *v.* to give or apply a tariff to something
tar-je-ta *f.* card
ta-rro *m.* jar
tar-ta *f.* pie
tar-ta-mu-de-o *m.* stammering
tar-tan *m.* tartan
tar-to-ro, -ra *adj.* tartar
ta-sa *f.* rate
ta-sa-cion *f.* appraisal
ta-sa-dor, -ra *adj.* appraising
ta-sa-je-ar *v.* to jerk something
ta-sa-jo *m.* jerky
tas-ca *f.* joint
ta-ta-ra-bue-la *f.* great-great-grandmother
ta-ta-ra-bue-lo *m.* great-great-grandfather
ta-ta-ra-nie-ta *f.* great-great-granddaughter
ta-ta-ra-nie-to *m.* great-great-grandson
ta-tau-je *m.* tattoo
ta-taur *v.* to tattoo
tau-ro-ma-quia *f.* bullfighting
ta-xi *m.* taxi
ta-xi-der-mia *f.* taxidermy
ta-xis-ta *m., f.* one who drives a taxie
ta-xo-no-mi-a *f.* taxonomy
ta-za *f.* bowl; cup
te *pron.* you
te-a *f.* torch
te-a-tral *adj.* theatrical
te-a-tra-li-dad *f.* theatricality
te-a-tro *m.* theater
te-cia *f.* key
te-cla-do *m.* keyboard
tec-ni-co, -ca *adj.* technical
tec-no-cra-cia *f.* technocracy
tec-no-lo-gi-a *f.* technology
tec-no-lo-gi-co, -ca *adj.* technological

te-char v. to roof a building
te-cho m. ceiling; roof
te-dio m. tedium
te-dio-so, -sa adj. tedious
te-ja f. tile
te-jar v. to tile
te-jer v. to knit
te-ji-do m. weave
te-jón m. badger
te-la f. fabric; film
te-la-ra-ña f. spider's web
te-le-co-mu-ni-ca-cion f. tele-
communication
te-le-di-fun-dir v. to telecast
te-le-di-fu-sion f. to telecast
te-le-fo-na-zo m. telephone
call
te-le-fo-ne-ar v. to phone
someone
te-le-fo-ni-ca-men-te adv. by
a phone
te-le-fo-nis-ta m., f. telephone operator
te-le-fo-no m. telephone
te-le-fo-to m. telephoto
te-le-gra-fi-a f. telegraphy
te-le-gra-fiar v. to telegraph
te-le-gra-fi-co, -ca adj. tele-
graphic
te-le-gra-fis-ta m., f. tele-
grapher
te-le-gra-fo m. telegraph
te-le-gra-ma f. telegram
te-le-man-do m. remote con-
trol
te-le-me-tri-a f. telemetry
te-le-pa-ti-a f. telepathy
te-le-pa-ti-co, -ca adj. tele-
pathic
te-les-co-pi-co, -ca adj. tele-
scopic
te-les-co-pio m. telescope
te-le-ti-po m. teletype
te-le-vi-sar v. to televise
te-le-vi-sion f. television
te-le-vi-sor m. television
te-lon m. curtain
te-lu-rio m. tellurium
te-ma f. subject; obsession
te-ma-ti-co, -ca adj. thematic
tem-blar v. to tremble
tem-ble-que-ar v. to tremble
tem-blor m. earthquake;

tremor
te-mer v. to be afraid of
te-me-ro-so-, sa adj. frigh-
tening
te-mor m. fear
tem-pe-ra-men-tal adj. temperamental
tem-pe-ra-men-to m.
weather
tem-pe-ran-cia f. tem-
perance
tem-pe-rar v. to calm
tem-pe-ra-tu-ra f. tempera-
ture
tem-pes-tad f. storm
tem-pes-tuo-so, -sa adj.
stormy
tem-pla-do, -da adj. mild
tem-plan-za f. moderation
tem-plar v. to temper; to
tune; to appease
tem-ple m. mood; temper
tem-plo m. temple
tem-po-ra-da f. season
tem-po-ral adj. temporal
tem-po-ra-ne-o, -a adj. temporary
tem-pra-ne-ro, -ra adj. early
tem-pra-no, -na adj. early
te-na-ci-dad f. tenacity
te-naz f. tenacious
ten-den-cia f. tendency
ten-der v. to stretch something out
ten-di-do, -da adj. spead out
ten-don m. tendon
te-ne-bro-so, -sa adj.
obscure; dark
te-ne-dor m. one who owns
te-nen-cia f. possession
te-ner v. to contain; to have;
to keep
te-nia f. tapeworm
te-nien-te m. lieutenant
te-nis m. tennis
te-nis-ta m., f. one who plays
tennis
ten-sar v. to stretch
ten-sion f. tension
ten-so, -sa adj. tense
ten-ta-cion f. temptation
ten-ta-cu-lo m. tentacle
ten-ta-dor, -ra adj. tempting

ten-ta-ti-vo, -va *adj.* tentative
te-ñir *v.* to make dark
te-o-cra-cia *f.* theocracy
te-o-lo-gi-a *f.* theology
te-o-lo-go, -ga *m., f.* theologian
te-o-re-ma *m.* theorem
te-o-re-ti-co, -ca *adj.* theoretical
te-o-ri-a *f.* theory
te-o-ri-co, -ca *adj.* theoretical
te-o-ri-zar *v.* to theorize
te-ó-so-fo, -fa *m., f.* theosophist
te-qui-la *f.* tequila
te-ra-peu-ta *m., f.* therapist
te-ra-péu-ti-co, -ca *adj.* therapeutic
te-ra-pia *f.* therapy
ter-ce-ro, -ra *adj.* third
ter-cia-do, -da *adj.* brown
ter-cio, -cia *adj.* third
ter-cio-pe-lo *m.* velvet
ter-co, -ca *adj.* stubborn
ter-gi-ver-sar *v.* to distort
ter-mal *adj.* thermal
ter-mi-na-cion *f.* ending; termination
ter-mi-nal *adj.* terminal
ter-mi-nar *v.* to complete; to end something
ter-mi-no *m.* ending
ter-mi-no-lo-gi-a *f.* terminology
ter-mi-ta *m.* termite
ter-mo-di-ná-mi-ca *f.* thermodynamics
ter-mo-e-lec-tri-co, -ca *adj.* thermoelectric
ter-mó-me-tro *m.* thermometer
ter-mos-ta-to *m.* thermostat
ter-no *m.* a set of three things
ter-nu-ra *f.* tenderness
te-rra-plen *m.* embankment
te-rra-que-o, -a *adj.* terrestrial
te-rra-za *f.* terrace
te-rre-mo-to *m.* earthquake
te-rre-nal *adj.* earthly
te-rre-no, -na *adj.* earthly

te-rres-tre *adj.* terrestrial
te-rri-ble *adj.* terrible
te-rri-to-rial *adj.* territorial
te-rri-to-rio *m.* territory
te-rror *m.* terror
te-rro-rí-fi-co, -ca *adj.* terrifying
te-rro-ris-ta *m., f.* terrorist
ter-so, -sa *adj.* smooth
te-sis *f.* thesis
te-son *m.* tenacity
te-so-ne-ro, -ra *adj.* tenacious
te-so-re-ri-a *f.* treasury
te-so-re-ro, -ra *m., f.* treasurer
te-so-ro *m.* treasure
tes-tí-cu-lo *m.* testicle
tes-ti-fi-car *v.* to testify
tes-ti-go *m.* one who sees something; witness
tes-ti-mo-niar *v.* to testify
tes-ti-mo-nio *m.* testimony
te-ta *f.* udder
té-ta-no *m.* tetanus
te-ti-lla *f.* teat
tex-til *adj.* textile
tex-to *m.* textbook
tex-tu-ra *f.* texture
tez *f.* complexion
ti *pron.* yourself
ti-a *f.* aunt
tia-ra *f.* tiara
ti-bia *f.* tibia
ti-bu-rón *m.* shark
tiem-po *m.* weather; time
tien-da *f.* store; shop
tien-to *m.* caution; touch
tier-no, -na *adj.* tender
tie-rra *f.* land; country
tie-so, -sa *adj.* arrogant
ties-to *m.* flowerpot
ti-foi-de-o, -a *adj.* typhoid
ti-fón *m.* typhoon
ti-fus *m.* typhus
ti-gre *m.* tiger
ti-gre-sa *f.* tigress
ti-je-re-te-ar *v.* to snip
ti-je-re-te-o *m.* snipping
ti-mar-dor, -ra *m., f.* cheat
ti-mar *v.* to cheat
tim-bra-do, -da *adj.* stamped
tim-brar *v.* to stamp

tim-bre *m.* ring
ti-mi-dez *f.* timidity
tí-mi-do, -da *adj.* timid
ti-mo *m.* thymus
ti-mo-ra-to, -ta *adj.* shy
tin-gla-do *m.* platform
ti-no *m.* good judgment
tin-ta *f.* dye
tin-te *m.* dye
tin-te-ro *m.* inkwell
tin-ti-nar *v.* to clink something
tin-tu-ra *f.* tincture
ti-ña *f.* ringworm
tí-o *m.* uncle
tí-pi-co, -ca *adj.* typical
ti-pi-fi-car *v.* to typify
ti-po *m.* type; kind
ti-po-gra-fí-a *f.* typofraphy
ti-ra-da *f.* distance
ti-ra-ní-a *f.* tyranny
ti-ra-ni-zar *v.* to tyrannize
ti-ra-no, -na *adj.* tyrannical
ti-ran-te *adj.* tight
ti-ran-tez *f.* tightness
ti-rar *v.* to throw
ti-ri-tar *v.* to shiver
ti-ro *m.* shot; throw
ti-ro-te-o *m.* shooting
ti-sis *f.* tuberculosis
ti-te-re *m.* puppet
ti-ti-lar *v.* to quiver
ti-ti-le-o *m.* quivering
ti-ti-ri-tar *v.* to tremble
ti-tu-be-o *m.* staggering
ti-tu-la-do, -da *adj.* titled
tí-tu-lo *m.* title
ti-za *f.* chalk
tiz-nar *v.* to smudge
to-a-lla *f.* towel
to-bi-llo *m.* ankle
to-bo-gán *m.* sled
to-ca-dor *m.* dressing room
to-car *v.* to ring; to handle; to touch
to-da-ví-a *adj.* every; all
to-do, -da *adj.* all; every
to-le-ran-cia *f.* tolerance
to-le-ran-te *adj.* tolerant
to-le-rar *v.* to tolerate
to-lon-dron, -ona *m., f.* scatterbrain
to-ma *f.* intake; taking

to-ma-dor, -ra *adj.* drinking
to-mar *v.* to have; to take
to-ma-te *m.* tomato
to-na-da *f.* tune
to-na-li-dad *f.* tonality
to-nel *m.* barrel
to-ne-la-da *f.* ton
to-ne-la-je *m.* tonnage
to-ni-fi-car *v.* to tone
to-ni-na *f.* tuna
to-no *m.* tone
ton-te-rí-a *f.* foolishness
ton-to *m.* fool
tó-pi-co *m.* topic
to-po *m.* mole
to-po-gra-fí-a *f.* topography
to-pó-gra-fo *m.* topographer
to-que *m.* beat; touch
to-que-te-ar *v.* to handle
to-que-te-o *m.* handling
to-ra-ci-co, -ca *adj.* thoracic
tor-ce-du-ra *f.* twist
tor-cer *v.* to sprain; to bend
to-re-a-dor *m.* toreador
to-re-ar *v.* to fight
to-re-o *m.* bullfighting
tor-men-ta *f.* storm
tor-men-to *m.* torment
tor-men-to-so, -sa *adj.* stormy
tor-na-do *m.* tornado
tor-na-sol *m.* sunflower
tor-na-so-la-do, -da *adj.* iridescent
tor-ne-ar *v.* to turn
tor-ne-o *m.* tournament
tor-ni-llo *m.* screw
tor-ni-que-te *m.* tourniquet
to-ro *m.* bull
to-ron-ja *f.* grapefruit
tor-pe-de-ar *v.* to torpedo
tor-pe-za *f.* stupidity
tor-por *m.* torpor
to-rrar *v.* to roast
to-rre *f.* castle
to-rren-cial *adj.* torrential
to-rren-te *m.* torrent
tó-rri-do, -da *adj.* torrid
tor-sión *f.* torsion
tor-so *m.* torso
tor-ta *f.* cake
tor-to-la *f.* turtledove
tor-tu-ga *f.* turtle

tor-tuo-so, -sa *adj.* tortuous
tor-tu-ra *f.* torture
tor-tu-rar *v.* to torture
tos *f.* coughing
tos-co, -ca *adj.* crude
to-ser *v.* to cough
tos-que-dad *f.* coarseness
tos-ta-do, -da *adj.* roasted
tos-ta-dor, -ra *m., f.* toaster
tos-tar *v.* to roast; to toast
to-tal *adj.* total
to-ta-li-dad *f.* totality
to-ta-li-ta-rio, -ria *adj.* totalitarian
to-ta-li-zar *v.* to total
to-xe-mia *f.* toxemia
to-xi-ci-dad *f.* toxicity
tó-xi-co, -ca *adj.* poison
to-xi-co-lo-go, -ga *m., f.* toxicologist
to-xi-na *f.* toxin
to-zu-do, -da *adj.* stubborn
tra-ba *f.* obstacle; bolt
tra-ba-ja-dor *m.* worker
tra-ba-jar *v.* to work
tra-ba-jo *m.* job; work
tra-ba-jo-so, -sa *adj.* demanding
tra-bar *v.* to fasten; to bolt
tra-bu-car *v.* to mix up
trac-ción *f.* traction
trac-tor *m.* tractor
tra-di-ción *f.* tradition
tra-di-cio-nal *f.* traditional
tra-duc-ción *f.* translation
tra-du-cir *v.* to express
tra-duc-tor, -ra *adj.* translating something
tra-er *v.* to wear; to carry; to bring
tra-fi-car *v.* to deal
trá-fi-co *m.* traffic
tra-gl-luz *v.* skylight
tra-gar *v.* to devour; swallow
tra-ge-dia *f.* tragedy
trá-gi-co, -ca *adj.* tragic
tra-gi-co-me-dia *f.* tragicomedy
tra-go *m.* gulp
trai-ción *f.* treason
trai-cio-nar *v.* to betray another
tra-je *m.* dress

tra-je-a-do, -da *adj.* dressed
tra-je-ar *v.* to dress
tra-ji-nar *v.* to carry
tra-ma *f.* plot
tra-ma-dor, -ra *m., f.* weaver
tra-mar *v.* to scheme
tra-mi-ta-ción *f.* transaction
tra-mi-tar *v.* to negotiate
tra-mo *m.* flight
tram-pa *f.* trap
tram-pc-ar *v.* to cheat
tram-po-lin *m.* trampoline
tram-po-so, -sa *adj.* cheating
tran-ce *m.* trance; crisis
tran-qui-li-dad *f.* tranquility
tran-qui-li-zan-te *adj.* tranquilizing
tran-qui-lo, -la *adj.* tranquil
tran-sac-ción *f.* transaction
tran-sat-lan-ti-co, -ca *adj.* transatlantic
trans-bor-dar *v.* to transfer
trans-bor-do *m.* transfer
trans-cen-den-cia *f.* transcendence
trans-cen-den-tal *adj.* transcendental
trans-cen-der *v.* to transcend
trans-con-ti-nen-tal *adj.* transcontinental
trans-cri-bir *v.* to transcribe
trans-crip-cion *f.* transcription
tran-se-un-te *adj.* transient
trans-fe-ren-cia *f.* transference
trans-fe-rir *v.* to transfer
trans-fi-gu-ra-ción *f.* transfiguration
trans-for-ma-ción *f.* transformation
trans-for-ma-dor, -ra *adj.* transforming
trans-for-mar *v.* to convert; to transform
trans-fun-dir *v.* to transfuse
trans-fu-sión *f.* transfusion
trans-gre-dir *v.* to transgress
trans-gre-sión *f.* transgression
tran-si-ción *f.* transition

tran-sis-tor *m.* transistor

tran-si-tar *v.* to travel

tran-si-ti-vo, -va *adj.* transitive

trán-si-to *m.* traffic

tran-si-to-rio, -ria *adj.* temporary

trans-la-ción *f.* translation

trans-lu-ci-do, -da *adj.* translucent

trans-mi-gra-ción *f.* tranmigration

trans-mi-grar *v.* to transmigrate

trans-mi-tir *v.* to transmit

trans-mu-tar *v.* to transmute

trans-pa-ren-te *adj.* transparent

trans-pi-ra-ción *f.* perspiration

trans-pi-rar *v.* to perspire

trans-plan-tar *v.* to transplant

trans-po-ner *v.* to transplant; to move

trans-por-ta-ción *f.* transportation

trans-por-tar *v.* to transport

trans-po-si-ción *f.* transposition

trans-ver-so, -sa *adj.* transverse

tran-vi-a *m.* streetcar

tra-pe-cio *m.* trapezoid

tra-pe-zoi-de *m.* trapezoid

trá-que-a *f.* trachea

tras *prep.* behind; after

tra-sat-lan-ti-co, -ca *adj.* transatlantic

tras-cen-den-te *adj.* transcendent

tras-cen-der *v.* to extend

tra-se-gar *v.* to decant

tras-fon-do *m.* background

tra-sie-go *m.* decanting

tras-la-ción *f.* translation

tras-la-dar *v.* to transcribe; to move

tras-la-do *m.* transfer

tras-no-cha-do, -da *adj.* trite

tras-pa-pe-lar *v.* to misplace something

tras-pa-pe-la-do, -da *adj.* misplaced

tras-pa-sar *v.* to break

tras-pa-so *m.* transfer

trans-plan-tar *v.* to transplant

tras-qui-lar *v.* to shear

tras-to-car *v.* to twist

tras-tor-nar *v.* to disrupt

tras-tro-car *v.* to twist

tra-sun-tar *v.* to summarize

tra-ta-mien-to *m.* treatment; process

tra-tar *v.* to process; to handle

tra-to *m.* treatment

trau-ma *m.* trauma

trau-má-ti-co, -ca *adj.* traumatic

trau-ma-ti-zar *v.* to traumatize

tra-ve-si-a *f.* crosswind; crossroad

tra-ve-su-ra *f.* mischief

tra-vie-so, -sa *adj.* mischievous

tra-yec-to *m.* way

tra-yec-to-ria *f.* trajectory

tra-za *f.* plan

tra-zar *v.* to outline something

tra-zo *m.* line

tré-bol *m.* clover

tre-ce *adj.* thirteen

tre-cho *m.* in parts; stretch

tre-gua *f.* rest

trein-ta *adj.* thirty

trein-ta-vo *f.* thirtieth

trein-te-na *f.* thirty

tre-men-do, -da *adj.* terrible; horrible

tre-men-ti-na *f.* turpentine

tre-mo-lar *v.* to wave

tre-mo-li-na *f.* rustling

tre-mor *m.* tremor

tren *m.* train

tren-ci-lla *f.* braid

tren-za *f.* braid

tren-zar *v.* to braid

tre-pi-dar *v.* to vibrate

tres *adj.* three

tres-cien-tos *adj.* three hundred

tres-pies *m.* tripod

tre-za-vo, -va *adj.* thirteenth
tri-a-da *f.* triad
trian-gu-lar *adj.* triangular
trián-gu-lo *m.* triangular
tri-bal *adj.* tribal
tri-bu *f.* tribe
tri-bu-la-ción *f.* tribulation
tri-bu-no *m.* tribune
tri-bu-tar *v.* to pay
tri-bu-ta-rio, -ria *adj.* tributary
tri-bu-to *m.* tribute
tri-cen-te-na-rio *m.* tricentennial
tri-ci-clo *m.* trcycle
tri-co-lor *adj.* tricolor
tri-cus-pi-de *adj.* tricuspid
tri-gal *m.* field of wheat
tri-ge-si-mo, -ma *adj.* thirtieth
tri-go *m.* wheat
tri-go-no-me-tri-a *f.* trigonometry
tri-lin-gue *adj.* trilingual
tri-lo-gi-a *f.* trilogy
tri-lla-dor, -ra *adj.* threshing
tri-lli-zo *m.* triplet
tri-mes-tral *adj.* quarterly
trin-cha-dor, -ra *adj.* carving
trin-char *v.* to carve
tri-no-mio *m.* trinomial
tri-o *m.* trio
tri-ple *adj.* triple
tri-pli-ca-ción *f.* triplication
tri-pli-ca-do *m.* triplicate
tri-pli-car *v.* to triplicate
tri-plo, -pla *adj.* triple
tri-po-de *m., f.* tripod
tri-qui-no-sis *f.* trichinosis
tris-ca *f.* crack
tris-car *v.* to stamp
tris-te *adj.* miserable; sad
tris-te-za *f.* sorrow
tri-tu-rar *v.* to chew; to triturate
triun-fa-dor, -ra *adj.* triumphant
triun-fan-te *adj.* triumphant
triun-fo *m.* triumph
tri-vial *adj.* trivial
tri-via-li-dad *f.* triviality
tri-za *f.* piece
tro-car *v.* to barter

tro-fe-o *m.* trophy
tro-glo-di-ta *adj.* barbarous
tro-le *m.* trolley
trom-bon *m.* trombone
trom-bo-sis *f.* thrombosis
trom-pa *f.* horn
trom-pe-ar *v.* to punch
trom-pe-ta *f.* trumpet
trom-pe-tis-ta *m., f.* trumpeter
trom-pi-car *v.* to trip
trom-po *m.* top
tro-na-da *f.* thunderstorm
tro-na-dor, -ra *adj.* thundering
tro-nan-te *adj.* thundering
tro-nar *v.* to thunder
tron-co *m.* trunk
tron-cha *f.* slice
tro-pel *m.* confusion
tro-pe-li-a *f.* violence
tro-pe-zar *v.* to trip
tro-pi-cal *adj.* tropical
tro-pi-co *m.* tropic
tro-pie-zo *m.* stumble
tro-po *m.* trope
tro-que-lar *v.* to mint
tro-ta-da *f.* trot
tro-ta-dor, -ra *adj.* trotting
tro-va *f.* ballad
tro-zo *m.* chunk; part; piece
tru-co *m.* trick
true-no *m.* thunder
try-far *v.* to lie
tú *pron.* you
tu-ba *f.* tuba
tu-ber-cu-li-na *f.* tuberculin
tu-ber-cu-lo-sis *f.* tuberculosis
tu-be-ro-so, -sa *adj.* tuberous
tu-bo *m.* tube
tu-bu-la-do, -da *adj.* tubular
tu-bu-lar *adj.* tubular
tu-can *m.* toucan
tues-te *m.* toasting
tu-fo *m.* fume
tu-li-pan *m.* tulip
tu-llir *v.* to cripple
tum-ba *f.* tomb
tum-bar *v.* to knock out
tum-bo *m.* jolt
tu-mes-cen-cia *f.* tumes-

cence

tu-mes-cen-te *adj.* tumescent

tu-mor *m.* tumor

tú-mu-lo *m.* tomb

tu-mul-to *m.* tumult

tu-mul-tuo-so, -sa *adj.* tumultuous

tu-nan-ta *adj.* cunning

tun-da *f.* beating

tun-de-ar *v.* to beat

tun-di-dor, -ra *m., f.* one who shears

tun-di-du-ra *f.* shearing

tun-dir *v.* to shear

tun-dra *f.* tundra

tú-nel *m.* tunnel

tungs-te-no *m.* tungsten

tu-ni-ca *f.* tunic

tu-pé *m.* toupee

tu-pi-do, -da *adj.* dense; thick

tu-pir *v.* to weave close together

tur-ba *f.* mob

tur-ba-cion *f.* confusion

tur-ba-dor, -ra *adj.* disturbing

tur-ban-te *m.* turban

tur-bar *v.* to embarrass; to upset another

tur-bie-dad *f.* opaqueness

tur-bi-na *f.* turbine

tur-bio, -bia *adj.* turbulent; muddy

tur-bión *m.* shower

tur-bu-len-cia *f.* turbulence

tur-bu-len-to, -ta *adj.* turbulent

tu-ris-ta *f.* tourist

tu-rís-ti-co, -ca *adj.* tourist

tur-nar *v.* taking turns at something

tur-no *m.* turn

tur-que-sa *f.* turquiose

tu-ru-la-to, -ta *adj.* being stunned

tu-sa *f.* cornhusk

tu-sar *v.* to trim

tu-te-ar *v.* to address another as tu

tu-tor, -ra *m., f.* guardian

tu-yo, -ya *adj.* yours

u-be-rri-mo, -ma *adj.* luxuriant

u-bi-ca-cion *f.* placing

u-bi-car *v.* to locate

u-bre *f.* udder

u-fa-nar-se *v.* to boast about something

u-fa-no, -na *adj.* pleased

ul-ce-ra *f.* ulcer

ul-ce-ra-cion *f.* ulceration

ul-ce-rar *v.* to ulcerate

ul-ce-ro-so, -sa *adj.* ulcerous

ul-te-rior *adj.* subsequent

ul-te-rior-men-te *adv.* subsequently

ul-ti-ma-men-te *adv.* finally

ul-ti-mar *v.* to finish; to conclude

ul-ti-ma-tum *m.* ultimatum

ul-ti-mo, -ma *adj.* final; last

ul-tra *adv.* besides

ul-tra-de-re-cha *f.* the far right

ul-tra-jan-te *adj.* outrageous

ul-tra-jar *v.* to insult

ul-tra-je *m.* insult

ul-tra-ma-ri-no, -na *adj.* overseas

ul-tra-mo-der-no, -na *adj.* ultramodern

ul-tra-so-ni-co, -ca *adj.* ultrasonic

ul-tra-so-ni-do *m.* ultrasound

ul-tra-vio-le-ta *adj.* ultraviolet

um-bi-li-cal *adj.* umbilical

um-bral *m.* threshold

um-brí-o, -a *adj.* shady

um-bro-so, -sa *adj.* shady

un *indef. art.* an; a

u-ña *indef. art.* an; a

u-ná-ni-me *adj.* unanimous

u-na-ni-mi-dad *f.* unanimity

un-cir *v.* to yoke

un-de-ci-mo, -ma *adj.* eleventh

un-du-lan-te *adj.* undulating

un-du-lar *v.* to undulate

un-güen-to *m.* ointment

u-ni-ce-lu-lar *adj.* unicellular

u-ni-ci-dad *f.* uniqueness

ú-ni-co, -ca *adj.* single; sole

u-ni-cor-nio *m.* unicorn

u-ni-dad *f.* unity; each

u-ni-do, -da *adj.* united
u-ni-fi-ca-cion *f.* unification
u-ni-fi-car *v.* to unify
u-ni-for-mar *v.* to make something uniform
u-ni-for-me *adj.* even; uniform
u-ni-for-mi-dad *f.* uniformity
u-ni-la-te-ral *adj.* unilateral
u-nion *f.* joint; unity
u-nir(se) *v.* to unite together
u-ni-se-xo *adj.* unisex
u-ni-so-no, -na *adj.* to be in unison with
u-ni-ta-rio, -ria *adj.* unified
u-ni-ver-sal *adj.* world-wide; universal
u-ni-ver-sa-li-dad *f.* universality
u-ni-ver-sa-li-zar *v.* to universalize
u-ni-ver-si-dad *f.* university
u-ni-ver-si-ta-rio, -ria *adj.* university
u-ni-ver-so *m.* universe
u-no, -na *adj.* one
un-tar *v.* to spread; to grease
un-to *m.* grease
un-tuo-si-dad *f.* greasiness
un-tuo-so, -sa *adj.* greasy
un-tu-ra *f.* greasing
u-na *f.* toenail; fingernail
u-ra-nio *m.* uranium
ur-ba-ni-dad *f.* urbanity
ur-ba-ni-za-cion *f.* urvanization
ur-ba-ni-zar *v.* to develop
ur-ba-no, -na *adj.* urban
u-re-a *f.* urea
u-re-ter *m.* ureter
u-re-tra *f.* urethra
ur-gen-cia *f.* urgency
ur-gen-te *adj.* urgent
u-ri-na-rio, -ria *adj.* urinary
u-san-za *f.* custom
u-sar *v.* to use
u-so *m.* use
us-ted *pron.* you
u-sual *adj.* usual
u-su-ra *f.* usury
u-sur-par *v.* to usurp
u-ten-si-lio *m.* utensil
ú-til *adj.* useful

va-ca *f.* cow
va-ca-cion *f.* vacation
va-can-te *adj.* vacant
va-cia-de-ro *m.* dump
va-cia-do *m.* cast
va-ciar *v.* to void; to empty; to drain
va-ci-la-ción *f.* vacillation; hesitation
va-ci-lan-te *adj.* hesitating
va-ci-lar *v.* to falter; to vacillate
va-ció, -cia *adj.* devoid; empty; void; hollow
va-cui-dad *f.* vacuity
va-cu-na-ción *f.* vaccination
va-cu-nar *v.* to vaccinate
va-cu-no, -na *adj.* bovine
va-cuo, -cua *adj.* vacuous
va-de-ar *v.* to overcome
va-ga-bun-do, -da *adj.* vagabond
va-ga-men-te *adv.* vaguely
va-gan-cia *f.* vagrancy
va-gar *v.* to roam; to stray; to wander
va-gi-do *m.* cry
va-go, -ga *adj.* hazy; wandering; vague
va-gón *m.* van
va-gue-ar *v.* to wander
va-gue-dad *f.* vagueness
va-ho *m.* vapor; steam
vai-ni-lla *f.* canilla
vai-vén *m.* fluctuation
va-le *m.* voucher
va-le-de-ro, -ra *adj.* valid
va-len-cia *f.* valence
va-len-tía *f.* courage; valor; bravery
va-len-tón, -ona *adj.* boastful
va-len-to-na *f.* boast
va-ler *v.* to be of value; to have authority over; to be of worth
va-le-ro-so, -sa *adj.* valorous; courageous
va-li-a *f.* worth
va-li-da-ción *f.* validation
va-li-dar *v.* to validate
va-li-dez *f.* validity
vá-li-do, -da *adj.* good
va-lien-te *adj.* brave; valiant

va-li-ja f. suitcase
va-lio-so, -sa adj. valuable
va-lor m. valor; worth; importance
va-lo-ra-ción f. appraisal
va-lo-rar v. to appraise something
va-lo-ri-za-ción f. appraisal
va-lo-ri-zar v. to appraise something
vals m. waltz
va-luar v. to value something
vál-vu-la f. valve
va-llar v. to put a fence around; to fence in
va-lle m. valley
vam-pi-ro m. vampire
va-na-glo-ria f. pride
va-na-glo-rio-so, -sa adj. boastful
va-na-men-te adv. foolishly; vainly
van-da-lis-mo m. vandalism
va-ni-dad f. vanity
va-ni-do-so, -sa m., f. one who is vain
va-no, -na adj. vain
va-por m. steam
va-po-ri-za-dor m. vaporizer
va-po-ri-zar v. to vaporize
va-po-ro-so, -sa adj. steamy; vaporous
va-que-ta f. hide of a cow
va-ra f. rod; stalk
va-rar v. to beach
va-re-a-dor, -ra m., f. cowhand
va-re-ar v. to cudgel
va-ria-ble adj. variable
va-ria-ción f. change; variation
va-ria-do, -da adj. varied
va-rien-te adj. varying
va-riar v. to change
va-rie-dad f. variety
va-ri-lla f. rob
va-rio, -ria adj. varied
va-ron m. man
va-ro-nil adj. virile
va-sa-llo, -lla adj. subordinate
vas-cu-lar adj. vascular
va-sec-to-mi-a f. vasectomy

va-si-ja f. container
va-so m. vessel; glass
vas-to, -ta adj. vast
va-ti-ci-nar v. to predict
va-ti-ci-nio m. prediction
va-tio m. watt
ve-ci-nal adj. local
ve-ci-na-men-te adv. next
ve-cin-dad f. vicinity
ve-ci-no, -na adj. near; next
vec-tor m. vector
ve-da f. prohibition
ve-da-do, -da adj. prohibited
ve-dar v. to suspend; to prohibit
ve-ge-ta-ción f. vegetation
ve-ge-tal adj. vegetable
ve-ge-tar v. to vegetate
ve-ge-ta-ria-no, -na adj. vegetarian
ve-ge-ta-ti-vo, -va adj. vegetative
ve-he-men-cia f. vehemence
ve-he-men-te adj. vehement
ve-hí-cu-lo m. vehicle
vein-te adj. twenty
ve-ja-ción f. vexation
ve-ja-men m. vezation
ve-jar v. to persecute; to vex
ve-jez f. old age
ve-li-ga f. bladder
ve-la f. sail
ve-la-da f. evening
ve-la-do, -da adj. veiled
ve-lar v. to guard
ve-lei-do-so, -sa adj. fickle
ve-lo m. viel
ve-lo-ci-dad f. velocity
ve-loz adj. swift
ve-llo m. fuzz
ve-llon m. sheepskin
ve-llu-do, -da adj. hairy
ve-na f. vein
ve-na-blo m. javelin
ve-na-do m. venison
ven-ce-dor, -ra m., f. conqueror
ven-cer v. to conquer; to beat another
ven-ci-do, -da adj. conquered; defeated
ven-ci-mien-to m. defeat; collapse

ven-da-je *m.* bandage
ven-dar *v.* to bandage
ven-de-dor, -ra *m., f.* seller
ven-der *v.* to sell
ven-di-mia-dor, -ar *m., f.* one who picks grapes
ve-ne-no *m.* poison
ve-ne-no-si-dad *f.* poisonousness
ve-ne-no-so, -sa *adj.* poisonous
ve-ne-ra-ble *adj.* venerable
ve-en-ra-ción *f.* veneration
ve-ne-rar *v.* to venerate
ven-gan-za *f.* revenge; vengeance
ven-gar *v.* to avenge
ve-nia *f.* forgiveness
ve-nial *adj.* venial
ve-ni-da *f.* return
ve-ni-de-ro, -ra *adj.* upcoming
ve-nir *v.* to come
ven-ta *f.* sale
ven-ta-ja *f.* benefit
ven-ta-jo-so, -sa *adj.* advantageous
ven-ta-na *f.* window
ven-ti-la-ción *f.* ventilation
ven-ti-la-dor *m.* fan
ven-ti-lar *v.* to air
ven-tis-ca *f.* blizzard
ven-tis-que-ro *m.* blizzard
ven-to-si-dad *f.* gas
ven-to-so, -sa *adj.* windy
ven-tri-cu-lar *adj.* ventricular
ven-trí-cu-lo *m.* ventricle
ven-tri-lo-cuo, -a *m., f.* ventriloquist
ven-tu-ra *f.* happiness
ven-tu-ro-so, -sa *adj.* fortunate
ver *v.* to sight; to see
ve-ra *f.* edge
ve-ra-ci-dad *f.* veracity
ve-ra-ne-o *m.* vacationing
ve-ra-no *m.* summer
ve-ras *f.* earnestness
ve-raz *adj.* truthful
ver-bal *adj.* verbal
ver-bal-men-te *adv.* verbally
ver-bo *m.* verb
ver-bo-rre-a *f.* verbosity

ver-bo-si-dad *f.* verbosity
ver-bo-so, -sa *adj.* verbose
ver-dad *f.* truth
ver-da-de-ro, -ra *adj.* truthful
ver-de *adj.* green
ver-dor *m.* verdancy
ver-do-so, -sa *adj.* greenish
ver-du-ra *f.* greenery
ve-re-dic-to *m.* verdict
ver-gel *m.* orchard
ver-gon-zo-so, -sa *adj.* shameful
ver-güen-za *f.* shyness
ve-ri-di-co, -ca *adj.* true
ve-ri-fi-ca-ción *f.* verification
ve-ri-fi-ca-dor, -ra *m., f.* checker
ve-ri-fi-car *v.* to check on; to verify something
ver-mi-ci-da *adj.* vermicidal
ver-nal *adj.* vernal
ve-ro-si-mi-li-tud *f.* probability
ver-sa-do, -da *adj.* versed
ver-sa-til *adj.* versatile
ver-sa-ti-li-dad *f.* versatility
ver-sí-cu-lo *m.* versicle
ver-si-fi-car *v.* to versify
ver-sión *f.* version
ver-so *m.* verse
ver-te-bra *f.* vertebra
ver-te-bra-do, -da *adj.* vertebrate
ver-te-bral *adj.* vertebral
ver-ter *v.* to shed
ver-ti-cal *adj.* vertical
ver-ti-ca-li-dad *f.* verticality
ver-tien-te *f.* spring
vér-ti-go *m.* vertigo
ve-sí-cu-la *f.* vesicle
ve-si-cu-lar *adj.* vesicular
ves-ti-bu-lo *m.* vestibule
ves-ti-do *m.* clothing; dress
ves-ti-du-ra *f.* garment
ves-ti-gio *m.* vestige
ves-ti-men-ta *f.* clothes
ves-tir *v.* to attire; to wear; to dress
ve-tar *v.* to veto
ve-te-ar *v.* to streak
ve-te-ra-no, -na *m., f., adj.* veteran
ve-te-ri-na-rio, -ria *m., f.* vet-

erinarian

vez f. time

vi-a f. means; way

via-ble adj. viable

via-jar v. to journey; to travel

via-je m. journey; trip

vial adj. traffic

vian-da f. food

vi-bo-ra f. viper

vi-bra-ción f. vibration

vi-brar v. to shake; to vibrate

vi-ce-pre-si-den-cia f. vice-presidency

vi-ce-pre-si-den-te m. vice-president

vi-ciar v. to corrupt; to falsify; to pollute

vi-cio m. vice

vi-cio-so, -sa adj. depraved

vi-ci-si-tud f. vicissitude

vic-ti-ma f., m. victim

vic-to-ra-ar v. to cheer

vic-to-ria f. victory

vic-to-rio-so, -sa adj. victorious

vid f. grapevine

vi-da f. life

vi-de-o m. video

vi-de-o-ca-se-te m. videocassette

vi-de-o-cin-ta f. videotape

vi-dria-do, -da adj. glazed

vi-drie-ro, -ra m., f. glazier

vi-drio m. glass

vi-drio-so, -sa adj. glassy

vie-jo, -ja adj. aged; old

vien-to m. wind

vier-nes m. Friday

vi-gen-cia f. force

vi-gi-lan-cia f. vigilance

vi-gi-lan-te adj. heedful; vigilant

vi-gi-lar v. to guard

vi-gi-lia f. vigil

vi-gor m. strength; vigor

vi-go-ro-so, -sa adj. forceful; vigorous

vi-hue-la f. guitar

vi-le-za f. vileness

vi-lla f. village

vi-lla-no, -na adj. peasant

vi-na-gre m. vinegar

vi-na-gre-ta f. vinaigrette

vin-cu-lar v. to link

vin-di-ca-ción f. cindication

vin-di-car v. to vindicate

vi-ni-lo m. vinyl

vi-no m. wine

vi-ne-do m. vineyard

vio-la f. viola

vio-la-ce-o, -a adj. violet

vio-la-ción f. violation

vio-lar v. to violate

vio-len-cia f. violence; enbarrassment; rape

vio-len-tar tr. to force; to distort; to break into

vio-len-to, -ta adj. violent

vio-le-ta f., adf violet

vio-lín f. violin

vio-li-nis-ta m., f. violinist

vio-lón m. double bass player; double bass

vi-pe-ri-no, adj. venomous

vi-ra-je m. turning point; veering turn

vi-rar tr. to turn; to tone; to swerve

vir-gen adf., f. virgin

vir-il adj. virile

vir-tual adj. virtual

vi-ru-len-to, -ta adj. virulent

vi-rus m., inv. virus

vi-ru-ta f. shavings

vi-sar tr. to sight; to endorse

vis-co-si-dad f. viscosity

vi-se-ra f. visor

vi-si-llo m. windo curtain

vi-sión f. vision

vi-si-tar v. to visit

vis-ta f. sight; view

vis-to-so, -a adj. colorful

vi-sual adj. visual

vi-tal adj. vital

vi-ta-mi-na f. vitamin

vi-to-re-ar tr. to cheer

vi-tral m. stained-glass window

viu-da f. widow

viu-do m. widower

vi-vaz adj. lively

vi-ven-cia f. experience

vi-ve-res m., pl. provisions

vi-ve-ro m., BOT. fish hatchery; nursery

vi-ve-za f. liveliness;

sharpness; quickness
vi-vi-do, -da *adj.* vivid
vi-vien-da *f.* dwelling; housing
vi-vien-te *adj.* living
vi-vi-fi-ca-dor, -ra *adj.* vivifying
vi-vir *v.* to reside; to live
vi-vo, -va *adj.* vivid; lively
vo-ca-blo *m.* term
vo-ca-bu-la-rio *m.* vocabulary
vo-ca-ción *f.* job; occupation; vocation
vo-cal *adj.* vocal
vo-ca-li-za-ción *f.* vocalization
vo-ce-ar *intr., tr.* to shout
vo-ce-o *m.* shouting
vo-ce-ro, -a *m., f.* spokesman; spokeswoman
vo-la-da *f.* short flight
vo-lan-do *adv.* in a flash
vo-lan-te *adj.* balance wheel; steering wheel
vo-lar *v.* to fly; to blow up; to disappear
vo-la-tín *m.* acrobatic stunt
vo-la-ti-ne-ro, -a *m., f.* tightrope walker
vol-cán *m.* volcano
vo-le-ar ARG. to scatter
vo-li-ción *f.* volition
vol-ta-je *m.* voltage
vol-te-ar *v.* to upset; to turn over
vol-te-re-ta *f.* somersault
vol-tí-me-tro *m.* voltmeter
vol-tio *m.* volt
vo-lu-ble *adj.* fickle; voluble
vo-lu-men *m.* volume
vo-lun-tad *f.* will; wish; intention
vo-lun-ta-rio, -ria *adj.* voluntary
vo-lun-ta-rio-so, -a *adj.* willing; willful
vo-lup-tuo-si-dad *f.* voluptuousness
vol-ver *v.* to turn; to return; to recur; to restore
vo-mi-tar *tr.* to spew; to vomit; to spill
vo-mi-ti-vo, -a *adj., m.* vomi-

tive
vo-ra-ci-dad *f.* voracity
vo-ra-gi-ne *f.* whirlpoool
vo-ra-gi-no-so, -a *adj.* turbulent
vo-raz *adj.* voracious
vór-ti-ce *m.* center of a cyclone; vortex
vos *pron., m., f.* you
vo-se-ar *tr.* to address
vo-se-o *m.* used in addressing someone
vo-so-tras *pron., f.* you
vo-so-tros *pron., m.* you
vo-ta-ción *f.* voting; vote
vo-tan-te *m., f.* voter
vo-tar *v.* to vote
vo-ti-vo *adj.* votive
voz *f.* voice
vo-za-rrón *m.* booming voice
vuel-co *m.* to overturn; overturning
vue-lo *m.* flight
vuel-to, -a *m., f.* revolution
vues-tra *adj.* your
vul-ca-ni-zar *tr.* to vulcanize
vul-gar *adj.* vulgar; common
vul-ga-ri-dad *f.* vulgarity
vul-ga-ris-mo *m.* vulgarism
vul-ga-ri-zar *tr.* to popularize; to vulgarize
vul-go *m.* masses
vul-ne-ra-bi-li-dad *f.* vulnerability
vul-ne-rar *tr.* to violate; to wound
vul-va *f.* vulva

wat *m.* watt
wel-ter *m.* welterweight
whis-ky *m.* whiskey

xe-no-fo-bia *f.* xenophobia
xi-ló-fo-no *m.* xylophone
xi-lo-gra-fí-a *f.* xylography

ya-ca-fe *m.* alligator
ya-cer *intr.* to lie; to be
ya-guar *m.* jaguar
yam-bi-co *adj.* iambic
yan-qui *adj., m., f.* Yankee
yar-da *f.* yard
ya-te *m.* yacht
ye-gua-da *f.* herd of horses
yel-mo *m.* helmet
ye-ma *f.* yolk
yen *m., FIN.* yen
yer-ba *f.* grass
yer-bal *m. F.P.* field of mate
yer-mar *tr.* to strip
yer-mo, -a *adj.* barren
yer-no *m.* son-in-law
ye-rra *f.* cattle branding
ye-rro *m.* fault; sin
yer-to *adj.* frozen stiff
ye-se-ro *adj.* plaster
ye-so *m.* gypsum
yo *pron.* I; me
yo-da-do, -a *adj.* iodized
yo-da-to *m.* iodate
yo-do *m.* iodine
yo-du-ro *m.* iodide
yo-ga *m.* yoga
yo-g(h)i *m.* yogi
yo-gur(t) *m.* yogurt
yo-yo *m.* yo-yo
yu-ca *f.* manioc
yu-cal *m.* yucca field
yu-do *m.* judo
yuu-ga-da *f.* day's plowing;
  yoke
yu-gu-lar *adj., f.* jugular
yun-que *m.* anvil
yun-ta *f.* yoke
yu-te *m.* jute

yux-ta-po-ner *tr* to juxtapose
yux-ta-po-si-cion *f.* jux-
  taposition
yu-yal *m.* weed patch
yu-yo *m.* weed
yu-yu-ba *f.* jujube

za-far(se) *v.* loosen
za-gal *m.* boy; lad
za-ga-la *f.* lass
za-ma-rro *m.* sheepskin
zam-bu-lli-da *f.* dive
zam-bu-llir *v.* plunge into
za-na-ho-ria *f.* carrot
zan-ja *f.* trench; ditch
za-pa-te-ria *f.* shoestore
za-pa-te-ro *m.* shoemaker
za-pa-ti-lla *v.* slipper
za-pa-to *m.* shoe
zar *m.* czar
za-ri-na *f.* czarina
zar-za-mo-ra *f.* blackberry
zo-co *adj.* left-handed
zo-dia-co *m.* zodiac
zo-na *f.* zone
zoo-lo-gia *f.* zoology
zoo-lo-gi-co *adj.* zoological
zoo-lo-go *m.* zoologist
zo-rra *f.* fox
zo-rro *m.* fox
zo-zo-brar *v.* overturn
zum-bar *v.* whirr; buzz
zu-mo *m.* juice
zu-mo-so *adj.* juicy
zur-cir *v.* stitch

a *indef. article* una; un
a-back *adv.* atras
a-ba-cus *n.* ábaco
a-ban-don *v.* abandonar
a-base *v.* humillar; rebajar
a-bate *v.* disminuir; reducir
ab-bey *n.* monasterio
ab-bre-vi-a-tion *n.* abreviación
ab-di-cate *v.* abdicar
ab-do-men *n.* abdomen
ab-duct *v.* secuestrar
ab-er-ra-tion *n.* aberración
a-bet *v.* instigar; ayudar
ab-hor *v.* aborrecer
a-bide *v.* habitar; soportar
a-bil-i-ty *n.* habilidad
ab-ject *adj.* abyecto
ab-jure *v.* abjurar
a-ble *adj.* capaz; competente
ab-ne-gate *v.* renunciar; negar
ab-nor-mal *adj.* anormal
a-board *adv.,prep.* a bordo
a-bode *n.* domicilio
a-bol-ish *v.* abolir
a-bom-i-nate *v.* abominar
ab-o-rig-i-nes *n.* aborigenes
a-bor-tion *n.* aborto
a-bound *v.* abundar
a-bout *prep.* sobre; alrededor de
a-bove *prep.* sobre; encima de
a-bra-sion *n.* abrasión
a-bra-sion *n.* abrasión
a-breast *adv.* de frente; al lado
a-bridge *v.* abreviar; resumir
a-broad *adv.* fuera de casa; en el extranjero
ab-ro-gate *v.* abrogar
ab-rupt *adj.* brusco
ab-scess *n.* absceso
ab-scond *v.* fugarse
ab-sent *adj.* ausente
ab-so-lute *adj.* completo; absoluto
ab-solve *v.* absolver
ab-sorb *v.* absorber
ab-stain *v.* abstenerse
ab-ste-mi-ous *adj.* abstemio
ab-stract *v.* abstraer
ab-surd *adj.* absurdo

a-bun-dant *adj.* abundante
a-buse *v.* abstraer
a-but *v.* confinar
a-byss *n.* abismo
ac-a-dem-ic *adj.* academico
a-cad-e-my *n.* academia
ac-cede *v.* acceder; consentir; subir
ac-cel-er-ate *v.* acelerar
ac-cent *n.* acento
ac-cept *v.* recibir
ac-cess *n.* acceso
ac-ces-si-ble *adj.* accesible
ac-ces-so-ry *n.,pl.* accesorios; complice
ac-ci-dent *n.* accidente
ac-claim *v.* aclamar
ac-cli-mate *v.* aclimatar
ac-co-lade *n.* acolada
ac-com-mo-date *v.* acomodar
ac-com-pa-ny *v.* acompanar
ac-com-plice *n.* cómlice
ac-com-plish *v.* cumplir; acabar
ac-cord *n.* acuerdo
ac-cor-di-on *n.* acordéon
ac-count *v.* explicar
ac-count-a-ble *adj.* responsable
ac-cum-u-late *v.* acumular
ac-cu-ra-cy *n.* exactitude
ac-cu-rate *adj.* exacto; fiel
ac-cuse *v.* acusar; culpar
ac-cus-tom *v.* acostumbrar
a-ce-tic *adj.* acetico
ac-c-tone *n.* acetone
ache *n.* dolor
a-chieve *v.* acabar
ac-id *adj.* ácido
ac-knowl-edge *v.* reconocer; confesar; agradecer
ac-me *n.* cima
ac-ne *n.* acne
ac-o-lyte *n.* acolito
a-corn *n.* bellota
a-cous-tics *n.* acustica
ac-quaint *v.* enterar
ac-quaint-ance *n.* conocido
ac-qui-esce *v.* consentir
ac-quire *v.* adquirir
ac-quit *v.* absolver
a-cre *n.* acre

ac-rid *adj.* acre
ac-ri-mo-ny *n.* acrimonia
ac-ro-bat *n.* acrobata
a-cross *prep.* a traves de
act *v.* fingir; hacer
ac-tion *n.* acción
ac-ti-vate *v.* activar
ac-tive *adj.* activo
ac-tor *n.* actor
ac-tress *n.* actriz
ac-tu-al *adj.* actual; real
a-cu-i-ty *n.* agudeza
a-cu-men *n.* agudeza
a-cute *adj.* agudo; fino
ad-age *n.* adagio
ad-a-mant *adj.* firme
a-dapt *v.* adaptar
add *v.* sumar; anadir
ad-di-tion *n.* adición
ad-dress *v.* dirigir (se a)
a-dept *n., adj.* experto
ad-e-quate *adj.* adecuado;
suficiente
ad-here *v.* adherirse;
pegarse; cumplir
ad-he-sive *adj., n.* adhesivo
ad-ja-cent *adj.* adyacente
ad-jec-tive *n.* adjetivo
ad-join *v.* juntar; estar con-
tiguo
ad-journ *v.* suspender
ad-judge *v.* juzgar; senten-
ciar
ad-just *v.* ajustar; adaptar
ad-ju-tant *n.* ayudante
ad-lib *v.* improvisar
admin-is-ter *v.* administrar
ad-min-is-tra-tion *n.* ad-
ministración
ad-mire *v.* admirar
ad-mis-si-ble *adj.* admisible
ad-mis-sion *n.* entrada;
confesion
ad-mit *v.* confesar; admitir
ad-mon-ish *v.* amonestar
a-do-be *n.* adobe
ad-o-les-cence *n.* adoles-
cencia
a-dopt *v.* adoptar; aceptar
a-dore *v.* adorar
a-dorn *v.* adornar
a-dren-a-line *n.* adrenalina
a-droit *adj.* habil; diestro

ad-u-la-tion *n.* adulación
a-dult *adj.* mayor
a-dul-ter-y *n.* adulterio
ad-vance *v.* avanzar
ad-van-tage *n.* ventaja
ad-ven-ture *n.* aventura
ad-ven-ture-some *adj.* aven-
turado
ad-verb *n.* adverbio
ad-ver-sar-y *n.* adversario
ad-verse *adj.* adverso; con-
trario
ad-ver-si-ty *n.* adversidad
ad-ver-tise *v.* publicar
ad-vice *n.* consejo
ad-vise *v.* avisar
ad-vo-cate *v.* abogar
adz, adze *n.* azuela
ae-gis *n.* egido
aer-ate *v.* airear
aer-i-al *adj.* aereo
aer-o-naut-ics *n. pl.*
aeronautica
aes-thete *n.* esteta
aes-thet-ic *adj.* estetico
a-far *adv.* lejos
af-fa-ble *adj.* afable; cortes
af-fair *n.* amorosa
af-fect *v.* afectar
af-fec-ta-tion *n.* afectación
af-fec-tion *n.* afeccion
af-fec-tion-ate *adj.* carinoso
af-fi-ance *v.* desposarse
af-fi-da-vit *n.* declaración
jurada
af-fil-i-ate *v.* afiliar
af-fin-i-ty *n.* afinidad
af-firm *v.* afirmar
af-firm-a-tive *adj.* aserción
af-fix *v.* anadir; fijar
af-flic-tion *n.* aflicción
af-flu-ence *n.* afluencia
af-flu-ent *adj.* rico; opulento
af-ford *v.* tener medios para;
dar
af-front *v.* afrentar
a-fire *adj., adv.* ardiendo
a-flame *adj., adv.* en llamas
a-float *adj., adv.* a flote
a-foul *adj., adv.* enredado
a-fraid *adj.* atemorizado
a-fresh *adv.* de nuevo; otra
vez

aft *adj., adv.* en (a) popa
af-ter *prep.* detras de
af-ter-birth *n.* secundinas
af-ter-noon *n.* tarde
af-ter-ward *adv.* despues
a-gain *adv.* otra vez
a-gainst *prep.* contra
a-gape *adj., adv.* boqui-
abierto
age *n.* edad
a-ged *adj.* viejo
a-gen-cy *n.* agencia; accion;
medio
a-gen-da *n. pl.* orden del dia
a-gent *n.* agente; repre-
sentante
ag-glom-er-ate *v.* aglomerar
ag-gran-dize *v.* engrandcer
ag-gra-vate *v.* agravar
ag-gre-gate *v.* agregar; jun-
ter
ag-gres-sion *n.* agresión
ag-gres-sive *adj.* agresivo
a-ghast *adj.* horrorizado
a-gil *adj.* agil
a-gil-i-ty *n.* agilidad
ag-i-tate *v.* agitar; inquietar
a-glow *adj.* ardiente
ag-nos-tic *n.* agnostico
a-go *adj.* pasado
ag-o-ny *n.* agonia; angustia
a-grar-i-an *adj.* agrario
a-gree *v.* acordar
a-gree-a-ble *adj.* agradable;
conforme
a-gree-ment *n.* acuerdo
ag-ri-cul-ture *n.* agricultura
a-gron-o-my *n.* agronomia
a-ground *adv.* encallado
a-head *adv.* al frente
aid *n.* ayuda
ail-ment *n.* enfermedad;
dolencia
aim *v.* aspirar
air *n.* aire
air con-di-tion-er *n.* acon-
dicionador de aire
air-plane *n.* avion
air-port *n.* aeropuerto
air-raid *n.* ataque aereo
air-y *adj.* ligero; alegre
aisle *n.* nave lateral; pasillo
a-jar *adj., adv.* entreabierto

a-kin *adj.* semejante; con-
sanguineo
al-a-bas-ter *n.* alabastro
a-lac-ri-ty *n.* alacridad
a-larm *n.* alarma
a-larm-ist *n.* alarmista
al-ba-tross *n.* albatros
al-be-it *conj.* aunque
al-bi-no *n.* albino
al-bum *n.* album
al-bu-men *n.* albumen
al-bu-min *n.* albumina
al-che-my *n.* alquimia
al-co-hol *n.* alcohol
ale *n.* cerveza
a-lee *adv.* a sotavento
a-lert *adj.* alerte
al-fal-fa *n.* alfalfa
al-ga *n.* alga
al-ge-bra *n.* algebra
a-li-as *n.* alias
al-i-bi *n.* coartada; excusa
al-ien *n.* extranjero
al-ien-ate *v.* enajenar
a-light *v.* bajar; posarse
a-lign *v.* alinera; aliar
a-like *adj.* semejante
al-i-ment *n.* alimento
al-i-men-ta-ry *adj.* alimen-
ticio
al-i-mo-ny *n.* alimentos
a-live *adj.* activo
al-ka-lize *v.* alcalizar
all *adj.* todo
al-lay *v.* aliviar; aquietar
al-le-ga-tion *n.* alegación
al-lege *v.* alegar; declarar
al-leged *adj.* supuesto;
alegado
al-le-giance *n.* lealtad
al-le-go-ry *n.* alegoria
al-ler-gy *n.* alergia
al-le-vi-ate *v.* calmar
al-le-vi-a-tion *n.*
aligeramiento
al-ley *n.* callejuela
al-li-ance *n.* alianza
al-li-ga-tor *n.* caiman
al-lo-cate *v.* asignar
al-lo-ca-tion *n.* reparto; cupo
al-lot *v.* asignar; distribuir;
adjudicar
al-low *v.* dar; permitir

al-low-ance n. ración; per-
  mision
al-loy n. aleación
al-lude v. aludir
al-lure v. tentar
al-lu-sion n. alusion
al-lu-vi-um n. derrubio
al-ly n. aliado; confederado
al-ma-nac n. almanaque
al-might-y adj. omnipotente;
  todopoderoso
al-mond n. almendra; al-
  mendro
al-most adv. casi
alms n. limosna
a-loft adv. en alto
a-lone adj. solo
a-long adv., con., prep. a lo
  largo
a-loof adv. lejos reservado
a-loud adv. en voz alta; alto
al-pha-bet n. alfabeto
al-read-y adv. ya
al-so adv. también; ademas
al-tar n. altar
al-ter v. cambiar; alterar;
  modificar
al-ter-a-tion n. alteración
al-ter-ca-tion n. altercación
al-ter e-go n. alter ego
al-ter-nate v. alternar
al-ter-na-tive n. alternativa
al-though conj. aunque
al-tim-e-ter n. altimetro
al-ti-tude n. altura; altitude
al-to n. alto; contralto
al-to-geth-er adv. en total
a-lu-mi-num n. aluminio
a-lum-na n., f. graduada
a-lum-nus n. graduado
al-ways adv. siempre
a.m. antemeridiano
a-mal-gam n. amalgama
a-mal-gam-ate v. amal-
  gamar
a-mass v. acumular; amon-
  tonar
am-a-teur n. aficionada
am-a-to-ry adj. amatorio
a-maze v. asombrar
a-maze-ment n. sorpresa
am-a-zon n. amazona
am-bas-sa-dor n. embajador

am-ber n. ambar
am-bi-dex-trous adj. am-
  bidextro
am-bi-gu-i-ty n. am-
  biguedad; doble sentido
am-big-u-ous adj. ambiguo
am-bi-tion n. ambición
am-bi-tious adj. ambicioso
am-biv-a-lence n. am-
  bivalencia
am-ble v. amblar; andar len-
  tamente
am-bu-late v. andar
am-bu-la-to-ry a. ambulante
am-bus-cade n. emboscada
am-bush n. emboscada;
  docil; respinsable
a-me-ba n. amiba
a-mel-io-rate v. mejorar
a-mel-io-ra-tion n. mejora;
  mejoramiento
a-men int. amen
a-me-na-ble adj. docil
a-mend v. enmendar; cor-
  regir
a-mends n., pl. compen-
  sación
a-men-i-ty n. amenidad
A-mer-i-can adj. americano
am-e-thyst n. amatista
a-mi-a-ble adj. amable
am-i-ca-ble adj. amistoso
a-mid prep. en medio de;
  entre.
a-mid-ships adv. en medio
  del navio
a-miss adv., adj. im-
  propiamente; mel
am-mo-nia n. municion
am-ne-sia n. amnesia
am-nes-ty n. amniastia
a-moe-ba n. amiba
a-mong prep. en medio de
a-mor-al adj. amoral
am-o-rous adj. amoroso
a-mor-phous adj. amoroso
am-or-tize v. amortizar
a-mount n. cantidad; suma
am-pere n. amperio *
am-phib-i-an adj., n. anfibio
am-phib-i-ous adj. anfibio
am-phi-the-a-ter n. an-
  fiteatro

am-ple *adj.* abundante
am-pli-fy *v.* amplificar
am-pli-tude *n.* amplitud; abundancia
am-pu-tate *v.* amputar
am-pu-ta-tion *n.* amputación
a-muck *adv.* furiosamente
am-u-let *n.* amuleto
a-muse-ment *n.* pasatiempo
an *indef. article* una; un; uno
a-nach-ro-nism *n.* anacronismo
an-a-con-da *n.* anaconda
a-nae-mi-a *n.* anemia
an-a-gram *n.* anagrama
a-nal *adj.* anal
an-al-ge-sic *adj.* analgesico
a-nal-o-gize *v.* analogizar
a-nal-o-gy *n.* analogia
a-nal-y-sis *n.* analisis
an-a-lyst *n.* analizador
an-a-lyze *v.* analizar
an-ar-chism *n.* anarquismo
an-ar-chist *n.* anarquista
an-ar-chy *n.* anarquia
a-nat-o-my *n.* anatomia
an-ces-tor *n.* antepasado
an-ces-try *n.* linaje; abolengo
an-chor *n.* ancla; ancora
an-cho-vy *n.* anchoa
an-cient *adj.* antiguo
and *conj.* y
an-ec-dote *n.* anecdota
a-ne-mi-a *n.* anemia
an-e-mon-e-ter *n.* anemometro
an-es-the-sia *n.* anestesia
an-es-thet-ic *n., adj.* anestesico
a-new *adv.* de nuevo; otra vez
an-gel *n.* angel
an-gel-ic *adj.* angelico
an-ger *n.* ira; colera
an-gle *n.* angulo
an-gle-worm *n.* lombriz
An-glo-Sax-on *v., adj.* anglosajon
an-gor-a *n.* angora
an-gry *adj.* enfadado
an-guish *n.* angustia; ansioa
an-gu-lar *adj.* angular; an-

guloso
an-hy-drous *adj.* anhidro
an-i-mad-ver-sion *n.* animadversion
an-i-mad-vert *v.* censurar
an-i-mal *n.* animal
an-i-mal-ize *v.* animalizar
an-i-mate *v.* dar vida
an-i-ma-tion *n.* animación
an-i-mos-i-ty *n.* animosidad
an-ise *n.* anis
an-kle *n.* tobillo
an-nals *n., pl.* anales
an-neal *v.* templar
an-nex *v.* anexar; adjuntar
an-nex-a-tion *n.* anexión
an-ni-hi-late *v.* aniquilar
an-ni-hi-la-tion *n.* aniquilación
an-ni-ver-sa-ry *n.* aniversario
an-no-tate *v.* anotar
an-nounce *v.* proclamar
an-nounce-ment *n.* anuncio
an-noy *v.* molestar
an-noy-ance *n.* fastidio
an-nu-al *adj.* anual
an-nu-i-ty *n.* renta vitalicia
an-nul *v.* anular
an-nul-ment *n.* anulación
an-nun-ci-ate *v.* anunciar
an-nun-ci-a-tion *n.* anunciación
an-ode *n.* anodo
a-noint *v.* untar; ungir
a-nom-a-lous *adj.* anomalo
a-nom-a-ly *n.* anomalia
a-non-y-mous *adj.* anonimo
an-oth-er *adj., pron.* otro
an-swer *v.* contestar; responder
ant *n.* hormiga
ant-ac-id *n.* antiacido
an-tag-o-nist *n.* antagonista
an-tag-o-nize *v.* contender
ant-arc-tic *adj.* antartico
ant-eat-er *n.* oso hormiguero
an-te-cede *v.* anteceder
an-te-ced-ent *n.* antecedente
an-te-date *v.* antedatar; preceder
an-te-di-lu-ve-an *adj.* antediluviano

an-te-lope *n.* antilope
an-ten-na *n.* antena
an-te-ri-or *adj.* anterior
an-te-room *n.* antecamara
an-them *n.* antifona. na-tion-al an-them himno nacional
an-ther *n.* antera
an-thol-o-gy *n.* antologia
an-thra-cite *n.* antracita
an-thrax *n.* antrax
an-thro-poid *adj.* antropoide
an-thro-pol-o-gist *n.* antropologo
an-thro-pol-o-gy *n.* antropologia
an-ti *prefix* anti; contra
an-ti-bi-ot-ic *n.* antibiotico
an-ti-bod-y *n.* anticuerpo
an-tic *n.* travewura; cabriola
an-tic-i-pate *v.* anticipar; esperar
an-tic-i-pa-tion *n.* anticipacion; expectacion
an-ti-cli-max *n.* anticlimax
an-ti-dote *n.* antidoto
an-tip-a-thy *n.* antipatia
an-tip-odes *n.* antipoda
an-ti-quate *v.* anticuar
an-ti-quat-ed *adj.* viejo; anticuado
an-tique *adj.* antiguo
an-tiq-ui-ty *n.* antiguedad
an-ti-Sem-i-tism *n.* antisemitismo
an-ti-sep-tic *adj., n.* antiseptico
an-ti-so-cial *adj.* antisocial
an-tith-e-sis *n.* antitesis
an-ti-tox-in *n.* antitoxina
ant-ler *n.* cuerna; asta
an-to-nym *n.* antonimo
a-nus *n.* ano
an-vil *n.* yunque
anx-i-e-ty *n.* inquietud; ansia
anx-ious *adj.* impaciente
an-y *adj., pron.* alguno; algun
an-y-bod-y *pron.* alguien
an-y-how *adv.* de cualquier modo; de todas formas
an-y-one *pron.* alguien; alguno
an-y-thing *pron.* algo

an-y-way *adv.* de cualquier modo; de todas formas
an-y-where *adv.* en todas partes; dondequiera
a-or-ta *n.* aorta
a-part *adv.* aparte. a-part from aparte de
a-part-ment *n.* apartamento
ap-a-thet-ic *adj.* indiferente
ap-a-thy *n.* apatia
ape *n.* mono
ap-er-ture *n.* abertura
a-pex *n.* apice
aph-o-rism *n.* aforismo
aph-ro-dis-i-ac *n.* afrodisiaco
a-pi-a-rist *n.* colmenero
a-pi-ar-y *n.* colmenar
a-piece *adv.* cada uño; por persona
a-plomb *n.* aplomo
a-poc-a-lypse *n.* apocalipsis
a-pol-o-gize *v.* disculparse
a-pol-o-gy *n.* apologia; disculpa
ap-o-plec-tic *adj.* apopletico
ap-o-plex-y *n.* apoplejia
a-port *adv.* a babor
a-pos-tate *n.* apostata
a-pos-ta-tize *v.* apostatar
a-pos-tle *n.* apostol
ap-os-tol-ic *adj.* apostolico
a-pos-tro-phe *n.* apostrofo
a-poth-e-car-y *n.* boticario
ap-pall, ap-pal *v.* aterrar
ap-pa-rat-us *n.* aparato
ap-pa-rel *n.* ropa
ap-par-ent *a.* claro; aparente
ap-pa-ri-tion *n.* fantasma
ap-peal *n.* apelacion
ap-pear *v.* parecer
ap-pear-ance *n.* apariencia
ap-pease *v.* apaciguar
ap-pel-lant *n.* apelante
ap-pel-la-tion *n.* nombre
ap-pend *v.* anexar
ap-pen-dage *n.* apendice
ap-pen-dec-to-my *n.* apendectomia
ap-pen-di-ci-tis *n.* apendicitis
ap-pen-dix *n.* apendice
ap-per-tain *v.* pertenecer

ap-pe-tite n. gana

ap-pe-tiz-ing adj. apetitoso; apetitivo

ap-plaud v. aplaudir

ap-plause n. aplauso

ap-ple n. manzana

ap-pli-cant n. suplicante

ap-pli-ca-tion n. aplicación

ap-ply v. aplicar

ap-point v. senalar; nombrar

ap-point-ment n. cita; nombramiento

ap-por-tion v. repartir

ap-po-si-tion n. aposición

ap-prais-al n. valoración

ap-praise v. valorar

ap-pre-ci-ate v. apreciar; volorar; agradecer

ap-pre-ci-a-tion n. aprecio; aumento en valor

ap-pre-hend v. entender

ap-pre-hen-sion n. aprenhension

ap-pren-tice n. aprendiz, v. poner de aprendize

ap-prixe, ap-prize v. informar

ap-proach v. aproximarse

ap-pro-ba-tion n. aporobación

ap-pro-pri-ate v. apropiarse; destinar. adj. apropiado

ap-prov-al n. aprobación

ap-prove v. aprobar

ap-prox-i-mate v. aproximar

ap-ri-cot n. albaricoque

A-pril n. abril

a-pron n. delantal, m.

ap-ro-pos of prep. a proposito de

apt adj. apto; listo

ap-ti-tude n. aptitud

a-quar-i-um n. acuario

a-quat-ic adj. acuatico

aq-ue-duct n. acueducto

a-que-ous adj. acueo

aq-ui-line adj. aguileño

Ar-ab n., adj. arabe, m., f.

Ar-a-bic nu-me-rals n. numeros arabigos

ar-a-ble adj. labrantio; cultivable

ar-bi-ter n. arbitro

ar-bi-trar-y adj. arbitrario

ar-bi-trate v. arbitrar

ar-bi-tra-tion n. arbitraje

ar-bo-re-al adj. arboreo

ar-bo-re-tum n. · jardin botanico

arc n. arce. v. formar un arco voltaico

ar-cade n. arcada; galeria

arch n. arco. v. arquear

arch- prefix principal

ar-chae-ol-o-gy, ar-che-ol-o-gy n. arqueología

ar-cha-ic adj. arcaico

arch-an-gel n. arcangel

arch-bish-op n. arzobispo

arch-duch-ess n. archiduquest

arch-duke n. archiduque

arch-er n. arquero

ar-cher-y n. bailesteria

ar-che-type n. arquetipo

ar-chi-pel-a-go n. archipielago

ar-chi-tect n. arquitecto

ar-chi-tec-tur-al adj. arquitectonico

ar-chi-tec-ture n. arquitectura

ar-chive n. archivo

arch-priest n. arcipreste

arc-tic adj. artico

ar-dent adj. ardiente; fervoroso

ar-dor n. ardor

ar-du-ous adj. arduo; difícil

a-re-na n. areña

ar-gon n. argo

ar-got n. jerga

ar-gue v. razonar

ar-gu-ment n. disputa

ar-gu-men-ta-tive adj. argumentador

a-ri-a n. aria

ar-id adj. arido

a-rid-i-ty n. aridez

a-rise v. alzarse; surgir

ar-is-toc-ra-cy n. aristocracía

a-ris-to-crat n. aristocrata

a-ris-to-crat-ic adj. aristocratico

a-rith-me-tic n. aritmetica

a-rith-me-ti-cian n. arit-

metico
ark *n.* arca
arm *n.* brazo
ar-ma-da *n.* armada
ar-ma-dil-lo *n.* armadillo
ar-ma-ment *n.* armamento
arm-ful *n.* brazado
ar-mi-stice *n.* armisticio
ar-moire *n.* armario
ar-mor *n.* armadura
ar-mored *adj.* blindado
ar-mor-y *n.* armeria
arm-pit *n.* sobaco
ar-my *n.* ejercito
a-ro-ma *n.* aroma
ar-o-mat-ic *adj.* aromatico
a-round *adv.* alrededor
a-rouse *v.* despertar; excitar
ar-range *v.* arreglar; prevenir
ar-range-ment *n.* orden
ar-rant *adj.* consumado
ar-ray *n* orden; formación;
    adorno. *v.* colocar; ataviar
ar-rest *v.* detener
ar-ri-val *n.* llegada
ar-rive *v.* llegar
ar-ro-gance *n.* arrogancia
ar-ro-gant *adj.* arrogante
ar-row *n.* flecha
ar-row-head *n.* punta de
    lfecha
ar-sen-al *n.* arsenal
ar-sen-ic *n.* arsenico
ar-son *n.* incendio
    premeditado
art *n.* arte
ar-te-ri-al *adj.* arterial
ar-ter-y *n.* arteria
art-ful *adj.* ingenioso; astuto
ar-thrit-ic *adj.* artrico
ar-thri-tis *n.* artritis, *f.*
ar-ti-cle *n.* articulo; objeto
ar-tic-u-late *v.* articular
ar-tic-u-la-tion *n.* ar-
    ticulación
ar-ti-fi-cial *adj.* artificial
ar-til-ler-y *n.* artilleria
art-ist *n.* artista
ar-tis-tic *adj.* artistic
as *conj., adv.* como
as-bes-tos, as-bes-tus *n.*
    asbesto
as-cend *v.* subir; ascender

as-cen-sion *n.* ascensión
as-cent *n.* subida; cuesta
as-cer-tain *v.* averiguar
as-ce-tic *adj.* ascetico. *n.*
    asceta *m., f.*
as-cet-i-cism *n.* ascetismo
a-scribe *v.* atribuir
a-sex-u-al *adj.* asexual
ash *n.* ceniza; fresno
a-shamed *adj.* avergonzado
a-side *adv.* a un lado *n.*
    aparte
as-i-nine *adj.* asnal
ask *v.* rogar; preguntar
a-skance *adv.* con recelo
a-slant *adv.* al sesgo. *prep.*
    a traves de
a-sleep *adv., adj.* dormido
asp *n.* aspid
as-par-a-gus *n.* esparrago
as-pect *n.* aspecto; aire
as-per-i-ty *n.* aspereze
as-per-sion *n.* calumnia
as-phalt *n.* asfalto
as-phyx-i-ate *v.* asfixiar
as-phyx-i-a-tion *n.* asfixia
as-pi-ra-tion *n.* aspiración;
    anhelo
as-pire *v.* aspirar
as-pl-rin *n.* aspirina
ass *n.* burro; tonto
as-sail *v.* acometer
as-sail-ant *n.* asaltador
as-sas-in *n.* asesino
as-sas-si-na-tion *n.*
    asesinato
as-sault *v.* atacar
as-sem-ble *v.* juntar
as-sem-bly *n.* asamblea
as-sent *n.* asentimiento
as-sert *v.* afirmar
as-sess *v.* fijar; tasar
as-set *n.* haber
as-sev-er-ate *v.* aseverar
as-sid-u-ous *adj.* asiduo
as-sign *v.* asignar
as-sign-ment *n.* asignación
as-sim-i-late *v.* asimilar
as-sist *v.* ayudar
as-sist-ance *n.* ayuda
asth-ma *n.* asma
asth-mat-ic *adj.* asmatico
as-ton-ish *v.* asombrar

as-ton-ish-ment *n.* asombro
as-trol-o-gy *n.* astrología
as-tron-o-my *n.* astronomia
at *prep.* a; en
ath-lete *n.* atleta
ath-let-ic *adj.* atletico
at-om *n.* atomo
a-tom-ic *adj.* atomico
a-top *prep.* sobre
at-tach *v.* pegar; sujetar
at-tack *v.* atacar
at-tempt *v.* intentar
at-tend *v.* asistir
at-ten-tion *n.* atención
at-tract *v.* atraer
at-trac-tion *n.* atracción
a-typ-i-cal *adj.* atipico
au-di-ence *n.* publico
au-di-tion *n.* audición
au-di-to-ry *adj.* auditivo
Au-gust *n.* agosto
aunt *n.* tia
au-then-tic-i-ty *n.* autenticidad
au-thor *n.* autor
au-thor-i-ty *n.* autoridad
au-thor-ize *v.* autorizar
au-to-bi-og-ra-pher *n.* autobiografo
au-to-bi-og-ra-phy *n.* autobiografia
au-to-mat-ic *adj.* automatico
au-to-ma-tion *n.* automatización
au-to-mo-bile *n.* automovil; coche
au-ton-o-mous *a.* autonomo
a-venge *v.* vengar
av-e-nue *n.* avenida
a-ver *v.* afirmar
av-er-age *adj.* medio
a-vert *v.* apartar
a-wait *v.* esperar
a-wake *v.* despertar(se)
a-way *adv.* lejos
aw-ful *adj.* horrible
awk-ward *adj.* embarazoso
ax-i-om *n.* axioma
ax-i-o-mat-ic *adj.* axiomatico
ax-is *n.* axis; eje
ax-le *n.* eje
aye, ay *int., n.* si
az-ure *adj., n.* azul celeste

bab-ble *v.* murmurar; barbotar; susurrar
ba-boon *n.* mandril
ba-bush-ka *n.* pañuelo
ba-by *n.* nino
ba-by-hood *n.* infancia
ba-by-ish *adj.* infantil
bac-cha-nal *n.* bacanal
bach-e-lor *n.* soltero
bach-e-lor-hood *n.* solteria
ba-cil-lus *n.* bacilo
back *n.* espalda
back-ache *n.* dolor de espalda
back-bit-ing *n.* murmuración
back-bone *n.* espinazo
back-break-ing *adj.* agobiador
back-date *v.* antedatar
back-er *n.* promotor
back-gam-mon *n.* chaquete
back-ground *n.* fondo
back-hand-ed *adj.* ambiguo
back-lash *n.* sacudida
back-pack *n.* mochila
back-side *n.* trasero
back-stairs *adj.* furtivo
back-track *v.* desandar
back-up *n.* suplente; reserva
back-ward *adv.* atras
back-ward-ness *n.* retraso
ba-con *n.* tocino
bac-te-ri-al *adj.* bacteriaño
bac-te-ri-cide *n.* bactericida
bac-ter-i-um *n.* bacteria
bad *adj.* malo
badge *n.* insignia
bad-ger *n.* tejon
bad-ly *adv.* mal
bad-min-ton *n.* volante
baf-fle *v.* desconcertar; confundir
baf-fle-ment *n.* confusion
baf-fling *adj.* desconcertante
bag *n.* bolso; saco
bag-gage *n.* equipaje
bag-pipe *n.* gaita
bail *v.* afianzar
bail-iff *n.* alguacil
bail-or *n.* fiador
bait *n.* carnada
bake *v.* cocer en horno
bak-er *n.* panadero

bak-er-y *n.* panaderia
bak-ing *n.* cocción
bal-ance *n.* equilibrio
bal-anced *adj.* balanceado
bal-co-ny *n.* balcon
bald *adj.* calvo
bald-ness *n.* calcicie
bale *n.* bala
bale-ful *adj.* funesto
balk *v.* oponerse
ball *n.* pelota
bal-lad *n.* balada
bal-le-ri-na *n.* bailarina
bal-let *n.* ballet
bal-lis-tic *adj.* balistico
bal-loon *n.* globo
bal-lot *n.* votación
balm *n.* balsamo
bal-sa *n.* balsa
bam-boo *n.* bambu
ban *v.* prohibir
ba-nal *adj.* banal
ba-nan-a *n.* platano
band *n.* banda
band-age *v.* vendar
ban-dit *n.* bandido
ban-do-leer *n.* bandolera
bane-ful *adj.* nocivo
bang *v.* golpear
bangs *n.* flequillo
ban-gle *n.* esclava
ban-ish *v.* desterrar
ban-ish-ment *n.* proscripción; exilio
ban-is-ter *n.* baranda
ban-jo *n.* banjo
bank *n.* banco
bank-er *n.* banquero
bank-ing *n.* banca
bank-rupt *adj.* arruinado
ban-ner *n.* bandera
ban-quet *n.* banquete
ban-ter *f.* broma
bap-tism *n.* bautismo
bap-tist *n.* bautista
bap-tis-ter-y *n.* baptisterio
bap-tize *v.* bautizar
bar *v.* excluir
bar-br-i-an *adj.* barbaro
bar-bar-ic *adj.* barbaro
bar-bar-i-ty *n.* barbaridad
bar-ba-rous *adj.* barbaro
bar-ber *n.* peluquero

bar-ber-shop *n.* peluqueria
bar-bi-tu-rate *n.* barbiturico
bare *adj.* desnudo; *v.* des nudar
bare-faced *adj.* descarado
bare-ly *adv.* simplemente; apneas
bar-gain *n.* ganga; convenio
bar-gain-ing *n.* negociación
barge *n.* gabarra
bar-i-tone *n.* baritono
bar-i-um *n.* bario
bark *v.* ladrar; *n.* ladrido
bar-ley *n.* cebada
bar-maid *n.* cantinera
barn *n.* granero
bar-na-cle *n.* percebe
ba-rom-et-er *n.* barometro
bar-o-met-ric *adj.* baro-metrico
bar-on *n.* baron
bar-on-ess *n.* baronesa
ba-roque *adj.* barroco
bar-racks *n.* barraca
bar-rel *n.* barril
bar-ren *adj.* infecundo; infructuoso; yermo
bar-ri-cade *n.* barricada
bar-ri-er *n.* barrear
bar-tend-er *n.* camarero
bar-ter *v.* trocar
bas-al *adj.* basico
ba-salt *n.* basalto
base *n.* base
base-ball *n.* béisbol
base-board *n.* zocalo
base-less *adj.* infundado
base-ment *n.* sotaño
bash *v.* golpear
bash-ful *adj.* timido
ba-sic *adj.* basico
ba-sic-i-ty *n.* basicidad
bas-il *n.* albahaca
ba-sil-i-ca *n.* basilica
ba-sin *n.* jofaina
ba-sis *n.* base
bask *v.* complacerse
bas-ket *n.* cesta
bas-ket-ball *n.* baloncesto
bas-ket-ry *n.* cesteria
baste *v.* hilvanar
bat *v.* golpear; *n.* maza
batch *n.* hornada

bate v. disminuir
bath n. baño
bathe v. bañar(se)
bath-ing suit n. traje de bano
bath-tub n. bañera
ba-ton n. batuta
bat-tal-ion n. batallon
bat-ter v. estropear; golpear
bat-ter-y n. bateria
bat-tle v. luchar, n. lucha
bat-tle-ground n. campo de batalla
bat-tle-ship n. acorazado
bau-ble n. baratija
baud n. baudio
bawl v. llorar
bay n. bahia
bay-o-net n. bayoneta
ba-zaar n. bazar
ba-zoo-ka n. bazuca
be v. estar; ser
beach n. playa
bea-con n. almenara; faro
bead n. abalorio
beak n. pico
beam n. rayo
bean n. frijol; habichuela
bear n. oso; v. llevar
bear-a-ble adj. soportable
beard n. barba
beard-ed adj. barbudo
bear-er n. portador
bear-ing n. porte
beast n. bestia
beast-ly adj. bestial
beat v. vencer; golpear
beat-en adj. derrotado
beat-er n. batidor
be-a-tif-ic adj. beatifico
be-at-i-fy v. beatificar
beat-ing n. latido; paliza
be-at-i-tude n. beatitud
beau-ti-ful adj. hermoso
beau-ti-ful-ly adj. ballamente
beau-ti-fy v. embellecer
beau-ty n. belleza
bea-ver n. castor
be-cause conj. porque
beck-on v. llamar
be-come v. hacer(se)
be-com-ing adj. apropiado
bed n. cama

be-daz-zle v. deslumbrar
bed-cham-ber n. alcoba
bed-lam n. alboroto
bed-room n. alcoba
bed-side adj. (de) cabecera
bee n. abeja
beech n. haya
beef-y adj. musculoso
bee-hive n. colmena
beer n. cerveza
bees-wax n. cera
beet n. remolacha
bee-tle n. escarabajo
be-fit v. convenir
be-fit-ting adj. conveniente
be-fore prep. antes de, adv. delante
be-fore-hand adv. antes
be-fud-dle v. confundir
beg v. pedir
beg-gar n. pobre
beg-gar-ly adj. misero
be-gin v. comenzar
be-gin-ner n. novato
be-gin-ning n. comienzo
be-grudge v. envidiar
be-guile v. seducir
be-have v. funcionar; comportarse
be-hav-ior n. comportamiento
be-head v. descabezar
be-hind adv. atras; detras; prep. detras de
be-hold v. contemplar
be-hold-en adj. obligado
be-hoove v. convenir
beige adj. beige
be-ing n. ser
be-la-bor v. machacar
be-lat-ed adj. tardio
be-lief n. fe
be-liev-a-ble adj. creible
be-lieve v. creer
be-liev-er n. creyente
bell n. cascabel
bellflower n. campanilla
bel-li-cose adj. belicoso
bel-lig-er-ence n. beligerancia
bel-lig-er-ent adj. beligerante
bel-low v. rugir

bel-ly *n.* estomago
be-long *v.* estar
be-long-ings *n.* pertenencias
be-lov-ed *adj.* querido
be-low *adv.* abajo, *prep.* debajo de
belt *n.* cinturon
be-moan *v.* lamentar
bench *n.* banco
bend *v.* doblar; inclinar
bend-er *n.* juerga
be-neath *prep.* debajo de
ben-e-dic-tion *n.* bendición
ben-e-fac-tor *n.* benefactor
ben-e-fice *n.* beneficio
be-nef-i-cent *adj.* benefico
ben-e-fi-cial *adj.* beneficioso
ben-e-fi-ci-ar-y *n.* beneficiario
ben-e-fit *n.* beneficio
be-nev-o-lence *n.* benevolencia
be-nev-o-lent *adj.* benevolo
be-nign *adj.* benigno
bent *adj.* empenado; torcido
be-numb *v.* entorpecer
be-queath *v.* legar
be-quest *n.* legado
be-rate *v.* reprender
be-reave-ment *n.* duelo
be-reft *adj.* privado
ber-ry *n.* baya
berth *n.* camarote
be-ryl-li-um *n.* berilio
be-seech *v.* implorar
be-set *v.* acosar
be-side *prep.* cerca
be-sides *prep.* ademas de
be-siege *v.* asediar
be-smirch *v.* manchar
best *adj.* mejor
bes-tial *adj.* bestial
bes-ti-al-i-ty *n.* bestialidad
be-stow *v.* conceder
bet *n.* apuesta
be-to-ken *v.* presagiar
be-tray *v.* revelar
be-tray-al *n.* traición
be-trothed *n.* novio
bet-ter *adv., adj.* mejor
bet-ter-ment *n.* mejoramiento
bet-tor *n.* apostador

be-tween *adv.* en medio; *prep.* entre
bev-eled *adj.* biselado
bev-er-age *n.* bebida
bev-y *n.* grupo
be-wail *v.* lamentar
be-wil-der *v.* aturdir
be-wil-der-ment *n.* aturdimiento
be-witch *v.* hechizar
be-witch-ment *n.* hechizo
be-yond *prep.* despues de
bi-an-nu-al *adj.* semestral
bi-as *n.* prejuicio
bib *n.* babero
Bi-ble *n.* Biblia
Bib-li-cal *adj.* biblico
bib-li-og-ra-pher *n.* bibliografo
bib-li-og-ra-phy *n.* bibliografia
bib-li-o-phile *n.* bibliofilo
bi-car-bon-ate *n.* bicarbonato
bi-cen-ten-ni-al *adj.* bicentario
bi-ceps *n.* biceps
bi-cy-cle *n.* bicicleta
bi-cy-clist *n.* biciclista
bid *n.* oferta; *v.* mandar
bid-ding *n.* oferta
bi-en-ni-al *adj.* bienal
bi-fo-cal *adj.* bifocal
bi-fur-cate *v.* bifurcarse
bi-fur-ca-tion *n.* bifurcación
big *adj.* grande
big-a-mist *n.* bigamo
big-a-my *n.* bigamia
big-ness *n.* grandeza
bike *n.* bicicleta
bik-er *n.* motociclista
bi-lat-er-al *adj.* bilateral
bile *n.* bilis
bi-lin-gual *adj.* bilingue
bil-ious *adj.* bilioso
bilk *v.* defraudar
bill *n.* pico; cuenta
bill-board *n.* cartelera
bil-let *v.* alojar
bill-fold *n.* cartera
bil-liards *n.* billar
bil-lion *n.* billon
bil-lion-aire *n.* billonario**

bil-low n. oleada
bil-low-y adj. ondulante
bi-month-ly adj. bimestram
bin n. cajon
bi-na-ry adj. binario
bind v. encuadernar; atar
bind-er n. atadura; encuadernador
bind-ing n. encuadernación
bin-oc-u-lar n. gemelos
bi-no-mi-al adj. binomio
bi-o-chem-i-cal adj. bioquimico
bi-o-chem-ist n. bioquimico
bi-o-chem-is-try n. bioquimica
bi-og-ra-pher n. biografo
bi-o-graph-ic adj. biografico
bi-og-ra-phy n. biografia
bi-o-log-ic adj. biologico
bi-ol-o-gist n. biologo
bi-ol-o-gy n. biologia
bi-on-ics n. bionica
bi-o-phys-ics n. biofisica
bi-op-sy n. biopsia
bi-par-tite adj. bipartito
bi-ped adj. bipedo
bi-plane n. biplaño
birch n. abedul
bird n. pajaro
bird-cage n. jaula
bird-seed n. alpiste
birth n. nacimiento
birth-day n. cumpleanos
bis-cuit n. bizcocho
bi-sect v. bisecar
bi-sec-tion n. bisección
bish-op n. obispo
bis-muth n. bismuto
bi-son n. bisonte
bit n. pedazo
bite v. picar
bit-ing adj. mordaz; cortante
bit-ter adj. cortante; implacable; amargo
bit-ter-ness n. rencor; encarnizamiento
bit-ter-sweet adj. agridulce
bi-tu-mi-nous adj. bituminoso
bi-va-lent adj. bivalente
bi-valve adj. bivalvo
bi-week-ly adj. quincenal

bi-zarre adj. raro
blab-ber v. cotorrear
black adj. negro
black-and-blue adj. amoratado
black-ber-ry n. zarzamora
black-bird n. mirlo
black-board n. pizarra
black-en v. difamar
black-head n. grano
black-mail v. chantajear
black-mail-er n. chantajista
black-smith n. herrero
black-top n. asfalto
blad-der n. vejiga
blade n. pala; hoja
blame v. culpar
bland adj. insulso
blank n., adj. blanco
blan-ket n. manta
blare v. resonar
blas-pheme v. blasfemar
blas-phe-mous adj. blasfemo
blas-phe-my n. blasfemia
blast v. destruir; n. explosion
blast-ed adj. maldito
bla-tant adj. patente
blaze n. joguera; llamarada; v. arder
bleach n. lejia; v. blanquear
bleach-ers n. gradas
blear adj. sombrio; frio
bleat v. balar
bleed v. sangrar
blem-ish v. manchar
blend n. mezcla; v. mezclar
blend-er n. licuadora
bless v. bandecir
bless-ed adj. santo
bless-ing n. bendición
blind v. cegar; adj. ciego
blind-ers n. anteojeras
blind-ing adj. cegador
blind-ly adv. ciegamente
blind-ness n. ceguera
blink v. pestanear; ceder
blink-ing adj. parpadeante
bliss n. felicidad
bliss-ful adj. feliz
blis-ter v. ampollar(se)
blis-ter-ing adj. forzado;

abrasador
bliz-zard *n.* ventisca
block *n.* manzana
block-ade *adj.* bloqueo
block-age *n.* obstrucción
blond *adj.* rubio
blonde *adj.* rubia
blood *n.* sangre
blood-less *adj.* exangue
blood-thirst-y *adj.* sanguinario
blood-y *adj.* sangriento
bloom *v.* florecer
blos-som *n.* flor
blot *n.* mancha
blotch *n.* mancha
blouse *n.* blusa
blow *v.* inflar; soplar
blow-gun *n.* cerbantana
blow-torch *n.* soplete
blow-up *n.* explosión
bludg-eon *v.* aporrear
blue *adj.* azul
blue-bell *n.* campanilla
blue-print *n.* cianotipo
blunt *adj.* abrupto
blur *v.* nublar
blur-ry *adj.* confuso
blush *n.* sonrojo
blus-ter *v.* bramar
boar *n.* verraco
board *n.* consejo
board-er *n.* pensionista
board-ing-house *n.* pensión
boast *v.* alardear
boast-ful *adj.* jactancioso
boast-ing *n.* jactancia
boat *n.* barco
boat-man *n.* lanchero
bob-ber *n.* flotador
bob-bin *n.* bobina
bod-ice *n.* cuerpo
bod-i-ly *adj.* corporal
bod-y *n.* cuerpo
bod-y-guard *n.* guardaespaldas
bog *n.* cienaga
bo-gus *adj.* falso
boil *v.* cocer; hervir
boil-er *n.* caldera
boil-ing *adj.* hirviente
bois-ter-ous *adj.* ruidoso; bullicioso

bold *adj.* descarado; intrepido
bod-ster *v.* apoyar
bolt *n.* perno; pestillo
bomb *n.* bomba
bom-bard *v.* acosar; bombardear
bom-bard-ment *n.* bombardeo
bomb-er *n.* bombardero
bomb-ing *n.* bombardero
bomb-shell *n.* bomba
bo-nan-za *n.* bonanza
bond *n.* atadura; bono
bone *n.* hueso
bon-fire *n.* hoguera
bon-net *n.* cofia
bo-nus *n.* sobresueldo
bon-y *adj.* huesudo
book *n.* libro
book-bind-ing *n.* encuadernación
book-end *n.* sujetalibros
book-ing *n.* reservación
book-sell-er *n.* librero
book-store *n.* libreria
boom *n.* prosperidad
boo-mer-ang *n.* bumerang
boor *n.* patan
boor-ish *adj.* tosco
boost *v.* levantar
boot *n.* bota
booth *n.* puesto; cabina
boot-leg *v.* contrabandear
boo-ty *n.* botin
bor-der *n.* borde; frontera
bor-der-line *n.* frontera
bore *v.* aburrir
bore-dom *n.* aburrimiento
bor-ing *adj.* aburrido
born *adj.* nacido
bor-ough *n.* municipio
bor-row *v.* apropiarse
bor-row-er *n.* prestatario
bos-om *n.* pecho
boss *n.* jefe
bo-tan-ic *adj.* botanico
bot-a-nist *n.* botanico
bot-a-ny *n.* botànica
botch *v.* chapucear
both *adj.* los dos
both-er *v.* molestar(se)
both-er-some *adj.* molesto

bot-tle n. botella
bot-tom n. base; fondo
bot-tom-less adj. sin fondo
bot-u-lism n. botulismo
bough n. rama
bouil-lon n. caldo
boul-e-vard n. avenida
bounce v. rebotar
bounc-ing adj. fuerte
bound v. saltar
bound-a-ry n. limite
bound-less adj. ilimitado
boun-te-ous adj. abundante
boun-ti-ful adj. generoso
boun-ty n. generosidad
bou-quet n. ramo
bour-geois n. burgues
bour-geoi-sie n. burguesia
bout n. ataque
bo-vine n. bovino
bow v. inclinarse; doblegarse
bow-el n. intestino
bowl n. tazon; fuente
bowl-ing n. bolos
box n. caja
box-er n. boxeador
box-ing n. boxeo
boy n. chico; niño
boy-cott v. boicotear
boy-friend n. novio
bra n. sosten
brace n. puntal
brace-let n. brazalete
brac-ing adj. fortificante
brack-et n. corchete
brack-ish adj. salino
brag v. jactarse
brain n. cerebro
brain-y adj. listo
brake v. frenar
bran n. salvado
branch n. rama
brand n. modo; marca
brand-ing n. hierra
bran-dish v. blandir
bran-dy n. conac
brash adj. insolente; impetuoso
brass n. laton
bras-siere n. sosten
brass-y adj. descarado
brave adj. valiente
brav-er-y n. valor

brawn-y adj. musculoso
bra-zen adj. descarado
bra-zier n. brasero
breach n. rupture; violación
bread n. pan
bread-bas-ket n. panera
breadth n. extension
break v. quebrar; romper
break-a-ble adj. rompible
break-age n. rotura
break-down n. depresión; desglose
break-fast n. desayuño
break-through n. adelanto
break-up n. desintegración; separacion
breast n. pecho
breast-bone n. esternon
breath n. respiración
breathe v. respirar
breath-ing n. respiración
breath-tak-ing adj. impresionante
breed v. criar; reproducirse
breed-er n. criador
breed-ing v. crianza
breeze n. brisa
breez-y adj. ventoso
brev-i-ty n. brevedad
brew-er n. cervecero
brew-er-y n. cerveceria
bribe v. cohechar
brick n. ladrillo
brick-lay-er n. albanil
bri-dal n. boda
bride n. novia
bridge n. puente
bri-dle n. brida
brief adj. breve
brief-case n. cartera
brief-ing n. reunion
bri-gade n. brigada
bright adj. brillante
bright-en v. iluminar(se)
bright-ness n. lustre
bril-liance n. brillo
bril-liant adj. brillante
brim n. borde
bring v. traer
bri-quet n. briqueta
brisk adj. vigoroso
bris-tle n. cerda
brit-tle adj. fragil

broach *n.* broche
broad *adj.* extenso; ancho
broad-cast *v.* transmitir; emitir
broad-cast-ing *n.* transmision
broad-en *v.* ensanchar(se)
broad-mind-ed *adj.* comprensivo
bro-cade *n.* brocado
broc-co-li *n.* brecol
bro-chure *n.* folleto
bro-ken *adj.* roto; quebrado
bro-ken-down *adj.* decrepito
bro-ker-age *n.* corretaje
bro-mide *n.* bromuro
bro-mine *n.* bromo
bron-chi-al *adj.* bronquial
bron-chi-tis *n.* bronquitis
bronze *n.* bronce
brook *n.* arroyo
broom *n.* escoba
broth *n.* caldo
broth-el *n.* burdel
broth-er *n.* hermano
broth-er-hood *n.* fraternidad
broth-er-in-law *n.* cuando
broth-er-ly *adj.* fraterno
brow *n.* ceja
brown *adj.* moreno
brown-out *n.* parcial
browse *v.* pacer; curiosear
bruise *n.* contusión
brunt *n.* impacto
brush *n.* cepillo
bru-tal *adj.* brutal
bru-tal-i-ty *n.* brutalidad
bru-tal-ize *v.* brutalizar
brute *n.* bruto
buc-ca-neer *n.* bucanero
buck-et *n.* balde
buck-le *n.* jebilla
bud *n.* yema
bud-dy *n.* compadre
budge *v.* ceder
budg-et *v.* presupuestar
buf-fa-lo *n.* bufalo
buff-er *n.* intercesor
buf-fet *n.* bofetada
buf-foon *n.* bufon
bug *n.* bicho
bu-gle *n.* clarin
build *v.* construir

build-er *n.* constructor
build-ing *n.* construcción
bulb *n.* bulbo
bulge *n.* bulto
bulk-y *adj.* pesado
bull *n.* toro
bull-dog *n.* buldog
bull-doz-er *n.* excavadora
bul-let *n.* bala
bul-le-tin *n.* boletin
bull-fight-er *n.* torero
bul-rush *n.* espadana
bul-wark *n.* baluarte
bum-ble-bee *n.* abejorro
bump *n.* choque
bump-y *adj.* agitado
bun *n.* bollo
bunch *n.* racimo
bun-dle *n.* fajo; bulto
bun-ny *n.* conejito
buoy *n.* boya
buoy-ant *adj.* boyante
bur *n.* erizo
bur-den *n.* carga
bu-reauc-ra-cy *n.* burocracía
bu-reau-crat *n.* burocrata
burg-er *n.* hamburguesa
bur-glar *n.* ladron
bur-glar-ize *v.* robar
bur-i-al *n.* entierro
bur-lap *n.* arpillera
bur-ly *adj.* robusto
burn *v.* incendiar
burn-er *n.* quemador
burn-ing *adj.* ardiente
burn-out *n.* extinción
burnt *adj.* quernado
burp *n.* eructo
bur-ro *n.* burro
burst *v.* romper
bur-y *v.* enterrar
bus *n.* autobus
bus-boy *n.* ayudante
bush *n.* arbusto
bushed *adj.* agotado
busi-ness *n.* oficio
but *conj.* pero
but-ter *n.* mantequilla
but-ter-fly *n.* mariposa
buy *v.* comprar
buy-er *n.* comprador
by *adv.* cerca, *prep.* cerca de; por

cab n. taxi
ca-bal n. cabala
cab-a-la n. cabala
cab-a-ret n. cabaret
cab-bage n. col
cab-driv-er n. taxista
cab-in n. cabana
cab-i-net n. gabinete
cab-i-net-mak-er n. ebanista
cab-i-net-work n. ebanisteria
ca-ble n. cable
ca-ble-gram n. cablegrama
ca-ca-o n. cacao
ca-chet n. cacareo
cac-tus n. cacto
ca-dav-er n. cadaver
ca-dav-er-ous adj. cadaverico
cad-die n. caddy
ca-dence n. cadencia
ca-det n. cadete
cad-mi-um n. cadmio
ca-du-ce-us n. caduceo
ca-fe n. cafe
caf-e-te-ri-a n. cafeteria
caf-feine n. cafeina
caf-tan n. tunica
cage n. jaula
ca-jole v. engatusar
cake n. pastel
cal-a-bash n. calabaza
cal-a-mine n. calamina
ca-lam-i-ty n. calamidad
cal-ci-fi-ca-tion n. calcificación
cal-ci-fy v. calcificar
cal-ci-um n. calcio
cal-cu-late v. calcular
cal-cu-lat-ed adj. intencional
cal-cu-lat-ing adj. calculador
cal-cu-la-tion n. calculo
cal-cu-la-tor n. calculadora
cal-dron n. caldera
cal-en-dar n. calendario
cal-i-ber n. calibre
cal-i-brate v. calibrar
cal-i-bra-tion n. calibración
cal-i-co n. calico
cal-i-per n. calibrador
ca-liph n. califa
cal-is-then-ics n. calistenia
ca-lix n. caliz
call v. llamar

call-er n. cisitante
cal-lig-ra-pher n. caligrafo
cal-lig-ra-phy n. caligrafia
call-ing n. vocación
cal-lous v. encallecerse
cal-low adj. inmaturo
cal-lus n. callo
calm v. calmar(se); n. calma
calm-ness n. tranquilidad
ca-lor-ic adj. calorico
cal-o-rie n. caloria
ca-lum-ni-ate v. calumniar
cal-va-ry n. calvario
ca-lyx n. caliz
ca-ma-ra-der-ie n. camaraderia
cam-bi-um n. cambium
cam-el n. camello
ça-mel-lia n. camelia
cam-e-o n. camafeo
cam-er-a n. camara
cam-ou-flage n. camuflaje
camp v. acampar
cam-paign n. campana
camp-er n. campista
cam-phor n. alcanfor
can v. poder
ca-nar-y n. canario
can-cel v. cancelar; matar; anular
can-cel-la-tion n. cancelacion
can-cer n. cancer
can-cer-ous adj. canceroso
can-des-cent adj. candente
can-did adj. franco
can-di-da-cy n. candidatura
can-di-date n. candidato
can-died adj. escarchado
can-dle n. cirio; vela
can-dle-hold-er n. candelero
can-dle-stick n. candelero
can-dor n. franqueza
can-dy n. azucar
cane n. cana; baston
ca-nine adj. canino
can-is-ter n. lata
canned adj. enlatado
can-ni-bal n. canibal
can-ni-bal-ism n. canibalismo
can-ni-bal-is-tic adj. canibal
can-non n. conon

ca-noe n. canoa
ca-non-i-za-tion n. canonización
can-on-ize v. canonizar
can-ta-loupe n. cantalupo
can-teen n. cantina
can-vas n. lona
can-yon n. canon
cap n. tapa
ca-pa-bil-i-ty n. capacidad
ca-pa-ble adj. capaz
ca-pa-cious adj. espacioso
ca-pac-i-ty n. capacidad
ca-per n. cabriola
cap-il-lar-y n. capilar
cap-i-tal n., adj. capital
cap-i-tal-ism n. capitalismo
cap-i-tal-ist n. capitalista
cap-i-tal-is-tic adj. capitalista
cap-i-tal-i-za-tion n. capitalización
cap-i-tal-ize v. capitalizar
cap-i-tal-ly adv. admirablemente
cap-i-tol n. capitolio
ca-pit-u-late v. capitular
ca-price n. capricho
ca-pri-cious adj. caprichoso
cap-sule n. capsula
cap-tain n. capitan
cap-tion n. subtitulo
cap-tious adj. capcioso
cap-ti-vate v. cautivar
cap-ti-va-tion n. encanto
cap-tive adj. cautivo
cap-tiv-i-ty n. cautividad
cap-tor n. capturador
cap-ture v. capturar
car n. coche
car-a-mel n. caramelo
car-at n. quilate
car-a-van n. caravana
car-bide n. carburo
car-bine n. carabina
car-bo-hy-drate n. carbohifrato
car-bon n. carbone
car-bon-ate v. carbonatar
car-bun-cle n. carbunco
car-bu-re-tor n. carburador
car-cin-o-gen-ic adj. cancerigeno
card n. tarjeta

car-di-ac adj. cardiaco
car-di-nal adj. cardinal
car-di-o-gram n. cardiograma
car-di-ol-o-gy n. cardiología
care v. cuidar
ca-reer n. carrera
care-free adj. despreocupado
care-ful adj. cuidadoso
care-less adj. espontaneo; descuidado
ca-ress n. caricia
care-tak-er n. portero
car-go n. carga
car-i-ca-ture n. caricatura
car-nage n. carniceria
car-nal adj. carnal
car-ni-vore n. carnivoro
car-niv-o-rous adj. carnivoro
ca-rous-al n. jarana
car-ou-sel n. carrusel
car-pen-try n. carpinteria
car-pet n. alfombra
car-riage n. carruaje
car-ri-er n. carrero
car-rot n. zanahoria
car-ry v. lograr; llevar
car-sick adj. mareado
cart n. carro
cart-age n. acarreo
car-tel n. cartel
car-ti-lage n. cartilago
cart-load n. carretada
car-toon n. tira
car-toon-ist n. caricaturista
car-tridge n. cartucho
carve v. esculpir
carv-ing n. escultura
case n. caja
cahs n. efectivo
cash-ew n. anacardo
cash-ier n. cajero
cash-mere n. cachemira
ca-si-no n. casino
cask n. barril
cas-se-role n. cacerola
cas-sette n. casete
cast v. dar; fundir; echar
cas-ta-nets n. castanuelas
caste n. casta
cas-ti-gate v. castigar

cas-tle n. castillo
cas-trate v. castrar
cas-tra-tion n. castración
ca-su-al adj. casual
cas-u-al-ly adv. casualmente
ca-su-ist-ry n. casuistica
cat n. gato
ca-tab-o-lism n. catabolismo
cat-a-log n. catalogo
cat-a-lyst n. catalizador
cat-a-lyt-ic adj. catalitico
cat-a-lyze v. catalizar
cat-a-pult n. catapulta
cat-a-ract n. catarata
ca-tas-tro-phe n. catastrofe
cat-a-stroph-ic adj. catastrofico
cat-a-ton-ic adj. catatonico
catch v. prender; coger
catch-er n. receptor
catch-ing adj. contagioso
catch-y adj. capcioso
cat-e-chism n. catecismo
cat-e-gor-ic adj. categorico
cat-e-gor-i-cal-ly adv. categoricamente
cat-e-go-rize v. clasificar
cat-e-go-ry n. categoria
cat-er-pil-lar n. oruga
cat-er-waul v. chillar
ca-thar-sis n. catarsis
ca-the-dral n. catedral
cath-ode n. catodo
cath-o-lic adj. catolico
ca-thol-i-cism n. catolicismo
cat-nip n. nebeda
cat-tail n. espadaña
cat-tle n. ganado
cat-tle-man n. ganadero
cau-li-flow-er n. coliflor
cau-sa-tion n. causalidad
caus-a-tive adj. causativo
cause n. razon; causa
cause-way n. elevada
caus-tic adj. caustico
cau-ter-ize v. cauterizar
cau-tion v. amonestar
cau-tion-ar-y adj. preventivo
cau-tious adj. cauteloso
cav-al-ry n. caballeria
cave n. cueva
cav-ern n. caverna
cav-ern-ous adj. cavernoso

cav-i-ty n. cavidad
ca-vort v. cabriolar
cay n. cayo
cease v. suspender
cease-less adj. continuo
ce-dar n. cedro
cede v. ceder
ceil-ing n. techo
cel-e-brant n. celebrante
cel-e-brate v. celebrar
cel-e-brat-ed adj. celebre
cel-e-bra-tion n. celebración
ce-leb-ri-ty n. celebridad
cel-er-y n. apio
ce-les-tial adj. celestial
cel-i-ba-cy n. celibato
cel-i-bate adj. celibe
cell n. celda
cel-lar n. sotano
cel-lo-phane n. celofan
cel-lu-lar adj. celular
cel-lu-loid n. celuloide
cel-lu-lose n. celulosa
ce-ment n. cemento
cem-e-ter-y n. cementerio
cen-ser n. insensario
cen-sor n. censor
cen-so-ri-ous adj. censurador
cen-sor-ship n. censura
cen-sure v. censurar
cen-sus n. censo
cent n. centavo
cen-taur n. centauro
cen-ten-ni-al adj. centenario
cen-ter n. centro
cen-ti-grade adj. centigrado
cen-ti-gram n. centiframo
cen-ti-li-ter n. centilitro
cen-ti-me-ter n. centimetro
cen-tral adj. central
cen-tral-ize v. centralizar(se)
cen-tric adj. centrico
cen-trif-u-gal adj. centrifugo
cen-tu-ry n. siglo
ce-phal-ic adj. cefalico
ce-ram-ic adj. ceramico
ce-re-al n. cereal
cer-e-bral adj. cerebral
cer-e-brum n. cerebro
cer-e-mo-ni-al adj. ceremonial
cer-e-mo-ni-ous adj. cere-

monioso
cer-e-mo-ny n. ceremonia
cer-tain adj. seguro; cierto
cer-tain-ly adv. ciertamente
cer-tain-ty n. certeza
cer-ti-fi-a-ble adj. certificable
cer-tif-i-cate n. certificado
cer-ti-fi-ca-tion n. certificación
cer-ti-fied adj. certificado
cer-ti-fy v. certificar
cer-ti-tude n. certidumbre
cer-vix n. cerviz
ces-sa-tion n. cesación
ces-sion n. cesion
chafe v. frotar; rozar
cha-grin v. desilusionar
chain n. cadena
chair n. silla
chair-man n. presidente
chair-man-ship n. presidencia
chair-wo-man n. presidenta
cha-let n. chalet
chal-ice n. caliz
chalk n. tiza
chalk-board n. pizarra
chal-lenge v. desafiar
chal-leng-er n. desafiador
cham-ber-lain n. chambelan
cha-me-leon n. camaleon
champ n. campeon
cham-pagne n. champana
cham-pi-on n. campeon
cham-pi-on-ship n. campeonato
chance n. oportunidad; casualidad
chan-cel-ler-y n. cancilleria
chan-cel-lor n. canciller
change v. transformar; cambiar
change-a-ble adj. cambiable
change-o-ver n. cambio
chang-er n. cambiador
chan-nel n. canal
chant n. canto
cha-os n. caos
cha-ot-ic adj. caotico
chap-el n. capilla
chap-er-one n. carabina
chap-lain n. capellan
chap-ter n. capitulo

char-ac-ter n. caracter
char-ac-ter-is-tic n. caracteristica
char-ac-ter-ize v. caracterizar
char-coal n. carboncillo
charge v. pedir; cargar
cha-ris-ma n. carisma
char-i-ta-ble adj. caritativo
char-i-ty n. caridad
charm n. encanto
charm-er n. encantador
charm-ing adj. encantador
chart v. trazar
char-ter n. carta
chase v. perseguir
chaste adj. casto
chas-ten v. castigar
chas-tise v. castigar
chas-ti-ty n. castidad
chat v. charlar
chat-ter v. charlar
chau-vin-ist n. chauvinista
chau-vin-is-tic adj. chauvinista
cheap adj. barato
cheap-en v. degradar(se)
cheap-ly adv. barato
cheap-ness n. tacaneria
cheat v. enganar
cheat-er n. tramposo
cheat-ing adj. tramposo
check n. cheque; parada; cuenta
check-book n. chequera
check-ered adj. a cuadros
cheek n. mejilla
cheep adj. piada
cheer v. alegrar; alentar
cheer-ful adj. alegre
cheer-i-ly adv. alegremente
cheer-less adj. triste
cheese n. queso
cheese-cake n. quesadilla
chef n. cocinero
chem-i-cal n. quimico
chem-ist n. quimico
chem-is-try n. quimica
che-mo-ther-a-py n. quimioterapia
cher-ish v. abrigar; querer
cher-ry n. cerezo
cher-ub n. querubin

che-ru-bic *adj.* querubico
chess *n.* ajedrez
chest *n.* pecho
chest-nut *n.* castaña
chew *v.* masticar
chew-ing *n.* masticación
chick-en *n.* pollo
chick-pea *n.* garbanzo
chief *n.* jefe
chif-fon *n.* chifon
child *n.* hijo; niño
child-birth *m.* parto
child-ish *adj.* aninado
child-like *adj.* infantil
chil-i *n.* chile
chill *n.* frio
chill-ing *adj.* frio
chime *n.* carillon
chim-ney *n.* chimenea
chim-pan-zee *n.* chimpance
chin *n.* barba
chi-na *n.* china
chip *n.* astilla; *v.* astillar
chip-per *adj.* jovial
chi-ro-prac-tor *n.* quiroprac-
tico
chirp *v.* gorjear
chis-el *n.* cincel
chis-el-er *n.* cincelador
chiv-al-rous *adj.* cabal-
leresco
chiv-al-ry *n.* caballerosidad
chive *n.* cebollino
chlo-ride *n.* cloruro
chlo-rine *n.* cloro
chlo-ro-phyll *n.* clorofila
choc-o-late *n.* chocolate
choice *adj.* selecto; *n.*
preferencia
choir *n.* coro
choke *v.* ahogar; atorar;
estrangular
chol-er-a *n.* colera
chol-er-ic *adj.* colerico
cho-les-ter-ol *n.* colesterol
chomp *v.* ronzar
choose *v.* escoger
choos-ing *n.* selección
chop *v.* cortar
cho-ral *n.* coral
cho-re-og-ra-pher *n.* coreo-
grafo
cho-re-og-ra-phy *n.* coreo-

grafia
cho-sen *adj.* escogido
chow *n.* comida
Christ *n.* Cristo
chris-ten *v.* bautizar
chris-ten-ing *n.* bautismo
Chris-tian *n.* cristiano
Chris-ti-an-i-ty *n.* cris-
tianismo
Christ-mas *n.* Navidad
chro-mat-ic *adj.* cromatico
chrome *n.* cromo
chro-mi-um *n.* cromo
chro-mo-some *n.* cro-
mosoma
chron-ic *adj.* cronico
chron-i-cle *n.* cronica
chron-o-log-ic *adj.* crono-
logico
chro-nol-o-gy *n.* cronologia
chrys-a-lis *n.* crisalida
chrys-an-the-mum *n.* crisan-
temo
chum *n.* compañero
chunk *n.* trozo
church *n.* iglesia
church-man *n.* clerigo
churn *n.* mantequera
chute *n.* conducto; rampa
ci-ca-da *n.* cigarra
ci-der *n.* sidra
ci-gar *n.* puro
cig-a-rette *n.* cigarrillo
cinch *n.* cincha
cin-der *n.* carbonilla
cin-e-ma *n.* cine
cin-e-mat-ic *adj.* filmico
cin-e-ma-tog-ra-phy *n.* cine-
matografia
cin-na-mon *n.* canela
ci-pher *v.* cifrar
cir-cle *n.* ciclo
cir-cuit *n.* circuito
cir-cu-lar *adj.* circular
cir-cu-late *v.* circular
cir-cu-lat-ing *adj.* circulante
cir-cu-la-tion *n.* circulación
cir-cum-cise *v.* circuncidar
cir-cum-cised *adj.* circunciso
cir-cum-ci-sion *n.* circunci-
sion
cir-cum-fer-ence *n.* circun-
ferencia

cir-cum-nav-i-gate v. circunnavegar

cir-cum-scribe v. circunscribir

cir-cum-spect adj. circunspecto

cir-cum-stance n. circunstancia

cir-cum-stan-tial adj. circunstancial

cir-cus n. circo

cir-rho-sis n. cirrosis

cir-rus n. cirro

cis-tern n. cisterna

cit-a-del n. ciudadela

ci-ta-tion n. citación

cite v. citar

cit-i-zen n. ciudadano

cit-i-zen-ship n. ciudadania

cit-rus adj. cítrico

cit-y n. ciudad

civ-et n. civeta

civ-ic adj. civico

civ-il adj. civil

ci-vil-ian n. civil

ci-vil-i-ty n. civilidad

civ-i-li-za-tion n. civilización

civ-i-lize v. civilizar

claim v. merecer; reclamar

clair-voy-ance n. clarividencia

clair-voy-ant adj. clarividente

clam n. almeja

clam-or n. clamor

clam-or-ous adj. clamoroso

clamp n. abrazadera

clan n. clan

clan-gor n. estruendo

clap v. aplaudir

clap-per n. badajo

clap-ping n. aplausos

clar-et n. clarete

clar-i-fi-ca-tion n. clarificación

clar-i-fy v. clarificar

clar-i-net n. clarinete

clar-i-on adj. sonoro

clar-i-ty n. claridad

clash v. entrechocarse

class n. clase

clas-sic adj. clasico

clas-si-cal adj. clasico

clas-si-cism n. clasicismo

clas-si-cist n. clasicista

clas-si-fi-ca-tion n. clasificación

clas-si-fied adj. clasificado

clas-si-fy v. clasificar

class-y adj. elegante

clause n. clausula

claus-tro-pho-bi-a n. claustrofobia

clav-i-chord n. clavicordio

clav-i-cle n. clavicula

claw n. garra

clay n. arcilla

clean v. limpiar

clean-cut adj. definido

clean-er n. limpiador

clean-ing n. limpieza

clean-li-ness n. limpieza

cleanse v. limpiar

cleans-er n. limpiador

clear adj. despejado; transparente

clear-cut adj. claro

clear-ing n. claro

clear-ly adv. claramente

cleav-age n. division

cleave v. adherir; partir

cleav-er n. cuchillo

clem-en-cy n. clemencia

cler-gyn. clero

cler-gy-man n. clerigo

cler-ic adj. clerigo

cler-i-cal adj. clerical

clerk n. oficinista

clev-er adj. listo

clev-er-ness n. inteligencia

cli-ent n. cliente

cli-mac-tic adj. culminante

cli-mate n. clima

cli-mat-ic adj. climatico

cli-max n. climax

climb v. trepar

climb-er n. alpinista

climb-ing adj. trepador

clin-ic n. clinica

clin-i-cal adj. clinico

cli-ni-cian n. clinico

clip v. cortar

cloak n. manto

clock n. reloj

clog n. atasco

clois-ter n. claustro

clone n. clon

close v. cerrar
closed adj. cerrado; vedado
close-down n. cierre
close-ly adv. atentamente; de cerca
close-ness n. proximidad
close-out n. liquidacion
clos-et n. armario
clos-ing n. cierre
clot n. coagulo
cloth n. tela
clothe v. arropar
clothes n. ropa
cloth-ing n. ropa
cloud n. nube
cloud-burst n. aguacero
cloud-y adj. nuboso
clout n. bofetada
clo-ver n. trebol
clown n. payaso
club n. palo; trebol
clue n. pista
clump n. grupo
clum-sy adj. pesado
coach n. vagon; coche
coach-man n. cochero
co-ag-u-late v. coagular(se)
co-ag-u-la-tion n. coagulación
coal n. carbon
co-a-lesce v. unirse
co-a-li-tion n. coalición
coarse adj. tosco
coars-en v. vulgarizar
coarse-ness n. aspereza
coast n. costa
coast-al adj. costero
coast-er n. trineo
coat n. pelo
coat-ed adj. banado
coat-ing n. capa; bano
coat-tail n. faldon
coax v. engatusar
coax-ing n. engatusamiento
cob n. elote
co-balt n. cobalto
cob-bler n. zapatero
co-bra n. cobra
cob-web n. telarana
co-caine n. cocaina
coc-cyx n. coccix
cock n. gallo
cock-ade n. escarapela

cock-a-too n. cacatua
cock-i-ness n. presunción
cock-le n. berberecho
cock-pit n. cancha
cock-roach n. cucaracha
cock-tail n. coctel
co-coa n. cacao
co-coa-nut n. coco
co-coon n. capullo
code n. codigo
co-de-fend-ant n. coacusado
co-deine n. codeina
cod-fish n. bacalao
cod-i-fy v. codificar
co-di-rec-tion n. codireccion
co-ed adj. coeducaciónal
co-ed-u-ca-tion n. coeducación
co-ed-u-ca-tion-al adj. coeducaciónal
co-ef-fi-cient n. coeficiente
co-erce v. coercer
co-er-cion n. coercion
co-ex-ist v. coexistir
co-ex-is-tence n. coexistencia
co-ex-ten-sive adj. coextenso
cof-fee n. cafe
cof-fer n. cofre
cof-fin n. ataud
cog n. diente
cog-i-tate v. meditar
cog-nac n. conac
cog-ni-tion n. cognición
cog-ni-zance n. conocimiento
cog-ni-zant adj. enterado
co-hab-it v. cohabitar
co-here v. adherirse
co-her-ence n. coherencia
co-her-ent adj. coherente
co-he-sion n. cohesion
co-he-sive adj. cohesivo
co-hort n. compañero
coil n. rollo
coin v. acunar; n. moneda
co-in-cide v. coincidir
co-in-ci-dence n. coincidencia
co-in-ci-den-tal adj. coincidente

co-la n. cola
col-an-der n. colador
cold n., adj. frio
cold-blood-ed adj. impasible
cold-heart-ed adj. insensible
cold-ness n. frialdad
col-ic n. colico
col-i-se-um n. coliseo
co-li-tis n. colitis
col-lab-o-rate v. colaborar
col-lab-o-ra-tion n. cola-
   boración
col-lab-o-ra-tion-ist n. cola-
   boracionista
col-lab-o-ra-tive adj. co-
   operativo
col-lab-o-ra-tor n. cola-
   borador
col-lage n. collage
col-lapse v. desplomarse;
   caerse
col-laps-i-ble adj. plegable
col-lar n. cuello
col-lar-bone n. clavicula
col-late v. colacionar
col-lat-er-al adj. colateral
col-league n. colega
col-lect v. recoger; reunir;
   coleccionar
col-lect-ed adj. sosegado
col-lec-tion n. coleccion
col-lec-tive adj. colectivo
col-lec-tiv-ist n. colectivista
col-lec-tiv-ize v. colectivizar
col-lec-tor n. colector
col-lege n. colegio
col-le-gian n. estudiante
col-le-giate adj. universitario
col-lide v. chocar
col-li-sion n. choque
col-loid n. coloide
col-lo-qui-al adj. familiar
col-lo-qui-um n. coloquio
col-lo-quy n. coloquio
col-lude v. confabularse
col-lu-sion n. confabulación
co-logne n. colonia
co-lon n. colon
colo-nel n. coronel
co-lo-ni-al adj. colonial
co-lo-ni-al-ist n. colonialista
col-o-nist n. colonizador
col-o-ni-za-tion n. colon-
   izacion
col-o-nize v. colonizar
col-o-niz-er n. colonizador
col-on-nade n. columnata
col-o-ny n. colonia
col-or v. colorear; n. color
col-or-a-tion n. coloración
col-ored adj. coloreado
col-or-ful adj. pintoresco
col-or-ing n. coloración
col-or-less adj. incoloro
co-los-sal adj. colosal
co-los-sus n. coloso
co-los-to-my n. colostomia
col-umn n. columna
col-umn-ist n. columnista
co-ma n. coma
co-ma-tose adj. comatoso
comb v. peinar; n. peine
com-bat v. conbatir
com-bat-ant n. combatiente
com-bat-ive adj. combativo
com-bi-na-tion n. com-
   binación
com-bine v. combinar
com-bo n. conjunto
com-bus-ti-ble adj. conbus-
   tible
com-bus-tion n. combustion
come v. llegar; venir
come-back n. replica
co-me-di-an n. comediante
co-me-di-enne n. come-
   dianta
com-e-dy n. comedia
come-on n. incentivo
com-et n. cometa
com-fort v. consolar
com-fort-a-ble adj. confort-
   able
com-fort-er n. consolador
com-ic adj. comico
com-i-cal adj. comico
com-ing adj. venidero
com-ma n. coma
com-mand n. mando; v.
   mandar
com-man-dant n. coman-
   dante
com-mand-er n. coman-
   dante
com-mand-ing adj. im-
   ponente

com-man-do *n.* comando

com-mem-o-rate *v.* conmemorar

com-mem-o-ra-tion *n.* conmemoración

com-mence *v.* comenzar

com-mence-ment *n.* comienzo

com-mend *v.* encomendar

com-men-da-tion *n.* recomendación

com-men-su-rate *adj.* proporcionado

com-ment *n.* observación

com-mem-tar-y *n.* comentario

com-men-tate *v.* comentar

com-merce *n.* comercio

com-mer-cial *adj.* comercial

com-mer-cial-ism *n.* comercialismo

com-mer-cial-ize *v.* comercializar

com-mis-er-ate *v.* compadecerse

com-mis-sar *n.* comisario

com-mis-sar-y *n.* economato

com-mis-sion *v.* encargar; *n.* comision

com-mis-sion-er *n.* comisario

com-mit *v.* entregar

com-mit-ment *n.* compromiso

com-mit-tal *n.* obligación

com-mit-ee *n.* comite

com-mode *n.* comoda

com-mo-dore *n.* comodoro

com-mon *adj.* comun

com-mon-place *adj.* ordinario

com-mon-wealth *n.* comunidad

com-mo-tion *n.* tumulto

com-mu-nal *adj.* comunal

com-mune *v.* comulgar

com-mu-ni-ca-ble *adj.* comunicable

com-mu-ni-cate *v.* comunicar(se)

com-mu-ni-ca-tion *n.* comunicación

com-mu-ni-ca-tive *adj.* comunicativo

com-nu-ca-tor *n.* comunicante

com-mun-ion *n.* comunion

com-mu-nism *n.* comunismo

com-mun-ist *n.* comunista

com-mu-nis-tic *adj.* comunista

com-mu-ni-ty *n.* comunidad

com-mu-ta-tion *n.* conmutación

com-mu-ta-tive *adj.* conmutativo

com-mute *v.* conmutar

com-pact *adj.* compacto

com-pan-ion *n.* companero

com-pan-ion-ship *n.* companerismo

com-pa-ny *n.* compañia

com-pa-ra-ble *adj.* comparable

com-par-a-tive *adj.* comparativo

com-pare *v.* comparar

com-par-i-son *n.* comparacion

com-part-ment *n.* compartimiento

com-pass *n.* compas

com-pas-sion *n.* compasión

com-pas-sion-ate *adj.* compasivo

com-pat-i-ble *adj.* compatible

com-pa-tri-ot *n.* compatriota

com-pel *v.* compeler

com-pel-ling *adj.* incontestable

com-pen-sate *v.* compensar

com-pen-sa-tion *n.* conpensación

com-pete *v.* competir

com-pe-tence *n.* competencia

com-pe-tent *adj.* competente

com-pe-ti-tion *n.* competencia

com-pet-i-tive *adj.* competitivo

com-pet-i-tor *n.* competidor

com-pi-la-tion *n.* com-

pilacion
com-plie v. compilar
com-plain v. quejarse
com-plain-ant n. demandante
com-plaint n. queja
com-plai-sant adj. complaciente
com-ple-ment n. complemento
com-ple-men-ta-ry adj. complementario
com-plete adj. completo
com-ple-tion n. terminación
com-plex adj. complejo
com-plex-ion n. caracter
com-plex-i-ty n. complejidad
com-pli-nance n. conformidad
com-pli-ant adj. obediente
com-pli-cate v. complicar
com-pli-cat-ed adj. complicado
com-pli-ca-tion n. complicación
com-plic-i-ty n. complicidad
com-pli-ment n. honor; elogio
com-pli-men-ta-ry adj. elogioso
com-ply v. obedecer
com-po-nent n. componente
com-port-ment n. comportamiento
com-pose v. redactar
com-posed adj. tranquilo
com-pos-er n. compositor
com-pos-ite adj. compuesto
com-po-si-tion n. composicion
com-po-sure n. serenidad
com-pound adj. compuesto
com-pre-hend v. comprender
com-pre-hen-si-ble adj. comprensible
com-pre-hen-sion n. comprensión
com-pre-hen-sive adj. comprensivo; general
com-press n. compresa
com-pressed adj. comprimido

com-pres-sion n. compresión
com-prise v. constar de; comprender
com-pro-mise n. compromiso; v. componer
com-pro-mis-ing adj. comprometedor
com-pul-sion n. compulsión
com-pul-sive adj. obsesivo
com-pul-so-ry adj. compulsorio
com-pu-ta-tion n. calculo
com-pute v. computar
com-put-er n. computador
com-put-er-ize v. computarizae
com-rade n. camarada
con adv. contra
con-cave adj. concavo
con-ceal v. ocultar
con-ceal-ment n. encubrimiento
con-cede v. conceder
con-ceit-ed adj. vanidoso
con-ceiv-a-ble adj. concebible
con-ceive v. concebir
con-cen-trate v. concentrar(se)
con-cen-tra-tion n. concentración
con-cen-tric adj. concentrico
con-cept n. concepto
con-cep-tion n. concepción
con-cep-tu-al adj. conceptual
con-cern v. concernir
con-cerned adj. preocupado
con-cern-ing prep. acerca de
con-cert n. concierto
con-cet-ed adj. conjunto
con-cer-to n. concierto
con-ces-sion n. concesión
con-cil-i-ate v. conciliar
con-cil-i-a-tion n. conciliacion
con-cise adj. conciso
con-clude v. concluir
con-clu-sion n. conclusión
con-clu-sive adj. concluyente

con-coc-tion *n.* confección
con-cord *n.* concordia
con-crete *adj.* concreto
con-cur *v.* concurrir
con-cur-rence *n.* concurrencia
con-cur-rent *adj.* concurrente
con-cus-sion *n.* concusión
con-dem-na-ble *adj.* condenable
con-den-sa-tion *n.* condensación
con-dense *v.* condensar(se)
con-dens-er *n.* condensador
con-de-scend-ing *adj.* condescendiente
con-di-ment *n.* condimento
con-di-tion *v.* condicionar
con-done *v.* condoñar
con-duc-tor *n.* cobrador
con-fed-er-a-cy *n.* confederación
con-fed-er-a-tion *n.* confederación
con-fer *v.* oferenciar
con-fess *v.* confesar
con-fide *v.* confiar
con-fi-dence *n.* confianza
con-fi-den-tial *adj.* confidencial
con-firm *v.* confirmar
con-flict *v.* chocar
con-form-i-ty *n.* conformidad
con-fron-ta-tion *n.* confrontación
con-fuse *v.* confundir
con-fu-sion *n.* confusión
con-gest *v.* acumular
con-ges-tion *n.* congestión
con-glom-er-a-tion *n.* conglomeración
con-grat-u-la-tion *n.* felicitación
con-gre-gate *v.* congregar(se)
con-junc-tion *n.* conjunción
con-jure *v.* conjurar
con-nect *v.* conectar
con-no-ta-tion *n.* connotación
con-note *v.* connotar

con-sec-u-tive *adj.* consecutivo
con-serv-a-to-ry *n.* conservatorio
con-serve *v.* conservar
con-sid-er *v.* considerar
con-sid-er-a-tion *n.* consideración
con-sist *v.* consistir
con-sol-i-date *v.* consolidar
con-sol-i-da-tion *n.* consolidación
con-stan-cy *n.* constancia
con-stant *adj.* continuo
con-sti-tu-tion *n.* constitución
con-struc-tion *n.* construcción
con-sult *v.* consultar
con-sume *v.* consumir
con-sump-tion *n.* consunción
con-tain *v.* contener
con-tam-i-na-tion *n.* contaminación
con-tem-plate *v.* proyectar
con-tem-po-rar-y *n.* contemplación
con-tend *v.* afirmar; contender
con-ti-nen-tal *adj.* continental
con-tin-gen-cy *n.* contingencia
con-tin-ue *v.* seguir; continuar
con-trac-tion *n.* contracción
con-tra-dict *v.* contradecir
con-trast *v.* contrastar
con-tri-bu-tion *n.* contribución
con-trol *v.* dirigir; controlar
con-va-lesce *v.* convalecer
con-ven-tion *n.* convención
con-verge *v.* convergir
con-ver-sa-tion *n.* conversación
con-verse *v.* conversar
con-ver-sion *n.* conversión
con-vey *v.* llevar
con-vic-tion *n.* convicción
con-vince *v.* convencer
con-vul-sion *n.* convulsión

cook n. cocinero; v. cocinar
cook-ie n. galleta
cool adj. fresco
co-or-di-nate v. coordinar
co-or-di-na-tion n. coordinación
cop-per n. cobre
cop-y v. copiar
cor-dial-i-ty n. cordialidad
corn n. maiz
cor-po-ral adj. corporal
cor-po-ra-tion n. corporación
cor-pu-lent adj. gordo
cor-pus-cu-lar adj. corpuscular
cor-ral v. acorralar
cor-rect v. corregir
cor-rec-tion n. corrección
cor-re-spond v. escribir
cor-re-spond-ence n. correspondencia
cor-rode v. corroer
cor-ro-sion n. corrosion
cor-rup-tion n. corrupción
cos-met-ic n. cosmetico
cos-mic adj. cosmico
cost v. costar; n. precio
couch n. sofa
count n. cuenta; v. contar
coun-try n. campo; pais
cou-ple n. pareja
cou-ra-geous adj. valiente
course n. plato; dirección
cous-in n. prima; primo
cov-er n. cubierta, v. cubrir
cow n. vaca
cow-boy n. vaquero
coy-o-te n. coyote
crab n. cangrejo
crack-er n. galleta
cra-dle v. mercer
crash n. choque; estallido
crate n. cajon
cra-ter n. crater
crave v. ansiar
crav-ing n. anhelo
crawl v. gatear; arrastrarse
cray-on n. pastel
craze v. enloquecer
crazed adj. loco
cra-zy adj. loco
cream n. crema

cream-y adj. cremoso
crease v. doblar
cre-ate v. producir; crear
cre-a-tion n. creación
cre-a-tive adj. creador
cre-a-tiv-i-ty n. originalidad
cre-a-tor n. creador
crea-ture n. criatura
cre-dence n. credito
cre-den-tial n. credencial
cred-i-ble adj. creible
cred-it n. credito; reconocimiento
cred-it-a-ble adj. loable
cred-u-lous adj. credulo
creed n. credo
creep-y adj. espeluznante
cre-mate v. incinerar
cre-ma-tion n. incineración
crepe n. crespon
cres-cent n. medialuna
crest n. cresta
cre-tin n. cretiño
crew n. equipo
crib n. pesebre
crick-et n. grillo
crime n. crimen
crim-i-nal n., adj. criminal
crin-kle v. arrugar(se)
crip-ple v. mutilar
cri-sis n. crisis
crisp adj. crespo
crisp-y adj. crujiente
crit-ic n. critico
crit-i-cal adj. critico
crit-i-cism n. critica
crit-i-cize v. criticar
cri-tique n. critica
croc-o-dile n. cocodrilo
cro-cus n. azafran
crook n. angulo; baculo
crook-ed adj. corvo
crop n. fusta; cultivo
cross-beam n. traviesa
cross-bow n. ballesta
cross-cur-rent n. contracorriente
cross-ex-am-ine v. interrogar
cross-ing n. cruce
cross-word puz-zle n. crucigrama
crouch v. acuclillarse

cross v. cruzar, n. cruz
crow v. cacarear
crowd n. gentio; multitud
crowd-ed adj. concurrido
crown n. corona
crown-ing n. coronación
cru-ci-ble n. crisol
cru-ci-fix n. crucifijo
cru-ci-fix-ion n. crucifixión
cru-ci-fy v. crucificar
crude adj. tosco; ordinario;
  crudo
crude-ness n. tosquedad
cru-el adj. cruel
cru-el-ty n. crueldad
cruise v. navegar
crumb n. migaja
crum-ble v. desmigajar(se)
crum-ple v. estrujar(se)
crunch-y adj. crujiente
cru-sade n. cruzada
cru-sad-er n. cruzado
crush v. aplastar
crust n. costra; corteza
crus-ta-cean n. crustaceo
crust-y adj. costroso
cry v. llorar
crypt n. cripta
crys-tal n. cristal
crys-tal-line adj. cristaliño
crys-tal-lize v. cristalizar(se)
crys-tal-log-ra-phy n. cris-
  talografia
cube n. cubo
cu-bic adj. cubico
cu-bi-cle n. compartimiento
cub-ist n. cubista
cu-cum-ber n. pepiño
cud-dle v. abrazar(se)
cue n. taco
cu-li-nar-y adj. culinario
cul-mi-nate v. culminar
cul-pa-ble adj. culpable
cul-prit n. culpable
cult n. culto
cul-ti-vate v. cultivar
cul-ti-va-tion n. cultivo
cul-ti-va-tor n. cultivador
cul-tur-al adj. cultural
cul-ture n. cultura
cul-tured adj. culto
cum-ber v. embarazar
cum-ber-some adj. em-

barazoso
cu-mu-late v. acumular
cu-mu-la-tive adj.
  acumulativo
cun-ning adj. habil; astuto
cup n. taza
cup-ful n. taza
cur-a-ble adj. curable
curb n. bordillo
curd n. cuajada
cure n. cura
cu-ri-os-i-ty n. curiosidad
cu-ri-ous adj. curioso
curl v. enrollar(se); rizar(se)
cur-ren-cy n. moneda
cur-rent n., adj. corriente
cur-rent-ly adj. actualmente
curse n. desgracia; mal-
  dición
curs-ed adj. maldito
cur-sor n. cursor
cur-tain n. telon
cur-va-ture n. curvatura
curve n. curva
curved adj. curvo
cus-to-di-an n. custodio
cus-to-dy n. custodia
cus-tom n. costumbre
cus-tom-ar-i-ly adv. acostumbrado
cut adj. cortado; n. cortadura;
  v. cortar
cu-ta-ne-ous adj. cutaneo
cute adj. mono
cu-ti-cle n. cuticula
cut-ler-y n. cubiertos
cy-a-nide n. cianuro
cy-cle n. ciclo
cy-clic adj. ciclico
cy-clist n. ciclista
cy-clone n. ciclón
cyl-in-der n. cilindro
cy-lin-dri-cal adj. cilindrico
cym-bal n. cimbalo
cyn-i-cal adj. cinico
cyn-i-cism n. cinismo
cy-press n. cipres
cyst n. quiste
cys-tic adj. enquistado
cys-ti-tis n. cistitis
cy-to-plasm n. citoplasma
czar n. zar
cza-ri-na n. zariña

dab v. tocar ligeramente
dab-ble v. salpicar
dad n. papa
daft adj. loco
dag-ger n. punal
dai-ly adj. diario
dain-ti-ness n. delicadeze
dain-ty adj. delicado
dair-y n. lecheria; queseria
dair-y-man n. lechero
da-is n. estrado
dale n. valle
dal-li-ance n. diversión
dal-ly v. perder tiempo; entretenerse
dam v. represar, n. presa
dam-age v. danar; perjudicar
damn v. condenar
dam-na-ble adj. detestable
damned adj. condenado
damp adj. humedo
damp-en v. mojar
dance n. baile, v. bailar
dan-cer n. bailador
dan-druff n. caspa
dan-ger n. peligro
dan-ger-ous adj. peligroso
dan-gle v. colgar
dank adj. liento
dap-pled adj. rodado
dare v. arriesgarse
dar-ing n. atrevimiento
dark n. oscuridad, adj. oscuro
dark-en v. oscurecer
dark-ness n. oscuridad
darl-ing n. querido
darn v. zurcir
dash v. precipitarse; romper
dash-board n. tablere de instrumentos
date n. cita; fecha
daub v. pintarrajar
daugh-ter n. hija
daugh-ter-in-law n. nuera
daunt-less adj. impavido
daw-dle v. perder el tiempo
dawn v. amanecer
day n. dia
day-break n. amanecer
day-dream n. ensueño
day-light n. luz del dia
day-time n. dia

daze v. aturdir
daz-zle v. deslumbrar
dea-con n. diacono
dea-con-ry n. diaconía
dead adj. muerto
dead-en v. amortiguar
dead-end n. calle sin salida
dead-ly adj. mortal
deaf adj. sordo
deaf-en v. ensordecer
deaf-ness n. sordera
deal n. cantidad; trato; reparto
deal-er n. tratante
dean n. decaño; dean
dear adj. querido; caro
dear-ness n. carestia
death n. muerte
death-less adj. inmortal
death-ly adj. mortal
de-ba-cle n. fracaso
de-bar v. prohibir
de-bate v. debatir
de-bauch v. corromper
de-bauch-er-y n. libertinaje
de-bil-i-tate v. debilitar
de-bil-i-ta-tion n. debilitación
de-bil-i-ty n. debilidad
deb-it n. debe
deb-o-nair adj. cortes; elegante
de-bris n. escombros
debt n. deuda
debt-or n. deudor
de-but, de-but n. presentación; estreno
deb-u-tant, deb-u-tante n. debutante
de-cade n. deceñio
dec-a-dence n. decadencía
dec-a-dent adj. decadente
de-can-ter n. garrafa
de-cay v. decaer; cariarse; deteriorar
de-cease v. morir
de-ceased adj. muerto
de-ceit n. engano
de-ceit-ful adj. enganoso
de-ceive v. enganar
De-cem-ber n. diciembre
de-cen-cy n. decencía
de-cent adj. decente

de-cep-tion *n.* fraude
de-cide *v.* decidir
de-cid-ed *adj.* decidido
de-cid-ed-ly *adv.* decididamente
dec-i-mal *n.* decimal
de-ci-pher *v.* descifrar
de-ci-sion *n.* decision; firmeze
de-ci-sive *adj.* decisivo
de-ci-sive-ly *adv.* con resolución
deck *v.* adornar
dec-la-ra-tion *n.* declaración
de-clare *v.* declarar
de-cline *v.* rehusar
de-com-pose *v.* descomponer(se)
de-com-po-si-tion *n.* descomposición
de-cor-ate *v.* adornar; condecorar
dec-o-ra-tion *n.* decoración; ornato
dec-o-ra-tor *n.* decorador
de-coy *n.* senuelo
de-crease *v.* disminuir(se)
de-creas-ing-ly *adv.* en disminucion
de-cree *n.* decreto
de-crep-it *adj.* decrepito
de-cry *v.* rebajar
de-duce *v.* deducir
de-duct *v.* restar
de-duc-tion *n.* descuento
deed *n.* hecho
deem *v.* juzgar
deep *adj.* profundo
deep-en *v.* intensificar
de-face *v.* desfigurar
def-a-ma-tion *n.* difamación
de-fame *v.* difamar
de-fault *n.* a falta de
de-feat *n.* derrota *v.* vencer; frustrar
de-fect *n.* defecto
de-fec-tion *n.* defección
de-fec-tive *adj.* defectuoso
de-fend *v.* defender
de-fend-ant *n.* demandado
de-fense, de-fence *n.* defensa
de-fen-sive *adj.* defensivo

de-fer *v.* diferir; aplazar
def-er-ence *n.* deferencia
de-fer-ment *n.* apazamiento
de-fi-ance *n.* desafio
de-fi-ant *adj.* provocativo
de-fi-cien-cy *n.* deficiencia
de-fi-cient *adj.* insuficiente
def-i-cit *n.* deficit
de-file *v.* manchar
de-fine *v.* definir
def-i-nite *adj.* concreto; definido
de-fi-ni-tion *n.* definición
de-fin-i-tive *adj.* definitivo
de-flate *v.* desinflar
de-fla-tion *n.* desinflación
de-flect *v.* desviar
de-form *v.* desfigurar; deformar
de-form-i-ty *n.* deformidad
de-fraud *v.* defraudar; estafar
de-fray *v.* pagar
deft *adj.* diestro
deft-ness *n.* habilidad
de-funct *adj.* difunto
de-fy *v.* desafiar; contravenir
de-gen-er-ate *v.* degenerar
deg-ra-da-tion *n.* degradación
de-grade *v.* degradar
de-gree *n.* rango
de-hy-drate *v.* deshidratar
de-hy-dra-tion *n.* deshidratación
de-i-fy *v.* deificar
deign *v.* dignarse
de-i-ty *n.* deidad
de-ject-ed *adj.* abatido
de-jec-tion *n.* melancolia; abatimiento
de-lay *v.* aplazar; demorar
de-lec-ta-ble *adj.* deleitable
de-le-gate *v.* delegar
de-le-ga-tion *n.* diputación
de-lete *v.* tachar
de-le-tion *n.* supresión; borradura
de-lib-er-ate *v.* deliberar
del-i-ca-cy *n.* delicadeze
del-i-cate *adj.* delicado; fino
de-li-cious *adj.* delicioso
de-light *v.* deleitar

de-light-ful *adj.* encantador

de-lin-e-ate *v.* delinear

de-lin-e-a-tion *n.* bosquejo

de-lin-quen-cy *n.* delincuencia

de-lin-quent *adj., n.* delincuente

de-lir-i-ous *adj.* delirante

de-lir-i-um *n.* delirio

de-liv-er *v.* entregar

de-liv-er-y *n.* entrega

del-ta *n.* delta

de-lude *v.* inganar

del-uge *n.* diluvio

de-lu-sion *n.* engano; ilusión

de-luxe *adj.* de lujo

delve *v.* cavar

de-mand *v.* demandar; exigir

de-moc-ra-cy *n.* democracia

dem-o-crat *n.* democrata

dem-o-crat-ic *adj.* democratico

dem-on-strate *v.* demostrar

dem-on-stra-tion *n.* demostración

de-mor-al-ize *v.* desmoralizar

dn *n.* estudio

de-nom-i-na-tion *n.* denominación

de-nom-i-na-tor *n.* denominador

de-note *v.* denotar

de-nounce *n.* denunciar

dense *adj.* denso

den-si-ty *n.* densidad

den-tist *n.* dentista

de-nun-ci-ate *v.* denunciar

de-nun-ci-a-tion *n.* denuncia

de-par-ture *n.* salida

de-pend-en-cy *n.* dependencia

de-port *v.* deportar

de-por-ta-tion *n.* deportación

de-prave *v.* depravar

de-praved *adj.* depravado

de-pres-sion *n.* desaliento

depth *n.* fondo

de-ride *v.* mofar

de-ri-sion *n.* irrision

der-i-va-tion *n.* derivación

de-rive *v.* derivar(se)

der-rick *n.* grua

de-scend *v.* bajar; descender

de-scend-ant *n.* descendiente

de-scribe *v.* describir

de-scrip-tion *n.* descripción

de-scrip-tive *adj.* descriptivo

des-ert *n.* desierto

de-sert-er *n.* desertor

de-serve *v.* merecer

de-sign *v.* idear; disenar

des-ig-nate *v.* senalar; nombrar

des-ig-na-tion *n.* nombramiento

de-sing-er *n.* disenador; dibujante

de-sire *v.* desear

de-sist *v.* desistir

desk *n.* pupitre

des-o-la-tion *n.* desolación

de-spair *v.* desesperar

des-per-ate *adj.* desesperado; arriesgado

des-per-a-tion *n.* desesperación

des-pi-ca-ble *adj.* despreciable

de-spise *v.* despreciar

de-spite *prep.* a pesar de

des-sert *n.* postre

de-stroy *v.* destruir

de-struct-i-ble *adj.* destructible

de-struc-tion *n.* destrucción

de-tain *v.* retener

de-ter *v.* disuadir

de-ter-mi-na-tion *n.* determinación

de-ter-mine *v.* resolver; determinar

de-test-a-ble *adj.* detestable

de-val-u-a-tion *n.* devaluación

dev-as-tate *v.* devastar

dev-as-ta-tion *n.* devastación

de-vel-op *v.* desenvolver

de-vice *n.* ingenio; estratagema

dev-il *n.* diablo

de-vi-ous *adj.* tortuoso

de-vise v. inventar
de-void adj. desprovisto
de-vote v. dedicar
dev-o-tee n. devoto
dev-o-tion n. devoción; lealtad
de-vour v. devorar
di-a-be-tes n. diabetes
di-a-bet-ic adj. diabetico
di-ag-nose v. diagnosticar
di-a-bol-ic adj. diabolico
di-a-dem n. diadema
di-ag-nose v. diagnosticar
di-ag-no-sis n. diagnostico
di-ag-o-na. adj., n. diagonal
di-a-gram n. diagrama
di-al v. marcar
di-a-lect n. dialecto
di-a-logue n. dialogo
di-am-e-ter n. diametro
di-a-met-ric adj. diametral
dia-mond n. diamante; oros
dia-per n. panal
di-a-phragm n. diafragma
di-ar-rhe-a n. diarrea
di-a-ry n. diario
dice n. dados
dick-er v. regatear
dic-tate v. mandar; dictar
dic-ta-tion n. dictado
dic-ta-tor n. dictador
dic-tion-ar-y n. diccionaio
die v. morir
dif-fer-ence n. diferencia
dif-fer-ent adj. diferente
dif-fi-cult adj. dificil
dif-fi-cul-ty n. dificultad
dif-fu-sion n. difusion
dig n. excavacion; v. extraer
di-ges-tion n. digestion
dig-it n. dedo
dig-ni-fy v. dignificar
di-lem-ma n. dilema
dil-i-gence n. diligencia
dil-i-gent adj. diligente
di-lute v. diluir
di-lu-tion n. dilución
dim adj. oscuro
di-min-ish v. disminuir(se)
dine v. cenar
din-ner n. cena
di-plo-ma-cy n. diplomacia
dip-lo-mat n. diplomatico

dip-lo-mat-ic adj. diplomatico
di-rect v. dirigir, adj. directo
di-rec-tion n. dirección
di-rec-tor n. director
dis-a-ble v. inutilizar
dis-ap-pear v. desaparecer
dis-ap-pear-ance n. desaparición
dis-as-trous adj. desastroso
dis-a-vow v. desconocer
dis-charge v. despedir
dis-ci-pli-nar-y adj. disciplinario
dis-ci-pline v. disciplinar, n. castigo
dis-con-nect v. desconectar
dis-con-tin-u-ous adj. discontinuo
dis-cov-er v. descubrir
dis-crep-an-cy n. discrepancia
dis-cus-sion n. discusión
dis-ease n. enfermedad
dis-guise n. disfraz, v. disfrazar
dish n. plato
dis-hon-or v. deshonrar
dis-hon-or-a-ble adj. deshonroso
dis-in-fect-ant n. desinfectante
dis-in-ter-est n. desinteres
disk n. disco
dis-lo-cate v. dislocar
dis-lo-ca-tion n. dislocación
dis-o-bey v. desobedecer
dis-or-der n. desorden
dis-pense v. dispensar
dis-play n. demostrar
dis-pute n. disputa, v. disputar
dis-qual-i-fy v. descalificar
dis-solve v. disolver(se)
dis-suade v. disuadir
dis-sua-sion n. disuasion
dis-tance n. distancia
dis-tant adj. distante
dis-till v. destilar
dis-till-er-y n. destileria
dis-tinc-tion n. distinción
dis-tin-guish v. distinguir
dis-tract v. distraer

dis-trac-tion *n.* distracción
dis-tri-bu-tion *n.* distribución
dis-turb *v.* perturbar
dis-turb-ance *n.* disturbio
di-verge *v.* divergir
di-ver-gence *n.* divergencia
di-ver-sion *n.* diversion
di-ver-si-ty *n.* diversidad
di-vert *v.* divertir
di-vide *v.* dividir(se)
di-vin-i-ty *n.* divinidad
diz-zy *adj.* mareado
do *v.* cumplir; hacer
doc-tor *n.* medico
doc-u-ment *n.* documentar
dog *n.* perro
dog-mat-ic *adj.* dogmatico
doll *n.* muneca
dol-lar *n.* dolar
do-mes-tic *adj.* domestico
do-mes-ti-cate *v.* domesticar
dom-i-nant *v.* dominar
dom-i-na-tion *n.* dominación
dom-i-neer *v.* tiranizar
dom-i-neer-ing *a.* dominante
do-min-ion *n.* dominio
don *v.* ponerse
do-nate *v.* donar
done *adj.* hecho
do-nor *n.* donante
doom *n.* juicio; suerte
door *n.* puerta
dope *n.* narcotico
dor-mi-to-ry *n.* dormitorio
dor-sal *adj.* dorsal
dos-age *n.* dosificación
dose *n.* dosis
dot *n.* punto
dot-age *n.* chochez
dou-ble *v.* doblar(se)
doubt *n.* duda, *v.* dudar
dough *n.* maxa
dough-nut *n.* buñuelo
dour *adj.* austero
douse *v.* mojar; zambullir
dow-a-ger *n.* vuida de un titulado
dow-dy *adj.* desalinado; poso elegante
down *prep., adv.* abajo
down-cast *adj.* abatido
down-fall *n.* caida
down-heart-ed *adj.* desa-
nimado
down-ward *adv.* hacia abajo
doze *v.* dormitar
doz-en *n.* doceña
drab *adj.* monotono
draft *n.* destacamento; giro; borrador
drag *v.* arrastar
drag-on *n.* dragon
drain *v.* agotar; desaguar
drain-age *n.* desague; drenaje
dra-ma *n.* drama
dra-mat-ic *adj.* dramatico
dram-a-tist *n.* dramaturgo
dram-a-tize *v.* dramatizar
drape *v.* poner colgaduras
dra-per-y *n.* paneria
dras-tic *a.* drastico; energico
draw *v.* sacar; dibujar; arrastrar
draw-back *n.* desventaja
draw-bridge *n.* puente levadizo
draw-er *n.* cajon
dread *v.* temer
dread-ful *adj.* terrible
dream *v.* sonar, *n.* sueño
dream-er *n.* sonador
dredge *v.* dragar
dreg *n.* heces
drench *v.* empapar
dress *n.* vestido, *v.* vestir(se)
dress-er *n.* aparador
drib-ble *v.* caer gota a gota
drift *n.* impulso de la corriente; monton
drift-wood *n.* madera llevada por el agua
drill *v.* taladrar
drink *n.* bebida, *v.* beber
drip *v.* gotear
drive *v.* manejar; empujar; conducir
driz-zle *v.* lloviznar
droll *adj.* gracioso
drone *n.* zangano
drool *v.* babear
droop *v.* inclinar
drop *n.* gota; declive
drop-sy *n.* hidropesia
dross *n.* escoria
drought *n.* sequia

drown v. ahogar; engar
drowse v. adormecer(se)
drow-sy adj. sonoliento
drudg-er-y n. faena penosa
drug n. droga
drug-gist n. farmaceutico; boticario
drum n. tambor
drum-stick n. baqueta
drunk adj. borracho
drunk-ard n. borracho
drunk-en adj. borracho
du-al-i-ty n. dualidad
dub v. armar caballero
du-bi-ous adj. dudoso
duch-ess n. duquesa
duck n. pato
duct n. conducto
dude n. petimetre
due adj. debido; oportuno
duel n. duelo
du-et n. duo
duke n. duque
dull adj. embotado; torpe
dumb adj. mudo
dum-found v. pasmar
dum-my n. maniqui
dump v. descargar
dump-ling n. bola de masa
dunce n. zopenco
dune n. duna
dung n. estiercol
dun-geon n. mazmorra
du-pli-cate adj. duplicado, v. duplicar
du-pli-ca-tion n. duplicación
du-ra-tion n. duración
dur-ing prep. durante
dusk n. crepusculo
dusk-y adj. oscuro
dust n. polvo
du-ti-ful adj. obediente
du-ty n. derechos
dwell v. habitar
dewll-ing n. morada
dwin-dle v. disminuir
dye n. tinte
dy-nam-ic adj. dinamico
dy-na-mite n. dinamita
dy-na-mo n. dinamo; dinamo
dy-nas-ty n. dinastia
dys-en-ter-y n. disenteria

each adv. para cada uño
ea-ger adj. impaciente
ea-ger-ness n. ansia
ea-gle n. aguila
ea-glet n. aguilucho
ear n. oido; oreja
ear-drum n. timpaño del oido
earl n. conde
ear-li-ness n. precocidad
ear-ly adj. primitivo adv., adj. temprano
earn v. merecer
ear-nest a. fervoroso; serio
ear-nest-ly adv. con seriedad
earn-ings n. sueldo
ear-ring n. pendiente
ear-shot n alcance del oido
earth n. mundo; tierra
earth-en-ware n. loza de barro
earth-ly adj. mundaño
earth-quake n. terremoto
earth-y a. terroso
ease v. facilitar, n. facilidad
ea=sel n. caballete
eas-i-ly adv. facilmente
eas-i-ness n. facilidad
east n. este
east-ern adj. del este
east-ward adv. hacia el este
eas-y adj. facil
eas-y-go-ing a. acomodadizo; de manga ancha
eat v. gastar; comer
eat-a-ble a. comestible
eaves n. alero
eaves-drop v. escuchar a escondidas; espiar
ebb v. menguar.; decaer
eb-on-y n. ebano
ec-cen-tric adj. excentrico
ec-cen-tric-i-ty n. ex-centricidad
ec-cle-si-as-tic a., n. eclesiastico
ech-o n. eco
e-clipse v. eclipsar
e-clip-tic adj. ecliptico
ec-o-lo-gic a. ecologiso
e-col-o-gist n. ecologo

e-col-o-gy n. ecologia
e-co-nom-ic adj. economico
e-co-nom-ic-al a. economico
e-co-nom-ics n. economia
e-con-o-mist n. economista
e-con-o-mize v. economizar
e-con-o-my n. economia
ec-sta-sy n. extasis
ec-stat-ic a. extatico
ec-u-men-i-cal n. ecumenico
ec-ze-ma n. eczema; eccema
ed-dy n. remolino
e-den-tate a. desdentado
edge n. filo; agudeza; borde
ed-i-ble a. comestible
e-dict n. edicto
ed-i-fi-ca-tion n. edificación
de-i-fice n. edificio
ed-i-fy v. edificar
ed-it v. editar
e-di-tion n. edición
ed-i-tor n. editor
ed-i-to-ri-al a. editorial
ed-i-to-ri-al-ist n. editorialista
ed-u-cate v. educar
ed-u-ca-tion n. educación
eel n. anguila
ee-rie a. espantoso; fantastico
ef-face v. borrar
ef-fect v. efectuar, n. resultado
ef-fec-tive a. efectivo; eficaz
ef-fec-tu-al a. eficaz
ef-fem-i-nate a. afeminado
ef-fer-vesce v. estar en efervescencia
ef-fer-ves-cence n. efervescencia
ef-fer-ves-cent adj. efervescente
ef-fe-ca-cious a. eficaz
ef-fi-cien-cy n. eficiencia
ef-fi-cient adj. eficiente
ef-fi-gy n. efigie
ef-fort n. esfuerzo
ef-fort-less a. sin esfuerzo
ef-fuse v. derramar
ef-fu-sion n. efusion

ef-fu-sive a.j exspansivo; efusivo
egg n. huevo
e-go n. el yo
e-go-tist n. egotista
e-gress n. salida
eight adj. ocho
eight-een adj. dieciocho
eighth adj. octavo
eight-y adj. ochenta
ei-ther adv. tampoco; tambien, adj. cualquier
e-ject v. echar; expulsar
e-jec-tion n. expusion
eke v. aumentar
e-lab-o-rate v. elaborar
e-lab-ra-tion n. elaboración
e-lapse v. pasar
e-last-ic a. elastico
e-las-tic-i-ty n. elasticidad
e-late v. alegrar
e-la-tion n. regocijo
el-bow n. codo
eld-er a. mayor
el-der-ly a. de edad
eld-est a. el major
e-lect v. elegir
e-lec-tion n. elección
e-lec-tive adj. electivo
e-lec-tor n. elector
e-lec-tor-ate n. electorado
e-lec-tric a. electrico; vivo
e-lec-tri-cian n. electricista
e-lec-tric-i-ty n. electricidad
e-lec-tro-cute v. electrocutar
e-lec-trode n. electrodo
e-lec-tron n. electron
e-lec-tron-ic a. electronico
el-e-gance n. elegancia
el-e-gant adj. elegante
el-e-gize v. hacer una elegia
el-e-gy n. elegia
el-e-ment n. elemento
el-e-men-ta-ry adj. elemental
el-e-phant n. elefante
el-e-vate v. elevar
el-e-va-tion n. elevación
el-e-va-tor n. ascensor
e-lev-en adj. once
e-lev-enth a.,n. undecimo

elf-in a. e elfo

e-lic-it v. sacar

el-i-gi-bil-i-ty n. elegibilidad

el-i-gi-ble a. elegible; deseable

e-lim-i-nate v. eliminar

e-lim-i-na-tion n. eliminación

e-lite n.
lo mejor

e-lix-ir n. elixir

elk n. alce

el-lipse n. elipse

el-lip-ti-cal a. eliptico

elm n. olmo

el-o-cu-tion n. elocución

e-lon-gate v. alargar

e-lope v. fugarse con su amante para casarse

e-lope-ment n. fuga

el-o-quence n. elocuencia

el-o-quent a. elocuente

else a. otro; mas

e-lu-ci-date v. elucidar

e-lude v. eludir; escapar de

e-lu-sive a. esquivo

e-ma-ci-ate v.
enflaquecer(se)

e-man-ci-pate v. emancipar

e-man-ci-pa-tion n. emancipación

em-balm v. embalsamar

em-bar-go n. embargo

em-bark v. embarcar(se)

em-bar-rass v. desconcertar

em-bas-sy n. embajada

em-ber n. ascua

em-bez-zle v. desfalcar

em-blem n. emblema

em-boss v. realzar

em-brace v. abrazar; aceptar; abarcar

em-broi-der v. recamar

em-bry-o n. embrion

em-er-ald n. esmeralda

e-merge v. salir

e-mer-gence n. salida

e-mer-gen-cy n. crisis

em-er-y n. esmeril

em-i-grant n. emigrante

em-i-grate v. emigrar

em-i-gra-tion n. emigración

em-i-nence n. eminencia

em-i-nent adj. eminente

em-is-sar-y n. emisario

e-mis-sion n. emision

e-mit v. emitir

e-mo-tion n. emoción

em-per-or n. empreador

em-pha-sis n. enfasis

em-pha-size v. acentuar; recalcar

em-phat-ic a. enfatico

em-pire n. imperio

em-ploy v. emplear

em-ploy-ee n. empleado

em-ploy-er n. amo; patron

em-ploy-ment n. empleo; colocacion

em-pow-er v. autorizar

em-press n. emperatriz

emp-ti-ness n. vacuidad; vacio

emp-ty v. vaciar, adj. desocupado

em-u-late v. emular

e-mul-sion n. emulsion

e-mul-sive a. emulsivo

en-a-ble v. hacer que; permitir

en-act v. decretar; hacer el papel de

e-nam-el n. esmalte

en-am-or v. enamorar

en-case v. encerrar; encajar

en-chant v. encantar

en-chant-ing adj. encantador

en-chant-ment n. encanto

en-cir-cle v. cenir; rodear

en-close v. cercar; encerrar; incluir

en-clo-sure n. cercamiento; carta adjunta

en-com-pass v. cercar; abarcar

en-core n. repeticion

en-coun-ter n. encuentro

en-cour-age v. animar; fomentar

en-croach v. usurpar; pasar los limites

en-cum-ber v. estorbor; gravar

en-cy-clo-pe-dia n. enciclopedia

end n. final; fin

en-dan-ger *v.* poner en peligro

en-dear *v.* hacer querer

en-deav-or *n.* esfuerzo

end-ing *n.* fin

en-dorse *v.* endosar

en-dorse-ment *n.* endoso

en-dow *v.* dotar

en-dur-ance *n.* resistencia

en-dure *v.* durar

en-e-my *n.* enemigo

en-er-get-ic *adj.* energico

en-er-gy *n.* energia

en-force *v.* hacer cumplir; exigir

en-gage *v.* engranar; apalabrar

en-gage-ment *n.* obligación

en-gine *n.* motor; locomotora

en-gi-neer *n.* ingeniero

en-gi-neer-ing *n.* ingenieria

Eng-lish *n.* ingles

en-grave *v.* grabar

en-gross *v.* absorber; monopolizar

en-hance *v.* aumentar

e-nig-ma *n.* enigma

en-join *v.* imponer

en-joy *v.* disfrutar

en-joy-ment *n.* disfrute

en-large *v.* extender(se)

en-large-ment *n.* aumento; ampliación

en-light-en *v.* iluminar; instruir

en-list *v.* alistar(se)

en-liv-en *v.* avivar

en-mi-ty *n.* enemistad

e-nor-mous *adj.* enorme

e-nough *adv.* bastante

en-slave *v.* entrar

en-ter-tain-ment *n.* espectaculo

en-thu-si-asm *n.* entusiasmo

en-thu-si-ast *n.* entusiasta

en-tire *adj.* entero

en-tire-ly *adv.* totalmente

en-trance *n.* entrada

en-trust *v.* entregar

en-try *n.* partida; entrada

en-vel-op *v.* envolver

en-zyme *n.* enzima

ep-i-dem-ic *n.* epidemia

ep-i-sode *n.* episodio

ep-och *n.* epoca

eq-ua-bil-i-ty *n.* uniformidad

eq-ua-ble *a.* uniforme

e-qual *v.* igualar, *n.* igual

e-qual-i-ty *adj.* igualdad

e-qual-ly *adv.* igualmente

e-qual-ize *v.* igualar

e-qual-ly *adv.* igualmente

e-qua-nim-i-ty *n.* ecuanimidad

e-quate *v.* comparar

e-qua-tion *n.* ecuación

e-qua-tor *n.* ecuador

e-ques-tri-enne *n.* jineta

e-qui-lib-ri-um *n.* equilibrio

e-quip *v.* proveer; equipar

e-quip-ment *n.* equipo

eq-ui-ta-ble *a.* equitat

eq-ui-ty *n.* equidad

e-quiv-a-lent *adj.* equivalente

e-ra *n.* era

e-rad-i-cate *v.* desarraigar

e-rase *v.* borrar

e-ras-er *n.* borrador

ere *conj.* antes de que

e-rect *v.* erigir

e-rec-tion *n.* erección

er-mine *n.* armino

e-rode *v.* corroer

e-ro-sion *n.* erosion

e-rot-ic *a.* erotico

err *v.* vagar; errar

er-rand *n.* recado

er-rant *a.* errante

er-ror *n.* error

er-u-dite *a.* erudito

er-u-di-tion *n.* erudicion

e-rupt *v.* estar en erupción

e-rup-tion *n.* erupción

es-ca-la-tor *n.* escalera movil

es-ca-pade *n.* aventura

es-cape *v.* escapar; huir

es-chew *v.* evitar

es-cort *v.* acompanar, *n.* acompanante

e-soph-a-gus, oe-soph-a-gus *n.* esofago

es-o-ter-ic *a.* esoterico

es-pe-cial *adj.* especial

es-pe-cial-ly adv. especialmente

es-pi-o-nage n. espionaje

es-pouse v. adherirse a; casarse

es-py v. divisar; percibir

es-say n. ensayo

es-sence n. esencia; perfume

es-sen-tial adj. esencial

es-tab-lish v. establecer; probar; fundar

es-tab-lish-ment n. establecimiento

es-tate n. finca; propiedad

es-teem v. estimar

es-thet-ic a. estetico

es-ti-ma-ble a. estimable

es-ti-mate v. calcular; estimar

es-ti-ma-tion n. juicio; aprecio

es-thet-ic adj. estetico

es-ti-mate v. estimar

es-ti-ma-tion n. juicio; aprecio

es-trange v. apartar

es-tu-ar-y n. estuario

et cet-er-a n. etcetera

etch v. grabar al agua fuerte

etch-ing n. aguafuerte

e-ter-nal adj. eterno

e-ter-nal-ly adv. eternamente

e-ter-ni-ty n. eternidad

e-ther n. eter

e-the-re-al a. etereo

eth-i-cal adj. etico

eth-ics n. etica

eth-nic a. etnico

eth-nol-o-gy n. etnologia

et-i-quette n. etiqueta

e-tude n. estudio

eu-lo-gize v. elogiar

eu-lo-gy n. elogio

eu-pho-ri-a n. euforia

eu-phor-ic adj. euforico

e-vac-u-ate v. evacuar

e-vac-u-a-tion n. evacuación

e-vade v. evadir

e-val-u-ate v. evaluar

e-val-u-a-tion n. evaluación

e-van-gel-i-cal a. evangelico

e-van-ge-list n. evangelista

e-vap-o-rate v. evaporar(se)

e-vap-o-ra-tion n. evaporación

e-va-sion n. evasion

e-va-sive a. evasivo

eve n. vispera

e-ven adj. igualar

eve-ning n. tarde

e-vent n. suceso

e-vent-ful a. memorable

e-ven-tu-al-i-ty n. eventualidad

ev-er adv. siempre; junca; jamas

eve-ry adj. todo

e-vict v. expulsar

e-vic-tion n. desahucio

ev-i-dence n. evidencia

ev-i-dent a. evidente

e-vil n. mal

e-vil-do-er n. malhechor

e-voke v. evocar

ev-o-lu-tion n. desarrollo; evolución

e-volve v. desarrollar

ewe n. oveja

ew-er n. aguamanil

ex-act adj. exacto

ex-act-ing a. exigente

ex-ag-ger-ate v. exagerar

ex-ag-ger-a-tion n. exageración

ex-alt v. exaltar; honrar

ex-al-ta-tion n. exaltacion

ex-am-in-a-tion n. examen

ex-am-ine v. examinar

ex-am-in-er n. examinador

ex-am-ple n. ejemplo

ex-as-per-ate v. exasperar

ex-as-per-a-tion n. exasperación

ex-ca-vate v. excavar

ex-ca-va-tion n. excavación

ex-ceed v. superar; exceder

ex-ceed-ing-ly adv. sumamente

ex-cel v. sobresalir; aventajar

ex-cel-lence n. excelencia

ex-cel-lent adj. excelente

ex-cept v. exceptuar

ex-cep-tion n. excepción

ex-cep-tion-al a. excepcional

ex-cerpt v. citar un texto
ex-cess n. exceso
ex-ces-sive adj. excesivo
ex-change v. cambiar
ex-cise n. impuestos sobre ciertos articulos
ex-cit-a-ble a. excitable
ex-cite v. excitar
ex-cite-ment n. agitacion; emocion
ex-cit-ing a. emocionante
ex-claim v. exclamar
ex-cla-ma-tion n. exclamacion
ex-clude v. excluir
ex-clu-sion n. exclusion
ex-clu-sive a. exclusivo
ex-com-mu-ni-cate v. excomulgar
ex-com-mu-ni-ca-tion n. excomunion
ex-cre-ment n. excremento
ex-cur-sion n. viaje; excursion
ex-cuse v. excusar; perdonar
ex-e-cute v. ejecutar; llevar a cabo
ex-e-cu-tion n. ejecución
ex-ec-u-tive a. ejecutivo
ex-ec-u-tor n. albacea
ex-em-pla-ry a. ejemplar
ex-er-cise n. ejercicio
ex-hale v. exhalar; espirar
ex-haust v. agotar
ex-hib-it v. mostrar; presentar
ex-hi-bi-tion n. exposición
ex-hil-a-rate v. vigorizar; alegrar
ex-hort v. exhortar
ex-i-gent a. exigente
ex-ile n. exilado; destierro
ex-ist v. existir
ex-ist-ence n. existencia
ex-it n. salida
ex-o-dus exoo
ex-or-bi-tant a. excesivo
ex-o-tic adj. exotico
ex-pand v. extendeer; ensanchar
ex-panse n. extensión
ex-pan-sion n. expansion
ex-pan-sive a. expansivo

ex-pect v. experar; contar con
ex-pect-an-cy n. expectacion
ex-pect-ant a. expectante
ex-pec-ta-tion n. expectacion
ex-pe-di-en-cy n. conveniencia
ex-pe-di-ent a. conveniente
ex-pe-dite v. facilitar; acelerar
ex-pe-di-tion n. expedición
ex-pel v. expulsar
ex-pend v. expender
ex-pend-i-ture n. gasto
ex-pe-ri-ence v. experimentar
ex-per-i-ment n. experimento
ex-pire v. terminar
ex-pla-na-tion n. explicación
ex-pli-cit a. explicito
ex-plode v. estallar; volar
ex-ploit n. hazaña
ex-plo-ra-tion n. exploracion
ex-plor v. explorar; examinar
ex-plor-er n. explorador
ex-plo-sion n. explosion
ex-po-nent n. exponente
ex-port v. exportar
ex-por-ta-tion n. exportacion
ex-pose v. exponer; desenmascarar
ex-press v. expresar
ex-pres-sion n. expresion
ex-pres-sive adj. expresion
ex-tend v. extender
ex-ten-sion n. extension
ex-te-ri-or adj. exterior
ex-tinct adj. extinto
ex-tinc-tion n. extinción
ex-tra n. extra
ex-tra-or-di-nar-y adj. extraordinario
ex-treme adj. extremo
ex-ul-ta-tion n. exultación
eye n. ojo
eye-let n. ojete
eye-sight n. vista
eye-tooth n. colmillo
eye-wit-ness n. testigo ocular

fa-ble n. fabula
fab-ric n. tela
fab-ri-cate v. inventar
fab-u-lous adj. fabuloso
fa-cade n. fachada
face n. cara
fa-cial adj. facial
fa-cile adj. facil
fa-cil-i-tate v. facilitar
fa-cil-i-ty n. facilida
fac-sim-i-le n. facsimile
fact n. hecho
fac-tion n. facción
fac-tor n. factor
fac-to-ry n. fabrica
fac-tu-al a. basado en datos
fac-ul-ty n. facultad
fad n. novedad
fade v. descolorar(se)
fag v. fatigar
fag-ot n. haz de lena
Fahr-en-heit adj. de Fahren-
heit
fail v. acabar; faltar
fail-ure n. fracaso
faint v. desmayarse
faint-ness n. debilidad
fair adj. justo; rubio
fair-ly adv. justamente
fair-y n. hada
faith n. fe
faith-ful adj. fiel
faith-less adj. desleal
fake n. impostura
fal-con n. halcon
fall v. caer(se)
fal-la-cious adj. enganoso
fal-la-cy n. error; falacia
fal-li-ble adj. falible
fal-low adj. en barbecho
false adj. falso
false-hood n. mentira
false-ly adv. falsamente
fal-si-fy v. falsificar
fal-si-ty n. falsedad
fal-ter v. vacilar; titubear
fame n. fama
fa-mil-iar adj. familiar
fa-mil-i-ar-i-ty n. familiaridad
fam-i-ly n. familia
fam-ine n. hambre
fam-ish v. morirse de
hambre

fa-mous adj. famoso
fan n. aficionado
fa-nat-ic n., adj. fanatico
fa-nat-i-cism n. fanatismo
fan-ci-er n. aficionado
fan-ci-ful adj. fantastico
fan-cy n. fantasia
fan-fare n. toque de trom-
petas
fang n. colmillo
fan-tas-tic adj. fan
fan-ta-sy n. fantasia
far adv. lejos
far-a-way adj. remoto
farce n. farsa
far-ci-cal adj. ridiculo
fare v. pasarlo
fare-well ent. adios
far-fetched adj. improbable
farm n. granja
farm-house n. alquería
far-off adj. lejano
fas-ci-nate v. fascinar
fas-cism n. fascismo
fas-cist n. facista
fash-ion n. estilo; moda; uso
fash-ion-a-ble adj. de moda
fast adj. rapidamente; rapido
fas-ten v. abrochar; asegurar
fas-tid-i-ous adj. fino;
esquilimoso
fat adj. gordo
fa-tal adj. fatal
fa-tal-ism n. fatalismo
fa-tal-ist n. fatalista
fa-tal-i-ty n. fatalidad
fate n. suerte
fate-ful adj. fatal
fa-ther n. padre
fa-ther-hood n. paternidad
fa-ther-in-law n. suegro
fath-om n. braza, v.
penetrar
fa-tigue n. fatiga
fat-ten v. engordar
fau-cet n. grifo
fault n. culpa; falta
fault-y adj. defectuoso
fa-vor n. favor
fa-vor-a-ble adj. favorable
fa-vored adj. favorecido
fa-vor-ite adj., n. favorito
fa-vor-it-ism n. favoritismo

fawn n. cervato
faze v. perturbar
fear n. miedo
fear-ful adj. temeroso
fear-less adj. intrepido
fear-some adj. temible
fea-si-bil-i-ty n. viabilidad
fea-si-ble adj. factible
feast n. banquete; fiesta
feat n. proeze
feath-er n. pluma
feath-er-y adj. plumoso
fea-ture n. facción; rasgo
Feb-ru-ar-y n. febrero
fe-ces n. excrementos
fe-cund adj. fecundo
fed-er-al adj. federal
fed-er-a-tion n. federación
fee n. honorario
fee-ble adj. debil
fee-bly adv. flojamente
feed v. alimentar
feel v. sentir(se)
feel-er n. antena
feel-ing n. emoción
feign v. fingir
feint n. treta
fe-lic-i-tate v. flicitar
fe-lic-i-tous a. oportuno; feliz
fe-lic-i-ty n. felicidad
fe-line adj. felino
fell v. talar
fel-low n. compañero
fel-low-ship n. com-
   panerismo
fel-on n. criminal
fel-o-ny n. crimen
felt n. fieltro
fe-male n. hembra
fem-i-nine adj. femenino
fe-mur n. femur
fence v. esgrimir
fenc-ing n. esgrima
fend v. rechazar
fen-der n. guardafango
fer-ment v. fermentar
fer-men-ta-tion n. fermen-
   tacion
fern n. helecho
fe-ro-cious adj. feroz
fe-ro-ci-ty n. ferocidad
fer-ret n. huron
fer-ry n. transbordador

fer-tile adj. fecundo; fertil
fer-til-i-ty n. fecundidad
fer-ti-lize v. fertilizar
fer-ti-liz-er n. abono
fer-vid adj. fervido
fer-vor n. fervor
fes-ter v. enconarse
fes-ti-val n. fiesta
fes-tive adj. festivo
fes-tiv-i-ty n. regocijo; fiesta
fes-toon n. feston
fetch v. ir por
fetch-ing adj. atractivo
fete, fete n. fiesta
fet-id adj. fetido
fet-ish n. fetiche
fet-it adj. fetido
fet-ter n. grillos
fet-tle n. condición
fe-tus n. feto
feud n. enemistad
feu-dal adj. feudal
feu-dal-ism n. feudalismo
fe-ver n. fiebre
fe-ver-ish adj. febril
few adj. pocos
fi-an-ce n. novio
fi-an-cee n. novia
fi-as-co n. fiasco
fi-at n. fiat
fib v. mentir
fi-ber, fi-bre n. fibra
fi-brous adj. fibroso
fick-le adj. inconstante
fic-tion n. ficcion
fic-tion-al adj. novelesco
fic-ti-tious adj. ficticio
fid-dle n. violin
fi-del-i-ty n. fidelidad
fidg-et v. inquietar
fidg-et-y adj. inquieto;
   azogado
field n. prado; campo
fiend n. demonio
fiend-ish adj. diabolico
fierce adj. feroz
fier-y a. ardiente; apaionado
fif-teen adj. quince
fif-teenth adj. decimoquinto
fifth adj. quinto
fif-ti-eth adj. quincuagesimo
fif-ty adj. cincuenta
fig n. higo

fight v. pelear; luchar, n. pelea; lucha

fight-er n. guerrero

fig-ment n. invención

fig-ur-a-tive adj. figuardo

fig-ure n. tipo; figura

fig-ure-head n. mascaron de proa

fig-ur-ine n. figurin

fil-a-ment n. filamento

filch v. ratear

file n. lima; archivo; fila

fi-let n. filete. Also fil-let

fil-i-bus-ter n. obstruccionist

fil-i-gree n. filigraña

fil-ings n. limaduras

fill v. llenar

fill-ing n. empaste; relleno

fil-ly n. potra

film n. película

fil-ter n. filtro

filth n. inmundicia

filth-y adj. sucio

fin n. aleta

fi-nal adj. final

fi-na-le n. final

fi-nal-ist n. finalista

fi-nal-i-ty n. finalidad

fi-nal-ly adv. finalmente; por fin

fi-nance n. finanzas

fi-nan-cial adj. financiero

fin-an-cier n. financiero

finch n. pinzón

find v. hallar; encontrar

fine adj. fino; admirable; multa, v. multar

fin-er-y n. adornos

fi-nesse n. sutileza; diplomacia

fin-ger n. dedo

fin-ger-nail n. uña

fin-ger-print n. huella dactilar

fin-ish v. terminar; acabar

fi-nite adj. finito

fir n. abeto

fire n. fuego

fire-arm n. arma de fuego

fire-crack-er n. petardo

fire en-gine n. bomba de incendios

fire-fly n. luciérnaga

fire-man n. bombero

fire-place n. hogar

firm adj. firme

fir-ma-ment n. firmamento

firm-ly adv. firmemente

firm-ness n. firmeza

first adj. primero

first-class adj. de primera clase

first-hand adj. de primera mano

first-rate a. de primera clase

fis-cal adj. fiscal

fish n. pez

fish-er-man n. pescador

fish-ery n. pesquera

fish-y adj. sospechoso

fis-sion n. fisión

fis-sure n. grieta

fist n. puño

fist-i-cuffs n. punetazor

fit v. probar; acomodar, adj. adecuado

fit-ful adj. espasmodico

fit-ting n. ajuste; adj. propio; conveniente

five adj. cinco

fix v. arreglar

fix-a-tion n. fijación

fix-ed adj. fijo

fix-ture n. cosa o instalación fija

fla-by adj. flojo; debil

flag n. bandera

flag-on n. jarro; frasco

fla-grant adj. notorio

flag-stone n. losa

flail n. mayal

flair n. instinto

flake n. escama, v. formar hojuelas

flak-y adj. escamoso

flam-boy-ant adj. llamativo

flame n. llama; v. flamear

flam-ma-ble adj. inflamable

flank n. ijada; lado, v. lindar; flanquear

flap v. ondear

flare v. brillar; fulgurar, n. bengala

flash n. relampago; rafaga, v. lanzar

flash-light n. linterna

electrica
flash-y *adj.* charro
flask *n.* frasco
flat *adj.* plano; llano
flat-ter-y *n.* adulación
flaunt *v.* lucir
fla-vor *n.* sabor
fla-vor-ing *n.* condimento
flaw *n.* imperfeccion
flax *n.* lino
flay *v.* desollar
flea *n.* pulga
fleck *n.* mancha
flee *v.* fugarse; huir
fleece *n.* vellon
fleec-y *adj.* lanudo
fleet *adj.* veloz
fleet-ing *adj.* fugaz
flesh *n.* carne
flex *v.* doblar
flex-i-ble *adj.* flexible
flick *n.* golpecito
fli-er *n.* aviador
flight *n.* vuelo
flim-sy *adj.* endeble
flinch *v.* acobardarse
fling *v.* arrojar
flint *n.* pedernal
flip *v.* mover de un tiron
flip-pant *adj.* ligero
flirt *v.* flirtear; coquetear
flit *v.* revolotear
float *v.* flotar; hacer flotar
flock *n.* rebanc
floe *n.* témpano
flog *v.* azotar
flood *n.* diluvio
floor *n.* suelo; piso
flop *v.* caer pesadamente; fracasar
flo-ra *n.* flora
flo-ral *adj.* floral
flor-id *adj.* florido
flo-rist *n.* florista
floss *n.* seda floja
flo-til-la *n.* flotilla
flounce *v.* moverse airadamente
floun-der *v.* tropezar
flour *n.* harina
flour-ish *v.* florecer; blandir
flout *v.* mofarse
flow *v.* fluir

flow-er *n.* flor
flu *n.* gripe
fluc-tu-ate *v.* fluctuar
flue *n.* canon de chimenea
flu-en-cy *n.* fluidez
flu-ent *adj.* facundo
fluff-y *adj.* plumosa
flu-id *adj.* fluido
flude *n.* chirpia
flunk *v.* no aprobar
flu-o-res-cent *adj.* fluores-cente
flur-ry *n.* rafaga; agitación
flush *adj.* nivelado
flus-ter *v.* aturdir
flute *n.* flauta
flut-ter *n.* aleteo, *v.* revolotear
flux *n.* mudanza; flujo
fly *v.* volar, *n.* mosca
fly-er *n.* aviador
fly-wheel *n.* rueda volante
foal *n.* potro
foam *n.* espuma
fo-cus *v.* enfocar
fod-der *n.* forraje
foe *n.* enemigo
fog *n.* niebla
fo-gy *n.* sona de ideas an-ticuadas
foi-ble *n.* flaco
foil *n.* hoja; florete
foist *v.* encajar
fold *v.* plegar; doblar
fold-er *n.* carpeta
fo-li-age *n.* follaje
folk *n.* gente
folk-lore *n.* folklore
fol-li-cle *n.* foliculo
fol-low *v.* perseguir; seguir
fol-low-er *n.* seguidor
fol-ly *n.* locura; tonteria
fo-ment *v.* fomentar
fond *adj.* carinoso
fon-dle *v.* acariciar
fond-ly *adv.* afectuosamente
food *n.* alimento
fool *n.* tonto
fool-har-dy *adj.* temerario
fool-ish *adj.* necio
fool-proof *adj.* infalible
foot *n.* pata; pie
foot-ball *n.* fútbol

foot-note n. nota
foot-print n. huella
foot-step n. paso
fop n. petimetre
for conj. pues, prep. para; por
for-age n. forraje
for-ay n. correria
for-bear v. contenerse
for-bid v. prohibir
for-bid-den adj. prohibido
for-ceps n. forceps
for-ci-ble a. energico; eficaz
ford n. vado
fore adj. anterior
fore-arm n. antebrazo
fore-bode v. presagiar
fore-cast v. pronosticar
fore-fa-ther n. antepasado
fore-fin-ger n. dede indice
fore-go v. preceder; renun- ciar
fore-gone a. predeterminado
fore-ground n. primer plano
fore-head n. frente
for-eign adj. extranjero
for-eign-er n. extranjero
fore-man n. capatiz
fore-most adj. primero
fore-run-ner n. precursor
fore-see v. prever
foresight n. prevision; perspicacia
fore-skin n. prepucio
for-est n. bosque
fore-tell v. predecir
for-ev-er adv. siempre
fore-word n. prefacio
for-feit v. perder
forge n. fragua
for-ger-y n. falsificación
for-get v. olvidar(se)
for-get-ful adj. olvidadizo
for-give v. perdonar
fork n. tenedor
for-lorn adj. abandonado
form n. forma
for-mal adj. ceremonioso
for-mal-i-ty n. formalidad
for-mat n. formato
for-ma-tion n. formación
for-mer adj. anterior
for-mer-ly adv. an-

tiguamente
for-mi-da-ble adj. formidable
for-mu-la n. formula
for-ni-cate v. fornicar
for-ni-ca-tion n. fornicación
for-sake v. abandonar
fort n. fuerte
forth adv. en adelante
forth-com-ing adj. próximo
forth-right adj. directo
for-ti-fi-ca-tion n. for- tificacion
for-tune n. fortuna
for-ty adj. cuarenta
for-ward adv. adelante
fos-sil n. fosil
foul adj. sucio
foun-da-tion n. fundación
foun-tain n. fuente
four adj. cuarto
four-teen adj. catorce
fourth adj. cuarto
fox n. zorra
fra-cas n. rina
frac-tion n. fracción
frac-ture v. quebrar, n. frac- tura
frag-ile adj. frágil
frag-ment n. fragmento
fra-grence n. fragancia
fra-grant adj. oloroso
frail adj. debil; fragil
frail-ty n. fragilidad
frame n. estructura; marco
fframe-work n. esqueleto
franc n. franco
fran-chise n. derecho de sufragio
frank adj. franco
frank-in-cense n. incienso
frank-ly adv. francamente
frank-ness n. franqueza
fran-tic adj. frenetico
fra-ter-ni-ty n. fraternidad
fraud n. fraude
fraught adj. lleno de
fray v. deshilacharse
freak n. monstruosidad; finomeno
freck-le n. peca
free v. libertar, adj. libre
free-dom n. libertad
free-way n. autopista

freeze v. helar(se); congelar
freight n. flete
freight-er n. buque de carga
French n., adj. frances
fre-net-ic adj. frenetico
fren-zy n. frenesi
fre-quen-cy n. frecuencia
fre-quent adj. frecuente
fres-co n. fresco
fresh adj. fresco
fresh-en v. refrescar
fret v. apararse
fret-ful adj. displicente
fri-ar n. fraile
fric-tion n. fricción
Friday n. viernes
friend n. amigo, amiga
friend-ly adj. amistoso
frieze n. friso
fright n. susto
fright-en v. asustar
frig-id adj. frio
frill n. lechuga
fringe n. orla; margen
frisk v. retoar
frit-ter v. desperdiciar
fro adv. atras
frock n. vestido
frog n. rana
from prep. desde; de
front n. frente
fron-tal adj. frontal
frown n. ceno
fru-gal adj. frugal
fruit n. fruta
frus-trate v. frustrar
frus-tra-tion n. frustración
fry v. freir
fu-gi-tive n., adj. fugitivo
full adj. completo; lleno
ful-ly adv. completamente
func-tion v. funcionar
func-tion-al adj. funcional
fun-da-men-tal adj. fun-
  damental
fun-ny adj. comico
fur n. piel
fu-ri-ous adj. furioso
fur-ni-ture n. mueblaje
fur-ther adj., adv. mas lejos
fuse n. fusible; espoleta
fu-tile adj. inutil
fuzz n. pelusa

gab-ar-dine n. gabardina
ga-ble n. aguilon; faldon
gad v. andorrear
gad-fly n. tabaon
gad-get n. aparato
gaff n. arpon
gag v. amordazar
gai-e-ty n. alegria
gai-ly adv. alegremente
gain v. ganar
gain-say v. contradecir
gait n. modo de andar
ga-la n. fiesta
gal-ax-y n. galaxia
gale n. ventarron
gall n. bilis
gal-lant adj. valeroso
gal-lant-ry n. galanteria
gal-ler-y n. galeria
gal-ley n. galera; fogón
gal-lon n. galón
gal-lop n. galope
gal-lows n. horca
gal-va-nize v. galvanizar
gam-bit n. gambito
gam-ble v. jugar
gam-bol v. brincar
game n. partido; juego
gam-ut n. gama
gan-der n. ganso
gang n. pandilla
gan-grene n. gangrena
gang-ster n. gangster; pis-
  tolero
gang-way n. pasillo
gap n. hueco
ga-rage n. garaje
garb n. vestido
gar-bage n. basura
gar-ble v. mutilar
gar-den n. jardin
gar-gan-tu-an a. colosal
gar-gle v. gargarizar
gar-ish v. llamativo
gar-land n. guirnalda
gar-ment n. prenda de vestir
gar-ner n. granero
gar-net n. granate
gar-nish v. adornar
gar-ret n. guardilla
gar-ri-son n. guarnición
gar-ru-lous adj. garrulo
gar-ter n. liga

gas *n.* gasolina

gas-e-ous *adj.* gaseous

gash *n.* cuchillada

gas-o-line *n.* gasolina

gasp *v.* boquear

gas-tric *adj.* gastrico

gas-tron-o-my *n.* gastronomia

gate *n.* puerta

gate-way *n.* paso

gath-er *v.* fruncir; reunir

gauche *adj.* torpe

gaud-y *adj.* chillón

gauge *n.* norma de medida; indicador

gaunt *adj.* flaco

gaunt-let *n.* guantelete

gauze *n.* gasa

gawk-y *adj.* desgarbado

gay *adj.* alegre; vistoso

gaze *v.* mirar

ga-zelle *n.* gacela

ga-zette *n.* gaceta

gaz-et-teer *n.* diccionario geografico

gear *v.* engranar

gel-a-tin *n.* gelatina

ge-lat-i-nous *adj.* gelatinoso

geld *v.* castrar

gem *n.* joya; gema

gen-der *n.* genero

gene *n.* gen

ge-ne-al-o-gy *n.* genealogia

gen-er-al *adj.* general

gen-er-al-i-ty *n.* generalidad

gen-er-al-ize *v.* generalizar

gen-er-ate *v.* generar

gen-er-tion *n.* generador

gen-er-a-tor *n.* generador

ge-ner-ic *adj.* generico

gen-er-os-i-ty *n.* generosidad

gen-er-ous *adj.* generoso

gen-e-sis *n.* genesis

ge-net-ic *adj.* genesico

gen-ial *adj.* afable

gen-i-tal *adj.* genital

gen-ius *n.* genio

gen-o-cide *n.* genocidio

gen-teel *adj.* elegante; bien criado

gen-til-i-ty *n.* gentilize

gen-tle *adj.* suave; apacible

gen-tle-man *n.* caballero

gen-tly *adv.* suavemente

gen-u-ine *adj.* genuino; sincero

ge-nus *n.* género

ge-o-gra-pher *n.* geógrafo

ge-o-gra-phic, ge-o-graph-i-cal *adj.* geografico

ge-o-gra-phy *n.* geografía

ge-o-log-ic *adj.* geologico

ge-ol-o-gist *n.* geologo

ge-ol-o-gy *n.* geologia

ge-o-met-ric *adj.* geométrico

ge-om-e-try *n.* geometria

ge-o-phys-i-cal *a.* geofisico

ge-o-phys-ics *n.* geofisica

ger-i-at-rics *n.* geriatria

germ *n.* germen

ger-mane *adj.* relativo

ger-mi-nate *v.* germinar

ger-mi-na-tion *n.* germinación

ger-und *n.* gerundio

ges-tic-u-late *v.* gesticular

ges-ture *n.* gesto

get *v.* lograr; obtener

gey-ser *n.* geiser

ghast-ly *adj.* horrible

gher-king *n.* pepinillo

ghost *n.* fantasma

ghost-ly *adj.* espectral

ghoul *n.* demonio

GI *n.* soldado

giant *adj.* gigantesco

gib-ber-ish *n.* galimatias; jerga

gib-bon *n.* gibón

gibe, jibe *v.* mofarse; burlarse

gib-let *n.* menudillos

gid-di-ness *n.* vertigo

gid-dy *adj.* mareado; ligero

gift *n.* regalo; don

gi-gan-tic *adj.* gigantesco

gig-gle *n.* risa sofocada

gild *v.* dorar

gill *n.* agalla

gilt *adj.* dorado

gim-mick *n.* truco

gin *n.* desmotadera de algodon; ginebra

gin-ger *n.* jengibre

gin-ger ale *n.* cerveza de

jengibre
gin-ger-bread n. pan de jengibre
gin-ger-ly adj. cauteloso
gip-sy n. gitano
gi-raffe n. jirafa
gird v. cenir
gird-er n. viga
gir-dle n. cinto; faja
girl n. chica; niña
girl-ish adj. de niña
girth n. cincha
gist n. esencial; clave
give v. entregar; dar
giv-en adj. citado
giz-zard n. molleja
gla-cial adj. glacial
gla-cier n. glaciar
glad adj. alegre
glad-den v. regocijar
glade n. claro
glad-ly adv. con mucho gusto
glad-ness n. alegria
glad-i-o-lus n. gladiolo
glam-our, glam-or n. encanto
glam-our-ous a. encantador
glance v. rebotar; mirar
gland n. glandula
glan-du-lar adj. glandular
glare v. relumbrar
glar-ing adj. evidente
glass n. vidrio; vaso
glass-y adj. vitreo
glau-co-ma n. glaucoma
glaze v. vidriar
gleam n. espigar
glee n. jubilo
glen n. jubilo
glide v. deslizarse
glim-mer v. brillar debilmente
glimpse n. vislumbre
glint v. destellar
glis-ten v. relucir
glit-ter v. relucir
gloat v. manifestar saticfacion maligna
globe n. globo; esfera
glob-ule n. globulo
gloom n. tristeza
gloom-y adj. lobrego;

melancolico
glo-ri-fy v. glorificar
glo-ri-ous adj. glorioso
glo-ry n. gloria
gloss n. lustre
glos-sa-ry n. glosario
gloss-y adj. lustroso
glot-tis n. glotis
glove n. guante
glow v. brillar
glow-er v. mirar con ceño
glow-worm n. luciernaga
glue v. encolar
glum adj. abatido
glut v. hartar
glut-ton n. glotón
glut-ton-y n. gula
gnarl v. torcer
gnash v. rechinar
gnat n. jejen
gnaw v. roer
gnome n. gnomo
go v. ir
goad n. aguijada; incitar
goal n. meta; gol
goat n. cabra
gob-ble v. engullir
gob-let n. copa
gob-lin n. trasgo
God n. Dios
god-child n. ahijado
god-daugh-ter n. ahijada
god-dess n. diosa
god-fa-ther n. padrino
god-ly adj. piadoso
god-moth-er n. madrina
god-par-ent n. padrino; madrina
god-send n. buena suerte
god-son n. ahijado
gog-gles n. anteojos
go-ing n. ida; estado del camino
gold n. oro
golf n. golf
gon-do-la n. gondola
gon-do-lier n. goldolero
gong n. gong
gon-or-rhe-a n. gonorrea
good n. bien
good-by; good-bye int. adios
good-heart-ed adj. amable

good-look-ing *adj.* guapo
good-ly *adj.* agradable; considerable
good-ness *n.* bondad
good-y *n.* golosina
goose *n.* ganso
goose-ber-ry *n.* uva espina
gore *n.* sangre
gorge *n.* barranco
gor-geous *adj.* magnifico; vistoso
gos-pel *n.* evangelio
gos-sa-mer *n.* gasa sutil
gos-sip *n.* chisme; comadre
gouge *n.* gubia
gourd *n.* calabaza
gour-met *n.* gastronomo
gout *n.* gota
gov-ern *v.* gobernar
gov-ern-ess *n.* institutriz
gov-ern-ment *n.* gobierno
gov-er-nor *n.* gobernador
gown *n.* vestido
grab *v.* asir; arrebatar
grace *n.* gracia
grace-ful *adj.* gracioso
gra-cious *adj.* agradable
gra-da-tion *n.* gradación
grade *n.* grado; clase
grad-u-al *adj.* gradual
grad-u-al-ly *adv.* poco a poco
grad-u-ate *v.* graduar(se)
grad-u-a-tion *n.* graduación
graft *n.* injerto; soborno
grain *n.* graño; bifra
gram *n.* gramo
gram-mar *n.* gramatica
gram-mat-i-cal *adj.* gramatical
gra-na-ry *n.* granero
grand *adj.* magnifico; grandioso
grand-child *n.* nieto
grand-daugh-ter *n.* nieta
grand-fa-ther *n.* abuelo
grand-moth-er *n.* abuela
grand-par-ent *n.* abuelo
grand-son *n.* nieto
grange *n.* cortijo
gran-ite *n.* granito
grant *v.* conferir; otorgar
gran-u-late *v.* granular

gran-ule *n.* grañulo
grape *n.* uva
grape-fruit *n.* toronja
graph *n.* grafica
graph-ic *adj.* grafico
graph-ite *n.* grafito
grap-nel *n.* arpeo
grap-ple *n.* arpeo
grasp *v.* agarrar; comprender
grasp-ing *adj.* codicioso
grass *n.* hierba
grass-hop-per *n.* saltamontes
grass-y *adj.* herboso
grate *n.* parrilla de hogar
grate-ful *adj.* agradecido
grat-i-fi-ca-tion *n.* gratificación; placer
grat-i-fy *v.* complacer; satisfacer
grat-ing *n.* reja
gra-tis *adj., adv.* gratis
grat-i-tude *n.* reconocimiento
gra-tu-i-tous *adj.* gratuito; injustificado
gra-tu-i-ty *n.* propina
grave *n.* sepultura
grav-el *n.* cascajo
grav-en *adj.* grabado
grave-yard *n.* cementerio
grav-i-tate *v.* gravitar
grav-i-ta-tion *n.* gravitación
grav-i-ty *n.* seriedad; gravedad
gra-vy *n.* salsa
gray, grey *adj., n.* gris
graze *v.* pacer; rozar
grease *n.* grasa
greas-y *adj.* grasiento
great *adj.* grande; gran
greed *n.* avaricia; codicia
greed-y *adj.* avaro; codicioso; goloso
green *adj., n.* verde
green-er-y *n.* verdura
greet *v.* saludar
greet-ing *n.* saludo
gre-gar-i-ous *a.* gregario
gre-nade *n.* granada de mano
grid *n.* reja; parrilla

grid-dle n. tortera

grid-i-ron n. campo de fútbol; parrilla

grief n. pesar

griev-ance n. agravio

grieve v. afligirse

griev-ous adj. grave; penoso

grif-fin, grif-fon n. grifo

grill v. asar a la parrilla

grille, grill n. verja

grim adj. inflexible; severo

grim-ace n. visaje

grime n. mugre

grim-y adj. mugriento

grin v. sonreir

grind v. moler; pulverizar

grind-stone n. muela

grip n. agarro; apreton; saco de mano

grippe n. gripe

gris-ly adj. horroroso

gris-tle n. cartilago

grit n. arena; firmeza

grit-ty adj. arenoso

griz-zled, griz-zly adj. gris

groan v. gemir

gro-cer n. abacero

gro-cer-y n. abaceria

groin n. ingle

groom n. novio; mozo de caballos

groove n. estria

grope v. buscar a tientas

gross adj. bruto; grosero; grueso

gro-tesque adj. grotesco

grot-to n. gruta

grouch v. refunfuñar

ground n. tierra; terreno; razon; poso

ground-work n. fundamento

group n. grupo

grouse v. quejarse

grove n. abbeleda

grov-el v. arrastrarse

gus-to n. entusiasmo

gym n. gimnasio

gym-nast n. gimnasta

gym-nas-tic adj. gimnastico

gy-ne-col-o-gy n. ginecologa

gyp v. estafar

gyp-sum n. jeso

hab-it n. costumbre

hab-it-a-ble adj. habitable

hab-i-tat n. habitación

hab-i-ta-tion n. habitación

ha-bit-u-al adj. habitual

ha-bit-u-ate v. acostumbrarse

hack v. acuchillar

hack-neyed adj. trillado

had v. pt. and pp. of have

hag n. bruja

hag-gard adj. ojeroso

hag-gle v. regatear

hail n. granizo, v. granizar

hail-stone n. piedra de granizo

hair n. pelo; cabello

hair-breadth n. ancho de un pelo

hair-dress-er n. peluquero

hair-pin n. horquilla

hale adj. robusto

half n. mitad

half-way n. pasillo

hall n. sala

hal-le-lu-jah int. aleluya

hal-low v. consagrar

hal-lu-cin-a-tion n. alucinación

hall-way n. pasillo

hal-o n. halo; aureola

halt v. parar

hal-ter n. cabestro

halve v. partir por mitad

ham n. jamón

ham-burg-er n. hamburguesa

ham-let n. aldehuela

ham-mer v. martillar, n. martillo

ham-mock n. hamaca

ham-per v. impedir

hand n. mano

hand-bag n. bolso

hand-book n. manual

hand-cuff n. esposas

hand-ful n. puñado

hand-i-cap n. desventaja

hand-ker-chief n. panuelo

han-dle n. mango; manubrio

hand-some adj. hermoso

hand-y adj. conveniente; prozimo; habil

hang v. pegar; colgar
hang-er-on n. pegote
hank-er v. anhelar
hap-haz-zard adj. fortuito
hap-pen v. pasar
hap-pen-ing n. acontecimiento
hap-pi-ly adv. alegremente
hap-pi-ness n. alegria
hap-py adj. feliz
har-bor n. puerto
hard adj. firme
har-dy adj. robusto
harm v. dañar
harm-ful adj. dañino
har-mo-ni-ous adj. armonioso
har-mo-ny n. armonia
harsh adj. severo
harsh-ness n. severidad
har-vest v. cosechar
hat n. sombrero
hatch v. empollar, n. portezuela
hatch-et n. machado
hate n. odio, v. odiar
hate-ful adj. odioso
have v. tener
hawk n. halcon
haz-ard v. arriesgar, n. azar
he pron. el
head n. cabeza
head-ache n. dolor de cabeza
head-ing n. titulo
head-land n. promontorio
head-light n. faro
head-quar-ters n. cuartel general
head-way n. progreso
heal v. sanar; curar
health n. salud
health-ful adj. sano
heap n. monton
hear v. oir
hear-ing n. oido
hear-say n. rumor
hearse n. coche funebre
heart n. corazon
heart-ache n. angustia
heart-break n. angustia
hearten v. alentar
heart-felt adj. sincero

hearth n. hogar
heat v. calentar, n. calor
heat-er n. calentador
heath n. brezal
heave v. levantar
heav-en n. cielo
heav-y adj. fuerte
heck-le v. interrumpor
hec-tic adj. febril
hedge n. seto
heed v. escuchar
heel n. talon
heft n. bulto
heif-er n. vaquilla
height n. altura
height-en v. elevar
hei-nous adj. atroz
heir n. heredero
heir-ess n. heredera
heir-loom n. herencia; reliquia de familia
hel-i-cop-ter n. helicoptero
he-li-um n. helio
he-lix n. helice
hell n. infierno
hell-ish adj. infernal
hel-lo int. hola
helm n. timon
hel-met n. casco
help n. ayuda, v. ayudar
help-ful adj. util
help-ing n. racion
help-less adj. incapaz
hem n. dobladillo
hem-i-sphere n. hemisferio
hem-i-spher-ic adj. hemisferico
hem-or-rhage n. hemorragia
hem-or-rhoid n. hemorroides
hemp n. cañamo
hen n. gallina
hence adv. de aqui; por lo tanto
her pron. obj. and poss. she
her-ald n. heraldo; precursor
he-ral-dic adj. heraldico
her-ald-ry n. heraldica
herb n. hierba
her-ba-ceous adj. herbáceo
her-cu-le-an adj. herculeo
herds-man n. pastor

here *adv.* aquí
here-af-ter *adv.* en el futuro
he-red-i-tar-y *adj.* hereditario
he-red-i-ty *n.* herencia
here-in *adv.* incluso
her-e-sy *n.* herejía
her-e-tic *n.* hereje
here-to-fore *adv.* hasta ahora
her-it-age *n.* herencia
her-mit *n.* ermitaño
her-mit-age *n.* ermita
her-ni-a *n.* hernia
he-ro *n.* heroe
he-ro-ic *adj.* heroico
her-o-ine *n.* heroína
her-o-ism *n.* heroísmo
her-on *n.* garszo
hers *pron. poss. of.* she
her-self *pron.* ella misma; si misma
hes-i-tant *adj.* vacilante
hes-i-tate *v.* vacilar
het-er-o-ge-ne-ous *adj.* heterogénio
hew *v.* tajar
hax-a-gon *n.* hexágono
hex-ag-o-nal *adj.* hexagonal
hi-ber-nate *v.* invernar
hic-cup *n.* hipo
hide *v.* ocultar(se)
hid-e-ous *adj.* horrible; feo
hi-er-ar-chy *n.* jerarquía
hi-er-ogyiphic *adj.* jeroglícifo
high *adj.* alto
hike *n.* caminata
hi-lar-i-ous *adj.* alegre
hi-lar-i-ty *n.* alegría
hill *n.* colina
hilt *n.* puño
him *pron. obj. of* he
him-self *pron.* el mismo
hind *adj.* trasero
hin-der *v.* impedir
hind-most *adj.* postrero
hinge *n.* gozne
hint *n.* indirecta
hip *n.* cadera
hip-po-pot-a-mus *n.* hipo-potamo
hire *v.* alquilar
hire-ling *n.* mercenario
his *pron.* suyo

hiss *v.* silbar
his-to-ri-an *n.* historiador
his-tor-ic *adj.* historico
his-to-ry *n.* historia
hit *n.* golpe, *v.* golpear
hitch *v.* atar
hitch-hike *v.* hace autostop
hith-er *adv.* aca
hive *n.* colmena
hoard *n.* provision
hoarse *adj.* ronco
hoax *n.* engaño
hob-ble *v.* cojear
hob-by *n.* pasatiempo
ho-bo *n.* vagabundo
hod *n.* azadon
hog *n.* puerco
hoist *v.* alzar
hold *v.* contener; tener
hold-ing *n.* tenencia
hole *n.* hoyo
hol-i-day *n.* día de fiesta
hol-low *adj.* vacío
hol-ly *n.* acebo
hol-o-caust *n.* holocausto
hol-ster *n.* pistolera
hom-age *n.* homenaje
home *n.* casa
home-ly *adj.* feo
home-sick *adj.* nostálgico
home-ward *adv.* hacia casa
home-y *adj.* comodo
hom-i-cide *adj.* homicidio
hom-i-ly *n.* homilia
ho-mo-gen-e-ous *adj.* homogéneo
hone *n.* piedra de afilar
hon-est *adj.* honrado
hon-es-ty *n.* honradez
hon-ey *n.* miel
hon-ey-comb *n.* panal
hon-ey-moon *n.* luna de miel
hon-ey-suck-le *n.* madre-selva
hon-or *v.* honrar, *n.* honor
hon-or-a-ble *adj.* honorable
hon-or-ar-y *adj.* honorario
hood *n.* capucha
hood-lum *n.* matón
hood-wink *v.* enganar
hoof *n.* casco
hook *n.* gancho, *v.*

enganchar; encorvar
hoop n. aro
hoot v. ulular, n. grito
hop n. salto, v. saltar
hope v. desear, n. esperanza
hope-less adj. desesperado
horde n. horda
ho-ri-zon n. horizonte
hor-i-zon-tal adj. horizontal
hor-mone n. hormona
horn n. cuerno
hor-o-scope n. horoscopo
hor-ri-ble adj. horrible
hor-ri-fy v. horrorizar
hor-ror n. horror
horse n. caballo
horse-man n. jinete
horse-pow-er n. caballo de fuerza
horse-rad-ish n. rabaño picante
horse-shoe n. herradura
hor-ti-cul-ture n. horticultura
hose n. medias
hose n. manga
ho-sier-y n. calcetería
hos-pi-ta-ble a. hospitalario
hos-pi-tal n. hospital
hos-pi-tal-i-ty n. hospitalidad
host n. anfitrion; patron; multitud
hos-tage n. rehén
host-ess n. huéspeda
hos-tile adj. hostil
hos-til-i-ty n. hostilidad
hot adj. caliente
ho-tel n. hotel
hot-house n. invernáculo
hound n. podenco, v. perseguir
hour n. hora
house n. casa
house-keep-er n. ama e llaves
hous-ing n. alojamiento
how adv. cómo
how-ev-er adv. en todo caso, conj. sin embargo
howl v. aullar
hub n. cubo
hud-dle v. amontonar(se)
hue n. color; matiz

hug v. abrazar
huge adj. enorme
hulk n. casco
hull n. cascara; casco
hum v. zumbar; canturrear
hu-man adj. humano
hu-man-i-ty n. humanidad
hum-ble adj. humilde
hu-mid adj. humedo
hu-mid-i-fy v. humdedecer
hu-mid-i-ty n. humedad
hu-mil-i-ate v. humillar
hu-mil-i-a-tion n. humillación
hu-mil-i-ty n. humildad
hum-ming-bird n. colibrí
hu-mor n. complacer
hump n. giba; joroba
hunch v. corazonada
hunch-back n. jorobado
hun-dred adj. ciento
hun-dredth adj. centesimo
hun-ger n. hambre
hun-gry adj. hambriento
hunt v. cazar
hunt-er n. cazador
hur-dle n. valla; zarzo
hurl v. lanzar
hur-ri-cane n. huracan
hur-ry v. apresurar; darse prisa
hurt v. hacer daño; doler; danar
hus-band n. esposo
hush n. cascara
husk-y adj. ronco
hus-sy n. picara
hus-tle v. empujar
hy-brid n. híbrido
hy-drant n. boca de reigo
hy-dro-gen n. hidrogeno
hy-e-na n. hiena
hy-giene n. higiene
hymn n. himno
hyp-no-sis n. hipnosis
hyp-no-tize v. hipnotizar
hyp-o-crite n. hipocrita
hy-po-der-mic adj. hipodérmico
hy-pot-e-nuse n. hipotenusa
hy-poth-e-sis n. hipotesis
hy-po-thet-i-cal a. hipotetico
hys-te-ri-a n. histerismo
hys-ter-ic adj. histérico

I *pron.* yo
i-bis *n.* ibis
ice *n.* hielo
ice-berg *n.* iceberg
ice cream *n.* helado
i-ci-cle *n.* carambano
ic-ing *n.* garapiña
i-con *n.* icono
i-con-o-clast *n.* iconoclasta
i-cy *adj.* helado
i-de-a *n.* idea
i-de-al *adj.* ideal
i-de-al-ize *v.* idealizar
i-den-ti-cal *adj.* idéntico
i-den-ti-fi-ca-tion *n.* identificación
i-den-ti-fy *v.* identificar
i-den-ti-ty *n.* identidad
i-de-ol-o-gy *n.* ideología
id-i-om *n.* idiotismo
id-i-o-mat-ic *adj.* idiomático
id-i-o-syn-cra-sy *n.* idiosincrasia
id-i-ot *n.* idiota
i-dle *adj.* ocioso
i-dol *n.* idolo
i-dol-a-trous *adj.* idolatra
i-dol-a-try *n.* idolatria
i-dol-ize *v.* idolatrar
if *conj.* si
ig-nite *v.* encender(se)
ig-no-ble *adj.* innoble
ig-no-min-y *n.* ignominia
ig-no-rance *n.* ignorancia
ig-no-rant *adj.* ignorante
ig-nore *v.* no hacer caso de
ill *adj.* enfermo
il-le-gal *adj.* ilegal
il-leg-i-ble *adj.* ilegible
il-le-git-i-ma-cy *n.* ilegitimidad
il-le-git-i-mate *adj.* ilegítimo
il-lic-it *adj.* ilícito
il-lit-er-ate *adj., m.* analfabeto
ill-ness *n.* enfermedad
il-lu-mi-nate *v.* iluminar
il-lu-sion *n.* ilusión
il-lus-trate *v.* ilustrar
il-lus-tra-tion *n.* ilustración; ejemplo
im-age *n.* imagen
im-ag-i-nar-y *adj.* imaginario

im-ag-i-na-tion *n.* imaginación
im-ag-ine *v.* imaginar
im-be-cile *n., adj.* imbécil
im-i-tate *v.* imitar
im-i-ta-tion *n.* imitación; copia
im-ma-ture *adj.* inmaturo
im-meas-ur-a-ble *a.* inmensurable
im-me-di-ate *adj.* inmediato
im-mense *adj.* inmenso
im-mer-sion *n.* inmersion
im-mi-grant *n.* inmigrante
im-mi-grate *v.* inmigrar
im-mi-gra-tion *n.* inmigración
im-mi-nent *adj.* inminente
im-mo-bile *adj.* inmovil
im-mo-dest *adj.* impudico
im-mor-al *adj.* inmoral
im-mor-tal *adj.* inmortal
im-mune *adj.* inmune
im-mu-ni-ty *n.* inmunidad
imp *n.* diablillo
im-pact *n.* impacto
im-pair *v.* deteriorar
im-part *v.* comunicar; relatar; dar
im-par-tial *n.* imparcial
im-pa-tient *a.* impaciente
im-peach *v.* acusar
im-pec-ca-ble *adj.* impecable
im-pede *v.* impedir; estorbr
im-ped-i-ment *n.* impedimento; estorbo
im-pel *v.* impulsar
im-pe-ri-al *a.* imperial
im-pe-ri-ous *adj.* imperioso
im-per-son-al *adj.* impersonal
im-per-ti-nent *a.* impertinente
im-per-vi-ous *a.* impenetrable
im-pe-tus *n.* impetu
im-pi-e-ty *n.* impiedad
im-ple-ment *n.* herramienta
im-pli-cate *v.* enredar
im-plore *v.* implorar
im-ply *v.* dar a entender; significar

im-po-lite *adj.* descortes
im-port *v.* importar
im-por-tance *n.* importancia
im-por-tant *adj.* importante
im-pose *v.* imponer
im-pos-si-ble *adj.* imposible
im-pos-ter *n.* impostor
im-pos-tor *n.* impostor
im-po-tence *n.* impotencia
im-pov-er-ish *v.* empobrecer
im-prac-ti-cal *adj.* impracticable
im-press *v.* estampar; imprimir; impresionar
im-pres-sion *n.* impresión
im-print *v.* imprimir
im-prove *v.* mejorar
im-prove-ment *n.* mejora
im-pro-vise *nl* improvisar
im-pulse *n.* impulso
in *adv.* dentro, *prep.* durante, en
in-a-bil-i-ty *n.* inhabilidad
in-ca-pac-i-tate *v.* incapacitar
inch *n.* pulgada
in-ci-den-tal *adj.* incidental
in-cin-er-ate *v.* incinerar
in-ci-sion *n.* incisión
in-cite *v.* incitar
in-cli-na-tion *n.* inclinación
in-clu-sion *n.* inclusión
in-com-pa-ra-ble *adj.* incomparable
in-com-pe-tent *adj.* incompetente
in-com-plete *adj.* incompleto
in-cor-rect *adj.* incorrecto
in-crease *v.* crecer; acrecentar
in-crim-i-nate *v.* incriminar
in-de-cen-cy *n.* indecencia
in-de-cent *adj.* indecente
in-deed *adv.* de veras
in-def-i-nite *adj.* indefinido
in-dem-ni-ty *n.* ondemnización
in-dent *v.* mellar
in-den-ta-tion *n.* mella
in-de-pend-ence *n.* independencia
in-de-pend-ent *adj.* independiente

in-de-struct-i-ble *a.* indestructible
in-dex *n.* indice
in-di-cate *v.* indicar
in-di-ca-tion *n.* indicación
in-dict *v.* acusar
in-dif-fer-ent *adj.* indiferente
in-dig-e-nous *a.* indigena
in-di-gent *a.* indigente
in-di-ges-tion *n.* indigestion
in-dig-nant *a.* indignado
in-dig-ni-ty *n.* indignidad
in-di-go *n.* anil.
in-di-rect *adj.* indirecto
in-dis-creet *a.* indiscreto
in-dis-cre-tion *n.* indiscrecion
in-dis-pen-sa-ble *a.* imprescindible
in-di-vid-u-al *n.* individuo
in-di-vid-u-al-i-ty *n.* individualidad
in-doc-tri-nate *v.* doctrinar
in-do-lent *a.* indolente
in-door *a.* interior; de puertas adentro
in-doors *adv.* dentro
in-duce *v.* inducir
in-duct *v.* iniciar
in-dulge *v.* satisfacer; consentir
in-dus-tri-al *adj.* industrial
in-er-tia *n.* inercia
in-ev-i-ta-ble *adj.* inevitable
in-fa-my *n.* infamia
in-fan-cy *n.* infancia
in-fect *v.* infectar
in-fec-tion *n.* infección
in-fe-ri-or *adj.* inferior
in-fi-del-i-ty *n.* infidelidad
in-fil-trate *v.* infiltrarse
in-fi-nite *adj.* infinito
in-fin-i-tive *n.* infinitivo
in-fin-i-ty *n.* infinidad
in-fir-ma-ry *n.* enfermeria
in-flame *v.* inflamar; provocar
in-flam-ma-ble *adj.* inflamable
in-flate *v.* inflar
in-fla-tion *n.* inflación
in-flec-tion *n.* inflexión
in-flict *v.* infligir; imponer

in-flu-ence *n.* influencia
in-flu-en-za *n.* gripe
in-form *v.* informar
in-for-mal *adj.* sin ceremonia
in-for-ma-tion *n.* informacion
in-for-ma-tive *adj.* informativo
in-fre-quent *adj.* infrecuente
in-fu-ri-ate *v.* enfurecer
in-fuse *v.* infundir
in-fu-sion *n.* infusion
in-gen-ious *adj.* ingenioso
in-ge-nu-i-ty *n.* ingeniosidad
in-got *n.* lingote
in-gre-di-ent *n.* ingrediente
in-hab-it *v.* habitar
in-hab-i-tant *n.* habitante
in-hale *v.* inhalar; aspirar
in-her-ent *a.* inmanente; inherente
in-her-it *v.* heredar
in-her-it-ance *n.* herencia
in-hib-it *v.* inhibir
in-hi-bi-tion *n.* inhibición
in-hu-man *a.* inhumano; cruel
in-iq-ui-ty *n.* iniquidad
in-i-tial *adj.* inicial
in-i-ti-ate *v.* iniciar
in-i-ti-a-tion *n.* iniciación
in-i-ti-a-tive *n.* iniciative
in-ject *v.* inyectar
in-jec-tion *n.* inyección
in-jure *v.* hacer daño a; ofender
in-ju-ry *n.* daño; injuria
in-jus-tice *n.* injusticia
ink *n.* tinta
ink-ling *n.* sospecha
in-let *n.* entrada; ensenada
in-mate *n.* inquilino
inn *n.* posada
in-nate *adj.* innato
in-ner *adj.* interior
in-no-cence *n.* inocencia
in-no-cent *adj.* inocente
in-no-va-tion *n.* innovación
in-nu-en-do *n.* indirecta
in-nu-mer-a-ble *a.* innumerable
in-oc-u-late *v.* inocular
in-oc-u-la-tion *n.* inoculación
in-quest *n.* pesquisa judicial

in-quire *v.* preguntar
in-quir-y *n.* indagación; pregunta
in-qui-si-tion *n.* inquisición
in-sane *adj.* insensato; loco
in-san-i-ty *n.* locura
in-scribe *v.* inscribir
in-scrip-tion *n.* inscripción
in-sect *n.* insecto
in-se-cure *a.* inseguro; precario
in-sert *v.* insertar; meter
in-ser-tion *n.* inserción
in-side *n.* interior
in-sight *n.* perspicacia
in-sig-ni-a *n.* insignias
in-sig-nif-i-cance *n.* insignificancia
in-sin-u-ate *v.* insinuar
in-sin-u-a-tion *n.* insinuación; indirecta
in-sip-id *adj.* insipido
in-sist *v.* insistir
in-sist-ent *a.* insistente; porfiado
in-so-lence *n.* insolencia
in-so-lent *adj.* insolente
in-som-ni-a *n.* insomnio
in-spect *v.* examinar; inspeccionar
in-spec-tion *n.* inspección
in-spi-ra-tion *n.* inspiración
in-spire *v.* inspirar; estimular
in-stall *v.* instalar
in-stall-ment *n.* plazo; entrega
in-stance *n.* ejemplo
in-stant *n.* instante
in-stan-ta-ne-ous *a.* instantaneo
in-stead *adv.* en lugar; en vez de
in-step *n.* empeine
in-sti-gate *v.* instigar
in-stinct *n.* instinto
in-stinc-tive *adj.* instintivo
in-sti-tute *v.* instituir; empezar
in-sti-tu-tion *n.* institución
in-struct *v.* instruir; enseñar
in-struc-tion *n.* instrucción
in-stru-ment *n.* instrumento
in-suf-fi-cient *adj.* in-

suficiente
in-su-late v. sislar
in-su-la-tion n. aislamiento
in-su-lin n. insulina
in-sult n. insulto; ultraje
in-sur-ance n. seguro
in-sure v. asegurar
in-sur-rec-tion n. insurección
in-tact adj. intacto
in-te-ger n. numero entero
in-te-grate v. integrar
in-te-gra-tion n. integración
in-teg-ri-ty n. integridad
in-tel-lect n. intelecto
in-tel-li-gence n. inteligencia
in-tel-li-gent adj. inteligente
in-tend v. proponerse; querer decir
in-tense adj. intenso
in-ten-si-ty n. intensidad
in-tent adj. atento; absorto
in-ter v. enterrar
in-ter-cede v. interceder
in-ter-cept v. interceptar
in-ter-ces-sion n. intercesión
in-ter-change v. intercambiar
in-ter-course n. comercio; trato; coito
in-ter-est n. interes
in-trer-fere v. intervenir; meterse
in-ter-im n. interin
in-te-ri-or adj. interior
in-ter-jec-tion n. interjección
in-ter-lude n. intemedio
in-ter-me-di-ate adj. intermedio
in-ter-mis-sion n. intermisión
in-tern n. interno
in-ter-nal adj. interior
in-ter-na-tion-al adj. internacional
in-ter-play n. interacción
in-ter-[pose v. interponer
in-ter-pret v. explicar; interpretar; entender
in-ter-pre-ta-tion n. interpretación
in-ter-ro-gate v. interrogar
in-ter-ro-ga-tion n. interrogación
in-ter-rupt v. interrumpir
in-ter-rup-tion n. interrupcion
in-ter-sec-tion n. intersección
in-ter-twine n. entretejer(se)
in-ter-val n. intervalo
in-ter-vene v. intervenir
in-ter-view n. entrevista
in-tes-tine n. intestino
in-ti-mate v. intimar
in-tim-i-date v. intimidar
in-to prep. en
in-tol-er-ant adj. intolerante
in-to-na-tion n. entonación
in-tox-i-cate v. emriagar; encitar
in-tran-si-tive adj. intransitivo
in-tra-ve-nous adj. intravenoso
in-trep-id adj. intrepido
in-tri-ca-cy n. complejidad; enredo
in-tri-cate adj. intrincado
in-trigue v. intrigar; fascinar
in-trin-sic adj. intrinseco
in-tro-duce v. introducir
in-tro-duc-tion n. introducción
in-trude v. entremeterse
in-tu-i-tion n. intuición
in-ure v. habituar
in-vade v. invadir
in-va-lid adj. invalido
in-var-i-a-ble adj. invariable
in-va-sion n. invasion
in-vent v. inventar
in-ven-tion n. invención
in-ven-to-ry n. inventario
in-ver-sion n. inversión
in-vert v. invertir
in-ver-te-brate a., n. invertebrado
in-vest v. investir
in-ves-ti-gate v. investigar
in-ves-ti-ga-tion n. investigacion
in-vig-or-ate v. vigorizar
in-vin-ci-ble adj. invencible
in-vis-i-ble adj. invisible
in-vi-ta-tion n. invitación

in-vite v. invitar
in-vo-ca-tion n. invocación
in-voice n. factura
in-voke v. invocar; implorar
in-vol-un-tar-y adj. involuntario
in-volve v. complicar; comprometer; enredar
in-ward adv. hacia dentro
i-o-dine n. yodo
i-on n. ion
i-ron v. planchar, n. plancha
i-ron-ic adj. ironica
i-ro-ny n. ironia
ir-ra-di-ate v. irradiar
ir-ra-tion-al adj. irracional
ir-rec-on-cil-a-ble adj. irreconciliable
ir-ref-u-ta-ble adj. irrefutable
ir-reg-u-lar adj. irregular
ir-rel-e-vant adj. inaplicable
ir-re-sist-i-ble adj. irresistible
ir-re-spon-si-ble adj. irresponsable
ir-ri-gate v. regar
ir-ri-tate v. irritar; provocar; molestar
is v. third person pres. sing of be
is-land n. isla
isle n. isla
i-so-late v. aislar
i-sos-ce-les adj. isosceles
is-sue v. publicar; salir, n. resultado; emision
isth-mus n. pl. istmo
it pron. le; la; lo; ello; ella; el
i-tal-ic n. usu. pl. letra bastardilla
i-tal-i-cize tr. imprimir en cursiva
itch v. picar
itch-y adj. que da picazon; impaciente
i-tem n. articulo; partida
i-tem-ize v. detallar
it-er-ate tr. iterar; repetir
i-tin-er-ar-y n. itinerario
its pron., adj. poss. case of it
it-self pron. el, ella, ello, o, so, mismo
i-vo-ry n. pl. marfil
i-vy n. hiedra

jab v. golpear
jab-ber v. farfullar
jack n. mozo; marinero; gato; sota
jack-al n. chacal
jack-ass n. burro
jack-et n. chaqueta
jack-nife n. navaja
jack-pot n. bote
jade n. jade
jag-uar n. jaguar
jail v. encarcelar, n. carcel
jam v. apinar; atascar
jamb n. jamba
jam-bo-ree n. francachela
angle n. sonido discordante
jan-i-tor n. portero
Jan-u-ar-y n. enero
jar n. jarra
jar-gon n. jerga
jas-mine n. jazmín
jaun-dice n. ictericia
jaunt n. excursión
jave-lin n. jabalina
jaw n. quijada
jay n. arrendajo
jazz n. jazz
jeal-ous adj. celoso
Jeep n. trademark. jeep
jeer v. mofarse; befar
jell v. cuajar(se)
jel-ly n. jalea
jel-ly-fish n. medusa
jeop-ar-dize v. arriesgar
jeop-ar-dy n. pelogro
jerk v. arrojar; sacudir
jer-kin n. justillo
jer-sey n. jersey
jest n. chanza
jet n. chorro; surtidor; avion; a reaccion; azabache
jet-same n. echazón
jet-ti-son n. echazón
jet-ty n. malecon; muelle
jew-el n. joya
jew-el-er n. joyero
jew-el-ry n. joyas
jif-fy n. instante
jib n. jiga
jig-saw n. sierra de vaiven
jig-saw puzzle n. rompecabezaw
jilt v. dar calcbazar

jim-my *n.* palanqueta
jin-gle *v.* retinir; tintinear
jinx *n.* gafe
jit-ters *n.* inquietud
ob *n.* trabajo
ock-ey *n.* jockey
o-cose *a.* jocoso
oc-u-lar *a.* jocoso
oc-und *a.* alegre
jog *v.* empujar; correr despacio
join *v.* unir(se)
oint *n.* juntura; union
oist *n.* viga
oke *n.* chiste; broma
ok-er *n.* bromista
ol-ly *adj.* alegre
jolt *v.* sacudir
on-quil *n.* junquillo
our-nal *n.* periodico
our-nal-ism *n.* periodismo
our-nal-ist *n.* periodista
our-ney *v.* viajar, *n.* viaje
oy-ous *adj.* alegre
udge *n.* juez; *v.* juzgar
u-di-cial *adj.* judicial
jug-gle *v.* hacer juegos malabares
jug-u-lar *adj.* yugular
juice *n.* jugo
July *n.* julio
jum-ble *v.* mezclar
jump *n.* salto, *v.* saltar
jump-er *n.* saltador
junc-tion *n.* juntura; empalme
junc-ture *n.* juntura; coyuntura
June *n.* junio
jun-gle *n.* selva
jun-ior *adj.* mas joven; menor
ju-ni-per *n.* enebro
junk *n.* trastos viejos; junco
ju-ris-dic-tion *n.* jurisdicción
ju-ris-pur-dene *n.* jurisprudencia
ju-rist *n.* jurista
ju-ror *n.* jurado
ju-ry *n.* jurado
just *adj.* justo; imparcial
us-ti-fy *v.* justificar
ju-ve-nile *adj.* joven

kale *n.* col rizada
ka-lei-do-scope *n.* calidoscopio
kan-ga-roo *n.* canguro
kar-at *n.* uilate
keel *n.* quilla
keen *adj.* agudo; perspicaz; entusiasta; afilado
keep *v.* detener; tener; cumplir
keep-ing *n.* custodia
keg *n.* cuñete
ken *v.* saver
ken-nel *n.* perrera
ker-chief *n.* pañuelo
ker-nel *n.* almendra; mucleo
ker-o-sene *n.* ueroseno
ketch *n.* queche
ketch-up *n.* salsa picante de tomate
ket-tle *n.* tetera
key *n.* llave
key-board *n.* teclado
key-stone *n.* piedra clave
khak-i *n.* caqui
kick *v.* dar patadas; dar un puntapie
kid *n.* cabrito
kid-nap *v.* secuestrar
kid-ney *n.* riñón
kill *v.* matar
kiln *n.* horno
kil-o-c-cle *n.* kilociclo
kil-o-gram *n.* kilogramo
kil-o-me-ter *n.* kilometro
kil-o-watt *n.* kilovation
kin *n.* parientes
kind *adj.* bueno; *n.* genero
kin-der-gar-ten *n.* jardín de la infancia
kind-heart-ed *a.* bondadoso
kin-dle *v.* encender
kind-ly *adj.* bondadoso
kind-ness *n.* benevolencia
kin-dred *n.* parientes
king *n.* rey
king-dom *n.* reino
kink *n.* coca; peculiaridad
kin-ship *n.* parentesco
kins-man *n.* pariente
kiss *n.* beso; *v.* besar
kit *n.* equipo; avios
kitch-en *n.* cocina

kite *n.* equipo; avios
kith *n.* amigos
kit-ten *n.* gatito
knack *n.* mana
knap-sack *n.* mochila
knave *n.* bribón
knav-er-y *n.* bellaquería
knav-ish *adj.* bellaco
knead *v.* amasar
knee *n.* rodilla
knee-cap *n.* rotula
kneel *n.* arrodillarse
knee-pad *n.* rodillera
knell *n.* doble
knick-ers *n.* bombachos
knick-knack *n.* chuchería
knife *v.* acuchillar, *n.* cuchillo
knight *n.* caballero
knight-hood *n.* caballerosidad
knit *v.* hacer punto; juntar
knit-ting *n.* tejido
knob *n.* tirador; buto
knock *v.* golpear
knock-down *adj.* que derriba
knock-er *n.* picaporte
knock-ing *n.* llamada
knoll *n.* otero
knot *v.* anudar
knot-hole *n.* agujero
knot-ted *adj.* anudado; nudoso
knot-ty *adj.* enredado; nudoso
know *v.* saber; conocer
know-a-ble *adj.* conocible
know-how *n.* pericia
know-ing *a.* astuto; habil
know-ing-ly *adv.* a sabiendas
knowl-edge *n.* saber
knowl-edge-a-ble *adj.* erudito
known *adj.* concido
know-noth-ing *n.* ighorante
knuck-le *n.* nudillo
ko-a-la *n.* koala
kook *n.* excentrico
Ko-ran *n.* Alcorán; Coran
ko-sher *adj.* legitimo; conforme a las reglas
kow-tow *v.* postarse

lab *n.* laboratorio
la-bel *v.* marcar; *n.* etiqueta; rotulo
la-bi-al *adj.* labial
la-bor *v.* trabajar, *n.* trabajo
lab-o-ra-to-ry *n.* laboratorio
la-bored *adj.* peon; trabajador; jornalero
la-bo-ri-ous *adj.* laborioso
lab-y-rinth *n.* laberinto
lac *n.* laca
lace *v.* encordonar; *n.* encaje
lac-er-ate *v.* lacerar
lac-er-ation *n.* laceración
lach-ry-mal *adj.* lagrimal
lack *v.* faltar; hacer falta; *n.* falta
lack-ey *n.* lacayo
lack-ing *adj.* deficiente; *prep.* sin
lack-lus-ter *adj.* deslucido
la-con-ic *adj.* laconico
lac-quer *n.* laca
lac-tase *n.* lactasa
lac-tate *v.* lactar
lac-ta-tion *n.* lactancia
lac-tic *adj.* lactico
lac-tose *n.* lactoxa
la-cu-na *n.* laguna
lac-y *adj.* de encaje
lad *n.* chico
lad-der *n.* escalera
lad-die *n.* chico
lade *v.* agobiar
lad-en *adj.* agobiado; cargado
la-dle *n.* cucharón
la-dy *n.* dama
la-dy-bug *n.* mariquita
lag *v.* trasarse; rezagarse
lag-gard *adj.* rezagado
la-goon *n.* laguna
la-ic *adj.* laico
lair *n.* madriguera
la-i-ty *n.* laicos
lake *n.* lago
lamb *n.* cordero
lame *v.* baldar; *adj.* renco; cojo
la-me *n.* lame
la-ment *v.* deplorar; lamentar
la-men-ta-ble *adj.* lamentable

lam-en-ta-tion *n.* lamentacion

la-ment-ed *adj.* lamentado

lam-i-na *n.* lamina

lam-i-nate *v.* laminar

lam-i-nat-ed *adj.* laminado

lam-i-na-tion *n.* laminación

lamp *n.* lampara

lam-poon *v.* satirizar; *n.* satira

lam-prey *n.* lamprea

lance *n.* lanza

lan-cet *n.* lanceta

land *v.* pais; tierra

land-ed *adj.* hacendado

land-fall *n.* recalada

land-hold-er *n.* terrateniente

land-ing *n.* amaraje; desembarco

land-lord *n.* arrendador

land-mark *n.* mojón

land-own-er *n.* terrateniente

land-scape *n.* panorama

lane *n.* ruta; vereda; camino

lan-guage *n.* lenguaje

lan-guid *adj.* lánguido

lan-guish *v.* decaer; languidecer

lan-guish-ing *adj.* lánguido

lan-guor *n.* languidez

lan-guor-ous *adj.* lánguido

lan-o-lin *n.* lanolina

lan-tern *n.* linterna

lap *n.* falda; *v.* plegar; doblar

la-pel *n.* solapa

lap-i-dar-y *n.* lapidario

lapse *v.* faltar; caer; decaer; deslizarse

lapsed *adj.* caduco

lar-ce-ny *adj.* robo

lard *n.* lardo

large *adj.* grande

lar-gess *n.* donativo; generosidad

lar-va *n.* larva

lar-val *adj.* larval

lar-yn-gi-tis *n.* laringitis

lar-y-nx *n.* laringe

la-ser *n.* laser

lash *n.* latigo; azote; latigazo

lash-ing *n.* fustigación; azotaina

lass *n.* muchacha

las-si-tude *n.* lasitude

las-so *n.* lazo

last *adv.* finalmente; *adj.* final

last-ing *adj.* duradero

last-ly *adv.* finalmente

latch *n.* aldabilla

late *adv.* tarde

late-ly *adv.* ultimamente

la-ten-cy *n.* latencia

late-enss *n.* tardanza

la-tent *adj.* latente

la-ter *adj.* posterior

lat-er-al *adj.* lateral

lat-est *adj.* último

la-tex *n.* latex

lath-er *n.* espuma

lat-i-tude *n.* latitud

la-trine *n.* letrina

lat-ter *adj.* ultimo

lat-ter-day *adj.* reciente

lat-tice *n.* celosia; *v.* enrejar

lat-tice-work *n.* enrejado

laud *v.* alabar; elogiar

laud-a-ble *adj.* laudable

laud-a-to-ry *adj.* laudatorio

laugh *n.* risa, *v.* reir(se)

laugh-a-ble *adj.* absurdo; comico

laugh-ing *adj.* risueño

laugh-ter *n.* risa

launch *v.* lanzar; iniciar; botar

launch-er *n.* lanzador

launch-ing *n.* lanzamiento

laun-der *v.* lavar(se)

laun-dered *adj.* lavado

laun-der-er *n.* lavandero

laun-dry *n.* lavanderia

lau-rel *n.* laurel

la-va *n.* lava

lav-en-der *n.* lavanda

lav-ish *adj.* espendido; generoso

law *n.* derecho; ley

law-ful *adj.* legitimo

law-less *adj.* sin leyes

law-mak-er *n.* legislador

lawn *n.* césped

law-yer *n.* abogado

lax *adj.* laxo

lax-a-tive *adj.* laxante

lax-i-ty n. laxitud
lay v. acostar; poner
lay-er n. estrato
lay-out n. distribución
la-zi-ness n. pereza
la-zy adj. perezoso
lead v. mandar; conducir
lead-en adj. plumbeo
lead-er n. lider
lead-er-ship n. mando
lead-ing n. emplomado
leaf n. hoja
leaf-let n. panfleto
leaf-y adj. hojoso
league n. liga
leak v. gotear; salirse; n. gotera; agujero
lean adj. magro
lean-ing n. inclinación
leap v. saltar
learn v. aprender
learn-ed adj. erudito
learn-er n. principiante
learn-ing n. aprendizaje
lease-hold n. arrendamiento
lease-hold-er n. arrendatario
leash n. trailla
leas-ing n. arrendamiento
least adv. menos, adj. menor
leath-er n. cuero
leath-er-y adj. curtido
leave v. salir; dejar; irse
leav-en v. leudar
leav-ing n. salida
lech-er-ous adj. lujurioso
lech-er-y n. lujuria
lec-tor n. lector
lec-ture v. sermonear; reprender; n. reprimenda; conferencia
lec-tur-er n. conferenciante
leech n. sanguijuela
leek n. puerro
left adj. izquierdo
left-o-ver adj. sobrante
left-y n. zirdo
leg n. pierna
leg-a-cy n. herencia
le-gal adj. legal
le-gal-ist n. legalista
le-gal-is-tic adj. legalista
le-gal-i-ty n. legalidad

le-gal-ize v. legalizar
leg-ate n. legado
le-ga-tion n. legación
leg-end n. leyenda
leg-end-ar-y adj. legendario
leg-gings n. polainas
leg-i-bil-i-ty n. legibilidad
leg-i-ble adj. legible
le-gion n. legion
le-gion-ar-y n. legionario
le-gion-naire n. legionario
leg-is-late v. legislar
leg-is-la-tion n. legislación
leg-is-la-tor n. legislador
le-git-i-ma-cy n. legitimidad
le-git-i-mate adj. legitimo
le-git-i-mize v. legitimar
lei-sure n. ocio
lem-on n. limon
lem-on-ade n. limonada
lend v. impartir; prestar
lend-er n. prestador
length n. extensión; longitud; tramo; largo
length-en v. prolongar(se); alargar(se)
length-y adj. prolongado
le-nient adj. indulgente
lens n. lente
len-til n. lenteja
le-o-nine adj. leonino
leop-ard n. leopardo
lep-er n. leproso
lep-ro-sy n. lepra
lep-rous adj. leproso
le-sion n. lesión
less adv., adj. menos
less-en v. disminuir
less-er adj. menor
les-son n. lección
let v. dejar; permitir
let-down n. desilusión
le-thal adj. letal
le-thar-gic adj. letargico
leth-ar-gy n. letargo
let-ter n. carta
let-tered adj. letrado
let-ter-ing n. rotulo
let-tuce n. lechuga
leu-ke-mi-a n. leucemia
lev-el n. llano; nivel
lev-i-ta-tion n. levitación
lev-y v. recaudar; exigir

lewd *adj.* lujurioso
lewd-ness *n.* lujuria
lex-i-cog-ra-phy *n.* lexicografia
lex-i-con *n.* lexicon
li-a-bil-i-ty *n.* obligación
li-a-ble *adj.* sujeto; responsable
li-ar *n.* mentiroso
li-ba-tion *n.* libación
lib-er-al *adj.* liberal
lib-er-ate *v.* libertar
lib-er-ty *n.* libertad
li-brar-y *n.* biblioteca
lie *v.* mentir; acostarse
life *n.* vida
lift *v.* levantar(se); elevar
light *n.* lampara; luz
light-ly *adv.* ligeramente
like *n.* gusto, *v.* gustar
like-ness *n.* semejanza
li-lac *n.* lila
lil-y *n.* lirio
lim-bo *n.* limbo
lime *n.* lima
lim-it *v.* limitar
lim-ou-sine *n.* limusina
line *v.* alinear; rayar, *n.* raya; linea
li-on *n.* león
lip *n.* labio
liq-uid *n.* liquido
liq-ui-date *v.* liquidar
liq-uor *n.* licor
list *n.* lista
lit-er-al *adj.* literal
lit-er-ar-y *adj.* literario
lit-er-a-ture *n.* literatura
lit-tle *n., adj., adv.* poco, *adj.* pequeno
live *v.* vivir
liz-ard *n.* lagarto
lob-ster *n.* langosta
lo-cal *adj.* local
lo-cal-i-ty *n.* localidad
lo-cate *v.* encontrar
lone *adj.* solitario
lone-ly *adj.* solo
lone-ly *adj.* solo
long *adj.* largo
look *n.* mirada, *v.* buscar; mirar
loose *v.* soltar, *adj.* disoluto; suelto
lost *adj.* perdido
lo-tion *n.* loción
lot-ter-y *n.* loteria
loud *adj.* alto
love *v.* amar; querer, *n.* amor
love-ly *adj.* hermoso
low *adv., adj.* bajo, *adv.* abajo
low-er *v.* bajar
loy-al *adj.* fiel
loy-al-ty *n.* fidelidad
lu-bri-cant *n.* lubricante
lu-bri-cate *v.* lubricar
lu-bri-cious *adj.* lúbrico
lu-cent *adj.* luminoso
lu-cid *adj.* cuerdo; lucido
lu-cid-i-ty *n.* lucidez
luck *n.* suerte
luck-less *adj.* desafortunado
luck-y *adj.* fortuito
lu-cra-tive *adj.* lucrativo
lu-di-crous *adj.* ridiculo
lug *v.* halar
lug-gage *n.* equipaje
luke-warm *adj.* tibio
lull *v.* sosegar; embaucar
lum-bar *adj.* lumbar
lum-ber *n.* leno
lum-ber-ing *adj.* torpe; pesado
lu-mi-nance *n.* luminancia
lu-mi-nar-y *n.* luminar
lu-mi-nes-cence *n.* luminiscente
lu-mi-nous *adj.* luminoso
lump *n.* masa; terron
lu-na-cy *n.* locura
lu-nar *adj.* lunar
lunch *v.* almorzar, *n.* almuerz
lus-ter *n.* lustre
lus-ty *a.* robusto
lute *n.* laud
lux-u-ri-ant *a.* lozano
lux-u-ry *n.* lujo
lye *n.* lejia
lymph *n.* linfa
lynch *n.* linchar
lynx *n.* lince
lyre *n.* lira
lyr-ic *adj.* lírico

ma-ca-bre *adj.* macabro
mac-a-ro-ni *n.* macarrones
mac-a-roon *n.* mostachon
ma-chaw *n.* guacamayo
mac-er-ate *v.* macerar(se)
ma-chet-e *n.* machete
mach-i-nate *v.* maquinar
mach-i-na-tion *n.* maquinacion
ma-chine *n.* maquina
ma-chine-gun *n.* ametrallar
ma-chin-er-y *n.* maquinaria
ma-chin-ist *n.* maquinista
mack-er-el *n.* caballa
mac-ra-me *n.* macrame
mac-ro-bi-ot-ics *n.* macrobiotica
mac-ro-cosm *n.* macrocosmo
mac-ro-scop-ic *adj.* macroscopico
mad *adj.* furioso
mad-cap *adj.* alocado
mad-den *v.* enloquecer
mad-den-ing *adj.* enloquecedor
made-up *adj.* incentado
mad-ness *n.* locura
mag-a-zine *n.* revista
mag-got *n.* gusano
mag-ic *n.* magia
mag-i-cal *adj.* mágico
ma-gi-cian *n.* mago
mag-is-te-ri-al *adj.* magistral
mag-is-trate *n.* magistrado
mag-nate *n.* magnate
mag-ne-si-um *n.* magnesio
mag-net-ic *adj.* magnetico
mag-net-ism *n.* magnetismo
mag-net-ize *v.* magnetizar
mag-ni-fi-ca-tion *n.* ampliación
mag-nif-i-cence *n.* magnificencia
mag-nif-i-cent *adj.* magnifico
mag-ni-fi-er *n.* amplificador
mag-ni-fy *v.* aumentar
mag-ni-tude *n.* magnitud
mag-num *n.* magnum
ma-hog-a-ny *n.* caoba
maid *n.* soltera
mail *n.* correo

mail-box *n.* buzón
mail-man *n.* cartero
main-tain *v.* mantener
main-te-nance *n.* mantenimiento
ma-jes-tic *adj.* majestuoso
maj-es-ty *n.* majestad
ma-jor *adj.* mayor
ma-jor-i-ty *n.* mayoria
make *v.* ganar; crear; hacer
mak-er *n.* fabricante
mak-ing *n.* fabricación
mal-a-dy *n.* dolencia
ma-lar-i-a *n.* malaria
mal-con-tent *adj.* malcontento
male *adj.* masculino; macho
mal-e-dic-tion *n.* maldición
ma-lev-o-lence *n.* malevolencia
ma-lev-o-lent *adj.* malévolo
mal-func-tion *v.* funcionar mal
mal-ice *n.* malicia
ma-li-cious *adj.* malicioso
ma-lig-nan-cy *n.* malignidad
ma-lig-nant *adj.* maligno
mall *n.* alameda
mal-le-a-ble *adj.* maleable
mal-nour-ished *adj.* desnutrido
mal-nu-tri-tion *n.* desnutrición
malt *n.* malta
mal-treat *v.* maltratar
mal-treat-ment *n.* maltratamiento
mam-mal *n.* mamifero
mam-ma-li-an *adj.* mamifero
mam-ma-ry *adj.* mamario
man *n.* hombre
man-age *v.* manejar
man-age-a-ble *adj.* manejable
man-age-ment *n.* gerencia
man-da-rin *n.* mandarin
man-date *n.* mandato
man-da-to-ry *adj.* mandante
man-do-lin *n.* mandolina
ma-neu-ver *v.* maniobrar
ma-neu-ner-a-ble *adj.* maniobrable
man-ga-nese *n.* manganeso

man-gle v. mutilar
man-go n. mango
man-hood n. madurez
ma-ni-a n. mania
ma-ni-ac adj. maniaco
ma-ni-a-cal adj. maniaco
man-ic adj. maniaco
man-i-cure n. manicura
man-i-cur-ist n. manicuro
man-i-fest adj. manifiesto
man-i-fes-ta-tion n. manifes-
  tación
man-i-fes-to n. manifiesto
ma-ni-kin n. maniqui
ma-nip-u-late v. manipular
ma-nip-u-la-tion n. mani-
  pulación
ma-nip-u-la-tive adj. de
  manipuleo
ma-nip-u-la-tor n. mani-
  pulador
man-li-ness n. hombria
man-ly adj. masculino
man-ne-quin n. maniqui
man-ner n. manera
man-nered adj. amanerado
m a n - n e r - i s m n .
  amaneramiento
man-nish adj. hombruno
man-tel n. manto
man-tle n. manto
man-u-al adj. manual
man-u-fac-ture n. manufac-
  tura
man-u-fac-tured adj. manu-
  facturado
m a n - u - f a c - t u r - i n g adj.
  manufacturero
man-u-script n. manuscrito
man-y adj. muchos
map n. mapa
ma-ple n. arce
map-mak-er n. cartografia
mar v. desfigurar
mar-a-thon n. maraton
ma-raud-er n. merodeador
mar-ble n. marmol
mar-bled adj. jaspeado
mar-bling n. marmoración
march v. marchar
March n. marzo
mar-ga-rine n. margarina
mar-gin s. margen

mar-gin-al adj. marginal
mar-i-gold n. maravilla
ma-ri-na n. marina
mar-i-nate v. marinar
ma-rine n. marino
mar-i-ner n. marinero
mar-i-tal adj. marital
mar-i-time adj. maritimo
mark n. marca
marked adj. marcado
mark-er n. marcador
mar-ket v. vender; n. mercado
mar-ket-a-ble adj. vendible
mar-ket-er n. vendedor
mark-ing n. marca
mar-ma-lade n. mermelada
ma-roon v. abandonar
mar-quis n. marques
mar-riage n. matrimonio
mar-ried adj. casado
mar-row n. medula
mar-ry v. casar(se)
marsh n. pantano
mar-shal n. mariscal
marsh-y adj. pantanoso
mar-su-pi-al adj. marsupial
mart n. mercado
mar-tial adj. marcial
mar-tyr n. martir
mar-tyr-dom n. martirio
mar-vel s. maravilla
mar-vel-lous adj. maravilloso
mas-cot n. mascota
mas-cu-line adj. masculion
mas-cu-lin-i-ty n. mas-
  culinidad
mash v. majar
mash-er n. majador
mask n. mascara
m a s - o c h - i s m n .
  masoquismo
mas-o-chist n. masoquista
m a s - o - c h i s - t i c adj.
  masoquista
ma-son-ary n. albanileria
mas-quer-ade n. mascarada
mass n. masa
mas-sa-cre n. masacre
mas-sage v. masajear
mas-sive adj. masivo
mast n. mastil
mas-tec-to-my n. mastec-

tomia
mas-ter n. maestro
mas-ter-ful adj. habil
mas-ter-ly adj. magistral
mas-ter-y n. maestria
mas-tic adj. mastique
mas-ti-cate v. masticar
mas-toid n. mastoides
mat n. estera
mate n. hembra; compañero
ma-te-ri-al adj., n. material
ma-te-ri-al-ist n. materialista
ma-te-ri-al-is-tic adj. materialista
ma-te-ri-al-i-ty n. materialidad
math n. matematicas
math-e-mat-i-cal adj. matematico
math-e-ma-ti-cian n. matematico
math-e-mat-ics n. matematicas
mat-i-nee n. matinee
ma-tri-arch n. matriarca
ma-tri-ar-chal adj. matriarcal
ma-tri-ar-chy n. matriarcado
ma-tric-u-late v. matricular(se)
ma-tric-u-la-tion n. matriculación
mat-ri-mo-ni-al adj. matrimonial
mat-ri-mo-ny n. matrimonio
ma-trix n. matriz
ma-tron n. matrona
ma-tron-ly adj. matronal
mat-ted adj. esterado
mat-ter n. materia
mat-ting n. estera
mat-tress n. colchon
mat-u-ra-tion n. maduración
ma-ture v. madurar, adj. maduro
ma-tur-i-ty n. madurez
maul v. maltratar
mauve n. malva
max-im n. máxima
max-i-mal adj. máximo
max-i-mum adj. máximo
May n. mayo
may v. poder
may-be adj. tal vez

may-on-naise n. mayonesa
may-or n. alcalde
may-or-al-ty n. alcadia
me pron. mi; me
mead-ow n. pradera
mea-ger adj. pobre; magro
meal n. comida
mean v. intentar
me-an-der v. vagar
mean-ing n. significado
mean-ing-ful adj. significativo
mean-ing-less adj. insignificante
mea-sles n. rubeola
meas-ure v. medir
meas-ured adj. mesurado
meas-ure-ment n. medición
meat n. carne
meat-y adj. carnoso
me-chan-ic n. mecánico
me-chan-i-cal adj. mecánico
mech-a-nism n. mecánismo
mech-a-nize v. mecanizar
med-al n. medalla
me-dal-lion n. medallon
med-dle v. entremeterse
med-dler n. entremetido
me-di-an adj. mediano
me-di-ate v. mediar
me-di-a-tion n. mediación
me-di-a-tor n. mediador
med-ic n. medico
med-i-cal adj. medico
med-i-cate v. medicinar
med-i-ca-tion n. medicación
med-i-cine n. medicina
me-di-e-val adj. midieval
me-di-o-cre adj. mediocre
me-di-oc-ri-ty n. mediocridad
med-i-tate v. meditar
med-i-ta-tion n. meditación
meet v. reunirse; encontras(se)
mel-o-dy n. melodia
mel-on n. melon
mem-ber n. miembro
mem-o-ra-ble adj. memorable
men-tal adj. mental
men-tion v. mencionar; n. mencion

mer-cu-ry *n.* mercurio
mer-it *v.* merecer
mer-ry *adj.* festivo
mes-sage *n.* comunicación
mes-sen-ger *n.* mensajero
met-al *n.* metal
me-te-or-ol-o-gy *n.* meteorologia
meth-od *n.* metodo
mi-crobe *n.* microbio
mi-cro-phone *n.* microfono
mi-cro-scope *n.* microscopio
mid-dle *n., adj.* medio
mid-night *n.* medianoche
mi-grate *v.* emigrar
mil-i-tar-y *adj.* militar
mi-li-tia *n.* milicia
milk *n.* leche
mil-lion *n.* millón
mil-lion-aire *n.* millonario
mind *v.* obedecer, *n.* mente
min-er-al *n.* mineral
min-is-ter *n.* ministro
mi-nor *adj.* menor
mi-nor-i-ty *n.* minoria
mi-nus *prep.* menos
mir-a-cle *n.* milagro
mir-ror *n.* espejo
mis-chie-vous *adj.* malicioso
miss *v.* perder
mis-sion *n.* misión
mis-sion-ar-y *n.* misionero
mis-take *v.* equivocar(se)
mis-ter *n.* senor
mis-treat *v.* maltratar
mit-i-gate *v.* mitigar
mit-ten *n.* mitón
mix *n.* mezcla, *v.* mezclar(se)
mix-ture *n.* mezcla
mod-el *v.* modelar, *n.* modelo
mod-er-ate *v.* moderar, *adj.* moderno
mod-ern *n.* moderno
mod-est *adj.* modesto
mod-i-fi-ca-tion *n.* modificación
mod-i-fy *v.* modificar
mod-u-late *v.* modular
moist *adj.* humedo
mois-ten *v.* humedecer(se)
moist-ness *n.* humedad

mois-ture *n.* humedad
mois-tur-iz-er *v.* humedecer
mo-lar *n.* molar
mo-las-ses *n.* melaza
mold *v.* moldear, *n.* molde
mold-er *v.* desmoronar(se)
mold-ing *n.* mohoso
mo-lec-u-lar *adj.* molecular
mol-e-cule *n.* molecula
mole-hill *n.* topera
mol-li-fy *v.* molificar
mol-lusk *n.* molusco
mol-ten *adj.* fundido
mom *n.* mama
mo-ment *n.* momento
mo-men-tar-i-ly *adv.* momentáneamente
mo-men-tar-y *adj.* momentaneo
mo-men-tum *n.* momento
mon-arch *n.* monarca
mo-nar-chic *adj.* monarquico
mon-ar-chist *n.* monarquico
mon-ar-chy *n.* monarquía
mon-as-ter-y *n.* monasterio
mo-nas-tic *adj.* monastico
Mon-day *n.* lunes
mon-e-tar-y *adj.* monetario
mon-ey *n.* dinero
mon-eyed *adj.* adinerado
mon-goose *n.* mangosta
mo-ni-tion *n.* admonición
mon-i-tor *n.* monitor
mon-i-to-ry *adj.* admonitorio
monk *n.* monje
mon-key *n.* mono
monk-hood *n.* monacato
monk-ish *adj.* monacal
mon-o-chro-mat-ic *adj.* monocromatico
mo-noc-u-lar *adj.* monocular
mo-nog-a-my *n.* monogamia
mon-o-gram *n.* monograma
mon-o-graph *n.* monografía
mon-o-lith *n.* monolito
mon-o-lith-ic *adj.* monolitico
mon-o-plane *n.* monoplano
mo-nop-o-lize *v.* monopolizar
mo-nop-o-ly *n.* monopolio
mon-o-rail *n.* monocarril
mo-no-tone *n.* monotonía

mo-not-o-nous adj. monotono

mo-not-o-ny n. monotonía

mon-ox-ide n. monoxido

mon-soon n. monzon

mon-ster n. monstruo

mon-stros-i-ty n. monstruosidad

mon-strous adj. monstruoso

mon-tage n. montaje

month n. mes

month-ly adj. mensual

mon-u-ment n. monumento

mon-u-men-tal adj. monumental

moo v. mugir

mood n. humor

moon n. luna

moor v. amarrar

moor-age n. amarradero

moor-ing n.n amarradero

moose n. anta

mop n. estropajo

mo-ped n. ciclomotor

mor-al adj. moral

mo-rale n. moral

mor-al-ist n. moralista

mor-al-is-tic adj. moralizador

mo-ral-i-ty n. moralidad

mor-al-ize v. moralizar

mor-bid adj. morboso

mor-bid-i-ty n. morbosidad

more n., adv., adj. mas

more-o-ver adv. ademas

morn-ing n. manana

mor-phine n. morfina

mor-phol-o-gy n. morfología

mor-tal n., adj. mortal

mor-tal-i-ty n. mortalidad

mor-tu-ar-y n. mortuorio

mos-qui-to n. mosquito

most adj. muy; mas

moth n. polilla

moth-er n. madre

moth-er-hood n. maternidad

moth-er-in-law n. suegra

mo-tor-cy-cle n. motocicleta

montain n. montaña

mouse n. ratón

mouth n. boca

move v. mundar; mover

mov-ie n. película

Mr. n. señor

Mrs. n. señora

Ms. n. señora

much adj. muy, n., adv., adj. mucho

mul-ti-ple adj. multiple

mul-ti-pli-ca-tion n. multiplicación

mul-ti-ply v. multiplicar

mul-ti-pur-pose adj. multiuso

mul-ti-tude n. multitud

mum-ble v. mascullar

mum-my n. momia

munch v. ronzar

mun-dane adj. mundaño

mu-nic-i-pal adj. municipal

mu-nic-i-pal-i-ty n. municipalidad

mu-ni-fi-cence n. munificencia

mu-nif-i-cent adj. munifico

mur-der v. matanza

mur-der-er n. asesiño

mur-der-ous adj asesiño

mur-mur v. murmurar

mus-cle n. musculo

mus-cu-lar adj. musculoso

muse v. meditar

mu-se-um n. museo

mu-sic n. musica

mu-si-cal adj. musical

mu-si-cal-i-ty n. musicalidad

mu-si-cian n. musico

mus-ing n. contemplación

mus-ket n. mosquete

mus-ket-eer n. mosquetero

mus-lin n. muselina

mus-sel n. mejillon

must v. deber

mus-tache n. bigote

mu-ti-late v. mutilar

muz-zle n. hocico; boca

my adj. mi

myr-i-ad n. miriada

my-self pron. yo mismo

mys-te-ri-ous a. misterioso

mys-ter-y n. misterio

mys-tic a. mistico

mys-ti-cism n. misticismo; mistica

myth n. mito

myth-ic a. mitico

my-thol-o-gy n. mitología

nab v. prender
na-dir n. nadir
nag n. jaca
nail v. clavar, n. clavo
na-ive adj. ingenuo
na-ive-te n. ingenuidad
naked adj. desnudo
name v. apellido; nombre
name-less adj. anonimo
name-ly adv. a saber
name-sake n. tocayo
nap n. siesta
nape n. nuca
nap-kin n. servilleta
nar-cis-sism n. narcisismo
nar-cis-sus n. narciso
nar-cot-ic n. narcotico
nar-rate v. narrar
nar-ra-tion n. narración
nar-ra-tive adj. narrativo
nar-ra-tor n. narrador
nar-row adj. estrecho;
   limitado; angosto
nar-row-ing n. limitación
na-sal adj. nasal
na-sal-i-ty n. nasalidad
nas-ty adj. antipatico; sucio;
   obsceno
na-tal adj. natal
na-tal-i-ty n. natalidad
na-tion n. nation
na-tion-al n., adj. nacional
na-tion-al-ist n. nacionalista
na-tion-al-is-tic adj.
   nacionalista
na-tion-al-i-ty n.
   nacionalidad
na-tion-al-ize v. nacionalizar
na-tive adj. natal; innato;
   nativo
na-tiv-i-ty n. natividad
nat-u-ral adj. natural
nat-u-ral-ist n. naturalista
nat-u-ral-is-tic adj.
   naturalista
nat-u-ral-ize v.
   naturalizar(se)
nat-u-ral-ly adv. natural-
   mente
na-ture n. genero;
   naturaleza
naught n. nada
naugh-ty adj. verde; travieso

nau-se-a n. nausea
nau-se-ate v. dar nauseas a
nau-se-at-ing adj.
   nauseabundo
nau-seous adj.
   nauseabundo
nau-ti-cal adj. nautico
na-val adj. naval
nav-i-ga-ble adj. navegable
nav-i-gate v. navegar
nav-i-ga-tion n. navegación
nav-i-ga-tor n. navegante
nay adv. no
near prep. cerca de, adv.
   cerca, adj. próximo
near-by adj. próximo
near-ly adj. caso
neat adj. claro; limpio; fantastico
neb-u-la n. nebulosa
neb-u-lar adj. nebuloso
nec-es-sar-y adj. necesario
ne-ces-si-tate v. necesitar
ne-ces-si-ty n. necesidad
neck n. cuello
neck-lace n. collar
neck-line n. escote
ne-crol-o-gy n. necrologia
ne-cro-sis n. necrosis
nec-tar n. nactar
nec-tar-ine n. pelon
need v. necesitar
need-ful adj. necessario
nee-dle n. aguja
need-less adj. superfluo
need-y adj. necesitado
ne-far-i-ous adj. nefario
ne-gate v. negar
ne-ga-tion n. negación
neg-a-tive n. negativa
ne-glect v. descuidar
ne-glect-ful adj. negligente
neg-li-gence n. negligencia
neg-li-gent adj. negligente
neg-li-gi-ble adj. insig-
   nificante
ne-go-tia-ble adj. negociable
ne-go-ti-ate v. negociar
ne-go-ti-a-tion n.
   negociación
ne-go-ti-a-tor n. negociador
neigh-bor n. projimo; vecino
neigh-bor-hood n. barrio

neigh-bor-ing adj. vecino
neigh-bor-ly adj. amable
nei-ther pron. ninguno, conj. tampoco; ni
ne-ol-o-gism n. neologismo
ne-ol-o-gist n. neologo
ne-on n. neon
ne-o-phyte n. neofito
neph-ew n. sobrino
nep-o-tism n. nepotismo
nerve n. nervio
nerve-less adj. sin nervios
nerv-ous adj. nervioso
nerv-ous-ness n. nerviosidad
nest n. nido
net n. red
net-ting n. red
net-tle n. ortiga
net-work n red
neu-ral-gia n. neuralgia
neu-ral-gic adj. neuralgico
neu-ri-tis n. neuritis
neu-ro-sis n. nervioso
neu-rol-o-gist n. neurólogo
neu-rol-o-gy n. neurólogia
neu-rot-ic adj. neurótico
neu-tral n., adj. neutral
neu-tral-i-ty n. neutralidad
neu-tral-ize v. neutralizar
neu-tral-iz-er n. neutralizador
neu-tron n. neutron
nev-er adv. jamás; nunca
nev-er-more adv. nunca mas
nev-er-the-less adv. sin embargo
new adj. nuevo
new-found adj. nuevo
new-ly adv. nuevamente
news n. nuevas
news-cast n. noticiario
news-cast-er n. locutor
news-pa-per n. diario
news-y adj. informativo
newt n. tritón
new-ton n. neutonio
next adj. próximo
nib-ble v. mordiscar
nice adj. agradable; amable
ni-ce-ty n. delicadeza; precisión
niche n. nicho

nick n. neusca; mella
nick-el n. niquel
nick-name n. apodo
nic-o-tine n. nicotina
niece n. sobrina
nigh adv. cerca
night n. noche
night-fall n. anochecer
night-gown n. camison
night-in-gale n. ruiseñor
night-light n. lamparilla
night-ly adj. nocturno
night-mare n. pesadilla
night-time n. noche
nine adj. nueve
nine-teen adj. diecinueve
nine-ty adj. noventa
ninth adj. noveno
no n., adv. no
no-bod-y n., pron. nadie
noise n. ruido
nois-y adj. ruidoso
none pron. nadie; nada
noon n. mediodia
nor conj. ni
nor-mal adj. normal
nor-mal-ly adv. normalmente
north n. norte
north-east n. nordeste
north-west n. noroeste
nose n. nariz
not adv. no
no-ta-ble adj. notable
no-ta-tion n. notación
note v. notar, n. nota
no-ti-fy v. notificar
no-tion n. nocion
no-to-ri-ous adj. notorio
No-vem-ber n. noviembre
now adv. ahora
nu-cle-ar adj. nuclear
nude n., adj. desnudo
num-ber v. numerar, n. numero
nu-mer-i-cal adj. numerico
nu-mer-ous adj. numeroso
nut n. nuez
nu-tri-tion n. nutrición
nu-tri-tion-al adj. nutritivo
nu-tri-tious adj. nutritivo
nu-tri-tive adj. nutritivo
nuz-zle v. hocicar
ny-lon n nailon

oak n. roble
oak-en adj. de roble
oar n. remo
o-a-sis n. oasis
oat n. avena
oath n. juramento
oat-meal n. gachas de avena
ob-du-ra-cy n. obstinación
ob-du-rate adj. obstinado; insensible
o-be-di-ence n. obediencia
o-be-di-ent adj. obediente
ob-e-lisk n. obelisco
o-bese adj. obeso
o-be-si-ty n. obesidad
o-bey v. obedecer
ob-fus-cate v. ofuscar
ob-fus-ca-tion n. ofuscación
o-bit-u-ar-y n. obituario
ob-ject v. desaprobar; n. objeto
ob-jec-tion n. objeción
ob-jec-tion-a-ble adj. ofensivo
ob-jec-tive n., adj. objetivo
ob-li-gate v. obligar
ob-li-ga-tion n. obligación
o-blig-a-to-ry adj. obligatorio
o-blige v. obligar
o-blig-ing adj. complaciente
o-blique adj. oblicuo
o-blit-er-ate v. aniquilar; arrasar
o-bliv-i-on n. olvido
o-bliv-i-ous adj. olvidadizo
ob-long adj. oblongo
o b - n o x - i o u s a d j. insoportable; desagradable
o-boe n. oboe
ob-scene adj. obsceno
ob-scen-i-ty n. obscenidad
ob-scure adj. imperceptible; oscuro
ob-scu-ri-ty n. oscuridad
ob-e-qui-ous adj. servil
o b - s e r - v a n c e n. observacion; cumplimiento
ob-ser-vant adj. observador
ob-ser-va-tion n. observación
ob-ser-va-to-ry n. observatorio
ob-serve v. cumplir; obser-

var
ob-serv-er n. observador
ob-sess v. obsesionar
ob-ses-sion n. obsesión
ob-ses-sive adj. obsesivo
ob-so-les-cence n. obsolencia
ob-so-lete adj. obsoleto
ob-sta-cle n. obstaculo
ob-stet-ric adj. obstetrico
ob-sti-na-cy n. obstinación
ob-sti-nate adj. obstinado
ob-struct v. obstruir
ob-struc-tion n. obstrucción
ob-struc-tion-ist n. obstruccionista
ob-tain v. obtener
ob-trude v. introducir
ob-tru-sion n. intrusión
ob-tuse adj. obtuso
ob-vi-ate v. obviar
ob-vi-ous adj. obvio
ob-vi-ous-ly adj. claro
oc-ca-sion n. ocasión
oc-ca-sion-al adj. ocasional
oc-clude v. ocluir
oc-cu-pan-cy n. ocupación
oc-cu-pant n. pasajero; inquilino
oc-cu-pa-tion n. ocupación
o c - c u - p a - t i o n - a l adj. ocupacional
oc-cu-pied adj. ocupado
oc-cu-py v. ocupar
oc-cur v. ocurrir
oc-cur-rence n. presencia; suceso
o-cean v. oceáno
o-ce-an-ic adj. oceánico
oc-ta-gon n. octagono
oc-tag-o-nal adj. octogonal
oc-tane n. octaño
oc-tave n. octavo
Oc-to-ber n. octubre
oc-to-ge-nar-i-an adj. octogenario
oc-to-pus n. pulpo
oc-u-lar adj. ocular
oc-u-lis n. oculista
odd adj. raro
odd-i-ty n. rareza
odds n. probabilidades
o-di-ous adj. odioso

o-di-um *n.* odio
o-dom-e-ter *n.* odometro
o-dor *n.* olor
o-dor-less *adj.* inoforo
o-dor-ous *adj.* fragante
od-ys-sey *n.* odisea
of *prep.* de
off *adv.* fuera
of-fend *v.* ofender
of-fend-er *n.* infractor
of-fense *n.* ofense
of-fen-sive *adj.* ofensivo
of-fer *n.* ofrecimiento, *v.* ofrecer
of-fer-ing *n.* ofrecimiento
of-fice *n.* oficina
of-fi-cer *n.* oficial
of-fi-cial *n., adj.* oficial
of-fi-ci-ate *v.* oficiar
of-fi-cious *adj.* oficioso
off-set *v.* compensar
of-ten *adv.* a menudo
oil *n.* aceite
oil-can *n.* alcuzq
oiled *adj.* aceitado
oil-y *adj.* aceitoso
oint-ment *n.* pomada
o-kra *n.* quingombo
old *adj.* anciano; viejo
old-en *adj.* pasado
old-fash-ioned *adj.* anticuado
ol-fac-to-ry *adj.* olfativo
ol-ive *n.* oliva
om-i-nous *adj.* ominoso
o-mis-sion *n.* omisión
o-mit *v.* omitir
om-ni-bus *n.* omnibus
om-nip-o-tence *n.* omnipotencia
om-nip-o-ten *adj.* omnipotente
on *prep.* sobre
once *n., adv.* una vez
on-col-o-gy *n.* oncologia
on-com-ing *adj.* que viene
one *adj.* uno; un
one-di-men-sion-al *adj.* unidimensional
on-er-ous *adj.* oneroso
one-self *pron.* uno
one-sid-ed *adj.* desigual
on-ion *n.* cebolla

on-look-er *n.* espectador
on-ly *adj., adv.* solo
on-rush *n.* embestida
on-to *prep.* sobre; en
on-ward *adj.* hacia adelante
on-yx *n.* onix
o-pac-i-ty *n.* opacidad
o-pal *n.* opalo
o-pal-es-cence *n.* opalescencia
o-paque *adj.* opaco
o-pen *v.* abrir, *adj.* abierto
o-pen-er *n.* abridor
o-pen-ing *n.* abertura
o-pen-mind-ed *adj.* receptivo
o-per-a *n.* opera
op-er-a-ble *adj.* operable
op-er-ate *v.* operar; actuar; manejar
op-er-at-ing *adj.* de mantenimiento
op-er-a-tion *n.* operación
op-er-a-tion-al *adj.* deoperacion
op-er-a-tive *adj.* operante
oph-thal-mol-o-gist *n.* oftalmolgo
oph-thal-mol-ogy *n.* oftalmologia
o-pi-ate *n.* opiato
o-pine *v.* opinar
o-pin-ion *n.* opinion
o-pi-um *n.* opio
op-po-nent *n.* adversario
op-por-tune *adj.* oportuno
op-por-tun-ist *n.* oportunista
op-por-tu-ni-ty *n.* oportunidad
op-pose *v.* oponerse
op-po-site *adj.* opuesto
op-po-si-tion *n.* oposición
op-press *v.* oprimir
op-pres-sion *n.* opresión
op-pres-sive *adj.* opresivo
op-pres-sor *n.* opresor
opt *v.* optar
op-yic *adj.* optico
op-ti-cal *adj.* optico
op-ti-cian *n.* optico
op-ti-mal *adj.* optimo
op-ti-mism *n.* optmismo
op-ti-mist *n.* optimista
op-ti-mis-tic *adj.* optimista

op-tion n. opción
op-tion-al adj. opcional
op-tom-e-try n. optometria
op-u-lent adj. opulento
or conj. u; o
o-ral adj. oral
or-ange adj. anaranjado, n. naranja
o-ra-tion n. oración
or-ches-tra n. orquesta
or-der n. orden
or-di-nar-y adj. ordinario
or-gan-ism n. organismo
or-gan-i-za-tion n. organización
or-gan-ize v. organizar
o-rig-i-nal adj. original
o-rig-i-nate v. originar
os-ten-ta-tion n. ostentación
oth-er prep. el otro, adj. otro
ounce n. onza
our adj. nuestro
our-selves pron. nosotros
out prep. fuera de, adv. fuera
out-er adj. externo
out-fit n. traje
out-line v. bosquejar, n. bosquejo
out-side adv. fuera, n. exterior
out-ward adj. exterior
o-va-ry n. ovario
o-va-tion n. ovación
ov-en n. horno
o-ver adj. otra vez, prep. sobre; encima de
o-ver-lap v. solapar
o-ver-night adj. de noche
o-ver-sight n. olvido
o-vert a. publico
o-ver-turn v. volcar
o-ver-weight adj. gordo
o-vum n. ovulo
owe v. tener deudas
owl n. buho
own v. reconocer
ox-ide n. oxido
ox-i-dize v. oxidar(se)
ox-y-gen n. oxigeno
ox-y-gen-ate v. oxigenar
oys-ter n. ostra
o-zone n. ozono

pa n. papá
pace n. paso
pa-cif-ic adj. pacifico
pac-i-fism n. pacifismo
pac-i-fy v. pacificar
pack n. fardo
pack-age n. paquete
pact n. pacto
pad n. almohadilla
pad-dle n. canalete
pad-lock n. candado
pa-gan n. pagano
page n. página
pag-eant n. espectaculo
pa-go-da n. pagoda
pail n. cubo
pain v. doler; n. dolor
pain-ful adj. doloroso
pains-tak-ing a. laborioso; esmerado
paint n. pintura, v. pintar
paint-ing n. pintura
pair n. pareja; par
pa-jam-as n. pijama
pal-ace n. palacio
pal-ate n. paladar
pale a. palido; claro
pa-le-on-tol-o-gy n. paleontologia
pal-ette n. paleta
pal-i-sade n. palizada
pall v. perder su sabor
pal-lid palido
pal-lor n. palidez
palm n. palma
palm-is-try n. quiromancia
pal-pa-ble adj. palpable
pal-pi-ta-tion n. palpitación
pal-try a. miserable
pam-per v. mimar
pam-phlet n. folleto
pan n. cazuela
pan-a-ce-a n. panacea
pan-cake n. hojuela
pan-cre-as n. pancreas
pan-de-mo-ni-um n. pandemonium
pane n. hoja de vidrio
pan-el n. panel
pang n. punzada; dolor
pan-han-dle v. mendigar
pan-ic n. terror
pan-o-ram-a n. panorama

pan-sy *n.* pensamiento
pant *n., pl.* pantalones
pan-the-ism *n.* panteismo
pan-ther *n.* pantera
pan-to-mime *n.* pantomima
pan-try *n.* despensa
pa-pa *n.* papa
pa-pa-cy *n.* papado; pontificado
pa-per *n.* papel
pa-pier-ma-che *n.* cartón piedra
pa-poose *n.* crio
pa-py-rus *n.* papiro
par *n.* par
par-a-ble *n.* parábola
par-a-chute *n.* paracaídas
pa-rade *n.* parada
par-a-dise *n.* paraiso
par-a-dox *n.* paradoja
par-af-fin *n.* paraffin
par-a-graph *n.* parrafo
par-al-lel *a.* paralelo
pa-ral-y-sis *n.* parálisis
pa-ra-lyze *v.* paralizar
par-ram-e-ter *n.* parametro; limite
par-a-noi-a *n.* paranoia
par-a-pher-nal-ia *n.* arreos
par-a-phrase *n.* parafrasis
par-a-site *n.* parásito
par-a-troop-er *n.* paracaidista
parcel *n.* paquete; bulto
parch *v.* secar
parch-ment *n.* pergamino
par-don *n.* perdón, *v.* perdonar
pare *v.* cortar
par-ent *n.* madre; padre
par-ren-the-sis *n.* parentesis
pa-ri-ah *n.* paria
par-ish *n.* parroquia
park *v.* aparcar, *n.* parque
par-ley *v.* parlamentar
par-lia-ment *n.* parlamento
par-lor *n.* sala de recibo
pa-ro-chi-al *a.* parroquial; estrecho
par-o-dy *n.* parodia
pa-role *n.* libertad bajo palabra
par-ox-ysm *n.* paroxismo

par-rot *n.* loro
par-ry *v.* parar
par-sley *n.* perejil
par-son *n.* clérigo
part *v.* separar(se); partir(se), *n.* parte
par-take *v.* tomar parte
par-tial *adj.* parcial
par-tial-i-ty *n.* parcialidad
par-tic-i-pant *a.* participe
par-tic-i-pate *v.* participar
par-tic-i-pa-tion *n.* participación
par-ti-ci-ple *n.* participio
par-ti-cle *n.* partículo
par-tic-u-lar *adj.* particular
par-tic-u-lar-i-ty *n.* particion; tabique
part-ing *a.* despendida
par-ti-san *n.* partidario
par-ti-tion *n.* partición; tabique
part-ner *n.* socio
par-tridge *n.* perdiz
par-ty *n.* fiesta
pass *v.* aprobar; pasar
pas-sage *n.* pasaje; travesia; pasadizo
pas-sen-ger *n.* pasajero; viajero
pas-sion *n.* pasión
pas-sion-ate *a.* apasionado
pas-sive *adj.* pasivo
pass-port *n.* pasaporte
pass-word *n.* santo y sena
past *n., adj.* pasado
paste *n.* enguido; pasta
paste-board *n.* carton
pas-teur-i-za-tion *n.* pasteurización
pas-teur-ize *v.* pasteurizar
pas-time *n.* pasatiempo
pas-tor *n.* pastor
pas-try *n.* pasteles
pas-ture *n.* pasto
pat *n.* golpecito; pastellillo
patch *n.* pedazo
pat-ent *n.* patente
pa-ter-nal *adj.* paterno
pa-ter-ni-ty *n.* paternidad
path *n.* senda
pa-thet-ic *a.* patético
pa-thol-o-gy *n.* patología

pa-tience n. paciencia
pa-tient a. paciente
pa-ti-o n. patio
pa-tri-ar-chy n. patriarcado
pat-ri-mo-ny n. patrimonio
pa-tri-ot n. patriota
pa-trol v. patrullar
pa-tron n. cliente
pat-tern n. patrón
pau-per n. pobre
pause n. pausa
pave v. empedrar; pavimentar
pave-ment n. pavimento
pa-vil-ion n. pabellon
paw v. manosear, n. pata
pawn v. empenar
pay v. pagar; ser provechoso
pay-roll n. nomina
pea n. guisante
peace n. paz
peace-ful a. tranquilo
peach n. melocoton
pea-cock n. pavo real; pavon
peak n. pico; cumbre
peal v. repicar
pea-nut n. cachuete
pear n. pera
pearl n. perla
peas-ant n. campesino
pab-ble n. guijarro
pec-ca-dil-lo n. pecadillo
pe-cu-liar adj. peculiar
pe-cu-li-ar-i-ty n. peculiaridad
ped-al n. pedal
ped-dle v. vender por las calles
ped-dler n. buhonero
ped-es-tal n. pedestal
pe-des-tri-an n. peaton
ped-i-gree n. genealogia
peel v. pelar
peer n. par
peg n. clavija; estaca
pel-let n. bolita; pella
pelt n. piel
pel-vis n. pelvis
pen n. pluma
pe-nal a. penal
pen-al-ty n. pena; castigo
pen-cil n. lápiz

pend-ant n. pendiente
pend-ing adj. pendiente
pen-du-lum n. péndulo
pen-e-trate v. penetrar
pen-i-cil-lin n. penicilina
pen-in-su-la n. península
pen-i-tent n. penitente
pen-i-ten-tia-ry n. presidio
pen-ny n. centavo
pen-sion n. pensión
pen-sive adj. pensativo
pen-ta-gon n. pentágono
pe-on n. peón
pe-o-ny n. peonía
peo-ple n. gente; pueblo
pep-per n. pimienta; pimiento
pep-per-mint n. menta
per prep. por
per-ceive v. percibir
per-cent n. por ciento
per-cent-age n. porcentaje
per-cep-tion n. percepción
perch n. percha; perca
per-di-tion n. perdición
per-en-ni-al a. perenne
per-fect adj. perfecto
per-fec-tion n. perfección
per-fo-rate v. perforar
per-form v. efectuar; hacer; representar
per-for-mance n. representación; función
per-fume n. perfume
per-il n. peligro
pe-rim-e-ter n. perimetro
pe-ri-od n. periodo
pe-ri-od-i-cal n. publicación periodica
pe-riph-er-y n. periferia
per-i-scope n. periscopia
per-ish v. perecer
per-jure v. perjurar(se)
per-ju-ry n. perjurio
per-ma-nent a. permanente
per-mis-sion n. permiso
per-mit v. permitir; tolerar
per-pen-dic-u-lar adj. perpendicular
per-pet-u-al a. perpetuo; continuo
per-plex v. confundir
per-se-cute v. perseguir

per-se-cu--tion n. persecución

per-sist v. persistir

per-son n. persona

per-son-al-i-ty n. personalidad

per-son-nel n. personal

per-spec-tive n. perspectiva

per-spi-ra-tion n. sudor

per-suade v. persuadi

per-spire v. sudar

per-ver-sion n. perversión

pe-ti-tion n. peticion

phar-ma-cy n. farmacia

phi-los-o-phy n. filosofía

pho-bi-a n. fobia

pho-to-cop-y n. fotocopia

pho-to-graph n. foto

pho-tog-ra-phy n. fotografia

phrase n. frase

phys-i-cal adj. fisico

phy-si-cian n. medico

pi-an-o n. piano

pick v. picar; elegir

pic-ture n. foto; cuadro; película

pie n. pastel

piece n. pedazo

pig n. cerdo

pi-geon n. paloma

pil-lar n. pilar

pine n. piño

pink adj. rosado

pipe n. pipa

pis-tol n. pistola

pit-y n. lástima

place v. poner, n. posición; sitio

plac-id adj. placido

plague n. plaga

plain adj., n. llano

plan v. planear, n. plano

plane n. avion; plano

plan-et n. planeta

plant v. plantar, n. planta

plas-ma n. plasma

plas-tic n., adj. plastico

plate n. plato

play v. tocar; jugar, n. juego

plea n. defensa

plead v. suplicar; defender

pleas-ure n. placer

plen-ti-ful adj. abundante

plen-ty n. abundancia

plum n. ciruela

plum-age n. plumaje

plu-ral n., adj. plural

pock-et n. bolsillo

po-em n. poema

po-et n. poeta

po-et-ic adj. poético

point n. punto

po-lice n. policía

po-lit-i-cal adj. politico

pol-i-ti-cian n. politico

pol-i-tics n. politicia

pol-lu-tion n. polución

pomp-ous adj. pomposo

pond n. estanque

po-ny n. jaca

pool n. piscina

poor adj. pobre

pop-u-lar adj. popular

pop-u-late v. poblar

pop-u-la-tion n. población

port n. puerto

por-tion n. parte

pose v. plantear

po-si-tion n. posición

pos-i-tive adj. positivo

pos-sess v. poseer

pos-ses-sion n. possesión

pos-si-bil-i-ty n. posibilidad

pos-si-ble adj. posible

post n. poste; puesto; correo

post-age n. porte; franqueo

post-card n. tarjeta

post-er n. cartel

pos-te-ri-or adj. posterior

post-man n. cartero

post-mark n. matasellos

post me-rid-i-em a. postmeridiano

post-mor-tem n. autopsia

post-pone v. alazar

post-script v. posdata

pos-ture n. postura

pot n. olla; tiesto

po-tas-si-um n. potasio

po-ta-to n. patata

po-tent a. potente; fuerte

po-ten-tial n. potencial

po-tion n. posion

pot-ter-y n. alfareria

pouch n. bolsa

poul-try n. aves de corral

pound n. libra
pour v. diluviar
pout v. hace puncheros
pov-er-ty n. pobreza
pow-der n. polvo
pow-er n. fuerza; poder
pow-er-ful a. potente; poderoso
prac-ti-cal adj. práctico
practice v. practicar; ejercer
prag-mat-ic a. pragmatico
pari-rie n. pradera
praise v. alabar
prank n. travesura
pray v. rezar
prayer n. oración
preach v. predicar
pre-am-ble n. preambulo
pre-cau-tion n. precaución
pre-dede v. preceder
prec-e-dent n. precedente
pre-cint n. recinto; distrito electoral
pre-cious adj. precioso
prec-i-pice n. precipicio
pre-cip-i-ta-tion n. precipitacion
pre-cise a. preciso; exacto
pre-co-cious a. precoz
pre-cur-sor n. precursor
pred-e-ces-sor n. predecesor
pre-des-ti-na-tion n. predestinación
pre-dic-a-ment n. apuro
pre-dict v. pronosticar
pre-dic-tion n. pronostico
pre-dom-i-nant a. predominante
pref-ace n. prologo; prefacio
pre-fer v. preferir
pref-er-ence n. preferencia
pre-fix n. prefijo
preg-nan-cy n. embarazo
preg-nant adj. embarazada
pre-his-tor-ic adj. prehistorico
prej-u-dice n. prejuicio
pre-lim-i-nar-y n. preliminar
pre-lude n. preludio
pre-med-i-tate v. premeditar
pre-miere n. estreno
pre-mi-um n. prima

pre-mo-ni-tion n. presentimiento
pre-oc-cu-pied adj. preocupado
prep-a-ra-tion n. preparación
pre-pare v. preparar(se)
prep-o-si-tion n. preposición
pre-pos-ter-ous a. absurdo
pre-req-ui-site a. requisito previo
pre-rog-a-tive n. prerrogative
pre-scribe v. prescribir
pre-scrip-tion n. recenta
pres-ence n. presencia
pre-sent adj. presente, v. presentar, n. regalo
pres-en-ta-tion n. presentación
pre-serv-a-tive a. preservativo
pre-serve v. preservar; conservar
pre-side v. presidir
pres-i-dent n. presidente
press n. prensa; imprenta
pres-sure n. presión; urgencia
pres-ti-gid-i-ta-tion n. prestidigitación
pres-tige n. prestigio
pre0sume v. presumir; suponer
pre-tend v. pretender
pre-tense n. pretexto
pret-ty a. guapo; bonito; mono
pre-vail v. prevalecer; predominar
pre-vent v. impedir
pre-vi-ous a. previo
prey n. presa
price n. precio
price-less a. inapreciable
prick v. punzar
pride n. orgullo
priest n. sacerdote
prim a. estirado
pri-ma-ry adj. primario
prime adj. primero
prim-i-tive adj. primitivo
pri-mo-gen-i-ture n.

primogeniture
prince n. principe
prin-cess n. princesa
prin-ci-pal n., adj. principal
prin-ci-pal-i-ty n. principado
prin-ci-ple n. principio
print v. imprimir
print-ing n. imprenta
pri-or a. anterior
pri-or-i-ty n. prioridad
pri-or-y n. priorato
prism n. prism
pris-on n. carcel
pri-va-cy n. soledad
pri-vate adj. privado
priv-i-lege n. privilegio
prize n. premio
prob-a-bil-i-ty n. probabilidad
prob-a-ble a. probable
probe n. sonda
prob-lem n. problema
pro-ce-dure n. procedimiento
pro-ceed v. proceder
proc-ess n. proceso
pro-claim v. proclamar
pro-cliv-i-ty n. proclividad; inclinación
pro-cras-ti-nate v. dilatar; aplazar
pro-cure v. obtener; alcahuetear
prod v. ponzar
prod-i-gal a. prodigo
pro-d-i-gy n. prodigio
pro-duce v. producir
prod-uct n. producto
pro-fane a. profano
pro-fan-i-ty n. profanidad
pro-fes-sion n. profesión
pro-fes-sor n. profesora; profesor
pro-fi-cien-cy n. pericia
pro-file n. perfil
prof-it n. ganancia; beneficio
pro-found a. profundo
pro-fuse a. profuso
pro-fu-sion n. profusion
prog-e-ny n. progenie
prog-no-sis n. pronostico
pro-gram n. programa
prog-ress n. progreso;

desarrollo
pro-gres-sive a. progresivo
pro-hib-it v. prohibir
pro-hi-bi-tion n. prohibición
pro-ject n. proyecto, v. proyectar
pro-jec-tile n. proyectile
pro-lif-ic adj. prolifico
pro-logue n. prolongar
pro-long v. prolongar
prom-i-nent a. prominente
pro-mis-cu-ous a. promiscuo; libertino
prom-ise v. prometer, n. promesa
prom-on-to-ry n. promontorio
pro-mote v. promover; fomentar; ascender
pro-mo-tion n. promoción
prompt a. puntual; pronto
pro-noun n. pronombre
pro-nounce v. pronunciar(se)
pro-nounced a. marcado
pro-nun-ci-a-tion n. pronunciación
proof n. prueba
proof-read-er n. corrector de pruebas
prop n. apoyo
prop-a-gan-da n. propaganda
pro-pel v. propulsar
pro-pel-ler n. helice
pro-pen-si-ty n. propensión; inclinación
prop-er a. propio; apropiado; decente
prop-er-ty n. propiedad
proph-e-cy n. profeciz
proph-e-sy v. profetizar
proph-et n. profeta
pro-phy-lac-tic a. profilatico
pro-pi-tious a. propicio
pro-por-tion n. proporción
pro-pose v. proponer(se); declararse
prop-o-si-tion n. proposición; propuesta
pro-pri-e-tor n. propietario
pro-pri-e-ty n. corrección; decoro

pro-scribe v. proscribir
prose n. prosa
pros-e-cute v. proseguir
pros-pect n. perspectiva
pros-per v. prosperar
pros-per-i-ty n. prosperidad
pros-ti-tute n. prostituta; ramera
pros-trate v. postrar(se); derribar
pro-tag-o-nist n. protagonista
pro-tect v. proteger
pro-tein n. proteina
pro-test n. protesta, v. protestar
pro-to-col n. protocolo
pro-ton n. proton
pro-to-plasm n. protoplasma
pro-trude v. salir fuera
proud a. orgulloso; arrogante
prove v. probar
pro-verb n. proverbio
pro-vide v. proveer
prov-ince n. provincia
pro-vi-sion n. provision
pro-voc-a-tive a. provocativa; provocador
pro-voke v. provocar
prow n. proa
prox-y n. poder; apoderado
prude n. gasmona
prune n. ciruela pasa
pry v. meterse; fisgonear
psalm n. salmo
pseu-do-nym n. seudonimo
psych-e-del-ic a. psiquedelico
psy-chi-a-trist n. psiquiatra
psy-chi-a-try n. psiquiatria
psy-cho-a-nal-y-sis n. psicoanalisis
psy-cho-an-a-lyze v. psicoanalizar
psy-cho-log-i-cal adj. psicológico
psy-chol-o-gy n. psicologia
psy-cho-sis n. psicosis
pto-maine n. ptomaina
pub n. taberna
pu-ber-ty n. pubertad
pub-lic n., adj. publico

pub-li-ca-tion n. publicación
pub-lish v. publicar
pub-lish-er n. editor
puck-er v. arrugar
pud-ding n. pudin
pud-dle n. charco
puff v. soplar; inflar
pug-na-cious a. pugnaz
puke v. vomitar
pull v. tirar; arrastrar
pul-ley n. polea
pul-mo-nar-y a. pulmonar
pulp n. pulpa
pul-pit n. pulpito
pulse n. pulso
pul-ver-ize v. pulverizar
pum-ice n. piedra pomez
pump n. bomba
pump-kin n. calabaza
pun n. juego de palabras o vocablos
punch v. punzar
punc-tu-al adj. puntual
punc-tu-a-tion n. puntuación
punc-ture n. pinchazo
pun-ish v. castigar
pu-ny a. encanijado
pu-pa n. crisalida
pu-pil n. estudiante; pupila
pup-pet n. titere
pur-chase v. comprar
pure adj. puro
pur-ga-to-ry n. purgatorio
pu-ri-fy v. purificar
pu-ri-tan n. puritano
pur-ple adj. purpureo
pur-pose n. fin; proposito; resolucion
purr n. ronreneo
purse n. bolsa
pur-sue v. perseguir
pur-suit n. perseguimiento; busca; ocupación
pus n. pus
push v. empujar; apretar
puss-y n. gatito
put v. meter; poner(se)
pu-tre-fy v. pudrir
pu-trid a. odrido
put-ty n. masilla
pyr-a-mid n. piramide
pyre n. pira
py-thon n. piton

quack v. graznar; n. graznido
quad-ran-gle n. cuadrangulo
quad-rant n. cuadrante
quad-rate adj. cuadrante
quad-rat-ic adj. cuadratico
quad-ri-ceps n. cuadriceps
quad-ri-lat-er-al n., adj. cuadrilátero
quad-ri-ple-gi-a n. cuadriplejia
quad-ri-ple-gic adj. cuadriplejico
quad-ru-ple v. cuadruplicar(se)
quag-mire n. pantano
quail n. codorniz
quake v. temblar
qual-i-fi-ca-tion n. calificacion
qual-i-fied adj. acreditado; capacitado
qual-i-fi-er n. calificativo
qual-i-fy v. habilitar
qual-i-fy-ing adj. eliminatoria
qual-i-ta-tive adj. cualitativo
qual-i-ty n. calidad
qualm n. duda
quan-ti-ta-tive adj. cuantitativo
quan-ti-ty n. cantidad
quar-an-tine n. cuarentena
quar-rel n. riña
quar-rel-er n. pendenciero
quar-rel-some adj. pendeciero
quar-ry n. cantera
quart n. cuarto
quar-ter n. cuarto
qua-ter-deck n. alcazar
quar-ter-ly adj. trimestral
quar-tet n. cuarteto
quartz n. cuarzo
qua-ver v. temblar
queen n. reina
quench v. matar; apagar
quench-a-ble adj. apagar
ques-tion n. pregunta
quick adj. listo; rapido
qui-et adj. silencioso
quit v. dejar; irse
quo-ta-tion n. cita
quote v. citar

rab-bi n. rabino
rab-bit n. conejo
rab-ble n. chusma
rab-id adj. rabioso
ra-bies n. rabia
rac-coon n. mapache
race v. correr de prisa, n. raza
rac-er n. corredor
race-track n. pista
ra-cial adj. racial
rac-ism n. racismo
ra-cist n. racista
rack n. potro
rack-et n. raqueta
rac-y adj. picante
ra-dar n. radar
ra-di-al adj. radial
ra-di-ance n. resplandor
ra-di-ant adj. radiante
ra-di-ate v. radiar; emitir; brillar
ra-di-a-tion n. radiación
ra-di-a-tor n. radiador
rad-i-cal n., adj. radical
rad-i-cle n. radícula
ra-di-o n. radio
ra-di-o-ac-tive adj. radiactivo
ra-di-o-ac-tiv-i-ty n. radiactividad
ra-di-o-broad-cast v. radiar
ra-di-o-gram n. radiograma
ra-di-o-graph n. radiografia
ra-di-ol-o-gist n. radiologo
ra-di-ol-o-gy n. radiologia
rad-ish n. rábano
ra-di-um n. radio
ra-di-us n. radio
ra-don n. radon
raff-ish adj. ostentoso
raf-fle n. rifa
raft n. balsa
raft-er n. cabrio
rag n. trapo
rage v. enfurecerse
rag-ged adj. desigual
raid v. atacar
rail n. carril
rail-ing n. baranda
rail-road n. ferrocarril
rail-way n. ferrocarril
rain v. llover, n. lluvia
rain-bow n. arco iris

rain-coat n. impereable
rain-drop n. gota de lluvia
rain-fall n. precipitación
rain-wear n. ropa impermeable
rain-y adj. lluvioso
raise v. criar; ;evantar
raised adj. repujado
rai-sin n. pasa
rake v. restrillar, n. rastro
ral-ly n. reunión, v. reunir(se)
ram n. carnero
ram-ble v. divagar
ram-bler n. vagabundo
ram-bunc-tious adj. alborotador
ram-i-fi-ca-tion n. ramificación
ramp n. rampa
ram-page n. alboroto
ramp-ant adj. destartalado
ranch n. hacienda
ranch-er n. hacendado
ran-cid adj. rancio
ran-cor n. rencor
ran-cor-ous adj. rencoroso
ran-dom adj. fortuito
range v. colocar; alinear
rang-er n. guardabosques
rank n. rango; fila
rank-ing adj. superior
ran-kle v. enconarse
ran-sack v. saquear
ran-som v. rescatar, n. rescate
rant v. vociferar
rap v. golpear
ra-pa-cious adj. rapaz
ra-pac-i-ty n. rapacidad
rape v. violar, n. violación
rap-id adj. rapido
ra-pid-i-ty n. rapidez
rap-ine n. rapiña
rap-ist n. violador
rap-port n. relación
rapt adj. absorto
rap-ture n. rapto
rap-tur-ous adj. extasiado
rare adj. poco; raro
rar-e-fied adj. refinado
rar-e-fy v. enrarecer(se)
rar-ing adj. impaciente

rar-i-ty n. rareza
ras-cal n. bribón
rash n. erupción
rash-er n. tocino
rasp-ber-ry n. frambuesa
rasp-y adj. aspero
rat n. rata
rate v. tasar, n. razón
rath-er adv. un poco
rat-i-fy v. ratificar
rat-ing n. popularidad; clasificación
ra-tio n. proporción
ra-ti-oc-i-nate v. raciocinar
ra-tion n. ración
ra-tion-al adj. racional
ra-tion-ale n. explicación; raxon
ra-tion-al-i-ty n. racionalidad
ra-tion-al-i-za-tion n. racionalización
ra-tion-al-ize v. racionalizar
ra-tion-ing n. racionamiento
rat-tle n. ruido
rat-trap n. ratonera
raun-chy adj. sucio
rav-age v. destruir, n. estrago
rave v. delirar
rav-el v. deshilar(se)
ra-ven n. cuervo
ra-ven-ous adj. coraz
ra-vine n. barranco
rav-ing adj. extraordinario
rav-ish v. raptar
rav-ish-ing adj. encantador
raw adj. novato; crudo
ray n. rayo
ray-on n. rayón
reach n. alcance, v. extenderse; alargar
re-act v. reaccionar
re-ac-tion n. reacción
re-ac-tion-ar-y n. reaccionario
re-ac-tor n. reactor
read v. decir; leer
read-ing n. lección
re-ad-just v. reajustar
read-y adj. pront; listo
re-al adj. real
re-al-i-ty n. realidad
re-al-ize v. realizar

re-al-ly adv. realmente
realm n. reino
ream n. resma
rea-son v. razonar, n. razon
rea-son-a-ble adj. razonable
reb-el adj., n. rebelde
re-bel-lion n. rebelión
re-buke n. reprimenda
re-call v. retirar; hacer
re-cant v. retractar(se)
re-cede v. retroceder
re-ceipt n. ingresos
re-ceive v. acoger; recibir
re-cent adj. reciente
re-cep-ta-cle n. receptaculo
re-cep-tion n. recepción
re-cess n. nicho
re-ces-sion n. retroceso
rec-i-pe n. receta
re-cip-ro-cal adj. reciproco
re-cit-al n. recital
rec-i-ta-tion n. recitación
re-cite v. recitar
reck-on v. considerar
re-claim v. reclamar
re-cline v. recostar(se)
rec-luse n. recluso
rec-og-ni-tion n. reconocimiento
rec-om-pense n. recompensa
rec-on-cile v. reconcinar
re-con-struct v. reconstruir
re-cord n. disco, v. registrar
re-course n. recurso
re-cov-er v. recobrar
re-cruit n. recluta
rec-tan-gle n. rectangulo
rec-ti-fy v. rectificar
re-cu-per-ate v. recuperar
re-cu-per-a-tion n. recuperación
red adj. rojo
red-dish adj. rojizo
re-deem v. redimir
re-demp-tion n. redención
re-do v. rehacer
re-duce v. disminuir; reducir
re-duc-tion n. reducción
reef n. escollo
reek n. olor
re-fer v. referir(se)
ref-er-ee n. arbitro

ref-er-ence n. referencia
re-fill v. rellenar
re-fine v. refinar
re-fin-er-y n. refinería
re-flect v. reflejar
re-flec-tion n. reflejo
re-flex adj. reflejo
re-flex-ive adj. reflexive
re-form n. reforma, v. reformarse
re-form-a-to-ry n. reformatorio
re-fract v. refractar
re-frain v. refrenar
re-fresh v. refrescar
re-fresh-ment n. refresco
re-frig-er-ate v. refrigerar
ref-uge n. refugio
ref-u-gee n. refugiado
re-fund n. reembolso
re-fuse v. rehusar
re-gain v. recobrar
re-gard v. considerar
re-gen-er-ate v. regenerar
re-gent n. regente
re-gime n. regimen
reg-i-men n. regimen
reg-i-ment n. regimiento
re-gion n. región
reg-is-ter v. registrar, n. registro
re-gret n. sentimiento
reg-u-lar adj. regular
reg-u-la-tion n. regulación
re-ha-bil-i-tate v. rehabilitar
re-ha-bil-i-ta-tion n. rehabilitacion
re-hearse v. ensayar
reign v. reinar, n. reinado
re-im-burse v. reembolsar
rein n. rienda
re-in-car-na-tion n. reencarnacion
re-in-force v. reforzar
re-it-er-ate v. reiterar
re-ject v. rechazar
re-lapse n. recaida, v. reincidir
re-late v. relatar
re-lat-ed adj. afin
re-la-tion n. relación
re-lax v. relajar
re-lease n. descargo

re-lent v. ceder
re-li-a-ble adj. confiable
rel-ic n. reliquia
re-lief n. alivio
re-lieve v. aliviar
re-li-gion n. religión
re-li-gious adj. religioso
rel-ish n. apetencia, v. gustar
re-ly v. contar; confiar
re-main v. quedar(se)
rem-e-dy n. remedio
re-mem-ber v. acordarse de
re-mem-brance n. recuerdo
re-mind v. recordar
rem-i-nis-cence n. reminiscencia
re-miss adj. descuidado
re-mit v. remitir
re-mit-tance n. remesa
re-morse n. remordimiento
re-mote adj. remoto
re-move v. apartar(se); quitar(se)
ren-ais-sance n. renacimiento
rend v. hender
ren-der v. volver
red-dez-vous v. reunirse
ren-e-gade n. renegado
re-new v. renovar(se)
re-nounce v. renunciar
re-nown n. renombre
rent v. alquilar, n. alquiler
re-pair v. remendar; reparar
re-pay v. pagar; recompensar
re-peat v. repetir(se)
re-pel v. repeler
re-per-cus-sion n. repersución
rep-er-toire n. repertorio
re-place v. reponer
re-ply n. respuesta
re-port v. informar
rep-re-hen-si-ble adj. reprensible
rep-re-sen-ta-tion n. representación
re-press v. reprimir
rep-ri-mand v. reprender
re-proach n. reproche
re-pro-duce v. reproducir

rep-tile n. reptil
re-pub-lic n. república
re-pulse n. repulsa
rep-u-ta-tion n. reputación
re-quest v. rogar
re-quire v. necesitar; exigir
res-cue n. rescate
re-search v. investigar
re-sent v. resentirse de
res-er-va-tion n. reservación
re-serve v. reservar
re-side v. vivir; residir
res-i-dent n., adj. residente
re-sign v. resignarse
res-ig-na-tion n. resignación
res-in n. resina
re-sist v. resistir
re-sist-ance n. resistencia
res-o-lu-tion n. resolución
re-solve v. resolver(se)
re-sort n. recurso
re-source n. recurso
re-spect n. respeto
re-spect-a-ble adj. respetable
re-spect-ful adj. respetuoso
re-spect-ing prep. respecto
re-spec-tive adj. respectivo
res-pi-ra-tion n. respiración
res-pi-ra-tor n. respirador
res-pi-ra-to-ry adj. respiratorio
re-spire v. respirar
res-pite n. respiro
re-splen-dent adj. resplandeciente
re-spond v. responder
re-spon-dent adj. resplandeciente
re-sponse n. respuesta
re-spon-si-bil-i-ty n. responsabilidad
re-spon-si-ble adj. responsable
rest n. descansar
res-tau-rant n. restaurante
rest-ful adj. sosegado
res-ti-tute v. restituir
res-ti-tu-tion n. restitución
rest-less adj. inquieto
res-to-ra-tion n. restauración
re-store v. restaurar
re-strain v. refrenar

re-strict v. restringir
re-stric-tion n. restricción
re-sult n. resultado, v. resultar
re-sus-ci-tate v. resucitar
re-tain v. retener
re-tard v. retardar
ret-i-na n. retina
re-tire v. retirarse
re-tract v. retractar(se)
re-trieve v. recobrar
ret-ro-ac-tive adj. retroactivo
re-turn v. volver
re-un-ion n. reunión
re-veal v. revelar
rev-e-la-tion n. revelación
re-venge v. vengar(se)
re-verse adj. inverso
re-view n. resena
re-vise v. repasar; revisar
re-vi-sion n. revisión
re-vive v. revivir
re-voke v. revocar
rev-o-lu-tion n. revolución
rev-o-lu-tion-ary n., adj. revolucionario
re-volve v. revolverse
re-volv-er n. revolver
re-ward n. recompensa
rhap-so-dy n. rapsodia
rhe-tor-i-cal adj. retorico
rheu-mat-ic adj. reumatico
rheu-ma-tism n. reumatismo
rhyme v. rimar, n. rima
rhythm n. ritmo
rib n. costilla
rib-bon n. cinta
rice n. arroz
rich adj. fertil; rico
rid v. librar(se)
rid-dle n. acertijo
ride v. montar
rid-i-cule v. ridiculizar
ri-dic-u-lous adj. ridiculo
ri-fle n. rifle
right adj. exacto; derecho
rig-id adj. rigido
rig-or-ous adj. riguroso
rind n. piel
ring v. sonar, n. anillo
rink n. pista
rip v. arrancar; rasgar
ripe adj. maduro

rise v. subir; levantarse
risk n. riesgo
rite n. rito
rit-u-al n., adj. ritual
ri-val-ry n. rivalidad
riv-er n. rio
roach n. cucaracha
road n. camino
roar v. rugir
rob v. robar
robe n. bata
ro-bust adj. robusto
rock n. roca
ro-dent n. roedor
roll n. rollo; lista
ro-mance n. amorio
ro-man-tic adj. romántico
ro-man-ti-cism n. romanticismo
roof n. tejado
room n. sitio; cuarto
roost-er n. gallo
root n. raiz
rope n. cuerda
rose n. rosa
ros-y adj. rosado
ro-tate v. girar
rough adj. tosco; aspero
rou-lette n. ruleta
round prep. alrededor de, adj. redondo
route n. ruta
rou-tine n. rutina
roy-al-ty n. realeza
rub v. rozar; fregar
rub-bish n. basura
ru-by n. rubi
rud-der n. timón
rude adj. tosco; rudo
ru-di-ment n. rudimento
rug n. alfombra
ru-in v. arruinar, n. ruina
rule v. gobernar, n. regla
rul-er n. regla
rum n. ron
ru-mor n. rumor
run v. correr
run-ning adj. corriente
ru-ral adj. rural
rust n. orin
rus-tic adj. rustico
ruth-less adj. despiadado
rye n. centeno

Sab-bath n. domingo
sa-ber n. sable
sa-ble n. cabellína
sab-o-tage v. sabotear, n. sabotaje
sac-cha-rin n. sacrina
sack n. saco
sac-ra-ment n. sacramento
sacred adj. sagrado
sac-ri-fice v. sacrificar, n. sacrificio
sac-ri-lege n. sacrilegio
sad adj. triste
sad-den v. entristecer
sad-dle v. ensillar
sad-ism n. sadismo
sa-fa-ri n. safari
safe adj. seguro
safe-ty n. seguridad
sag v. combar(se)
sa-ga n. saga
sage n., adj. sabio
sail v. nevegar, n. vela
sail-or n. marinero
saint n., adj. santo
sake n. consideración; motivo
sal-ad n. ensalada
sal-a-man-der n. salamandra
sal-a-ry n. salario
sale n. venta
sa-line n. salino
sa-li-va n. saliva
sal-low n. cetrino
sal-ly n. salida
salm-on n. salmón
sa-lon n. salón
sa-loon n. salón
salt n. sal
sal-u-tar-y adj. saludable ·
sal-u-ta-tion n. saludo
sa-lute v. sakudar
sal-vage n. salvamento
sal-va-tion n. salvación
salve n. unguento
sal-vo n. salva
same adj. mismo
sam-ple v. probar
san-a-to-ri-um n. sanatorio
sanc-ti-fy v. santificar
sanc-tion n. sanción
sanc-ti-ty n. santidad

sanc-tu-ar-y n. santuario
sand n. arena
san-dal n. sandalia
sand-stone n. arenisca
sand-wich n. bocadillo
sand-y adj. arenoso
sane adj. sano
san-gui-nar-y a. sanguinario
san-i-tar-i-um n. sanatorio
san-i-tar-y adj. sanitario
san-i-ta-tion n. instalación sanitaria
san-i-ty n. juicio sano
sap n. savia
sa-pi-ent a. sabio
sap-phire n. zafiro
sar-casm n. sarcasmo
sar-cas-tic adj. sarcastico
sar-coph-a-gus n. sarcofago
sar-dine n. sardina
sa-ri, sa-ree n. sari
sash n. faja
sas-sy adj. descarado
sa-tan n. Satanas
sa-tan-ic a. satanico
sate v. saciar; dsatisfacer
sat-el-lite n. satelite
sa-ti-ate v. saciar
sat-in n. raso
sa-tire n. satira
sat-is-fac-tion n. satisfacción
sat-is-fy v. satisfacer
sat-u-rate v. saturar
Sat-ur-day n. sabado
sa-tyr n. satiro
sauce n. salsa
sau-cer n. platillo
sau-sage n. salchicha
sav-age n., adj. salvaje
save v. ahorrar; salvar
sav-ing n. economia
sav-ior n. salvador
sa-vor n. sabor
saw n. sierra
sax-o-phone n. saxofón
say v. decir
say-ing n. dicho
scab n. costra
scaf-fold n. andamio
scald v. escaldar
scale n. escala
scal-lop n. venera; feston
scalp n. pericraneo

scal-pel n. escalpelo
scan v. escundrinar
scan-dal n. escandalo
scan-dal-ize v. escandalizar
scant adj. escaso
scant-y adj. escaso
scape-goat n. cabeza de turco
scar n. cicatriz
scarce adj. escaso
scare v. asustar
scare-crow n. espantajo; espantapajaros
scarf n. bufanda
scar-let n. escarlata
scat-ter v. esparcir
scav-en-ger n. basurero
scene n. vista; escena
scen-er-y n. paisaje
scent n. pista; olor
sched-ule n. horario
scheme v. intrigar
schism n. cisma
schiz-o-phre-ni-a n. esquizofrenia
schol-ar n. erudito; alumno
schol-ar-ship n. erudición; beca
scho-las-tic adj. escolar
school n. escuela
sci-ence n. ciencia
sci-en-tist n. cientifico
scim-i-tar n. cimitarra
scis-sors n. tijeras
scoff v. mofarse
scold v. reganar
scoop n. paleta
scoot-er n. patinete
scope n. alcance
scorch v. chamuscar
score n. cuenta
scorn n. desden
scor-pi-on n. escorpión
scotch v. frustrar
scoun-drel n. canalla
scour v. fregar; recorrer
scout n. explorador
scowl v. poner mal gesto
scrag-gy a. escamado
scram-ble v. revolver
scrap n. fragmento; sobras
scrape v. raer
scratch v. rayar; rasgunar; rascar

scrawl n. garrabatos; garrapatos
scream n. grito
screen n. biombo; pantalla
screw v. atornillar, n. tornillo
scrib-ble v. garrapatear
scrim-mage n. arrebatina
script n. letra cursiva; guion
scrip-ture n. Sagrada Escritura
scroll n. rollo de pergamino
scrub v. fregar
scru-ple n. escrupulo
scru-ti-nize v. escundrinar
scru-ti-ny n. escrutinio
scuf-fle v. pelear
sculp-tor n. escultor
sculp-ture v. esculpir, n. escultura
scum n. espuma
scur-ry v. darse prisa
scur-vy n. escorbuto
scut-tle v. echar a pique
scythe n. guadana
sea n. mar
seal n. foca
seal n. sello v. cerrar
seam n. costura
sea-man n. marinero
seam-stress n. costurera
seam-y a. asqueroso
se-ance n. sesión de espiritistas
sea-port n. puerto de mar
sear v. marchitar; chamuscar
search v. buscar
sea-shore n. orilla del mar
sea-sick-ness n. mareo
sea-son n. estación
sea-son-ing n. condimento
seat v. sentar, n. asiento
sea-weed n. alga marina
se-clude v. aislar
se-clu-sion n. retiro
sec-ond n., adj. segundo
sec-ond-ar-y adj. secundario
sec-ond-hand a. de segunda mano
sec-ond-rate a. inferior
se-cre-cy n. secreto
se-cret n., adj. secreto
sec-re-tar-y n. secretario

se-crete v. secretar; ovultar

se-cre-tion n. secreción

sect n. secta

sec-tion n. sección

sec-tor n. sector

sec-u-lar adj. secular

se-cure adj. seguro

se-cu-ri-ty n. seguridad

se-date adj. sosegado

sed-a-tive n. sedativo

sed-en-tar-y a. sedentario

sed-i-ment n. sedimento

se-di-tion n. sedición

se-duce v. seducir

se-duc-tion n. seducción

see v. percibir; ver

seed n. semilla; simiente

seed-y a. desharrapado

seek v. buscar; solicitar

seem v. parecer

seem-ly a. decoroso; correcto

seep v. rezumarse

se-er n. profeta

seg-ment n. segmento

seg-re-gate v. segregar

seg-re-ga-tion n. segregación

seis-mo-graph n. sismografo

seize v. apoderarse de; asir

sei-zure n. asimiento

sel-dom adv. rarmente

se-lect adj. selecto, v. elegir

se-lec-tion n. selección

self n. See my-self, yourself

self-cen-tered a. egocentrico

self-com-mand n. dominio de si mismo

self-con-fi-dence n. confianza en si mismo

self con-scious a. timido

self-control n. dominio de si mismo

self-ev-i-dent a. patente

self-ex-plan-a-to-ry a. evidente; obvio

self-gov-ern-ment n. autonomia

self-im-por-tance n. presunción

self-ish a. egoista; interesado

self-less a. desinteresado

self-re-li-ance n. confianza en si mismo

self-same a. mismo

self-suf-fi-cient adj. independiente

self-will n. terquedad

sell v. vender

se-man-tics n. semantica

sem-blance n. parecido; apariencia

se-men n. semen

se-mes-ter n. semestre

sem-i-cir-cle n. semicirculo

sem-i-co-lon n. punto y coma

sem-i-fi-nal adj. semifinal

sem-i-nar n. seminario

sem-i-nar-y n. seminario

sem-i-of-fi-cial adj. semioficial

sem-i-pre-cious adj. semiprecioso

sem-i-week-ly a. bisemanal

sen-ate n. senado

sen-a-tor n. senador

send v. mandar; enviar

se-nile adj. senil

sen-ior adj. superior

sen-ior-i-ty n. antiguedad

sen-sa-tion n. sensación

sense v. percibir, n. sentido

sense-less a. sin sentido; insensato

sen-si-bil-i-ty n. sensibilidad

sen-si-ble adj. razonable

sen-si-tive adj. delicado

sen-si-tiv-i-ty n. delicadeza

sen-so-ry adj. sensorio

sen-su-al adj. sensual

sen-su-ous adj. sensorio

sen-tence n. frase

sen-ti-ment n. sentimiento

sen-ti-nel n. centinela

sen-try n. centinela

se-pal n. sepalo

sep-a-rate v. separar(se)

sep-a-ra-tion n. separación

Sep-tem-ber n. septiembre

sep-tic adj. septico

sep-ul-cher n. sepulcro

se-quel n. resultado

se-quence n. sucesión
sequestered a. aislado
se-ques-ter v. separar; aislar
se-quin n. lentejuela
ser-aph n. serafín
ser-e-nade n. serenata
se-rene n. sereno
se-ren-i-ty n. serenidad
serf n. siervo
ser-geant n. sargento
se-ri-al a. en serie
se-ries n. serie
se-ri-ous adj. serio
ser-mon n. sermon
ser-pent n. serpiente
se-rum n. suero
serv-ant n. serviente; servidor
serve v. servir
serv-ice n. servicio
serv-ice-man n. militar
ser-vile a. servil
ses-sion n. sesion
set v. fijar; poner(se)
set-back n. revés
set-ting n. engaste
set-tle v. arreglar; resolver
set-tle-ment n. colonización
set-tler n. colono
seven adj., n. siete
sev-en-teen adj. diecisiete
sev-enth n., adj. séptimo
sev-en-ty n., adj. setenta
sev-er v. cortar
sev-er-al a. varios; diversos
se-vere adj. severo
se-ver-i-ty n. severidad
sew v. coser
sew-er n. albañal
sex n. sexo
sex-tet n. sexteto
sex-u-al adj. sexual
sex-y a. provocativo
shab-by a. raído; en mal estado
shack n. choza
shack-le n. grillete
shade v. sombrear, n. sombra
shad-ing n. degradación
shad-ow n. sombra
shadowy a. umbroso; vago
shad-y adj. sombreado

shaft n. eje; pozo
shag-gy adj. velludo
shake v. estrechar; temblar
shak-y a. poso profundo
sham v. fingir(se), adj. fingido
sham-bles n. desorden
shame n. verguenza
shame-less al desvergonzado
sham-poo n. champú
shan-ty n. choza
shape v. formar, n. forma
shape-ly a. bien formado
share n. parte
shark n. tiburón
sharp adj. vivo; cortante
sharp-en v. afilar; sacar punta
shat-ter v. hacer(se) pedazos
shave v. afeitar(se)
shav-er n. maquina de afeitar
shawl n. chal
she pron. ella
shears n. tijeras grandes
shed v. quitarse; verter
sheen n. lustre
sheep n. oveja
sheep-ish a. timido
sheer adj. escarpado
sheet n. sábana; hoja; lamina
sheik, sheikh n. jeque
shelf n. estante
shell n. cascara
shel-lac, shel-lack n. goma laca
shell-fish n. marisco
shel-ter n. refugio
shep-herd n. pastor
sher-bet n. sorbete
sher-iff n. sheriff
sher-ry n. jerez
shield n. escudo
shift v. mover(se); cambiar
shil-ly-shal-ly v. vacilar
shim-mer v. rielar
shin n. espinilla
shine v. pulir; brillar
shin-gle n. ripia; tejamanil
shin-y adj. brillante

ship *n.* barco
ship-ment *n.* embarque; envio
ship-shape *a.* en buen orden
ship-wreck *n.* naufragio
shirk *v.* evitar; esquivar
shirt *n.* camisa
shiv-er *v.* temblar
shock *n.* susto; choque; postracion nerviosa
shod-dy *a.* de pacotilla; falso
shoe *n.* zapato
shoe-horn *n.* calzador
shoe-lace *n.* cordon
shoot *v.* espigar; disparar
shoot-ing *n.* tiro; caza con escopeta
shoot-ing star *n.* estrella fugaz
shop *n.* taller; tienda
shop-keep-er *n.* tendero
shore *n.* playa
short *adj.* breve; corto
short-age *n.* deficienca; escasez
short cir-cuit *n.* corto circuito
short-com-ing *n.* defecto
short-cut *n.* atajo
short-en *v.* acortar(se)
short-hand *n.* taquigrafia
short-lived *a.* de breve duración
short-tem-pered *a.* de mal genio
shot *n.* tiro; tirador
shot-gun *n.* escopeta
should *aux. v. past form of* **shall**
shoul-der *n.* hombro
shout *v.* gritar, *n.* grito
shov-el *n.* pala
show *v.* mostrar(se)
show-er *v.* ducharse, *n.* ducha
show-man *n.* director de espectaculos
shred *v.* hacer tiras
shrew *n.* arpia
shrewd *a.* sagaz; prudente
shriek *n.* chillar
shril *a.* estridente

shrimp *n.* camarón
shrine *n.* relicario
shrink *v.* encoger(se)
shriv-el *v.* encoger(se); secar(se)
shroud *n.* mortaja
shrub *n.* arbusto
shrub-ber-y *n.* arbustos
shrug *v.* encogerse de hombros
shud-der *v.* extremecerse
shuf-fle *v.* arrastrar los pies; *(cards)* barajar
shun *v.* evitar; apartarse de
shut *v.* cerrar(se)
shut-ter *n.* contraventana
shut-tle *n.* lanzadera
shy *adj.* timido
sic *v.* atacar
sick *adj.* enfermo
sick-en *v.* enfermar(se)
sick-le *n.* hoz
sick-ness *n.* enfermedad
side *n.* partido; lado
side-burns *n.* patillas
side-long *a.* lateral
side-track *v.* desviar
side-walk *n.* acera
side-ways *adv.* oblicuamente
siege *n.* sitio; cerco
sieve *n.* coladera; tamiz
sift *v.* tamizar
sigh *n.* suspiro, *v.* suspirar
sight *n.* visión; vista
sight-less *adj.* ciego
sight-see-ing *n.* visita de puntos de interes
sign *n.* signo; senal
sig-nal *n.* senal
sig-na-ture *n.* firma
sig-nif-i-cance *n.* significación
sig-ni-fy *v.* significar
si-lence *n.* silencio
si-lent *adj.* silencioso
sil-hou-ette *n.* silueta
sil-ic-a *n.* silice
sil-i-con *n.* silicio
silk *n.* seda
silk-y *adj.* sedoso
sil-ly *adj.* bobo
si-lo *n.* silo

silt *n.* sedimento

sil-ver *n.* plata

sil-ver-smith *n.* platero

sil-ver-ware *n.* vajilla de plata

sim-i-an *a.* simico

sim-i-lar *adj.* similar

sim-i-lar-i-ty *n.* semejanza

sim-mer *v.* hervir a fuego lento

sim-per *v.* sonreirse afectadamente

sim-ple *adj.* simple; facil

sim-pli-fy *v.* simplificar

sim-ply *adv.* sencillamente

sim-u-late *v.* simular

si-mul-ta-ne-ous *a.* simultaneo

sin *n.* pecado; transgresion

since *conj.* puesto que, *prep.* despues; desde

sin-cere *adj.* sincero

sin-cer-i-ty *n.* sinceridad

si-ne-cure *n.* sinecura

sin-ew *n.* tendón

sing *v.* cantar

sing-er *n.* cantante

sin-gle *adj.* único; soltero

sin-gle-hand-ed *a.* sin ayuda

sin-gu-lar *adj.* singular

sin-is-ter *adj.* siniestro

sink *v.* hundir(se)

sin-ner *n.* pecador

si-nus *n.* seno

sip *n.* sorbo, *v.* sorber

sir *n.* señor

sire *n.* padre

si-ren *n.* sirena

sir-loin *n.* solomillo

sis-ter *n.* hermana

sis-ter-in-law *n.* cuñada

sit *v.* sentar(se)

site *n.* sitio

sit-u-a-tion *n.* situacion

six *adj., n.* seis

six-teen *adj., n.* dieciséis

sixth *n., adj.* sexto

six-ty *adj., n.* sesenta

size *n.* talla

siz-zle *v.* chisporrotear

skate *v.* patinar

skel-e-ton *n.* esqueleto

skep-tic *n.* esceptico

skep-ti-cal *adj.* esceptico

sketch *n.* esbozo; bosquejo

skew-er *n.* broqueta

ski *v.* esquiar

skid *n.* patinazo

skill *n.* destreza; habilidad

skil-let *n.* sarten

skim *v.* expumar; desnatar; hojear

skin *n.* piel

skin-ny *adj.* flaco

skip *v.* saltar; pasar por alto

skir-mish *n.* escaramuza

skirt *n.* falda

skit *n.* parodia

skull *n.* cráneo

skunk *n.* mofeta

sky *n.* cielo

sky-rock-et *n.* cohete

sky-scrap-er *n.* rascacielos

slab *n.* table; plancha

slack *a.* flojo; negligente

slack-en *v.* aflojar

slacks *n.* pantalones

slag *n.* excoria

slam *v.* cerrarse de golpe

slan-der *v.* calumniar, *n.* calumnia

slang *n.* argot

slant *v.* inclinar(se); sesgar(se)

slap *v.* pegar

slash *v.* acuchillar

slat *n.* tabilla

slate *n.* pizarra; lista de candidatos

slaugh-ter *v.* matar

slave *n.* esclavo

slav-er-y *n.* esclavitud

slay *v.* matar

sled *n.* trineo

sleek *a.* liso; pulcro

sleep *v.* dormir

sleep-y *a.* sonoliento

sleet *n.* aguanieve

sleeve *n.* manga

sleigh *n.* trineo

slen-der *adj.* delgado

sleuth *n. inf.* detective

slice *v.* tajar, *n.* tajada

slide *v.* deslizarse

slight *a.* pequeño; de poco importancia

slim *adj.* delgado
slime *n.* legamo
sling *v.* tirar; suspender
slip *v.* introducir; deslizar(se); resbalar; escaparse
slip-knot *n.* nudo corredizo
slip-per *n.* zapatilla
slip-per-y *adj.* resbaladizo
slip-up *n. inf.* equivocación
slit *v.* cortar
sliv-er *n.* astilla
slob-ber *v.* babear; babosear
slo-gan *n.* mote
slop *v.* verter
slope *v.* inclinar(se), *n.* inclinación
slot *n.* ranura
slov-en-ly *a.* descuidado; desadeado
slow *adj.* torpe; lento
slow-ly *adv.* despacio
slung *n.* posta
slug-gish *a.* perezoso; lento
slum *n.* barrio bajo
slump *v.* hundires
slur *v.* comerse palabras; calumniar
slut *n.* pazpuerca; perra
sly *a.* astuto; disimulado
smack *v.* pegar
small *adj.* pequeño
small-pox *n.* viruelas
smart *adj.* listo; fresco
smash *v.* romper(se)
smear *v.* manchar; untar
smell *v.* oler
smile *n.* sonrisa, *v.* sonreir(se)
smirk *n.* sonrisa afectada
smith *n.* herrero
smock *n.* blusa de labrador
smog *n.* niebla y humo mezclados
smoke *v.* fumar, *n.* humo
smol-der *v.* arder sin llamas
smooch *v. inf.* besar
smooth *adj.* suave
smooth-er *v.* ahogar(se); sofocar(se)
smudge *n.* mancha
smug *a.* papado de si mismo

smug-gle *v.* pasar de (o hacer) contrabando
snack *n.* merienda
snag *n.* obstaculo; rasgon
snail *n.* caracol
snake *n.* culebra
snap-shot *n.* foto
snare *n.* trampa
snatch *n.* fragmento; trocito
sneak *v.* moverse a hurtadillas
sneer *v.* mofarse
sneeze *n.* estornudo, *v.* estornudar
sniff *v.* husmear; oler
snip *v.* tijeretear
snob *n.* esnob
snooze *v. inf.* dormitar
snore *n.* ronquido, *v.* roncar
snow *v.* nevar, *n.* nieve
snow-ball *n.* bola de nieve
snow-flake *n.* copo de nieve
snow-man *n.* figura de nieve
snub *v.* desairar
snug-gle *v.* arrimarse
so *conj.* por tanto, *adv.* asi; tan
soak *v.* remojar
soap *n.* jabón
soar *v.* remontarse
sob *v.* sollozar
so-ber *adj.* sobrio
so-bri-quet, sou-bri-quet *n.* apodo
so-called *a.* llamado; supuesto
soc-cer *n.* fútbol
so-cia-ble *adj.* sociable
so-cial *adj.* social
so-cial-ism *n.* socialismo
so-cial-ize *v.* socializar
so-ci-e-ty *n.* sociedad
so-di-um *n.* sodio
so-fa *n.* sofa
soil *v.* manchar, *n.* tierra
so-lar *adj.* solar
sol-dier *n.* soldado
sole-ly *adv.* solamente
sol-emn *adj.* solemne
so-lic-it *v.* solicitar
sol-id *n., adj.* solido
sol-i-dar-i-ty *n.* solidaridad
sol-i-tar-y *adj.* solitario

sol-u-ble adj. soluble
so-lu-tion n. solución
solve v. resolver
sol-vent adj. solvente
som-ber adj. sombrío
some pron. algunos, adj. alguno
some-bo-dy pron. alguien
some-day adv. algún día
some-one pron. alguién
some-thing n. algo
some-times adv. a veces
son n. hijo
song n. canción
son-in-law n. yerno
soon adv. pronto
soothe v. calmar
so-pran-o n. soprano
sor-did adj. vil
sor-ry adj. triste
so-so adv. así así
soul n. alma
sound n. ruido
soup n. sopa
sour adj. agrio
south n. sur
south-east n. sudeste
south-ern adj. del sur
south-west n. sudoeste
sov-er-eign n., adj. soberano
space v. espaciar, n. espacio
spa-cious adj. espacioso
spa-ghet-ti n. espagueti
spasm n. espasmo
spas-mod-ic adj. espasmodico
spas-tic adj. espastico
spat-u-la n. espatula
speak v. decir; hablar
spear n. lanza
spe-cial adj. especial
spe-cial-ist n. especialista
spe-cial-ize v. especializar(se)
spe-cial-ty n. especialidad
spe-cies n. especie
spe-cif-ic adj. especifico
spec-i-fy v. especificar
spec-ta-cle n. espectaculo
spec-tac-u-lar adj. espectacular
speech-less adj. mudo

speed v. apresurarse; acelerar
spell v. deletrear
spell-bind v. encantar
spell-ing n. ortografía
spend v. gastar
sperm n. esperma
sperm-whale n. cachalote
sphere n. esfera
spher-i-cal adj. esferico
spice n. especia
spic-y adj. picante
spi-der n. arana
spill v. verter(se)
spin-ach n. espinaca
spi-nal adj. espinal
spine n. espinazo
spi-ral adj., n. espiral
spir-it n. espiritu
spir-it-u-al adj. espiritual
spir-it-u-al-ism n. espiritismo
spit v. escupir
spite n. rencor
splin-ter n. astilla
split v. dividir; separarse
spoil v. echar(se); estropear(se)
spo-ken adj. hablado
sponge n. esponja
spon-gy adj. esponjoso
spon-ta-ne-i-ty n. espontaneidad
spon-ta-ne-ous adj. espontaneo
spoon n. cuchara
spoon-ful n. cucharada
spo-rad-ic adj. esporadico
spore n. espora
sport n. deporte
sports-man n. deportista
spot n. mancha
spot-ty adj. manchado
spouse n. esposa; esposo
spread v. diseminar
spring n. primavera, v. saltar
spring-time n. primavera
spruce n. picea
spu-ri-ous adj. espurio
spy v. espiar
squad-ron n. escuadron
squal-id adj. desalinado
square adj., n. cuadrado

squeak n. chirrido, v. chillar
sta-bil-i-ty n. estabilidad
sta-ble adj. estable
sta-di-um n. estadio
stage n. etapa
stain n. mancha
stair n. escalón
stair-way n. escalera
stamp n. sello
stam-pede n. estampida
stand v. colocar
stand-ing adj. derecho
sta-ple n. grapa
sta-pler n. grabadora
star n. estrella
star-less adj. sin estrellas
star-ry adj. estrellado
start v. comenzar; empezar
state n. estado
stat-ic adj. estatico
sta-tion n. estación
sta-tis-tic n. estadistico
stat-ue n. estatua
stay v. quedar(se)
steal v. robar
steam v. empanar, n. vapor
steam-y adj. vaporoso
stem n. tallo
step n. escalera
step-broth-er n. hermanastro
step-daugh-ter n. hijastra
step-fa-ther n. padrastro
step-moth-er n. madrastra
step-sis-ter n. hermanastra
step-son n. hijastro
ste-ril-i-ty n. esterilidad
stick n. palo
stick-y adj. viscoso
stiff adj. rigido
still adj. tranquilo
stim-u-lant n. estimulante
stim-u-late v. estimular
stink v. hedor
stip-u-late v. estipular
stip-u-la-tion n. estipulación
stock-ing n. media
sto-i-cal adj. estoico
stom-ach n. estomago
stone n. piedra
stop v. terminar
stop-light n. semaforo
store n. almacen; tienda

stork n. cigüeña
storm n. tempestad
sto-ry n. piso; historia
stove n. estufa
straight adj. directo
strange adj. extraño; raro
stra-te-gic adj. estrategico
strat-e-gy n. estrategia
straw n. pajilla
straw-ber-ry n. fresa
stream n. arroyo
street n. calle
strength n. vigor; fuerza
strict adj. estricto
strike v. atacar; golpear
string n. cordel
stripe n. raya
striped adj. rayado
strong adj. robusto; fuerte
struc-tur-al adj. estructural
stu-dent n. estudiante
stu-di-o n. estudio
stud-y v. estudiar
stu-pen-dous adj. estupendo
stu-pid adj. estupido
style n. modo; estilo
sub-di-vide v. subdividir
sub-ject adj., n. sujeto
sub-jec-tive adj. subjetivo
sub-lease v. subarrendar
sub-let v. subarrendar
sub-li-mate v. sublimar
sub-li-ma-tion n. sublimación
sub-lime a. sublime
sub-lim-i-ty n. sublimidad
sub-ma-rine n. submarino
sub-merge v. sumergir(se)
sub-mer-gence n. sumersión
sub-merse v. sumergir(se)
sub-mer-sion n. sumersión
sub-mis-sion n. sumisión
sub-mis-sive a. sumiso
sub-mit v. someter(se); presentar
sub-nor-mal adj. anormal
sub-or-di-nate a. subordinado; secundario; dependiente
sub-or-di-na-tion n. subordinacion

sub-poe-na, sub-pe-na *n.* citación; comparendo

sub-scribe *v.* subscribir(se)

sub-scrip-tion *n.* subscripción

sub-se-quent *a.* subsiguiente

sub-ser-vi-ent *a.* servil

sub-side *v.* bajar; calmarse

sub-sid-i-ar-y *a.* ubsidiario

sub-si-dize *v.* subvencional

sub-si-dy *n.* subvención; subsidio

sub-sist *v.* subsistir; existir

sub-sis-tence *n.* subsistencia

sub-stance *n.* esencia; substancia

sub-stan-tial *adj.* substancial

sub-stan-ti-a-tion *n.* comprobación; justificación

sub-stan-tive *n.* substantivo

sub-sti-tute *n.* substituto, *v.* substituir

sub-sti-tu-tion *n.* substitución; reemplazo

sub-ter-fuge *n.* subterfugio

sub-ter-ra-ne-an *a.* subterraneo

sub-ti-tle *n.* subtitulo

sub-tle *a.* sutil; ingenioso; delicado; astuto

sub-tle-ty *n.* sutileza

sub-tract *v.* substraer

sub-trac-tion *n.* substracción; resta

sub-urb *n.* suburbio

sub-ur-ban *a.* suburbano

sub-ver-sion *n.* subversión

sub-ver-sive *a.* sobversivo

sub-vert *v.* subvertir

sub-way *n.* metro

suc-ceed *v.* suceder

suc-cess *n.* exito

suc-cess-ful *a.* prospero; afortunado

suc-ces-sion *n.* sucesión

suc-ces-sor *n.* sucesor

suc-cinct *a.* sucinto

suc-cor *n.* soccorro; auxilio

suc-cu-lent *a.* suculento

suc-cumb *v.* sucumbir

such *adv.* tan, *pron., adj.* tal

suck *v.* chupar; mamar

suck-er *n.* piruli

suck-le *v.* lactar; amamantar

suc-tion *n.* succión

suf-fer *v.* sufrir

suf-fer-ance *n.* tolerancia

suf-fice *v.* bastar

suf-fi-cien-cy *n.* suficiencia

suf-fix *n.* sufijo

suf-fo-cate *v.* sofocar; asfixiar

suf-frage *n.* sufragio

suf-fuse *v.* extender; banar

suf-fu-sion *n.* difusión

sug-ar *n.* azucar

sug-ar-y *adj.* azucarado

sug-gest *v.* sugerir

sug-ges-tion *n.* sugestión

sug-ges-tive *a.* sugestivo

su-i-cide *n.* suicida

suit *n.* traje

suit-a-ble *a.* apropiado

suit-case *n.* maleta

suite *n.* juego; serie

sul-fur, sul-phur *n.* azufre

sul-fu-ric ac-id *n.* acido sulfurico

sulk *v.* estar de mal humor

sul-len *a.* hosco

sul-ly *v.* manchar

sul-tan *n.* sultan

sul-tan-ate *n.* sultanato

sul-try *a.* bochornoso

sum *v.* sumar, *n.* suma

sum-ma-ry *n.* sumario

sum-mer *n.* verano

sun *n.* sol

Sun-day *n.* domingo

sun-down *n.* puesta del sol

sun-flow-er *n.* girasol

sun-glass-es *n.* gafas de sol

sun-light *n.* luz del sol

sun-rise *n.* salida del sol

su-per-fi-cial *adj.* superficial

su-per-in-tend *v.* superentender

su-pe-ri-or *n., adj.* superior

su-pe-ri-or-i-ty *n.* superioridad

su-per-mar-ket *n.* supermercado

su-per-sti-tion *n.* superstición

su-per-sti-tious adj. supersticioso
su-pine adj. supino
sup-per n. cena
sup-ple-ment n. suplemento
sup-pli-cate v. suplicar
sup-pose v. suponer
sup-pres-sion n. supresión
su-prem-a-cy n. supremacia
su-preme adj. supremo
sure adj. seguro
sure-ly adv. seguramente
sur-face n. superficie
sur-geon n. cirujano
sur-ger-y n. cirugía
sur-name n. apellido
sur-prise v. sorprender, n. sorpresa
sur-vive v. sobrevivir
sus-cep-ti-ble adj. susceptible
sus-pend v. suspender
sus-pense n. incertidumbre
sus-pen-sion adj. suspensión
sus-pi-cion n. sospecha; sombra
sus-pi-cious adj. sospechoso
sus-tain v. sustentar
sus-te-nance n. sustento
svelte a. esbelto
swab n. torunda
swan n. cisne
swap v. cambiar
swarm n. enjambre
swash-buck-ler n. espadachin
swat v. matar
sway v. bambolearse; inclinar
swear v. jurar
swear-word n. palabrota
sweat n. sudor, v. sudar
sweat-y adj. sudoroso
sweet adj. dulce
sweet-en v. azucarar; endulzar
sweet-heart n. querida; novia
sweet-meat n. dulce
swell v. hinchar(se)
swerve v. torcer(se); desviar(se)
swift a. veloz
swig v. beber a grandes tagos
swill n. bazofia
swim n. natación, v. nadar
swim-mer n. nadador
switch v. cambiar
swiv-el n. alacran, torniquete; girar
swoon n. desmayo
sword n. espada
sword-belt n. talabarte
sword-fish n. pez espads
sword-play n. esgrima
swordsman n. espadachin
syc-a-more n. sicomoro
syc-o-phant n. adulador
syl-lab-i-cate v. silabear
syl-lab-i-ca-tion n. silabeo
syl-lab-i-fy v. silabear
syl-la-ble n. silaba
syl-la-bus n. resumen; programa
syl-van a. silvestre
sym-bol n. simbolo
sym-bol-ic adj. simbolico
sym-bol-ism n. simbolismo
sym-bol-ize v. simbolizar
sym-me-try n. simetria
sym-pa-thet-ic a. compasivo; sompatico
sym-pa-thy n. simpatia
sym-pho-ny n. sinfonia
symp-ton n. sintoma
syn-a-gogue n. sinagoga
syn-chro-nize v. sincronizar(se)
syn-di-cate v. sindicar
syn-od n. sinodo
syn-o-nym n. sinonimo
syn-on-y-mous adj. sinonimo
syn-op-sis n. sinopsis
syn-the-sis n. sintresis
syn-thet-ic adj. sintetico
syph-i-lis n. sifilis
sy-ringe n. jeringa
sy-rup n. jarabe; almibar
sys-tem n. sistema
sys-tem-at-ic a. sistemático
sys-tem-a-tize v. sistematizar

tab 211 teamwork

tab *n.* cuenta
tab-er-nac-le *n.* tabernáculo
ta-ble *n.* mesa
ta-ble-spoon-ful *n.* cucharada
tab-let *n.* tableta
ta-boo, ta-bu *a.* tabú
tab-u-lar *adj.* tabular
tab-u-late *y.* tabular
tac-it *a.* tácito
tac-i-turn *adj.* taciturno
tack *n.* tachuela; virada
tack-le *n.* equipo; carga
tact *n.* tacto
tac-tics *n.* tactica
tad-pole *n.* renacuajo
taf-fe-ta *n.* tafetan
taf-fy *n.* caramelo
tag *n.* etiqueta; marbete
tail *n.* cola; rabo
tai-lor *n.* sastre
taint *v.* inficionar(se); corromper(se)
take *v.* coger; tomar; sacar
take-off *n.* despegue
tal-cum pow-der *n.* polvo de talco
tale *n.* cuenta
tal-ent *n.* talento
tal-ent-ed *adj.* talentoso
tal-is-man *n.* talismán
talk *v.* decir; hablar
talk-a-tive *adj.* hablador
tall *a.* alto
tal-low *n.* sebo
tal-ly *n.* cuenta
tal-on *n.* garra
tam-bou-rine *n.* pandereta
tame *a.* domesticado; manso; soso
tam-per *v.* estropear; falsificar
tan *v.* curtir; tostar
tan-dem *adv.* en tandem
tang *n.* sabor fuerte
tan-gent *n., adj.* alto
tan-ge-rine *n.* naranja mandarina o tangerina
tan-gi-ble *adj.* tangente
tan-gle *v.* enredar(se)
tan-go *n.* tango
tank *n.* tangible
tan-ta-lize *v.* atormentar

tan-ta-mount *a.* equivalente
tan-trum *n.* rabieta; berrinche
tap *n.* grifo; golpecito
tape *n.* tanque
ta-per *v.* afilar
tap-es-try *n.* tapiz
tape-worm *n.* cinta
tap-i-o-ca *n.* tenia
ta-pir *n.* tapir
tar *v.* alquitranar; embrear
ta-ran-tu-la *n.* tapioca
tar-dy *adj.* tarantula
tar-get *n.* blanco
tar-iff *n.* tardio
tar-nish *v.* deslustrar(se); empanar
tar-ry *v.* tardar; detenerse
tart *n.* tarifa
tar-tar *n.* tartaro
task *n.* tarea; labor
task-mas-ter *n.* capataz
tas-sel *n.* borla
taste *n.* sabor
tast-y *adj.* sabroso
tat-ter *n.* andrajo
tat-tered *a.* harapiento; andrajoso
tat-too *n.* tatuaje
taunt *n.* mofa; sarcasmo; escarnio
taut *a.* tieso; tirante
tav-ern *n.* taberna
taw-dry *a.* charro
taw-ny *a.* leonado
tax *n.* impuesto; contribución; carga
tax-i *n.* taxi
tax-i-cab *n.* taxi
tea *n.* té
tea-bag *n.* sobre de té; muñeca de te
teach *v.* instruir
teach-er *n.* maestro; profesora; profesor
tea-cup *n.* taza para te
tea-ket-tle *n.* tetera
team *n.* equipo
team-mate *n.* compañero de equipo
team-ster *n.* camionero; camionista
team-work *n.* cooperación

tea-pot n. tetera
tear n. lágrima
tear v. rasgar(se); romper(se)
tease v. tomar el pelo; atormentar
tea-spoon n. cucharilla
tea-spoon-ful n. cucharadita
tech-ni-cal adj. técnico
tech-ni-cian n. tecnico
tech-nol-o-gy n. tecnología
te-di-ous adj. tedioso
tel-e-gram n. telegrama
tel-e-graph n. telegrafo
te-leg-ra-phy n. telegrafía
tel-e-phone n. telefono
tel-e-scope n. telescopio
tel-e-vi-sion n. televisión
tell v. mandar; decir
tem-per-a-ment-al adj. temperamental
tem-per-a-ture n. fiebre
tem-pes-tu-ous adj. tempestuoso
tem-ple n. templo
tem-po n. tiempo
tem-po-ral adj. temporal
temp-ta-tion n. tentación
ten adj., n. diez
tend v. tender
ten-den-cy n. tendencia
ten-der-ly adv. tiernamente
ten-don n. tendón
ten-nis n. tenis
tense v. tensar, adj. tenso
ten-sion n. tensión
ter-mi-nal adj., n. terminal
ter-mi-nate v. terminar
ter-mi-nol-o-gy n. terminología
ter-rain n. terreno.
ter-res-tri-al adj. terrestre
ter-ri-ble adj. terrible
ter-rif-ic adj. terrifico
ter-ror n. terror
ter-ror-ism n. terrorismo
ter-ror-ist n. terrorista
test v. examinar, n. examen
tes-ti-fy v. testificar
text n. texto
tex-ture n. textura
than conj. de; que

thanks n. gracias
that adj. aquella; aquel; esa; ese
the def. art. la; le; las; los; lo
the-a-ter n. teatro
them pron. las; les; los; ellas; ellos
then adv. luego; entonces
the-ol-o-gy n. teología
the-o-rize v. teorizar
the-o-ry n. teoría
there adv. ahi; allí; allá
ther-mal adj. termal
ther-mom-e-ter n. termometro
the-sau-rus n. tesauro
these pron. estas; estos
they pron. ellas; ellos
thick adj. denso
thief n. ladrón
thigh n. muslo
thin adj. escaso; delgado
thing n. cosa
think v. creer; pensar
third adj. tercero
thirst n. sed
thir-teen n., adj. trece
thir-ty n., adj. treinta
this adj. esta; este, pron. esto; esta; este
thorn n. espina
thorn-y adj. espinoso
thor-ough adj. completo
though adv. sin embargo, conj. aunque
thought-ful adj. pensativo
thou-sand n., adj. mil
threat-en v. amenazar
three n., adj. tres
throat n. garganta
throne n. trono
through prep. por
throw v. lanzar; echar
thumb n. pulgar
Thurs-day n. jueves
tib-i-a n. tibia
tick-le v. cosquillear
tide n. marea
ti-ger n. tigre
till prep. hasta
tim-ber n. madero
time n. hora; tiempo; vez
tim-id adj. timido

tim-id-i-ty *n.* timidez
tip *n.* propina
tire *v.* cansar(se)
tired *adj.* cansado
tire-some *a.* molesto
tis-sue *n.* tisu
ti-tan-ic *adj.* titanico
tithe *n.* diezmo
ti-tle *v.* titular, *n.* titulo
tit-ter *v.* reir a medias
tit-u-lar *a.* titular
TNT, T.N.T. *n.* explosivo
to *adv., prep.* hacia, *prep.* hasta; a
toad *n.* sapo
toad-stool *n.* hongo; hongo venenoso
toast *v.* tostar; brindar
to-bac-co *n.* tabaco
to-bog-gan *n.* tobogan
to-day *n., adv.* hoy
toe *n.* dedo del pie
tof-fee, tof-fy *n.* caramelo
to-ga *n.* toga
to-geth-er *adv.* juntos
toil *v.* trabajar asiduamente; afanarse
toi-let *n.* retrete; water; tacado
toi-let-ry *n.* articulo de tocador
to-ken *n.* indicio; prenda; señal
tol-er-a-ble *a.* tolerable; regular
tol-er-ance *n.* tolerancia
tol-er-ant *a.* tolerante
tol-er-ate *v.* permitir; tolerar
toll *n.* peaje
to-ma-to *n.* tomate
tomb *n.* tumba
tomb-stone *n.* lapida sepulcral
to-mor-row *adv., n.* mañana
ton *n.* tonelada
tone *n.* tono; tendencia
tongs *n.* tenazas
tongue *n.* lengua
ton-ic *n.* tonico
to-night *adv.* esta noche
ton-nage *n.* tonelaje
ton-sil *n.* amigdala; tonsila
ton-sil-li-tis *n.* amigdalitis

too *adv.* ademas; tambien
tool *n.* herramienta
tooth *n.* diente
tooth-ache *n.* dolor de muelas
tooth-brush *n.* cepillo de dientes
top *n.* tapa
to-paz *n.* topacio
top-coat *n.* sobretodo
top-hat *n.* chistera
top-ic *n.* tema
top-i-cal *adj.* topico
to-pop-ra-phy *n.* topografia
top-ple *v.* venirse abajo
top-sy-tur-vy *adv.* patas arri ba
torch *n.* antorcha; hacha
tor-ment *v.* atormentar
tor-na-do *n.* tormento
tor-pe-do *n.* torpedo
tor-rent *n.* torrente
tor-rid *a.* torrido
tor-so *n.* torso
tor-toise *n.* tortuga
tor-tu-ous *a.* tortuoso
tor-ture *v.* torturar
toss *v.* echar
tot *n.* nene; nena
to-tal *n., adj.* total
to-tal-i-tar-i-an *a.* totalitario
to-tal-ly *adv.* totalmente
tote *v. inf.* llevar
to-tem *n.* totem
tot-ter *v.* bambolearse
touch *v.* tocar(se)
touch-y *a.* irritable
tough *adj.* dificil
tough-en *v.* endurecer(se); hacer(se)
tour *n.* viaje; excursion
tour-ism *n.* turismo
tour-ist *n.* turista
tour-na-ment *n.* torneo
tour-ni-quet *n.* torniquete
tou-sle *v.* despeinar
tow *v.* llevar a remolque
to-ward *prep.* cerca de
tow-el *n.* toalla
tow-er *n.* torre
town *n.* pueblo; ciudad
tox-ic *a.* toxico
tox-in *n.* toxina

toy n. juguete

trace n. indicio; huella; rastro

tra-che-a n. tráquea

track n. via; pista; senda

tract n. extensión; tratado

trac-tor n. tractor

trade v. comerciar

trade-mark n. marca de fabrica; marca registrado

trade un-ion n. sindicato

tra-di-tion n. tradición

tra-di-tion-al adj. tradicional

tra-duce v. calumniar

traf-fic n. tráfico

trag-e-dy n. tragedia

trag-ic adj. trágico

trail v. arrastrar(se); rastrear

trail-er n. remolque

train n. tren

trait n. caracteristica; rasgo

trai-tor n. traidor

tra-jec-to-ry n. trayectoria

tramp v. andar con pasos pesados

tram-ple v. pisotear

trance n. arrobamiento; estado hipnotico

tran-quil adj. tranquilo

tran-quil-li-ty n. tranquilidad

tran-quil-lize v. tranquilizar

tran-quil-iz-er n. tranquilizante

trans-act v. despachar

trans-ac-tion n. transacción

tran-scend v. sobresalir

tran-scribe v. transcribir

tran-script n. trasunto

tran-scrip-tion n. transcripción

trans-fer v. transferir; trasladar

trans-fer-ence n. transferencia

trans-form v. transformar

trans-for-ma-tion n. transcripción; copia

trans-form-er n. transformador

trans-fu-sion n. transfusión

trans-gress v. traspasar; pecar

trans-gres-sion n. transgresion

tran-sient a. transitorio; pasajero

tran-sis-tor n. transistor

trans-it n. transito

tran-si-tion n. transito

tran-si-tive a. transiotivo

tran-si-to-ry adj. transitorio

trans-late v. traducir

trans-la-tion n. traducción

trans-lu-cent a. translucido

trans-mis-sion n. transmision

trans-mit v. transmitir

trans-mit-ter n. transmisor

tran-som n. travesano

trans-par-ent a. transparente, claro; obvio

tran-spire v. transpirar; suceder

trans-plant v. trasplantar

trans-port n. transporte, v. transportar

trans-por-ta-tion n. transporte

trans-pose v. transponer

trans-verse a. transversal

trap v. entrampar

tra-peze n. trapecio

trap-e-zoid n. trap-e-zoid

trash n. basura

trau-ma n. trauma

trau-mat-ic adj. traumatico

trav-el v. viajar

trea-son n. traición

treas-ure n. tesoro

treas-ur-er n. tesorero

treas-ur-y n. tesoro

treat v. tratar

trea-tise n.n tratado

treat-ment n. tratamiento

trea-ty n. tratado; pacto

tre-ble a. triple

tree n. arbol

trek v. caminar

trel-lis n. enrejado; espaldera

trem-ble v. temblar

tre-men-dous a. tremendo

trem-or n. temblor

trench n. foso; trinchera

tri-al n. prueba

tri-an-gle n. triángulo

tri-an-gu-lar *adj.* triangular

tri-bu-nal *n.* tribunal

trib-ute *n.* tributo

trick *n.* trucio; trampa; engano

trick-le *v.* gotear

tri-cy-cle *n.* triciclo

tried *adj.* probado

tri-fle *n.* bagatela

tri-fling *a.* sin importancia

trig-ger *n.* gatillo

trig-o-nom-e-try *n.* trigonometria

tril-lion *n.* billon

trim *v.* guarnecer

trin-ket *n.* dije

tri-o *n.* trio

trip *n.* viaje

tri-ple *v.* triplicar(se)

trip-let *n.* trillizo

trip-li-cate *v.* triplicar

tri-pod *n.* tripode

trite *a.* gastado

tri-umph *n.* triunfo

tri-um-phant *adj.* triunfante

triv-i-al *a.* trivial; frivolo

triv-i-al-i-ty *n.* trivialidad

trol-ley *n.* tranvia

trom-bone *n.* trombon

troop *n.* tropa; escuadron

troop-er *n.* soldado de caballeria

tro-phy *n.* trofeo

trop-ic *n.* tropico

trop-i-cal *adj.* tropical

trot *v.* ir al trote; hacer trotar

trou-ba-dour *n.* trovador

trou-ble *v.* molestar(se)

trou-ble-some *a.* molesto

trough *n.* abrevadero

troupe *n.* compania

trou-sers *n.* pantalones

trous-seau *n.* ajuar

trout *n.* trucha

trow-el *n.* paleta; desplantador

tru-ant *n.* novillero

truce *n.* tregua

truck *n.* camion

true *adj.* verdadero

tru-ly *adv.* verdaderamente; realmente

trump *n.* triumfo

trum-pet *n.* trompeta

trun-cate *v.* truncar

trunk *n.* tronco; baul

trus *v.* empaquetear

trust *v.* esperar, *n.* fideicomiso

trus-tee *n.* fideicomisario

trust-wor-thy *a.* fidedigno; confiable

trust-y *adj.* seguro

truth *n.* verdad

trugh-ful *a.* veraz

try *v.* probar

try-ing *a.* dificil; penoso

tryst *n.* cita

T-shirt *n.* camiseta

tub *n.* baño; tina

tu-ba *n.* tuba

tube *n.* tubo

tu-ber-cu-lo-sis *n.* tuberculosis

tuck *v.* alforzar

Tues-day *n.* martes

tuft *n.* copete

tug *v.* tirar con fuerza; remolcar

tug-boat *n.* remolcador

tu-i-tion *n.* ensenanza

tu-lip *n.* tulipan

tum-ble *v.* caer(se)

tum-bler *n.* volteador; vaso

tu-mor *n.* tumor

tu-mult *n.* tumulto

tu-mul-tu-ous *a.* tumultuoso

tu-na *n.* atun

tun-dra *n.* tundra

tune *n.* aire; afinacion

tu-nic *n.* tunica

tun-nel *n.* tunel

tur-ban *n.* turbante

tur-bid *adj.* turbido

tur-bine *n.* turbina

tur-bu-lence *n.* turbulencia; confusion

tur-bu-lent *adj.* turbulento

tu-reen *n.* sopera

turf *n.* cesped

tur-key *n.* pavo

tur-moil *n.* tumulto

turn *v.* volver(se); girar

turn-coat *n.* traidor

tur-nip *n.* nabo

turn-out *n.* ocncurrencia;

producción

turn-pike *n.* autopista de peaje

turn-stile *n.* torniquete

tur-pen-tin *n.* trementina

tur-quoise *n.* turquesa

tur-ret *n.* turrecilla

tur-tle *n.* tortuga

tusk *n.* colmillo

tus-sle *n.* agarrada

tu-te-lage *n.* tutela

tu-tor *n.* tutor

tux-e-do *n.* smoking

TV *n.* televisión

twang *n.* tanido; timbre nasal

tweed *n.* mezcla de lana

tweez-ers *n.* bruselas

twelfth *adj.* duodecimo

twelve *adj., n.* doce

twen-ty *adj., n.* veinte

twice *adv.* dos veces

twig *n.* ramita

twi-light *n.* crepusculo

twill *n.* tela cruzada

twin *adj., n.* gemelo

twine *n.* guita; bramante

twinge *n.* dolor agudo

twin-kle *v.* centellear

twirl *v.* girar; piruetear

twist *v.* torcer(se)

twitch *v.* crisparse

twit-ter *v.* gorjear

two *adj., n.* dos

two-faced *a.* falso; hipoocrita

ty-coon *n.* magnate

type *n.* tipo

type-write *v.* escribir a maquina

type-writ-er *n.* maquina de escribir

ty-phoid *n.* fiebre tifoidea

ty-phoon *n.* tifón

ty-phus *n.* tifus

typ-i-cal *adj.* típico

typ-i-fy *v.* simbolizar

typ-ist *n.* mecanografo

ty-pog-ra-phy *n.* tipografía

ty-ran-ni-cal *a.* tiránico; despotico

tyr-an-nize *v.* tiranizar

tyr-an-ny *n.* tirania

u-biq-ui-tous *adj.* ubicuo

u-biq-ui-ty *n.* ubicuidad

ud-der *n.* ubre

ug-li-ness *n.* fealdad

ug-ly *adj.* feo

u-ku-le-le *n.* ukelele

ul-cer *n.* úlcera

ul-cer-ate *v.* ulcerar(se)

ul-cer-ous *adj.* ulceroso

ul-na *n.* cúbito

ul-te-ri-or *adj.* ulterior

ul-ti-mate *adj.* último

ul-ti-ma-tum *n.* ultimatum

ul-tra *adj.* excesivo

ul-tra-mod-ern *adj.* ultramoderno

ul-tra-son-ic *adj.* ultrasonico

ul-tra-sound *n.* ultrasonido

ul-tra-vi-o-let *adj.* ultravioleta

ul-u-late *v.* ulular

um-bil-i-cal *adj.* umbilical

um-bil-i-cus *n.* ombligo

um-brel-la *n.* paraguas

um-pire *n.* arbitro

ump-teen *a.* muchos

un-a-bashed *a.* desvergonzado; descarado

un-a-ble *adj.* incapaz

un-a-bridged *adj.* no abreviado

un-ac-cent-ed *adj.* sin acento

un-ac-cept-a-ble *adj.* inaceptable

un-ac-count-a-ble *adj.* inexplicable

un-ac-cus-tomed *adj.* no acostumbrado

un-ac-knowl-edged *adj.* no econocido

un-a-dorned *adj.* sin adorno

un-a-dul-ter-at-ed *adj.* no adulterado

un-af-fect-ed *adj.* sin afectación

un-a-fraid *adj.* sin temor

un-aid-ed *adj.* sin ayuda

un-am-big-u-ous *adj.* sin ambiguedad

u-nan-i-mous *adj.* unanime

un-an-swer-a-ble *adj.* incontestable

un-ap-proach-a-ble *adj.* inaccesible

un-armed *adj.* desarmado

un-as-sail-a-ble *adj.* inexpugnable

un-as-sist-ed *adj.* sin ayuda

un-as-sum-ing *a.* modesto; sencillo

un-at-tached *adj.* suelto

un-at-tend-ed *adj.* desatendido

un-at-trac-tive *adj.* inatractivo

un-au-thor-ized *adj.* sin autorización

un-a-void-a-ble *adj.* inevitable

un-a-ware *adj.* ignorante

un-a-wares *adv.* de improviso

un-bal-anced *adj.* desequilibrado

un-beat-a-ble *adj.* invencible

un-beat-en *adj.* invicto

un-be-com-ing *a.* que sienta mal

un-be-lief *n.* incredulidad

un-be-liev-a-ble *adj.* increíble

un-be-liev-er *n.* descreído

un-be-liev-ing *adj.* incrédulo

un-bend *v.* desencorvar; aflojar

un-bend-ing *adj.* inflexible

un-bi-ased *a.* imparcial

un-bind *v.* desatar

un-blem-ished *adj.* puro

un-born *a.* no nacido

un-bos-om *v.* revelar

un-bound-ed *adj.* ilimitado

un-bowed *adj.* recto

un-break-a-ble *adj.* irrompible

un-breath-a-ble *adj.* irrespirable

un-bri-dled *adj.* desenfrenado

un-bro-ken *adj.* inviolado; sin romper

un-buck-le *v.* deshebillar

un-bur-den *v.* descargar

un-bot-ton *v.* desabotonar(se)

un-caged *adj.* suelto

un-called-for *a.* inmerecido

un-can-ny *a.* extraño; misterioso

un-cap *v.* destapar

un-ceas-ing *adj.* incesante

un-cer-e-mo-ni-ous *a.* informal

un-cer-tain *adj.* indeciso

un-cer-tain-ty *n.* incertidumbre

un-change-a-ble *adj.* inalterable

un-changed *adj.* inalterado

un-chang-ing *adj.* invariable

un-chart-ed *adj.* desconocido

un-civ-il *adj.* incivil

un-civ-i-lized *adj.* incivilizado

un-clad *adj.* desnudo

un-clasp *v.* separar

un-cle *n.* tío

un-clean *adj.* sucio

un-clear *adj.* confuso

un-clog *v.* desatascar

un-com-fort-a-ble *adj.* incomodo

un-com-mon *adj.* raro

un-com-mu-ni-ca-tive *a.* poco comunicativo

un-com-pro-mis-ing *a.* inflexible

un-con-cern *n.* indiferencia

un-con-nect-ed *adj.* inconexo

un-con-scious *adj.* inconsciente

un-con-sid-ered *adj.* inconsiderado

un-con-trolled *adj.* desenfrenado

un-cooked *adj.* crudo

un-count-ed *adj.* innumerable

un-cross *v.* descruzar

un-de-cid-ed *adj.* indeciso

un-der-es-ti-mate *v.* subestimar

un-der-ground *adj.* subterráneo

un-der-line *v.* subrayar

un-der-neath *adv.* debajo, *prep.* bajo

un-der-wear *n.* ropa interior

un-do v. desatar
un-fin-ished adj. incompleto
unn-fold v. extender; abrir
u-ni-form n. uniforme
un-ion n. unión
u-ni-ted adj. unido
u-ni-ver-sal adj. universal
un-luck-y adj. desdichado
un-rest n. inquietud
un-sa-vor-y adj. desagradable
un-seem-ly adj. indecoroso
un-skilled adj. inexperto
un-so-phis-ti-cat-ed adj. candido
un-sta-ble adj. inestable
un-stead-y adj. inseguro
un-til prep. hasta
un-truth-ful adj. mentiroso
un-u-su-al adj. raro
un-wrap v. desenvolver
up prep. subiendo, adj. ascendente, adv. acabado; arriba
up-hill adj. ascendente
up-hol-ster-y n. tapiceria
up-on prep. sobre; encima de
up-per adj. alto
up-per-cut n. gancho
up-roar n. alboroto
up-set n. trastorno; v. volcar
up-stairs adj. arriba
u-ra-ni-um n. uranio
U-ra-nus n. Urano
ur-ban adj. urbano
urge n. impulso, v. incitar
ur-gent adj. urgente
u-rine n. orina
urn n. urna
us pron. nosotras; nosotros; nos
use n. uso, v. utilizar; usar
use-less adj. inútil
u-su-al adj. usual
u-ten-sil n. utensilio
utilitarian n. utilitario
u-til-i-ty n. utilidad
u-til-ize v.t. utilizar
ut-ter-ance n. expresion
u-ter-us n. útero
uxorious a. uxorio; gurromino

va-can-cy n. vacante
va-cant adj. vacío
va-ca-tion n. vacación
vac-ci-nate v. vacunar
vac-ci-na-tion n. vacunación
vac-cine n. vacuna
vac-il-late v. vacilar
vac-il-la-tion n. vacilacon; fluctuación
va-cu-i-ty n. vacuidad
vac-u-um n. vacío
va-gar-y n. capricho
va-grant n. vagabundo
vague adj. incierto; vago
vain adj. vano
vale n. valle
val-e-dic-to-ry n. discurso de despedida
val-en-tine n. novia o novio en el dia de San Valentine
val-id adj. valido
val-i-date v. validar
va-lid-i-ty n. validez
va-lise n. maleta
val-ley n. valle
val-or n. valor; valentia
val-u-a-ble a. valioso; costoso; precioso
val-u-a-tion n. valuación
val-ue v. valuar, n. valor
valve n. valvula
vam-pire n. vampiro
van n. vanguardia; camion de mudanzas
van-dal n. vandalo
van-dal-ism n. vandalismo
vane n. veleta
van-guard n. vanguardia
va-nil-la n. vainilla
van-ish v. desaparecer
van-i-ty n. vanidad
van-quish v. vencer; conquistar
van-tage n. ventaja; provecho
vap-id a. insipido
va-por n. vapor
va-por-ize v. vaporizar(se)
va-por-ous adj. vaporoso
var-i-a-bil-i-ty n. variabilidad
var-i-a-ble n., adj. variable
var-i-a-tion n. variación
var-i-cose a. varicoso

var-ied *adj.* variado
va-ri-e-ty *n.* variedad
var-i-ous *adj.* variado
var-nish *n.* barniz
var-si-ty *n.* equip principal de una universidad
var-y *v.* variar; desviarse; cambiar
vase *n.* jarrón
vast *adj.* vasto
veal *n.* ternera
veg-e-ta-ble *n.* legumbre
veg-e-tar-i-an *n.* vegetariano
veg-e-tate *v.* vegetar
veg-e-ta-tion *n.* vegetacion
ve-hi-cle *n.* vehículo
vein *n.* vena
ve-loc-i-ty *n.* velocidad
ve-nal-i-ty *n.* venalidad
vend *v.* vender
ven-er-a-ble *adj.* venerable
ven-er-a-tion *n.* veneración
ve-ni-al *adj.* venial
ven-om *n.* veneno
ven-om-ous *adj.* venenoso
ven-ti-late *v.* ventilar
ven-tral *adj.* ventral
ven-tri-cle *n.* ventrículo
ven-ture-some *adj.* aventurero
Ve-nus *n.* Venus
ve-ra-cious *adj.* veraz
verb *n.* verbo
ver-bal *adj.* verbal
ver-bose *adj.* verboso
ver-bos-i-ty *n.* verbosidad
ver-dict *n.* veredicto
ver-i-fy *v.* verificar
ver-mouth *n.* vermut
ver-nal *adj.* vernal
ver-sa-til-i-ty *n.* adaptabilidad
verse *n.* versiculo
ver-sion *n.* versión
ver-te-bra *n.* vertebra
ver-te-brate *adj.* vertebrado
ver-ti-cal *adj.* vertical
ver-y *adj.* mismo, *adv.* muy
ves-sel *n.* vaso
vest *n.* chaleco
vet *n.* veterinario
vet-er-an *adj., n.* veterano
vet-er-i-nar-i-an *n.*

veterinario
vet-er-i-nar-y *adj., n.* veterinario
vi-brant *adj.* vibrante
vi-brate *v.* oscilar
vi-bra-tion *n.* vibración
vic-ar *n.* vicario
vi-car-i-ous *a.* substituto
vice *n.* vicio
vice-pres-i-dent *n.* vicepresidente
vice-roy *n.* virrey
vice ver-sa *adv.* viceversa
vi-cin-i-ty *n.* vecindad
vi-cious *a.* depravado; vicioso; cruel
vic-tim *n.* victima
vic-tim-ize *v.* hacer victima
vic-to-ri-ous *adj.* victorioso
vic-to-ry *n.* victoria
view *v.* ver, *n.* escena
vig-i-lance *n.* vigilancia
vig-or *n.* vigor
vig-or-ous *adj.* vigoroso
vil-lage *n.* aldea
vin-di-cate *v.* vindicar
vine *n.* vid
vin-e-gar *n.* vinagre
vi-o-la *n.* viola
vi-o-la-tion *n.* violación
vi-o-lent *adj.* violento
vi-o-let *adj.* violado
vi-o-lin *n.* violín
vir-ile *adj.* viril
vi-ril-i-ty *n.* virilidad
vir-tu-al *adj.* virtual
vir-tu-al-ly *adv.* virtualmente
vir-u-lent *adj.* virulento
vi-rus *n.* virus
vis-cos-i-ty *n.* viscosidad
vis-count *n.* vizconde
vis-count-ess *n.* vizcondesa
vise *n.* tornillo
vis-i-bil-i-ty *n.* visibilidad
vis-i-ble *a.* visible; conspicuo
vi-sion *n.* visión
vi-sion-ar-y *n.* visionario
vis-it *n.* visita, *v.* visitar
vis-it-a-tion *n.* visitación
vi-sor *n.* visera
vis-u-al *adj.* visual
vis-u-al-ize *v.* representarse en la mente

vi-tal *adj.* vital
vi-tal-i-ty *n.* vitalidad
vi-ta-min *n.* vitamina
vit-re-ous *a.* vitreo
vit-ri-ol *n.* vitriolo
vi-tu-per-ate *v.* vituperar
vi-va-cious *a.* vivaz; animado; vivaracho
vi-vac-i-ty *n.* vivacidad; animacion
viv-id *adj.* intenso; vivo
vix-en *n.* arpia; zorra
vo-cab-u-lar-y *n.* vocabulario
vo-cal *adj.* vocal
vo-cal-ist *n.* cantante
vo-ca-tion *n.* vocación
vod-ka *n.* vodka
vogue *n.* moda; boga
voice *n.* voz
void *a.* nulo; vacio
vol-can-ic *adj.* volcanico
vol-ca-no *n.* volcan
vo-li-tion *n.* voluntad; volicion
vol-ley *n.* descarga; voleo
volt *n.* voltio
volt-age *n.* voltaje
vol-u-ble *a.* hablador
vol-ume *n.* cantidad; volumen
vol-un-tar-y *adj.* voluntario
vol-un-teer *n.* voluntario
vo-lup-tu-ar-y *n.* voluptuoso
vo-lup-tu-ous *a.* voluptuoso
vom-it *n.* vomito; *v.* vomitar
vom-it-ing *n.* vomito
voo-doo *n.* vodu
vo-ra-cious *a.* voraz
voracity *n.* voracidad
vor-tex *n.* vortice
votary *n.* devoto; partidario
vote *v.* votar, *n.* voto
vo-ter *n.* votante
vot-ing *n.* votacion
vo-tive *a.* votivo; exvoto
vouch *v.i.* afirmar
vouch-er *n.* comprobante
vow-el *n.* vocal
voy-age *v.* viajar, *n.* viaje
vul-gar *adj.* vulgar
vul-gar-ize *v.* vulgarizar
vul-ner-a-ble *a.* vulnerable
vul-ture *n.* buitre

wack-y *a.* loco; chiflado
wad *n.* fajo; taco; rollo; bolita
wad-dle *v.* anadear
wade *v.* vadear; pasar con dificultad
wag *v.* menear(se)
wage *n.* salario
wag-er *n.* apostar
wag-on *n.* carro
waif *n.* nino abandonado
wail *v.* lamentarse; sollozar
wain-scot *n.* friso de madera
waist *n.* cintura
waist-coat *n.* chaleco
waist-line *n.* talle
wait *n.* espera, *v.* esperar
wait-er *n.* camarero
wait-ress *n.* camarera
waive *v.* renunciar a; abandonar
waiv-er *n.* renuncia
wake *v.* despertar(se)
wake-ful *a.* vigilante
wak-en *v.* despertar(se)
walk *n.* caminata, *v.* caminar; andar
walk-out *n.* huelga
walk-o-ver *n.* triunfo facil
wall *n.* pared
wall-board *n.* carton de yeso
wal-let *n.* cartera
wal-lop *v.* zurrar
wal-low *v.* revp;carse
wall-pa-per *n.* papel pintado
wal-nut *n.* nogal
wal-rus *n.* morsa
waltz *n.* vals
wan *a.* palido
wan-der *v.* desviarse
wan-der-lust *n.* deseo de viajar
wane *v.* disminuir; menguar
want *v.* querer; requerir; desear
want-ing *a.* deficiente
wan-ton *a.* lascivo; desenfrenado
war *v.* guerrear, *n.* guerra
war-ble *v.* trinar
war-cry *n.* grito de guerra
ward *v.* desviar
war-den *n.* guardián; alsaide
ward-robe *n.* guardarropa;

vestuario
ware *n.* mercancias
ware-house *n.* almacén
war-fare *n.* guerra
war-lock *n.* hechicero
warm *v.* calentar(se), *adj.* caluroso; caliente
warm-heart-ed *a.* afectuoso
war-mong-er *n.* belicista
warmth *n.* calor
warn *v.* advertir
warn-ing *n.* advertencia; aviso
warp *v.* albearse; pervertir
war-rant *n.* autorizacion; garantia
war-ran-ty *n.* garantia
war-ren *n.* conejera
war-ri-or *n.* guerrero
wart *n.* verruga
war-y *a.* cauteloso
was *pret of* be
wash *v.* lavar(se)
wash-cloth *n.* paño para lavarse
wash-er *n.* lavadora
wash-ing *n.* lavado
wash-room *n.* lavabo
wash-stand *n.* lavamanos
wash-tub *n.* tin o cuba de lavar
wasp *n.* avispa
wast-age *n.* desgaste; merma
waste *n.* perdida, *v.* desperdiciar
wast-rel *n.* derrochador
watch *n.* reloj, *v.* mirar; observar
watch-ful *a.* vigilante; desvelado
watch-man *n.* vigilante
watch-word *n.* santo y sena
wa-ter *n.* agua
wa-ter-col-or *n.* acuarela
wa-ter-course *n.* corriente
wa-ter-fall *n.* cascada
wa-ter-fowl *n.* ave acuantica
wa-ter-front *n.* terreno rebereno
wa-ter lil-y *n.* nenufar
wa-ter-logged *a.* anegado
wa-ter-mark *n.* nivel de

agua; filigrana
wa-ter-mel-on *n.* sandia
wa-ter-proof *a.* impermeable
wa-ter-side *n.* orilla del agua
wa-ter sof-ten-er *n.* ablandador quimico de agua
wa-ter-spout *n.* tromba marina; mangua
wa-ter-tight *a.* estanco; seguro
wa-ter-way *n.* canal
wa-ter-y *adj.* insipido
watt *n.* vatio
wave *v.* ondular, *n.* onda
wa-ver *v.* oscilar; vacilar
wav-y *a.* ondulado
wax *n.* cera
wax-en *a.* de cara; palido
wax-work *n.* figura de cera
way *n.* camino; modo; direccion
way-far-er *n.* viajero
way-lay *v.* asaltar
way-side *n.* borde del camino
way-ward *a.* voluntarioso; travieso
we *pron.* nosotras; nosotros
weak *adj.* débil
weak-en *v.* debilitar(se)
weak-ling *n.* alfenique
weak-ly *a.* achacoso
weak-mind-ed *a.* sin voluntad
weak-ness *n.* debilidad
wealth *n.* riqueza
wealth-y *adj.* rico
wean *v.* destetar
weap-on *n.* arma
weap-on-ry *n.* armas
wear *v.* desgastar(se); llevar
wear-ing *adj.* penoso
wea-ri-some *a.* fastidioso
wea-ry *a.* fatigado; aburrido
wea-sel *n.* comadreja
weath-er *n.* tiempo
weath-er-beat-en *a.* curtido pro la intemperie
weath-er-glass *n.* barometro
weath-er-man *n.* pronosticador de tiempo
weave *v.* tejido
web *n.* tela

web-bing *n.* cincha
wed *v.* casar(se)
wed-ding *n.* boda
wedge *n.* cuña
wed-lock *n.* matrimonio
Wednes-day *n.* miércoles
wee *a.* pequeñito
weed *v.* escardar
week *n.* semana
week-day *n.* día laborable o de trabajo
week-end *n.* fin de la semana
week-ly *a.* semanal
weep *v.* llorar
wee-vil *n.* gorgojo
weigh *v.* pesar
weight *n.* pesa
weight-y *adj.* pesado
weird *adj.* extraño
wel-come *adj.* agradable
weld *v.* soldar
wel-fare *n.* bienestar
well *adv.* pues, *n.* fuente
well-be-ing *n.* bienestar
well-bred *a.* bien criado
well-dis-posed *a.* bien dispuesto
well-known *adj.* famoso
well-off *a.* adimerado
well-read *a.* leído
well-thought-of *a.* bien mirado
well-timed *a.* oportuno
well-to-do *a.* acaudalado
welt *n.* verdugón
wel-ter *v.* revolcar(se)
wench *n.* moza
were *pret. of* be
were-wolf *n.* hombre que puede transformarse en lobo
west *n.* oeste
west-ern *adj.* occidental
wet *v.* mojar(se)
whack *v.* golpear
whale *n.* ballena
whale-bone *n.* ballena
wharf *n.* muelle
what *pron.* qué; lo que; cual
what-ev-er *pron.* todo lo que
what-not *n.* estante; juguetero

wheat *n.* trigo
whee-dle *v.* engatusar; halagar
wheel *n.* rueda
wheel-bar-row *n.* carretilla
wheel-chair *n.* silla de ruedas
wheeze *v.* respirar asmáticamente
when *conj.* cuando
whence *adv.* de donde; de que
when-ev-er *adv.* siempre que
where *conj., adv.* donde, *adv.* adonde
where-a-bouts *n.* paradero
where-as *conj.* visto que
where-up-on *adv.* con lo cual
wher-ev-er *adv.* dondequiera
wheth-er *conj.* si
whey *n.* suero de la leche
which *pron.* lo que; cual; la; le
which-ev-er *pron.* cualquiera
whiff *n.* olorcillo
while *conj.* mientras
whim *v.* lloriquear
whim-per *v.* lloriquear
whim-si-cal *a.* caprichoso
whine *v.* gimotear
whin-ny *n.* relincho
whip *v.* batir
whir *v.* zumbar; batir
whirl *v.* girar repidamente
whirl-pool *n.* remolino
whirl-wind *n.* torbellino
whisk-ers *n.* barbas; bigotes
whis-key *n.* whisky
whis-per *n.* cuchicheo, *v.* cuchichear
whis-tle *v.* silbar
white *n., adj.* blanco
white-col-lar *a.* oficinesco
whit-en *v.* blanquear
white-wash *n.* jalbeque
whith-er *conj.* adonde
whit-tle *v.* cortar poco a poco
whiz *v.* silbar; rehilar
who *pron.* la; el; lo; quién;

que

who-ev-er *pron.* quienquiere que

whole *n., adj.* todo

whole-heart-ed *a.* sincero; incondicional

whole-sale *n.* venta al por menor

whole-some *a.* saludable

whol-ly *adv.* completamente

whom *pron.* a quién

whom-ev-er *pron.* a quienquiera

whoop *n.* alarido

whore *n.* puta; prostituta

whose *pron.* cuyo

why *adv.* ¿por qué?

wick *n.* mecha

wick-ed *adj.* malicioso

wick-er *a.* de mimbre

wide *adj.* ancho

wide-a-wake *a.* despabilado

wid-en *v.* ensanchar(se)

wide-spread *a.* extendido; difuso

wid-ow *n.* viuda

wid-ow-er *n.* viudo

width *n.* anchura

wield *v.* ejercer; mandar; manejar

wife *n.* esposa

wig *n.* peluca

wig-gle *v.* menear(se); cimbrearse

wild *adj.* descabellado

wild boar *n.* jabali

wil-der-ness *n.* yermo; desierto

wile *n.* ardid

will *v.* querer

will-ful *a.* voluntarioso; terco; premeditado

will-ing *a.* dispuesto; complanciente

wil-low *n.* sauce

wil-low-y *a.* esbelto

wil-ly-nil-ly *adv.* de grado o por fuerza

wilt *v.* marchitar(se)

win *n.* victoria, *v.* lograr; ganar

wince *v.* estremecerse; respingar

winch *n.* torno

wind *n.* viento

wind *v.* arrollar(se)

wind-fall *n.* ganacia inesperada

wind-mill *n.* molino de viento

win-dow *n.* ventana

win-dow-pane *n.* cristal

wind-shield *n.* parabrisas

wind-y *adj.* ventoso

wine *n.* vino

win-er-y *n.* lagar; candiotera

wing *n.* ala

wink *v.* guinar; pestanear

win-ner *n.* ganador

win-ning *n.* ganancias

win-now *v.* aventar

win-some *a.* atractivo; alegre

win-ter *n.* invierno

win-try *adj.* invernal

wipe *v.* enjugar; secar; borrar

wire *n.* alambre

wire-tap *v.* intervenir

wir-ing *n.* instalación de alambres

wir-y *a.* nervudo

wis-dom *n.* sabiduria

wise *adj.* acertado; sabio

wise-crack *n.* cuchufleta; pulla

wish *n.* deseo, *v.* desear

wish-ful *adj.* deseoso

wit *n.* sal

witch *n.* bruja

witch-craft *n.* brujeria

with *prep.* con

with-draw-al *n.* retirada

with-drawn *a.* ensimismado

with-er *v.* marchitar(se); secarse

with-hold *v.* retener

with-in *adv.* dentro

with-out *adv.* por fuera

with-stand *v.* resistir

wit-less *a.* tonto

wit-ness *n.* testigo

wi-ti-cism *n.* dicho gracioso

wit-ty *a.* salado; ingenioso

wiz-ard *n.* hechicero

wob-ble *v.* bambolear; bailar

woe *n.* aflicción; infortunio

wolf *n.* lobo

wom-an *n.* mujer

wom-an-kind *n.* sexo femenino

womb *n.* matriz

wom-en's rights *n.* derechos de la mujer

won-der *v.* asombrarse

won-der-ful *adj.* maravilloso

woo *v.* cortejar

wood *n.* madera

wood-en *a.* de madera; sin expresión

wood-land *n.* monte

w o o d - p e c k - e r *n.* picamaderos

wood-y *adj.* lenoso

wool *n.* lana

wool-ly *adj.* lanudo

word *n.* palabra

work *v.* trabajar, *n.* obra; trabajo

work-book *n.* cuaderno

work-er *n.* trabajador

work-shop *n.* taller

world *n.* mundo

world-ly *adj.* mundano

world-wide *a.* mundial

worm *n.* gusano

worm-eaten *a.* carcomido

wormwood *n.* ajenjo

worn *adj.* usado

worrier *n.* aprensivo; pesimista

wor-ry *v.* inquietar(se)

wors-en *v.* empeorar

wor-ship *v.* venerar

worth *n.* valor

worth-less *adj.* despreciable

wound *v.* herir

wrap *v.* envolver

wreck *v.* naufragar, *n.* ruina

wrin-kle *v.* arrugar(se), *n.* arruga

wrist *n.* muñeca

write *v.* escribir

writ-er *n.* escritora; escritor

writ-ing *n.* escrito

wrong *adj.* equivocado

wrong-ful *a.* injusto; falso

wrong-head-ed *a.* terco

w r o u g h t *a.* forjado; trabajado

wry *a.* torcido; ironico; mueca

x-ray *v.* radiografiar, *n.* radiografia

yank *v.* sacar de un tirón

Yan-kee *n.* yanqui

yard *n.* yarda

yard-goods *n.* tejidos

yard-stick *n.* vara de medir

yarn *n.* hilaza

yar-row *n.* milenrama

yawn *n.* bostezo, *v.* bostezar

ye *pron.* vosotros

yea *adv.* sí

year *n.* año

year-ling *n.* primal

year-ly *adv.* anualmente

yearn *v.* suspirar; anhelar

yearn-ing *n.* anhelo

yeast *n.* levadura

yell *n.* grito, *v.* gritar

yel-low *n., adj.* amarillo

yes *adv.* sí

yes-ter-day *n.* ayer

yet *adv.* todavía

yew *n.* tejo

yield *v.* rendir(se)

yolk *n.* yema

yon-der *adv.* allí; allá

yore *n.* antaño

you *pron.* vosotras; vosotros; tu

young *adj.* joven

young-ster *n.* jovencito

your *adj.* sus; tus; vuestras; vuestros

yours *pron.* tu; vos; vosotros; vosotras

your-self *pron.* usted mismo; tu mismo

youth *n.* jovenes

youth-ful *adj.* juvenil

zeal *n.* ardor

zeal-ous *adj.* celoso

ze-bra *n.* cebra

ze-nith *n.* cenit

ze-ro *n.* cero

ze-ro hour *n.* hora de ataque

zest *n.* gusto

zone *n.* zona

zoo *n.* jardín zoologico

zo-o-log-i-cal *adj.* zoologico

zuc-chi-ni *n.* cidracayote de verano